Praise for
THE PERFECT HORSE

"A truly fascinating chronicle of a dedicated group of horsemen and the risks they were willing to take to preserve the equine icon that is the Lipizzaner . . . I was hooked from start to finish by Letts's incredible attention to detail and her gripping account of the events surrounding and leading up to the rescue mission." —*Horse Nation*

"A brilliantly written story about Hitler's effort to build an equine master race with the finest horses in Europe gathered in one place . . . As the end neared, these beautiful animals were within days of being slaughtered when a controversial covert mission was planned to rescue the horses and smuggle them to safety." —*PineStraw Magazine*

"A wholly original, illuminating perspective on the war . . . *The Perfect Horse* tells a fascinating story of bravery and benevolence that has gone far too long without reaching an audience. Full of action, heartbreak and well-developed characters, it has everything needed to be adapted into an outstanding war movie. To anyone with a love of horses or other animals, Letts' fantastic, almost humanizing characterizations of some of the horses will make this book an instant favorite. And to history buffs, *The Perfect Horse* provides a totally fresh look at WWII that can't be found anywhere else." —*Bookreporter*

"A riveting and touching piece of equestrian history beautifully told . . . [Letts makes] long dead characters come alive, revealing their passions and fears and flashes of uncommon valor for the sake of horses whose fate lay in their hands. The horses, too, are vivid and unforgettable. . . . Don't miss it." —*EquiSearch*

"An absorbing history of an unusual rescue mission in the closing days of the war in Europe . . . Letts does an excellent job of bringing the various players to life." —*BookPage*

"[Elizabeth] Letts, a lifelong equestrienne, eloquently brings together the many facets of this unlikely, poignant story underscoring the love and respect of man for horses. . . . The author's elegant narrative conveys how the love for these amazing creatures transcends national animosities."

—*Kirkus Reviews*

"*The Perfect Horse* raises the narrative bar. Applying her skills as a researcher, storyteller and horsewoman, Letts provides context that makes this account spellbinding."

—*Culturess*

"*The Perfect Horse* is an enthralling and moving story that I could not put down. This is a riveting and unique perspective on World War II. History buffs and horse lovers will enjoy this amazing tale."

—MOLLY GUPTILL MANNING, author of *When Books Went to War*

"Passionately told and dazzling in scope, *The Perfect Horse* charges headlong into an unforgettable tale of World War II, when good men were given a final mission—to save beloved horses—at an hour when no one wanted to die. In Elizabeth Letts, the saga of World War II's white stallions has found its perfect guardian."

—ADAM MAKOS, author of *A Higher Call*

"Elizabeth Letts's beautiful prose, woven together with meticulous research, takes you for a ride that will keep you on the edge of your seat until the end."

—ROBIN HUTTON, author of *Sgt. Reckless*

"Letts deftly tells the harrowing tale of a little-known wartime mission and its unlikely heroes, who understood that the treasures they risked their lives for—some of the world's finest-bred horses—were a keystone of civilization during a time of perilous threat. This is the best kind of storytelling."

—JOE DRAPE, author of *American Pharoah*

"In Elizabeth Letts's engrossing, richly researched book—a story of horses and heroism during the final days of World War II—we learn that our human instinct to protect our equine friends can cause us to risk even our own lives for their sake. This relatively unknown episode is as moving as it is dramatic."

—WENDY WILLIAMS, author of *The Horse*

BY
ELIZABETH LETTS

The Perfect Horse

The Eighty-Dollar Champion

Family Planning

Quality of Care

THE
PERFECT
HORSE

THE PERFECT HORSE

THE DARING
U.S. MISSION TO
RESCUE THE
PRICELESS STALLIONS
KIDNAPPED BY
THE NAZIS

Elizabeth Letts

BALLANTINE BOOKS
New York

2017 Ballantine Books Trade Paperback Edition

Copyright © 2016 by Elizabeth Letts
Map copyright © 2016 by Mapping Specialists, Ltd., Madison, Wisconsin

Published in the United States by Ballantine Books, an imprint of Random House, a division of Penguin Random House LLC, New York.

BALLANTINE and the HOUSE colophon are registered trademarks of Penguin Random House LLC.

Originally published in hardcover in the United States by Ballantine Books, an imprint of Random House, a division of Penguin Random House LLC, in 2016.

LIBRARY OF CONGRESS CATALOGING-IN-PUBLICATION DATA
NAMES: Letts, Elizabeth, author.
TITLE: The perfect horse : the daring U.S. mission to rescue the priceless stallions kidnapped by the Nazis / Elizabeth Letts.
DESCRIPTION: First edition. | New York : Ballantine Books, [2016] | Includes bibliographical references and index. | Description based on print version record and CIP data provided by publisher; resource not viewed.
IDENTIFIERS: LCCN 2016030226 (print) | LCCN 2016010501 (ebook) | ISBN 9780345544827 (paperback) | ISBN 9780345544803 (hardcover : alk. paper)
SUBJECTS: LCSH: World War, 1939–1945—Confiscations and contributions—United States. | World War, 1939–1945—Commando operations—Czech Republic—Hostouň. | Lipizzaner horse—Austria—History—20th century. | Arabian horse—Poland—History—20th century. | World War, 1939–1945—Confiscations and contributions—Germany. | Spanische Reitschule (Vienna, Austria)—History—20th century. | Podhajsky, Alois. | World War, 1939–1945—Austria. | Reed, Charles Hancock, 1900–1980. | United States. Army. Cavalry Regiment, Mechanized, 2nd—History.
CLASSIFICATION: LCC D810.C8 (print) | LCC D810.C8 L46 2016 (ebook) | DDC 940.54/213714—dc23
LC record available at https://lccn.loc.gov/2016030226

Printed in the United States of America on acid-free paper

randomhousebooks.com

246897531

Title-page photo: Associated Press

Book design by Barbara M. Bachman

COURAGE IS BEING
SCARED TO DEATH . . . AND
SADDLING UP ANYWAY.

—*John Wayne*

CONTENTS

PART FOUR: HOMECOMING

LIST OF CHARACTERS

THE EUROPEANS

Andrzej Kristalovich (Andrzej Krzysztalowicz): /Ahn-jay Kshee-stal-o-veech/ Director of Poland's national stud farm.

Rudolf Lessing: German army veterinarian stationed at the Hostau stud farm in Czechoslovakia.

Alois Podhajsky: /Ah-loys Pod-hey-skee/ Austrian director of the Spanish Riding School of Vienna.

Gustav Rau: German horse expert. Chief equerry in charge of all horse breeding in the Third Reich.

Hubert Rudofsky: Czech-born ethnic German. Director of the stud farm in Hostau, Czechoslovakia.

Jan Ziniewicz: /Yahn Zee-nee-ev-eech/ Chief groom of Poland's National Stud Farm.

THE AMERICANS

Major James Pitman: West Point graduate, lover of dogs and horses. Executive officer of the 42nd Squadron of the 2nd Cavalry.

Lieutenant William Donald "Quin" Quinlivan: Career cavalryman. Assigned to the 42nd Squadron of the 2nd Cavalry.

Colonel Charles Hancock "Hank" Reed: Virginia-born, expert horseman, commanding officer of the 2nd Cavalry.

Captain Ferdinand Sperl: Swiss-born naturalized U.S. citizen. Interrogator attached to the 2nd Cavalry.

Captain Thomas Stewart: Son of a Tennessee senator. Intelligence officer in the 2nd Cavalry.

THE HORSES

Lotnik: Gray Arabian stallion foaled in Poland.

Neapolitano Africa: Austrian Lipizzaner performing stallion, one of Alois Podhajsky's personal mounts.

Pluto Theodorosta: Austrian Lipizzaner performing stallion, one of Alois Podhajsky's personal mounts.

Witez: /Vee-tezh/ Bay Arabian stallion foaled in Poland in 1938. His official registered name was Witez II.

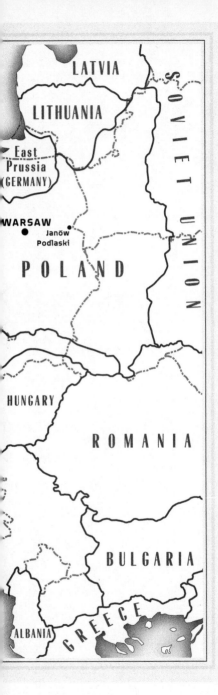

CENTRAL EUROPE

1938

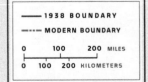

——— 1938 BOUNDARY

-------- MODERN BOUNDARY

0   100   200 MILES

0   100   200 KILOMETERS

BOMBARDMENT

A shrill air raid signal pierced the quiet of the cobblestoned Michaelerplatz, a plaza in the heart of central Vienna. A moment later, the grand baroque edifices ringing the square shuddered in violent reverberation. Vienna was under siege. On the grounds of the Hofburg Palace, tucked away from view in the ornate stables that once belonged to an emperor, thirty-three majestic white stallions startled, pawing and rearing, their eyes white-rimmed with fear.

Peering out of a box stall, one eight-year-old Lipizzaner stood perfectly still, his white coat glowing in the stable's dim light. His ears pricked forward as he tried to pick out the soft tread of his master's footsteps through the sound of airplanes roaring overhead. Next to his stall, on a small black slate, his name, Neapolitano Africa, and his birthdate, 1935, were neatly stenciled in white paint. A moment later, a slim middle-aged gentleman rushed to Africa's side, whispering a word of reassurance, then placing a warm hand on the stallion's shoulder. Alois Podhajsky was utterly concentrated on a single goal—to keep his stallions safe. With a deft motion, Podhajsky slipped the polished leather halter from its peg next to the stall. The stallion lowered his head and placed his speckled muzzle through the leather noseband, helping to make the task easier. His eyes seemed to say, "I know what's going on here. Let me help."

By now the entire stable, with its marble water basins and neatly hung tack, its wide aisles and airy stalls, was a hive of activity: Grooms in gray uniforms quickly haltered some of the stallions while riders, in their buckskin britches and jackets, took charge of others. Around them, bits of plaster broke free and a powdery residue sifted down like snow.

In single file, the horses and men crossed a large courtyard, passed through heavy iron-studded wooden doors, and then clattered across a city street, now deserted. The horses filed through a second set of doors and into a sheltered hallway. The stallions had calmed and didn't shy or balk even as the loud booms and crashes almost drowned out the ringing of their iron shoes on the cobblestones. The last to enter the shelter of the hallway was Alois Podhajsky, Olympic bronze medal winner and director of the Spanish Riding School of Vienna. The enormous wooden doors swung shut behind them; here, the thick walls muffled the sounds a little bit. For the first moment since hearing the air raid signal, Podhajsky took a deep breath. He reached into the leather pouch at his hip, extracted a sugar lump, and offered it to Africa, feeling the tickle of the horse's whiskers as he lipped it up from Podhajsky's bare palm. Horse and man were clearly intimate and seemed to converse without words, the man promising protection and the horse evidently comforted by his silent reassurance.

The Spanish Riding School of Vienna was one of Austria's most beloved institutions. Named for the Spanish provenance of the original horses, the school famously showcased the finest specimens of the equine species' most rarefied breed: the royal Lipizzaner. As priceless as any of the masterpieces that hung in Vienna's museums, from their snow-white coats to their large aristocratic heads and deep brown eyes, the horses were unlike any others in the world.

The horses and masters huddled here were at the center of a maelstrom. Around them, war raged in all directions. These royal horses had escaped danger on numerous previous occasions, fleeing for their lives and safety from the armies of Napoleon and again during the Great War. Each time they had been able to find safe haven. But now, in the all-out war of air and ground that was engulfing Europe, where could they go? No obvious path to safety lay before them.

A loud boom ripped through the building. Next came a deafening thud; glass shattered high above them. A cacophony of terrified neighs tore through the dust-choked air. Podhajsky and Africa turned to look at each other. Podhajsky gripped the sturdy lead rope, held his breath, and waited.

PART ONE

The Europeans

Equestrian art, perhaps more than any other,
is closely related to the wisdom of life.

—ALOIS PODHAJSKY

ALOIS PODHAJSKY INSTRUCTS
HIS RIDERS AT THE
SPANISH RIDING SCHOOL
IN VIENNA.

1.

AN UNLIKELY OLYMPIAN

BERLIN, GERMANY, 1936

Alois Podhajsky wore the cares of the world on his narrow, melancholy face. His gaze was like a poet's, directed inward. His oeuvre was the art of classical dressage. His verses danced on four legs. Podhajsky looked as if he'd been born to sit astride a horse. His long straight torso had no awkward angles, no rounded curves, nothing to detract from its elegant lines. But to look at the Austrian officer's forlorn expression was to understand that within, he carried a shadow. In 1918, after being severely wounded in the neck while serving in the trenches in Flanders, he had suffered from shell shock. His love for horses had brought him slowly back, but the deep stillness of a defeated warrior never left him.

On June 12, 1936, Alois Podhajsky sat astride his mount, Nero, ready to enter the rectangular dressage arena that had been set out with meticulous precision on May Field, a twenty-eight-acre lawn just to the east of the Olympic stadium; it was the site of the Olympic competition in equestrian dressage. The fact that this pair was competing here, in the eleventh Olympic Games, against the top equestrian contenders from around the world, was unlikely indeed. Nero, a gangly brown Thoroughbred, had been bred to race, but having proven slow, he had been cast off for use as an army cavalry mount. The gelding had shown equally little talent as a soldier's charger, and the army had nearly sold him off before Podhajsky decided that the horse showed potential and saved him from the auction block. Podhajsky too was an almost-reject, kicked out of Austria's prestigious cavalry officer training school after a back injury made him unable to bend at the waist, forcing him to abandon his first love—jumping. Unwilling to give up his passion, he kept riding even though he had to be lifted onto his horse. He would never forget the day in 1928, during a cavalry school lesson, when his riding instructor scrutinized Podhajsky's stiff form in the saddle and said, "You're finished." But Podhajsky had pressed on, working with his reject mount, dedicating his energy to the art of dressage. Just three years later, Podhajsky had received the Austrian cavalry's highest honor: In 1931, he was sent to study for two years at the world's oldest academy of classical riding, the Spanish Riding School. The instruction he received in the classical art of horsemanship was as much a spiritual education as a physical one. Students neither entered their horses in competitions nor vied for any medals. They pursued perfection as an end unto itself. Podhajsky's love for horses, for riding, for life, had been restored. Five years after being expelled from the cavalry school, Podhajsky was representing his country at the Olympics. While Nero was neither flashy nor handsome, the gelding was willing and cooperative, and after several years of training, they had risen to the top of the sport: Today, they entered the arena as favorites.

Although Podhajsky believed that the Austrian tradition of riding was without peer, he knew that many found his country's traditions backward-looking. One of Podhajsky's teammates was the oldest competitor at the entire Games, born way back in 1864. Podhajsky's own love of Austria's equestrian traditions had started during his boyhood, and at eighteen, he'd joined the cavalry. Posing for a portrait in 1916, wearing the uniform of his regiment, he looked younger than his eighteen years. His ornate uniform—fur-muffed, spike-helmeted, brass-buttoned—could be mistaken for a costume. In his right hand, he held white gloves; at his left hip, a sword and scabbard. He resembled a boy playing dress-up in his father's clothes. But Austria lost both the Great War and its empire, and the pomp and traditions to which he had sworn boyhood allegiance were mostly gone. What remained of the great Austrian empire was its tradition of horsemanship, which Podhajsky still believed was the best in the world. Now was his chance to prove it with the eyes of the world upon him.

SEVENTEEN-
YEAR-OLD
ALOIS
PODHAJSKY
DRESSED IN
HIS
WORLD WAR I
UNIFORM.

Nero's turnout was impeccable, each of his braids carefully wrapped in snow-white adhesive tape, setting off the arched carriage of his neck. Podhajsky looked resplendent in the olive uniform of the Austrian Republic. The failed racehorse and his reject rider were preparing to compete in one of the most complex and demanding sports. Of all equestrian sports, dressage requires the most discipline. Descended from intricate military maneuvers developed in ancient times, dressage asks horse and rider to execute a series of carefully prescribed movements. Just as ballroom dancing and pair skating command partners to work together seamlessly, in the sport of dressage, the rider performs an intricate pas de deux with his partner—a twelve-hundred-pound four-footed beast. Great dressage demands more than skill; it engages a rider's inner wisdom and his ability to communicate with a mount in the silent language of horsemanship.

The arena was laid out with geometrical precision on the clipped lawn of May Field. Large pots of flowers were set up at intervals around the perimeter, adding vibrant splashes of color. In the distance, the impressive hulk of Olympia Stadium filled the horizon, festooned with the flags of many nations. Evenly spaced scarlet Nazi swastika banners stained its perimeter. Inside, a hundred thousand seats were filled to capacity for the track and field events. The crowd assembled to watch the dressage competition, though a quarter that size, was no less fervent. Men in white fedoras and women in colorful summer dresses speckled the field's stands like rainbow sprinkles on ice cream. Podhajsky had committed to memory the complex series of movements that he would need to execute perfectly in the seventeen minutes allotted to him. If his horse stepped out of the low barriers that marked the boundaries of the twenty-by-sixty-meter ring, he would be eliminated. Surrounding the arena were points marked by letters of the alphabet: If the program specified that a movement be completed as he passed that mark, the horse needed to begin or end the movement just as the rider's boot passed the marker.

In the sport of dressage, the rider spends years teaching a horse to perform movements on command that come naturally to horses in the wild. The horse has four ordinary paces: walk, trot, canter, and gallop, each with a different cadence. But in each of these paces, a wild horse will perform the gaits with a variety of nuances. For example, when a horse trots, it moves its legs in diagonal pairs with a two-beat cadence. A wild stallion, showing off, sometimes elevates the simple trot to an art form—he coils his powerful haunches underneath him, slows down the tempo, and elevates each step, transforming the workaday gait into a balletic art. These exaggerated movements are innate in certain circumstances, but to coax a horse to perform them on command takes the utmost tact, sympathy, and meticulous training from a rider. In an advanced dressage test, a rider may ask a horse to perform a pirouette, whereby the horse's hindquarters remain almost in place while his forelegs canter a full circle around them, or a half-pass, where a horse moves both forward and sideways, his body slightly bent around his rider's leg, his legs crossing each other. Each of these movements has been inculcated slowly, painstakingly, in a step-by-step process that takes years to complete.

As he awaited his turn, Podhajsky hoped that his own long years of practice would pay off. His thoughts turned inward as he listened to the voice of his instructor at the Spanish Riding School, the man who had taught him to tap into riding's most ancient traditions. Every competitor on May Field had trained hard to be here. Everyone hoped to win an Olympic medal. But Podhajsky had more at stake than the desire to win a prize: He believed that the deep communion between rider and horse was something exalted. In an indifferent and sometimes cruel world, he wanted to embody what his years of patient training stood for—discipline, tradition, perfection for its own sake, passion given form. Winning a medal might be the final outcome of this endeavor, but for Podhajsky, the endeavor itself mattered most.

Podhajsky lifted his eyes to look over risers jammed with spectators. So strange that such a large crowd was gathered here to watch a spectacle that in some ways was so private. As Podhajsky himself later commented, "Excited applause does not help in the least; what is needed is perfect sympathy and harmony with one's partner." Practicing this most delicate art, Podhajsky had learned to turn himself into an animal psychologist; he knew that success belonged to those riders who were able to ally themselves with their mounts. Today Podhajsky would ride for Austria, but more than anything, he would seek to enter into an almost mystical state of union with his horse.

As Podhajsky waited his turn to enter the arena, he watched the other competitors with a practiced eye. He knew that his stiffest competition came from the Germans, who had a home field advantage. He was certain that he and Nero could compete with the world's best, though as he looked across the field at the international panel of judges assembled there, he knew that this was not just a competition but also an elaborate game of political chess.

One hundred and thirty-three riders from twenty-one countries had gathered to compete in the equestrian events at the summer '36 Games. Three years earlier, the National Socialist Party had catapulted Hitler into power. Designed to showcase the Nazi Party's Aryan ideals, the Berlin Olympics were a piece of nationalistic theater dressed up as a sporting event. The Nazis, in a clever propaganda move, had camouflaged many of the blatant anti-Jewish policies that were already being enforced, removing anti-Semitic street signs in Berlin and even toning down the rhetoric in the newspapers, but a latent menace and violence lurked just beneath the whitewashed surface.

On this very public stage, the equestrian events had a particular significance: The competitions were open only to members of the military. Uniformed officers rode their best horses in contests specifically designed to test the mettle of equestrian soldiers. The three different sports—dressage, Three-Day Eventing (also called "the Military"), and Prix des Nations (stadium jumping)—could easily be viewed as a stage for international battle writ small. To mark this importance, the Prix des Nations, or Nations Cup, had been given the prime spot: just before the closing ceremonies, when the eyes of the world would be watching. For centuries, men had measured their military might by the worth of their horses. In 1936 Berlin, the equestrian competitions were psychological war games: a dress rehearsal for the much larger cataclysm that lay just over the horizon.

AT ONE END OF THE JUDGES' DAIS, his face in a concentrated scowl, sat the most influential person at the equestrian site, Gustav Rau. Clad in a dark suit, his bald head covered by a felt fedora, Rau lacked the long limbs and regal bearing of a horseman, but what he lacked in panache, he more than made up for in acumen. This fifty-six-year-old German was the mastermind behind every one of the equestrian competitions at the Olympics. Gustav Rau had overseen each detail of the equestrian events: from the selection of the judges to the layout of the courses, a preparation that had consumed the previous two years. In spite of being a civilian, he relied on the close cooperation of high-ranking Nazi officials, in particular Hermann Fegelein, head of the SS Cavalry. Fegelein was the special protégé of Heinrich Himmler, Reich leader of the SS.

Gustav Rau watched from the dais as the next competitor prepared to enter the ring. He recognized Podhajsky and Nero as the winners of several important competitions leading up to the Olympics, beating out top German entries. Today's test called for Podhajsky and Nero to enter the ring at an extended canter and then stop on a dime precisely in the center of the arena.

Even though Podhajsky wore white gloves, his movements were

barely perceptible as he shortened his reins, a signal to Nero that they were soon to begin. The press had called the ex-racehorse "a long-legged gelding without charm or personality," and indeed, Nero once was flighty and nervous, afraid of his own shadow. Just as they prepared to enter the arena, the words of the oldest groom from the Spanish Riding School came into Podhajsky's head: "Don't be nervous. The horse is all right." He relaxed his thighs and sank deeper into his saddle; he turned inward, listening to his mount. An old adage says that a good rider can hear his horse speak and a great rider can hear his horse whisper. As Podhajsky listened to Nero's whisper, the whole world fell away, the flags, the crowds, even his own will to win. All that was left was himself, his horse, and the signal that passed between them, like a radio tuned to a frequency that only the two of them could hear. He was scarcely aware of the five judges lined up at the far end of the arena, one each from France, Germany, Sweden, Austria, and Great Britain. He took no notice of the German observer, Rau.

When the ringmaster gave the signal, Podhajsky and Nero entered on a straight line at a controlled gallop, stopping smoothly so that Podhajsky's riding boot was centered at the exact midpoint of the arena, on the spot that, though unmarked, was known as X. Nero stood as still as a bronze statue while Podhajsky swept off his visored military cap to salute the judges. Then the pair continued at a free walk, a deceptively simple movement that tested a horse's perfect obedience. Podhajsky sensed Nero relaxing, elongating his neck as he felt the reins slacken just a bit. The horse seemed to take no notice of the fluttering flags, the crowds of people, or the roaring from the track-and-field events in the distance. With no obvious cue from his rider, Nero picked up a floating trot and proceeded to crisscross and zigzag through the arena, flawlessly executing each of the complicated prescribed movements as the twenty-thousand-plus members of the crowd leaned forward in their seats in a collective spellbound hush. Nero, unprepossessing when standing still, now looked bright and lively, while his rider remained so motionless that he almost seemed to disappear.

For more than a year after Podhajsky returned from the front in 1918, the injury to his neck prevented him from speaking above a whisper; he was mired in depression about the loss of the great empire that he had sworn his young life to serve. Only rekindling his love of horses had slowly pulled him out of his pit of despair. Now, as he neared the end of his ride, turning back down the centerline of the arena and halting once more at the X while doffing his hat in salute, the world seemed to glow in vivid hues. His ride had gone flawlessly, and as he dismounted, well-wishers crowded around him, assuring him that he was certain to take home the gold medal. But Podhajsky had no time to listen. He stripped off one white glove and reached into the hidden pocket sewn into the interior of his jacket. He extracted a sugar lump from his pocket, and the adoring crowd watched quietly while Nero daintily nuzzled up the treat from the palm of his master's outstretched hand. Podhajsky laid his other hand on his horse's shoulder. The two had eyes only for each other.

Seated on the dais, the German judge was adding up his marks (each individual movement was scored separately, with some given more weight than others). When the German judge realized that the Austrian had the best score, he stealthily erased a few marks on his scorecard and penciled in a lower mark.

The following day, on June 13, 1936, Alois Podhajsky stood on the podium watching the red and white flag of his country shimmer against the Berlin sky. The pair had finished in third place, behind the two German riders. He was a representative of a young democracy, the Republic of Austria, and had demonstrated one of Austria's greatest prides, its equestrian prowess, in front of the world. As he bowed his head to receive his medal, he instantly became one of his country's most famous citizens. In the end, Germany gained all of the individual and team gold medals in all three equestrian events, a clean sweep never equaled before or since. Later, when Gustav Rau penned the official review of the Olympic equestrian events, he claimed that only German superiority, not any inherent unfairness, had led to the lopsided medal count, though in the annals of Olympic equestrian history, the 1936 results have remained controversial. Of Podhajsky's ride, Rau wrote only, "His appearance had attracted notice." Nevertheless, Podhajsky and Nero, two ugly ducklings, had won the world's attention with their swanlike performance.

Podhajsky returned to Austria a national hero. The success of the German equestrian team had burnished Gustav Rau's reputation to a high shine. Neither of these men knew that their paths would cross again. Each man would have a mission: Alois Podhajsky would soon be entrusted to safeguard one of his nation's most important cultural treasures. Gustav Rau would be hell-bent on seizing those treasures for Nazi Germany.

2.

THE MASTER OF
ALL HORSES

On May 8, 1938, two months after Hitler's Reich annexed Austria, Gustav Rau docked at New York Harbor on the German luxury liner *Bremen*. Rau's lofty new title, chief equerry of Germany and master of the horse, barely fit in the small space allotted for "profession" on the ship's log. Ever since his triumph in Berlin in '36, the fifty-eight-year-old Rau had assumed the manner of the powerful and influential man he had become. Despite his generally jovial air, he was quick to spot weakness in both men and horses. Where he saw flaws in horses, he bred around them; when he saw them in humans, he administered verbal jabs like a stinging whip to a horse's flank. Accompanying Rau was his wife, Helga, herself an accomplished horsewoman, along with more than a dozen of Germany's most prominent horse lovers. Among the group was General Curt Freiherr von Gienanth, recently retired from the cavalry after a distinguished career that included the directorship of the German Cavalry School (although he was to be pressed back into service for the Third Reich the following year). *The New York Times* trumpeted the group's arrival with the headline "Reich Equestrians Arrive for Shows."

Just three years later, the two countries would be at war, but in May 1938 there was no sign of tension as the *Bremen* tied up at the busy New York Harbor and the privileged, well-dressed German men and women preened down the gangplank, ready to commence an itinerary packed with festivities. The group checked into the sumptuous Hotel Biltmore in Manhattan, home base for their eighteen-day equestrian sightseeing tour of America.

GUSTAV RAU KNEW HORSES, but he was a particular expert on breeding. He had started his career as a journalist, and one of his early assignments was to cover the first Olympic equestrian events in 1912 in Stockholm, Sweden. Germany had made a poor showing in the world's inaugural international riding competition. Since then, Rau had developed an obsession: He wanted the German horse to be the best in the world, a goal he meant to accomplish by utilizing the still poorly understood principles of genetic inheritance.

Rau had begun developing his theories in the 1920s, when his greatest hope was to revitalize Germany's horse-breeding industry by promoting an interest in horseback riding. After World War I, several factors combined to almost destroy horse breeding and equestrian sports in Germany. The numbers of equine casualties were so high during the war that the horse population declined by half. In addition, the inflationary conditions in Germany made the sale and upkeep of horses difficult, and to further complicate matters, Germany was required to export horses as part of the reparations imposed by the Treaty of Versailles. So, Rau's goal to increase the demand for horses by promoting the popularity of equestrian sports in rural Germany was an excellent idea.

As the National Socialist Party came into power, Rau found that the Nazis shared his enthusiasm for this goal. Hitler's National Socialists were eager to establish themselves with the prestige of international military competitions, and soon the SS riders, known as "the Blacks," were fielding teams to compete with the German Army teams, known as "the Grays." German equestrians increasingly made their mark in international competitions. In 1930 the German Army team won the prestigious international jumping competition at the National Horse Show in New York, and their triumph was touted in newspapers on both sides of the Atlantic. As the decade continued, these two top-notch military teams brought international prestige to Germany at a time when the country was struggling to recover from its devastating defeat in World War I.

On the cover of its April 3, 1933, issue, Germany's most influential horse magazine featured Hitler's portrait, captioned: "The Man Who Put Germany Back in the Saddle." That same season, the German riders won the prestigious Italian Mussolini Gold Cup for the third time, snatching it away from the Italian hosts, who had long dominated the contest. On May 24, 1933, the winning rider wrote a letter to Hitler offering him his champion horse, Wotan the "wonder horse," as a gift. The following day, before an audience of more than a thousand horsemen gathered for a large horse show in Berlin, Gustav Rau read Hitler's telegraphed acceptance aloud. A photograph of the event shows the small man wearing a white suit, his bald head shining in the spring sunshine, his right arm raised in the Hitler salute, the führer's telegram clutched in his other hand.

BREEDING HORSES FOR SPECIFIC purposes had been pursued avidly in Europe for several hundred years. Human and equine life were deeply

GUSTAV RAU
EXPLAINS
THE FINE
POINTS OF
BREEDING AND
CONFORMATION.

intertwined, since human enterprise required equestrian help for almost every task, from transportation to heavy work to engaging in warfare. Through trial and error, men had managed to make significant modifications in their equestrian companions. Riding horses need speed and good temperaments, plow horses need brute strength, military horses are best if they have hearty constitutions and don't require much food. Breeders used observation and trial and error to perfect horses to type, but the science was poorly understood. At the time of Gustav Rau's visit to America, many still believed that a breed's traits were related to the environment in which it was bred—climate, elevation, and type of feed—and that a change in environment might cause a breed to lose its characteristic features.

Rau's horse-breeding expertise was entirely self-taught, his theories a hodgepodge of seat-of-the-pants observation, established traditions, and pseudo-science. He believed that breeding closely related horses was the surest way to the best-quality progeny with a high degree of uniformity, aiming to create "a whole race comparatively fast and so even and identical that one horse looks like another."

Rau's horse-breeding theories soon caught the eye of Richard Walther Darré, one of the primary architects of the Nazi ideology known as *Blut und Boden,* or blood and land, which mythologized the "purity" of the German rural people and folkways. As minister of food and agriculture, Darré appointed Rau to be the chief equerry of the German state of Prussia in 1934. More than any other Nazi theorist, Darré provided the ideological background for the Nazi policy of expansion, known as *Lebensraum* (living space), which purported that strong, healthy "Nordic-type" people needed more territory in which to expand and grow, hence justifying their wars of aggression and occupation. Darré's theories strongly influenced Himmler, Reich leader of the SS, providing an ideological framework to bolster Himmler's desire to create a German nation based on a purely Nordic or Aryan race.

Rau seemed only too happy to associate himself with these powerful allies. In 1934, he published a book entitled *Horsebreeding in the National Socialist State.* Reaching beyond its title, the book expanded his breeding theories to include beliefs about the racial purity of people, declaring that only farmers whose family trees had "unmixed blood" would "have the sense to breed pureblooded horses." The English were renowned for their Thoroughbreds; Poland bred the world's finest

Arabian horses; Rau's dream was that the German nation would produce the greatest military horse.

By May 1938, when Rau and his party arrived in New York, events
in Nazi Germany were taking an ominous turn. In March, Germany
had invaded Austria; by the following September, Hitler would have
annexed large portions of Czechoslovakia, and by signing the Munich
Agreement, France, Great Britain, and Italy would let him get away
with it. By November 1938, the persecution of Jews could be hidden
no more as crazed mobs stormed the streets of Berlin and other large
cities, burning synagogues and smashing Jewish-owned store windows
during the night of broken glass known as *Kristallnacht*.

But in America, the atmosphere was finally lightening a bit after
years of severe economic woes. Howard Hughes set an airspeed record,
flying his H-1 Racer around the world in just ninety-one hours. The
federal minimum wage was established, providing unprecedented protection for American workers, and Walt Disney released his first short
cartoon that featured Donald Duck. But amid this brightening landscape, an urgent debate was growing. Many declared that Americans
should take a stand against Hitler's aggressive aims; an equally vocal
group took a strict isolationist stance.

The first event on the Reich equestrians' American tour was a motor
trip to nearby Elmont, New York, for a visit to the iconic Gilded Age
racetrack Belmont Park. This elegant venue attracted members of the
American aristocracy who had long been passionate about horses, as
well as the new-moneyed industrial titans who aped these patricians to
improve their social standing. "The sport of kings" was an ostentatious
way for the country's nouveau riche to flaunt their wealth, and Belmont was built in 1906 to be their own private playground. According
to track historian Paul Moran, "From concept to completion in its
original form, the new racecourse that would be named Belmont Park
in honor of the first August Belmont, was a project by, of, and for the
American aristocracy, which was defined strictly by wealth, position
and lineage." In truth, Belmont's Jockey Club, the organization that
controlled Thoroughbred racing in America, was founded by a mix of

people. Some were blue-blooded Americans who traced their ancestry to *Mayflower* voyagers and Puritan founding fathers, and others were nouveau riche industrialists who wished to ally themselves—through marriages to aristocrats, membership in the Episcopal Church, and associations with the elite sport of horse racing—to the American upper crust.

At Belmont Park, the races were run clockwise, known as "English-style," so that the well-heeled spectators could see the finish line from their vantage point in the posh clubhouse. Rau and his guests settled into the covered clubhouse, eager to see American Thoroughbred horseracing on display. The Thoroughbred was originally an English breed, and to this day, all so-named horses trace their lineage back to three stallions imported into England from the Middle East in the late seventeenth and early eighteenth centuries. When bred to the heavier English draft horse, the result was a lighter, faster, more hot-blooded horse that proved adept at racing. By the middle of the nineteenth century, Thoroughbred horses could reach sixteen hands, a full four inches taller than the size of the foundational sires: Selective breeding had produced a bigger, speedier horse, and one so highly strung and sensitive that it wanted to break out fast and keep on going. Perhaps nowhere more than in the field of horse racing had the concepts of selective breeding been so assiduously applied. To create the highest-quality animals, breeders relied on two principles, superior bloodlines and demonstrated performance, to get the swiftest possible horses. A seasoned horse could be evaluated on his track record, but each time an untested two-year-old pranced out onto the racetrack, everyone from the owners to the breeders to the ordinary folk who wagered on the outcomes turned into an amateur scientist in the inheritance of genetic traits. In many ways, the trial-and-error successes of horse breeding had surpassed the state of the science. Prior to the discovery of DNA, scientists did not know exactly how traits were transmitted from parent to offspring, but the refinement of the Thoroughbred horse had demonstrated that both basic qualities, such as size and color, and more complex qualities, like heart and temperament, seemed heritable through judicious choices in breeding.

Belmont Park was not the only place on Long Island where people were taking an interest in the results of selective breeding. Twenty-five miles away, in Cold Spring Harbor, New York, Mary Harriman, widow of railroad magnate E. H. Harriman, had donated the funds to found a brand-new "scientific" research center: the Eugenics Record Office. The director, Charles B. Davenport, a Harvard-trained professor of zoology, held the zealous belief that principles of breeding developed for livestock could be applied to humankind. The goal of the ERO was to train "eugenic field-workers" who would create pedigree records for American families to replicate the kind of breeding records that already existed for horses, with the aim of identifying both strong bloodlines and weak ones. The proximity of the two endeavors, the racetrack and the Eugenics Record Office, was more than coincidental. A conservative upper-class faction, many of whom kept baronial estates on Long Island, shared both a keen interest in horse breeding and a desire to improve American human bloodstock by applying the racist and pseudo-scientific concepts of eugenics.

Sir Francis Galton, a cousin of Charles Darwin, first coined the term "eugenics" in his 1883 book *Human Faculty and Its Development*. Galton was a statistician who, among other endeavors, developed formulas that helped to predict the outcome of horse races. Galton theorized that just as the natural world benefited from the process of natural selection, so would human society benefit from weeding out weaker elements: Eugenicists believed that just as horse breeders could breed a bigger, swifter, better racehorse, scientists could eventually eliminate from the human population those considered "undesirables"—which he defined with fuzzy terms such as "feeble-minded" (which could run the gamut from the severely developmentally delayed, to epileptics, to unwed mothers) and "degenerate" (from drunks, to petty thieves, to the unemployed). Galton and his followers imagined a future in which society had become homogenized and social ills had been quite simply bred out of the population.

In 1930, Alfred Frank Tredgold, a physician at London University Hospital, referred to Britain's most important horse race—the Grand National—in his address to the British Eugenics Society on Racial Fitness: "It is safe to say that if the principles of eugenics had not been applied to horses there would have been no Grand National at all." Charles B. Davenport once remarked to a prospective donor that the most "progressive revolution in human history" would be attained "if human matings could be placed upon the same high plane as those of horse-breeding."

The notion that mankind could be improved by using similar principles to those that had created the Thoroughbred horse was enjoying an intellectual vogue, and in the United States, the idea had gained favor with some of the very plutocrats who would have been sitting in the stands hobnobbing with the German visitors in 1938.

The Reich visitors would have been familiar already with the concept of a human pedigree. In order to be accepted as a member of the Nazi Party, an individual needed to be able to demonstrate that he or she had "pure blood" that went back at least four generations. Aspiring civil servants, especially those who came from German-speaking regions of Slavic countries, were required to carry a document to prove their Aryan ancestry.

THE SECOND DAY OF the Reich equestrians' visit was spent away from horses, touring the metropolis of New York City, a glittering testament to modern industrial power. The Empire State Building and the Chrysler Building rose sparkling above the skyline, each under a decade old. From its bustling harbor to its coin-operated Automat restaurants, New York seemed to the Old World European visitors to burst with novelty.

And here, in America's largest and most modern city, the science of eugenics had its own temple. The American Museum of Natural History filled most of Manhattan Square, its Victorian Gothic visage glowering over Central Park like a disapproving schoolmarm. The grand new entrance on Central Park West was a memorial to the famous naturalist and statesman Theodore Roosevelt, and was home to one of the most impressive collections of natural artifacts in the world. Effectively a shrine to the principles of evolution, housing a dinosaur collection that was arguably the finest in the world, the museum was also the display place for the skeleton of the American racehorse Sysonby, famed for winning fourteen of fifteen starts. (His groom later admitted to being bribed to ensure the stallion's single loss by drugging him before the race.) Sysonby's scientific contribution was to furnish "the most perfect example of the bony frame of the modern racehorse in existence as he was a horse of perfect conformation and size, aside from his superior qualities as a racehorse."

From 1908 to 1933, the museum's director was Henry Fairfield Os-

SYSONBY'S SKELETON ON DISPLAY AT THE
AMERICAN MUSEUM OF NATURAL HISTORY, 1908.

born, whose significant contribution to the study of dinosaurs was marred by his devotion to eugenics and his admiration for Hitler. In 1921, to great fanfare, the museum opened the director's brainchild, an exhibit called Osborn's Hall of the Age of Man, which purported to show the evolution of the "human races" from "primitive" to "advanced" expressions of humanity. The entire show was based upon flawed science—in particular, Osborn's embrace of "the Piltdown Man," bits of fossilized bone fragments that were popularly believed to provide the "missing link" between apes and humans. While other contemporary scientists questioned the validity of the findings (which were later proved to be a deliberate hoax—an ape's mandible fused to a human skull), Osborn attested that the skull proved the primeval ancestor of modern man was not an African or Asian but an Anglo-Saxon. In August 1932, the Museum of Natural History had played host to the Third International Congress on Eugenics, at which Elmont's E. H. Harriman was the keynote speaker. Among the scheduled events, alongside lectures on the dangers of race mixing and the benefits of involuntary sterilization, was a presentation about horse racing. Here again, the science of breeding a better horse was deeply intertwined with the parallel push to understand and improve the human race.

After a day of sightseeing in Manhattan, the German equestrians' next stop on the tour was a visit north to Goshen, New York, to see a famous stable of American trotting horses bred by another Harriman—E. Roland Harriman, the late E. H. Harriman's brother. Throughout the nineteenth century, harness racing was one of America's favorite homegrown sports. Popular in agrarian towns, harness racing started to decline as the country industrialized. One of the country's biggest promoters of trotting races was E. Roland Harriman, who invested in the breeding of trotters and served as president of the American Trotting Horse Association, thus almost single-handedly keeping interest alive in this quintessentially Yankee sport. Seated in the grandstand donated in 1911 by his sister-in-law Mary Harriman, the same philanthropist who had donated the funds to found the Eugenics Record Office at Cold Spring Harbor, the Reich equestrians would have the opportunity to see modern breeding at its most refined level.

The American Standardbred differs in important ways from his more storied racing brother, the Thoroughbred. The Standardbred is judged not by his noble ancestry but by his ability to perform a specific task: to trot the distance of one mile in less than two minutes and thirty seconds. The differences between the Thoroughbred and Standardbred are evident in the names of the breeds: "Thoroughbred," denoting purity of blood; "Standardbred," denoting a close match to a breed standard. Standardbred racing, perhaps not surprisingly, had a particular popularity among American industrialists who seemed drawn to the idea of horses being produced for reliability and standardization, like factory output. Unlike the principle of pure bloodlines underlying Thoroughbred horse breeding, the line of reasoning for breeders of Standardbreds was somewhat different: To breed a standardized horse with uniform skills, they selected horses that most closely met their target criteria. This practice would have been of much interest to Rau, whose dream was to create a breed of German military horses that would be as closely matched as industrially produced machines.

From Goshen, Rau's group headed to the Devon Horse Show on Philadelphia's tony Main Line, then continued to Baltimore. Off Reisterstown Road in the Worthington Valley north of Baltimore, Alfred Vanderbilt's Sagamore Farms spread out over more than five hundred acres. The farm had more than eighteen miles of white fences, and its distinctive red-roofed training stable had ninety stalls and a quarter-mile indoor track. There was a good bit of cross-pollination between European and American Thoroughbreds at that time, as wealthy breeders from the United States attended the best Thoroughbred horse auctions on the Continent. Vanderbilt, who received the farm as a twenty-first-birthday gift from his mother, had acquired from the Aga Khan the breeding rights to one of Europe's finest Thoroughbreds, the English Triple Crown winner Bahram. After they surveyed the grandeur of Vanderbilt's farm, the equestrians' next stop was the bluegrass of Lexington, Kentucky, heart of American Thoroughbred breeding. At each stop on the tour, the Germans toured stables, watched displays of fine horsemanship, and discussed the finer points of breeding and training.

When Rau's group reached their final destination, the cavalry base at Fort Leavenworth, Kansas, they stepped off the train into a landscape so different from Germany's that their senses must have been reeling. An enormous blue sky arched over the wide-open expanses surrounding the rural town where they would tour one of the U.S. Army's impressive western cavalry schools. In his notes on the 1936 Olympic competition, Rau was proud to note how many contenders from other countries rode German-bred mounts. Not so the Americans, who brought their own U.S. Army–bred chargers to Berlin. At Fort Leavenworth, Rau could observe firsthand the Americans' breeding program, which operated on a principle quite different from the models that stressed the "pure-bloodedness" so prized by Rau. The Americans had started their program in 1918, inspired, just as Rau was, by seeing the world's horses gathered together at the 1912 Olympics. But the Americans adopted a completely different approach with the establishment of the army's Remount Division in 1918, which sought out stallions with desirable characteristics such as hardiness, good temperament, soundness, and medium stature. The breeds varied, and included Thoroughbreds, Morgans, Quarter Horses, and Arabians. These stallions were disbursed throughout the country—on loan to ranchers, especially in the Western Plains, where most of the nation's horses were raised. Any local could breed a mare to one of the army's stallions for a nominal stud fee, as long as the mare was considered fit for breeding. At Rau's Olympics, one of these mixed-blood remount horses, Jenny Camp, had captured the silver medal after a brilliant performance in the grueling three-day competition. This little mare had proven that a range-bred horse, the product of a Thoroughbred sire and dam of unknown breeding, could compete against the world's most rarefied purebreds.

In the United States and Britain, the vogue for applying principles of selective horse breeding to human society would never fully take hold, thankfully; while the interest lingered among the more conservative elements of the American upper class, by the mid-1930s the ideas had begun to generally fall from favor. The exhibits in Osborn's Hall of the Age of Man would be taken down and the "science" behind them discredited. But in Adolf Hitler's Third Reich, these ideas would take hold and thrive, with disastrous results for both people and horses.

AS RAU STEAMED BACK across the Atlantic with his entourage, he hoped to bring some of these modern American ideas to Germany, tempered with his own belief in the superiority of the European (particularly German) horses. Soon history would give him the opportunity to put his theories to work on an unprecedented scale.

By the time the Reich equestrians docked in Bremerhaven, they had seen most of what America's finest horse breeders had to offer. The group had returned to a Germany that was teetering on the brink of a modern war in which the breeding of horses would nonetheless play a central role in the Reich's logistical planning. The German Army was known for its technological prowess, yet it still relied heavily on horses for the transport of heavy artillery and supplies. The military needed to rapidly increase the number of horses at the army's disposal. In 1938, the peacetime German Army possessed only 183,000 horses (including donkeys). By 1945, the Germans would employ 2.7 million horses in the war effort, more than double the number used in World War I. Just back from his American reconnaissance trip, Rau was in an ideal position to put his horse-breeding skills to work for the German military machine.

Hitler would invade Poland in just six months. In the blueprint forged for its occupation, a plan was put into place for the "rebuilding of Poland's horse-breeding industry" for the "interest of the German nation." To head up that program, the German Army High Command chose Gustav Rau.

3.

THE POLISH PRINCE

Four hundred and thirty-five miles due east of the plotters at Berlin's Army High Command, the staff of Janów Podlaski Stud Farm had no idea that the Germans had designs on their purebred Arabians. The horses here at Poland's only national stud farm lived in lush meadows that bordered the sparkling Bug River. Galloping across the farm's grassy fields, they seemed to float on an ethereal plane—their silken tails caught the wind like unfurled banners; their tread was light enough to dance a Chopin polonaise.

Inside one of the stud farm's roomy box stalls, at four-thirty A.M. on April 30, 1938, a gray mare delivered a colt onto a thick bed of clean straw. From the moment he struggled upright on long, awkward legs and his luminous dark brown eyes gazed out upon the world, he attracted notice, his perfect proportions immediately marking him as one of the most promising foals of the year. On his wide forehead, he had a large white star that looked remarkably like an outline of his native Poland, and his feet were white up to his fetlocks—a marking known as socks. These would add extra flash each time he lifted his hooves. Between his two nostrils, he had one more bright spot of white—a snip—which accentuated his delicate flaring nostrils, coal black on the outside, pink as a conch on the inside. His grand name, Witez, was fitting for such a fine foal. It was an old Polish word meaning "warrior, chieftain, knight," and wrapped up in the name were the concepts of honor, courage, and loyalty.

Established in 1817, the white brick stables at Janów Podlaski formed a U around a large courtyard; its central stable was named Zegarowa—the Clock Stable—for the square clock tower that crowned its center. The buildings' gray slate roofs reflected the spring sunshine. Flanked on all sides by ample pastures, the breeding stables at Janów followed traditional precepts.

The first mentions of Arabian horses bred in Poland date back to the late seventeenth century. Introduced into Poland by the Ottoman Turks, they became so sought after that in the nineteenth century, a handful of wealthy Polish noblemen traveled to Arabia in search of purebreds, bringing them home to create breeding stables on their large estates. Bolshevik marauders in 1917 raided most of the large Polish stud farms and slaughtered the horses, which they viewed as playthings of princes. Horses hung from the barn rafters, their throats slit. Stable courtyards turned into lakes of blood. Of the five hundred registered purebred Arabians in Poland prior to 1917, only fifty survived the raids. In 1918, at the close of World War I, the count of purebred horses at Janów was zero. Painstakingly, the farm's director, Stanislaw Pohoski, had rebuilt this stud farm from the ground up. It had taken almost twenty years to recover, but now, in the spring of 1938, Poland's national breeding program was in full swing, with thirty-three broodmares producing a bumper crop of promising foals.

The stud farm's assistant director, Andrzej Kristalovich, was a quiet young man with a serious angular face. Born in Vienna, Andrzej had grown up around horses, as his father worked on some of Poland's greatest horse estates. As a boy, fascinated with machines and flight, Andrzej first wanted to become an aviator, but his love for horses won out. (Still, he indulged his fondness for machines by tooling around in a shiny new American Ford car.)

In December 1938, Kristalovich arrived at Janów to take up his position as assistant director of the stud farm. Witez was not yet a year old. The young Pole quickly decided that the bay colt with the white star was the cream of that year's crop and that Janów Podlaski would soon regain the stature it had enjoyed before the Great War. This year, the best stallion, Ofir, had produced three magnificent colts: Witez and his two half brothers, Witraz (Stained Glass) and Wielki Szjlam (Grand Slam). The farm's director, forty-three-year-old Stanislaw Pohoski, was twenty years his senior and would eventually retire. Kristalovich hoped that he would one day succeed him as director of Poland's national stud farm, and that together, he and the three colts of 1938 and those to come would build up Polish Arabian horse breeding to new heights. Kristalovich lingered next to the pasture fence as Witez cavorted alongside his mother, Federajca. The dam, a gray mare, had a rare marking called "the bloody shoulder." According to Arabian lore, a mare with this distinctive patch of reddish hair would give birth to horses that would win glory in battle.

At the beginning of 1939, though everything at Janów appeared prosperous and serene, dark clouds of trouble were massing all around the peaceful stables. Within just six months, by the last week in August, the Germans and Russians would sign a non-aggression pact, secretly agreeing that they would not fight over Poland but, rather, divide the country into two spheres of influence. One week later, on September 1, 1939, Germany invaded Poland from the west. Witez and his brothers were just a year old.

Janów Podlaski was situated five miles from the Bug River, which formed the border with its eastern neighbor, Russia. Any thought that the Germans would be slow to venture so far east was soon dispelled. In just five days, the German blitzkrieg had broken across the Vistula River, which roughly parallels the Bug, running through Poland's center. It had seemed like an impenetrable barrier. The Germans were 150 miles from Janów and advancing rapidly.

As the situation grew more threatening, the stud farm's small staff huddled together, discussing their plans in worried whispers. Kristalovich listened carefully as Pohoski weighed their options. The stud farm's director was old enough to remember the depredations visited upon them the last time the horses of Janów Podlaski had been trapped in a war zone. As they talked, the men surveyed the fruits of their labor: the dappled mares with foals at their sides, the regal stallion Ofir, the three glorious yearling colts. The thought of them being slaughtered was devastating. To embark on a long overland trip with the horses would be fraught with difficulty, but the director feared staying put even more. No good solution presented itself. After days of wavering, Pohoski made a final decision. They would evacuate the entire staff and all of the horses. Their route would take them east over the Bug River, then south toward Romania, where they hoped to find refuge—a trek of more than five hundred overland miles.

On the morning of September 11, 1939, the unlikely group set off on the highway: Pohoski took the lead, driving a carriage containing their belongings, pulled by two horses; next came the stallion manager on foot, leading the boisterous group of more than a dozen stallions. A young groom had hold of Witez's lead rope. As the prince waltzed out of the stable, eyes bright and tail held high, he looked as if he were embarking on a joyful promenade instead of the flight of his life. Kristalovich led the last group—the most vulnerable, the mares with frolicking foals at their sides.

The long line of 250 fine-boned Arabians snaked down the narrow, rutted country roads; the percussive sound of their hoofbeats filled the air as they passed humble farms and simple dwellings whose inhabitants startled at the sight of the prancing equine princes and princesses, as out of place as a royal entourage driving through a peasant village. But when they reached the main east-west highway, the group from Janów joined a flood of desperate people—some on foot, others with horse-drawn carts overloaded with their possessions. The roads were filled with refugees streaming east from the German advance. Their fellow travelers shared terrifying tales—the German Luftwaffe had been strafing refugee columns and attacking civilians. The roads were not safe. The group from Janów decided to travel only at night.

Witez's groom watched him with a worried eye. The colt was high-spirited, but after hours of trekking, his fatigue was evident. Soon Witez and his two half brothers were having trouble keeping pace with the older stallions. On the crowded roadways, the horses were difficult to control. Kristalovich tried to keep a head count, but the grooms handling the horses could only look on helplessly if one started and broke away. Soon some of the youngest foals were dragging behind as their mares nudged and pushed them along. Before long, a few started to stumble and fall, unable to take another step.

Then, as they crested a hill, disaster struck. The group came upon an enormous Polish military convoy blocking the center of the road. The horses in front panicked at the unexpected sight and started to rear and bolt. A moment later, in a chain reaction, the roadway became a battlefield of horses with flailing hooves turning and spinning in all directions. It was complete pandemonium. Grooms tried desperately to hold on to their charges, but in the confusion, a large group of horses broke away. Kristalovich watched helplessly as Witez tore off, heading toward the deepest reaches of the forest. By the time the Janów men gained control, more than eighty horses had fled—including the three most precious, Witez, Stained Glass, and Grand Slam.

Unable to leave the main road or abandon their horses in order to search the woods, the diminished group from Janów had no choice but to keep moving forward. Kristalovich vowed that when they had reached a safe place, he would return to search out the left-behind horses. As they moved on, the air sounded with the whinnies of the remaining horses, crying for their lost comrades. Somewhere in the forest, Witez wandered alone. Devastated, Stanislaw Pohoski pulled out his pistol and pointed it at his temple, determined to kill himself as a matter of honor. Kristalovich spoke to him softly but urgently. His duty was to save the remaining horses. They could not give up now. After a pause that seemed to last forever, Pohoski lowered his pistol and returned it to his holster.

The group forged on, watching as the younger foals continued to struggle, their tender hooves deteriorating from the long journey. After a while they noticed that refugees were now moving in both directions—some fleeing east, others moving west. Everyone seemed confused about which way might lead to safety. The roads were cluttered with people and blockades hastily thrown up by the out-gunned Polish forces. The low visibility at night posed its own dangers. One night, they stumbled into barbed wire strung across the road. Before they realized what had happened, eight of the horses were so badly entangled that no one could extricate them. Shrill cries rent the air, their terror only serving to bind the wires more tightly around them. Silently, Kristalovich pulled out his pistol. Eight single well-placed shots rang out in the night. The screams ceased, but the night became heavier, blacker, and more desperate for the refugees from Janów.

There was no promise of relief. Word soon reached the group that the Russians had crossed Poland's eastern border on September 17 and were heading toward them. After three exhausting days of trekking, the riders, grooms, and remaining horses finally made it to a small wooden bridge that led over the Bug River. Safety from the Germans lay on the other side. When the last of the horses safely crossed the bridge, the men of Janów thought their worst troubles were behind them. With renewed hope, they headed toward the village of Kovol, a couple of miles down the road, hoping to find a place to rest and shelter the horses. But as they neared the village, they saw that something was terribly wrong. Orange flames stood out against the sky: The village was on fire. The sound of artillery boomed deafeningly close and was getting closer. After days of exhausting and dangerous travel, no safer than when they started off, the group could advance no farther.

Not seeing any alternative, Pohoski made an agonizing decision: They would return to Janów, collecting the left-behind horses as they went. Footsore, hungry, the dwindling group headed back along the same crowded road. As they began to retrace their steps, they felt as if the road were under a shadow. The entire journey, the loss of the young horses—it had all been for nothing. After a few miles, they were back at the place where they had crossed the Bug, but now the bridge lay in rubble. The river was impassable. Heartsick, they turned south. They would not even have the chance to retrieve the horses left along the road. A few miles downstream, unable to find an intact bridge, the men forced the tired horses to ford the river.

Thin, lame, and exhausted, the decimated group arrived at Janów a few days later, hobbled through the gates of their home, and started a period of tense waiting, knowing that the invading army would soon arrive. The white buildings and green fields appeared unchanged. The tall clock tower over the stable measured out the slow tick of time. On September 25, the waiting ended: Six Russian tanks appeared on the horizon. Janów Podlaski was under Russian occupation.

At first, the Russian troops showed little interest in the horses. Kristalovich and Pohoski and the rest of the staff tried to stay out of sight, emerging only to feed and care for their animals. Warily, they watched, wondering what would happen next. On the morning of October 5, the Polish inhabitants of Janów noted with some relief that the Russians appeared to be getting ready to leave. But their relief soon turned to terror: The soldiers were preparing to take the horses with them—no matter that the animals were in no condition to travel. But the Poles' protests were fruitless. The small staff of the stud farm was no match for a regiment of Russian soldiers.

Kristalovich watched in horror as a brutish Russian soldier tramped into the stall of a small gray mare named Nejada. As he attempted to put on her halter, the mare, seeming to understand the danger, lashed out—striking the Russian and injuring him so severely that he decided to leave her alone. The troops torched the stables as they left, destroying everything they could before leaving. They even wrenched the windows from the frames.

By the afternoon of October 5, Nejada was the only remaining equine inhabitant of Janów. The wrecked white stables, badly scorched from the fires, stood empty. The rest of the farm was eerily peaceful. Swans floated on a pond that lazily lapped the edges of the verdant pastures. Janów's inhabitants had watched the horses' hindquarters, their high-carried tails and springy powerful hocks, head east in the company of Russian tanks and disappear. (Only after the war would the Poles learn that their final destination was the Tersk stud farm in Russia, almost a thousand miles away.) Kristalovich and his staff had done everything they could to protect the horses. Now, just five short weeks since the invasion had started, they were left with nothing but empty stables. Where just a few weeks ago Poland's most beautiful living treasures had galloped across the meadows, their coats shining in the sunlight, now barn cats wandered through the stable aisles, past lifeless stalls where half-eaten rations of oats lay untouched in the mangers and water buckets remained half full.

Just a few weeks after the Russian departure, a different enemy approached from the opposite direction. A shiny black chauffeur-driven limousine rolled up the drive and into the eerily quiet stable yard. As the car braked in front of Janów's tall clock tower, out stepped the newly appointed commissioner for horse breeding and stud farming in the former Poland. Gustav Rau, dressed in his Sumatra greatcoat, rolling a cigar between his fingers, had arrived at the scorched and looted stables of Janów Podlaski ready to take charge. His task was to reassemble the Polish horse-breeding industry for the glory of the Third Reich.

It was a quirk of Nazi philosophy, so inhumane to humans, that animals were treated with the utmost care and kindness. Nazi Germany was the first government to outlaw vivisection, the practice of experimenting on animals while they were still alive. The Nazis also reformed the definitions of humane treatment of animals and put into place safeguards for animal welfare that predated reforms adopted by other countries. Adolf Hitler was a vegetarian, and while he was not a horseman and did not appear to take a direct interest in the horse-breeding operations, he supported rebuilding the Polish breeding programs, as they went directly along with his greater reprehensible aims for the Polish territories. In a cruel and ironic twist of fate, the German invaders, whose express aim was to relocate, enslave, massacre, and eventually annihilate Poland's human inhabitants, prized the well-bred Polish horses. The goal for the Polish horse industry under German rule was twofold: first, to breed horses to keep up with the insatiable need for horses used for transport and logistics; and second, to provide workhorses to help cultivate the seized Polish lands.

Gustav Rau, Olympic organizer, connoisseur of fine horses, had a rapacious appetite for the world's most elegant specimens. The Arabian was known by horse breeders as "the great improver." Breeding Arabian stallions with the mares of other breeds tended to improve conformation, temperament, and rideability—all characteristics prized in the military horse. In the convoluted logic that ruled the concept of pure-bloodedness, Arabian horses were deemed to have pure blood, so they could be paired with other breeds without affecting the breed's integrity. In the words of Hans Fellgiebel, Janów's new Rau-appointed director, Janów had been, before the war, "the continued source of the cleanest and purest blood which made the domestic country horse what it is today." Rau immediately set to work restoring Poland's premier stud farm. With the organizational skills that had allowed him to put together the equestrian competitions at the Olympics, he set out to find the horses lost along the route when the Poles had tried to flee, and bring them back to German-run Janów.

All along the escape route, patriotic Poles, recognizing that these horses were Polish treasure, had found and stashed the runaways in barns and sheds, daubing them with mud to disguise their beauty and hide their distinctive brands. But the Polish peasants were afraid of the new German overlords and handed over the horses when asked. Even so, eighty percent of the Arabians from Janów were never recovered. Among those lost forever was Witez's dam, Federajca. Witez, thin, bedraggled, and pitiably weak, limped back into Janów Podlaski along with his two half brothers, lucky to be among the thirty-odd young horses that were found scattered about the Polish countryside. The son of Federajca, the mare with the bloody shoulder, had survived his first battle.

The Polish employees of Janów hung back at first, unsure of their welcome and afraid of the German intruders. But Kristalovich's passion for his horses was too great for him to stay away long. Seeing that Hans Fellgiebel, Rau's appointee to run Janów, appeared fair-minded, he stepped forward and volunteered his services as a humble groom— a huge step down from his previous position as assistant director, but the best he could do if he wanted to stay with the horses. After a while the farm returned to a topsy-turvy kind of normal. At least the horses were no longer in direct danger.

Janów Podlaski was not the only stud farm taken over by Rau. All over Poland, carefully tended equestrian stud farms were coming under siege, some invaded by Russian forces, others seized by Germans. Neither fared uniformly well. Still, as a general rule, the Germans looked after the horses, which they considered to be valuable assets, whereas those horses in the pathway of Russian troops were more likely to be lost or killed. The Arabians seized at Janów and transported to the Tersk stud farm in Russia (and then eventually moved again, on foot, all the way to Kazakhstan) fared poorly. Of the twenty-seven mares seized by the Russians at Janów, only nine lived longer than three years. All in all, the horses and the staff of the Polish stud farms suffered greatly during the war years. Relative to the other farms, those in Gustav Rau's dominion fared better than most. The native Poles worked tirelessly, cooperating with those who had come as conquerors, and made tremendous personal sacrifice on behalf of the horses.

Rau watched over an expanding network of German-controlled horse-breeding establishments in Poland. His sumptuous lodgings, seized from a wealthy Jewish textile merchant in Lodz, were within view of the barbed-wire fences of the city's ghetto. He bragged to those in his dominion that he had "a direct line to the führer." The high-handed chief of horse breeding was described by one who knew him as "a man in love with power" as he made the rounds of his new dominion, carefully documenting the details of all the horses in the territories seized by Germany. Since Rau had first observed the top equine specimens of all nations at the 1912 Olympic Games, he had dreamed of being able to breed the perfect horse for Germany. Now, with all of Poland's 3.9 million horses under his jurisdiction, he had an unparalleled opportunity to try to do so. At Janów Podlaski, the luminous, intelligent, light-footed Witez had not escaped his notice. Those who knew Rau said he never forgot a horse, and indeed, he would not forget the Polish prince, Witez.

To gaze upon the blood bay Arabian Witez was to imagine how nobility made flesh would appear. But what did the stallion see as he gazed at the chaotic world around him? His country of birth was under siege, scene of more death, willful destruction, mayhem, and darkness than any other country in Europe. His father had been carried off like looted treasure; his mother had been lost in the turmoil and would never be found. Every morning, he whickered when he saw his groom coming to feed him. He needed what all horses need—care and kindness, fresh oats, clean straw, exercise, a loving word, and a gentle pat. Around him swirled the dark forces of war: men driven by a lust for

WITEZ IN GERMANY.

power. Of this, Witez, now two years old, knew nothing. Squeezed between Russia and Germany, two great powers, Polish citizens, both equine and human, were caught in the middle. Gustav Rau had imposed an artificial peace on the stables of Janów Podlaski, but their war was not yet over. It had only just begun.

4.

RAU'S DOMINION

Veterinarian Rudolf Lessing looked out from a train that was paused in the station, en route to a German-run stud farm in Debica, Poland. Lessing served as adjutant to Gustav Rau. In his German Army uniform, he was clean and well fed, a tall, handsome man with light blue eyes, sandy hair, and a long chiseled face. From his train window, Lessing could see black ashes spewing into the air, blackening the gray sky like a spreading blot of ink. He couldn't help recoiling at the sight of the murky sky, but he could not avert his eyes. Out the window, above the busy platform, the sign read "Auschwitz." Beyond heavy barbed-wire fences, a huge German industrial complex spread out toward the horizon. Lessing knew that at this "agricultural station," a gruesome truth was unfolding. On a recent trip home to Mecklenburg, east of Berlin, he had tried to explain what was happening in Poland to his father: "They're gassing the Jews. So many people know what's going on." His father had refused to believe him, but Lessing could not afford the luxury of disbelief. The smell clung to the inside of his nostrils, and the smoky residue settled into his uniform. The train rolled out of Auschwitz station.

If the Germans win this war, there is no God Almighty, he thought.

In 1942, the Axis was at the height of its powers as Hitler's stranglehold stretched across Europe, from France to the Ukraine, from Norway to Italy. In occupied Poland, Rau's German-run horse-breeding enterprise was flourishing. The sleek, well-tended horses and the manicured grounds of these stud farms existed, in a through-the-lookingglass juxtaposition, not far from the barbed wire of concentration camps and death camps that latticed occupied Poland after 1939. Karl Koch, the camp commander of Buchenwald, erected on the grounds a riding stable, a racetrack, and an indoor riding hall for himself and his wife. Germans lavished money and attention on breeding farms, horse shows, races, and pleasure riding that they enjoyed during their occupation of Poland. With a cold-blooded hubris, the Third Reich had created a vast kingdom of horses, and Rau was its emperor.

Three years had passed since Gustav Rau first arrived at Janów Podlaski, restoring the stud farm and finding the lost horses. His dominion had spread out across the vast expanse of Poland; he had fourteen stud farms and more than seventy people in his employ. The most notorious was on the grounds of Auschwitz, a four-hundred-acre experimental farm, as well as stables for horses ridden by the SS Totenkopf, or Death's Head, squadrons, known for perpetrating some of the Third Reich's most heinous atrocities. The Germans were churning through horses at an astonishing rate—the army demanded six thousand fresh ones per month to replace those killed or lost to disease.

Gustav Rau had limitless funds at his disposal. Together with Lessing and other members of his staff, he traveled all over Europe, attending the largest horse sales, seizing the horses from state-owned stud farms in occupied territories, or "purchasing," often well below the actual value, from private owners. Rau's acquisitiveness focused on horses characterized by highly refined pedigrees; he was hoping to capture their vaunted pure blood for his mission to create the quintessentially German warhorse. Soon his interest began to center more and more on the Lipizzaner. He sent one of his adjutants on a buying mission to Yugoslavia, where he procured for the Reich all of the Lipizzaner stock from the royal Yugoslavian stud farms, as well as the private Lipizzaner stud owned by Count Eltz of Vukovar, in Croatia. Rau sent some of these horses to a stud farm in Czechoslovakia for safekeeping. Others were fanned out across Poland and the Ukraine, where Rau proudly oversaw the organization of grand parades that featured imperial carriages pulled by teams of Lipizzaner and driven by his highly trained staff, with uniformed SS riding the elegant white horses in formation.

———

RUDOLF LESSING, RAU'S ADJUTANT, toured the vast domain alongside him, assisting in veterinary matters. At first, Rau traveled in a chauffeured limousine, but as his territory expanded into the Ukraine, he was given a personal airplane. This posh setup was a far cry from what Lessing was used to. Only twenty-six, Lessing had spent the first years of the war as a field veterinarian on the Eastern Front, where he had tended to sick and injured horses at field hospitals. His every waking moment had been taken up with his duties, blessedly leaving him little opportunity to think about the war's larger aims.

Lessing hailed from Mecklenburg, an area well known for its horse farms. He grew up on a farm, clambering on horseback as soon as he could walk and spending much of his childhood there. As a young man, he was persuaded by the National Socialist rhetoric and, against his own father's wishes, joined the Hitler Youth. At eighteen, he decided to attend the veterinary school in Hamburg—the military demand for veterinarians was great and the army would pay his tuition. His father advised him not to accept the offer of tuition, telling him that the Nazis wanted war, but Lessing brushed aside his father's admonitions. Later, he would characterize his own and his contemporaries' enthusiasm for Hitler as inexplicable.

After graduating from the veterinary academy in 1939, Lessing was first sent to Norway, then to Russia, where the Germans were engaged in a bitter fight against Red Army forces. His father's prophecy had come true. The experience had marked Lessing deeply—he had witnessed the misery of suffering men, wounded and killed, and had also seen up close the agony of horses on the battlefield. Lessing had nursed feverish horses as epidemics of strangles, also known as equine distemper, filled their tracheas with so much pus they could barely breathe. He had rigged a metal detector to find embedded bullets in their flesh, and operated on twelve-hundred-pound beasts in improvised field hospitals that lacked proper equipment. He had seen exhausted horses, pulling artillery wagons, stuck in the mud and lacking the will to pull themselves out. While most people tend to associate warhorses with World War I, during World War II, the German Army used 2,750,000 horses, double the number in World War I. Over sixty percent of them ended up as casualties—the average life expectancy of a horse was only about four years. On the front lines, Lessing worked in the mud and cold to alleviate the horses' suffering.

In spite of his father's objections, Lessing never questioned the legitimacy of the purpose they were fighting for—he had accepted Hitler's aims without questioning them, too immersed in his daily struggles to consider the dark side of the fanatical ideology of the Nazi Party. As a veterinary officer, he was occupied with the animals and had never seen the Nazi leadership up close. This all changed when Gustav Rau recruited Lessing to work in his horse-breeding domain. For the young veterinarian, it was a dream job. But as he later described in his memoirs, it was not possible to work in Poland without realizing the horrific truth of what was going on there.

The social and sporting realm that swirled around the horses included some of the most heinous elements of the Nazi state. For over a decade, the SS, with Heinrich Himmler at the helm, had pursued prestige for their organization by becoming involved in riding competitions through their equestrian arm, the Rider SS. The German Army—an entirely separate organization—had not been quick to embrace the rival SS riders, who had not been allowed to compete in the Berlin Olympics in 1936. By 1939, however, the German Olympic Committee had promised to include SS riders on the German equestrian teams, marking their increased legitimacy within the equestrian world.

Just as before the war, the army and SS kept up a friendly rivalry in the field of equine sport. In 1940, the Polish occupation police force organized a four-day riding, jumping, and driving competition in Kraków, in which 438 riders competed: Competitors were drawn from the army, the SS, the police force, the air force, and even the railway guards. The four-man team of judges was made up of the best-known equestrian names in German-occupied Poland: the head of the SS Cavalry and close Hitler confidant Hermann Fegelein; two of the most celebrated equestrian SS riders; and the chief equerry, Gustav Rau. The *Black Corps,* an official publication of the SS, reported that this tournament provided "a demonstration of German war readiness . . . a great proof of the German pacifying work in the East of the German realm of power." Gustav Rau had come to Poland to breed horses, but what mattered to the High Command were the prestige and propaganda power his activities lent to the occupying forces.

Rudolf Lessing had been at his new job only a few months when he started to see the truth that lay behind the Nazi occupation. One day in 1942, he and Rau set off on a horse-buying expedition to the Ukraine. Traveling with them was Erich Koch, a barrel-chested, mustached Nazi who controlled the Gestapo and police as *Reichskommissar* of the Ukraine. The group was journeying in great luxury on a train that had been seized from Poland's deposed leader. During a pause while they were held in the Brest-Litovsk station in the middle of the war zone, Koch, whose uniform was studded with medals and had the vaunted cluster of oak leaves on his lapels, poured out champagne. The mood in the train car was light and pleasant as the travelers were joined by several high-ranking German officers, all chatting and sipping from their crystal flutes. Lessing was by far the youngest and felt thoroughly intimidated, being more accustomed to spending his time in stable yards than hobnobbing with the top brass.

Just then a medical train car rolled up on a track alongside. Through the windows, Lessing could see wounded soldiers from the Eastern Front, stacked three deep on tiered bunks inside the train car. The men, pitiful and exhausted, wrapped in tattered bandages sodden with blood, looked only half-alive. Lessing glanced down at the champagne flute in his hand, and his face turned scarlet as he imagined what the wounded men must have been thinking when they gazed inside the saloon car and watched the officers smoking and drinking.

Koch turned his ice-blue eyes toward the wounded soldiers and then turned away without any expression. "Johann," he barked to his white-uniformed valet, "close the curtains. Those men have no understanding of the National Socialist lifestyle." But Lessing could not get the memory of the wounded soldiers out of his thoughts. For the first time, he had seen up close with what ruthless contempt the party leaders viewed even their own men who were suffering and dying.

Rudolf Lessing, who had made it his life's work to care for animals, had a front-row seat for the depredations being visited upon Poland. After the war, Lessing was adamant that during his time there, he had been well aware of the atrocities being committed. Speaking about Auschwitz, he said, "I just don't understand that today anyone can say that it is in doubt that the Jews were killed there. This is all documented. There are thousands of contemporary witnesses who know this."

Lessing's job as a veterinarian took him all over Rau's realm, including frequent visits to the stables at Janów Podlaski, where the friendly face of Witez was a familiar sight as he toured through the stallion barns. During that time, Lessing's home base was another one of Rau's stud farms, located in Debica, in eastern Poland near the Ukraine. One day, Hermann Fegelein, an *Obersturmbannführer* in the SS, came to see him. Fegelein's thin blond hair swooped back from his high forehead in a pronounced widow's peak. He was a skilled equestrian but a brutal and fanatical henchman of the Nazi regime. Fegelein was part of Hitler's inner circle—a protégé of Heinrich Himmler; he was married to Gretl Braun, the sister of Hitler's mistress.

Lessing had recently been issued new leather for riding boots, and Fegelein started questioning him about it.

"Have you received the boots yet?" Fegelein asked.

"Not yet," Lessing said, as the boots weren't due to be finished for a few days. "But there's no rush."

"Tell the Polack that if the boots are not ready the day after tomorrow, I will have him hanged," Fegelein said.

"The man is doing his work, and everything is going well," Lessing replied nervously.

The Nazi focused his cool blue eyes on the veterinarian and said without a trace of compassion, "Yes, but we need to show the Polacks how it's done."

Lessing was overwhelmed with anger as he regarded Fegelein's expression; he saw that the man had nothing but utter contempt for these human beings. Lessing had made it his life's work to care for those who could not speak for themselves—his quiet ways and deft hands had soothed and quieted panicked horses who were in pain after being put in harm's way by the plans of men that these beasts knew nothing about. Lessing had a natural sympathy for those who could not protect themselves—yet now he found himself working within a system that made brutality its central premise.

Despite the mayhem that rocked Poland, Rau's horse-breeding enterprise continued unimpeded—he had ample resources not just to care for the horses but to move them around in style. Because horse breeding was a specialized task requiring skilled labor, Rau and his staff had made few enemies. None of them would be directly implicated in the criminal activities that swirled around them. They worked closely with the highly skilled local horsemen and craftspeople they needed to keep their farms running. But the truth was still unpleasant and bleak. Lessing realized that Rau was not encouraging Polish horse breeding for the benefit of the Polish nation but only for the glorification of the Third Reich. While human beings were being transported in cattle cars, horses moved about in plush padded train cars, specially equipped for their protection, always accompanied by grooms who cared for their every need. After working with Rau for under a year, Lessing had given up believing in the Nazi cause. His vow of loyalty, in his own mind, was no longer to the führer but only to the horses.

THE SPANISH RIDING SCHOOL OF VIENNA

Five hundred miles away from Witez's war-torn home in Poland, the magnificent Lipizzaner stallion Neapolitano Africa floated across the tanbark inside the Spanish Riding School in Vienna. The vast white hall was silent but for the hollow thumping of hoofbeats, the slight creak of leather, and an occasional almost inaudible whisper of praise. Enormous arched windows bathed the hall in a golden glow that sparked up fiery points of light on the stallion's all-white coat. From the saddle, Alois Podhajsky, clad in a brown uniform jacket, white buckskin breeches, and tall black riding boots, made a series of minute adjustments, communicating with the stallion in a language—small shifts of weight, light contact on the reins, and slight pressure of the lower legs—that both he and the stallion spoke fluently. Africa was high-strung and sensitive—a prima donna, Podhajsky called him, so eager to please that his teeth started to chatter with excitement when he successfully performed a difficult movement. Podhajsky and Africa shared a special bond. This was the first horse that Podhajsky had trained himself, from the first day the eager young stallion arrived at the Spanish Riding School. According to the school's ancient traditions, a single rider formed a lifetime partnership with his mount, training him from the very beginning and riding him until the day the horse retired. This commitment—a marriage between man and beast that lasted a lifetime—was the bond that joined Podhajsky to this beautiful animal.

The stallion's crest was arched, his nose was perpendicular to the floor, and his hind legs were gathered underneath him, showing off the powerfully developed muscles in his massive hindquarters. His ears cocked back toward his rider—he was concentrating. With no obvious cue from the rider, the stallion sank back on his haunches and began to circle around his hind hooves, which continued to canter in place: a movement known as a pirouette. Around them in the arena, other uniformed riders practiced diligently astride similar white stallions, while other riders guided horses attached to long reins that allowed them to put the horses through their paces while walking behind them. Despite the large number of horses and uniformed men in the hall, the feeling was hushed, as in a library, the essence of peace and harmony. But deep in the back of his mind, Alois Podhajsky was worried.

An observer in the Riding Hall during one of the morning practice sessions in 1942 would have noticed little amiss. Unlike the depredations that had been unleashed against both horses and humans at Janów Podlaski in Poland, the white Lipizzaner stallions that lived at the Spanish Riding School in Vienna had thrived since the Nazi occupation of Austria in March 1938. They had been lavished with attention and taken on tours to perform for crowds in Berlin and East Prussia. The school was spruce with fresh paint and renovated living quarters for the riders. Not since the days of the Habsburg Empire had the Spanish Riding School been in such excellent repair.

The beauty and order apparent here now was in tremendous contrast to the spring of 1939, when Podhajsky took over as director. At that time, the school was in chaos. Only the three oldest riders remained; the rest had been called up to military service. The stallions were restless in the abandoned stables. The three riders struggled to keep all of the horses exercised, while the few remaining grooms, also older men, tried to keep them cleaned up and fed. Occupied with their voracious war of conquest, the Nazis at first paid no attention to the school and even considered shutting it down. The traditions and routines that had existed over three centuries prior to the Anschluss had nearly broken down.

Realizing that he could not run the school without better resources, Podhajsky lobbied for more manpower and much-needed repairs to the school, and he soon discovered that the German Army was responsive to his needs, sending him the funds he needed and even sparing that most scarce resource in wartime—cavalry soldiers, assigned to be riders in training at the school. In return, Podhajsky was expected only to continue training the Lipizzaner and putting on performances as usual. The Germans clearly understood that the beloved white stallions of Vienna contributed to the morale of the brutalized occupied city.

From the outside, the school appeared to be humming along and prospering under the German regime, but Podhajsky knew that in spite of appearances, the future of the institution was deeply uncertain. He was painfully aware that most of the horses at the riding school were growing old; since the war started, the supply of new stallions for training had dwindled almost to zero. Since 1920, all stallions used at the school had been bred and raised at the National Stud Farm in the Styrian village of Piber, Austria. Before the war, the Spanish Riding School and the stud farm had worked together seamlessly, ensuring that a fine crop of new stallions arrived for training each year. But Germany's takeover of Austria had changed everything. In 1942, the stud farm at Piber was repurposed as an army military breeding establishment, its primary purpose to breed horses suitable for trekking in mountainous territory. The school's need for stallions to train for riding was no longer given priority.

Since 1939, though Gustav Rau had been moving horses, including Lipizzaner, like chess pieces all over the German-occupied territories, he had not interfered with the running of the Spanish Riding School. Nor had he taken Podhajsky's stallions, or the mares from Piber, and sent them east to Poland, the destination for many of his prize horses. But Podhajsky was hearing a persistent rumor that Rau planned to move all of the Lipizzaner mares and foals from Piber to a location outside of Austria.

This concern was on Podhajsky's mind as he patiently worked through his practice session on Neapolitano Africa. Intensely focused, neither horse nor rider was conscious of the beauty that surrounded them. The Winter Riding Hall was one of Vienna's architectural marvels. The grand hall was painted entirely white, from its coffered plaster ceilings to its colonnaded second- and third-floor balconies. The only splashes of color came from the portrait of Charles VI, the school's founder, and from the red Nazi swastika flags that adorned two wooden training pillars that stood precisely 1.45 meters apart in the center of the arena. The ornate expanse of the Winter Riding Hall's ceiling soared seventeen feet above the ground floor, floating above them with no central support columns. When the riding hall was first built in 1736, it was considered a feat of engineering wizardry. At the time, it was Vienna's single largest structure—a palace built by the powerful Habsburg monarchs for the express purpose of showcasing the equestrian arts, the grand jewel of their empire.

ALOIS PODHAJSKY OBSERVES A TRAINING SESSION AT
THE SPANISH RIDING SCHOOL IN VIENNA.

The purebred Lipizzaner practicing here were descended from horses originally bred in Spain during the Renaissance. These Spanish horses uniquely combined the heavier-boned bloodlines of European horses with the swift, fleet, and intelligent Arabian and Moorish breeds to create an entirely new equine type. The popularity of these animals spread like wildfire all over Europe, and soon every principality had its own nursery for Spanish horses. Among the twentieth-century descendants of the Spanish horse, the Lipizzaner was the most rarefied. Each had its royal pedigree tattooed upon it: the birthplace on the right shoulder; the dam, or mother, on the left flank and the sire on the right flank; and the letter L, marking it as a purebred Lipizzaner, on the cheek. Each was descended from one of six original sires, all born between 1765 and 1810.

These snow-white horses are born dark. Their coats whiten slowly with age, except for about one in a hundred that don't change—making them highly sought after, as they are believed to bring good luck. At the beginning of the twentieth century, there were only three to four thousand of these purebred specimens in the entire world. The breed took its name from the village of Lipica, Italy (in current-day Slovenia), where, beginning in the sixteenth century, the horses were bred and refined. After the fall of the Habsburgs at the end of World War I, the horses from Lipica were divided among the former nations of the empire. Some stayed in Lipica, others were moved to Piber in Austria, and still others were given to the monarch of Yugoslavia. The result was that this already tiny breed was divided into three different strains. It was the Austrian strain, the stallions bred at Piber, that performed at the Spanish Riding School; in addition to the marks found on all Lipizzaner, they were also branded with the farm's symbol: the letter P beneath an imperial crown.

The art that was practiced there, known as classical riding, was first refined in antiquity, when its most notable proponent was a student of Socrates, the Greek military and equestrian expert Xenophon. As he explained in his two hugely influential treatises on horsemanship, only through a partnership of mutual respect could a man fully rely on a horse in battle. Xenophon was strictly opposed to any kind of violence toward horses. For the achievement of true beauty on horseback, he observed, the animal must be a willing participant, "for what the horse does under compulsion is done without understanding; and there is no beauty in it either, any more than if one should whip and spur a dancer." As Podhajsky crossed the grand hall on Africa, the stallion's power was entirely harnessed while Podhajsky's hand maintained the lightest contact on the reins and his spurs never touched the horse's barrel—the perfect exemplar of Xenophon's ancient philosophy.

At the Spanish Riding School, then and now, stallions (no mares are used at the school) begin their training only at age three and a half, then gradually progress through a routine that takes years to perfect. Just as a ballerina spends years learning the basic positions before ever learning to dance on her toes, so a stallion needs to start with basic skills. The training proceeds in three stages. First is straight-line training, where a young horse is taught the basic paces (walk, trot, and canter) and learns to carry a rider on his back. Next is *campagne* school, where horses learn collection and balance while developing the muscles and flexibility needed for the higher-level movements; this allows them to shift their center of balance to their haunches in order to free up the forelegs' action. The final stage is the *haute école,* or high school, which encompasses training in the most complex and difficult movements. Not every stallion has the temperament to progress to the high school. The movements taught at this stage, such as the slow-motion elevated trot named *passage,* and the prancing in place called *piaffe,* are among the most difficult in the equestrian domain.

A few of the exceptionally talented stallions—the stars of the show—are tapped to learn the most difficult movements of all, the airs above the ground. First developed to give an advantage on the battlefield, these complicated leaps require exceptional strength, trust in the rider, and willingness. When performing, these stallions raise their forelegs off the ground entirely, balancing only on the hind legs. From this position they leap from the ground in a variety of different combinations, such as the leap and kick called *capriole,* or a magnificent jump from a rearing position known as the *courbette.* Sometimes these movements are performed riderless; sometimes horses are able to lift not just their own weight but also that of a perfectly coordinated rider who does not use stirrups but maintains his position by balance alone. At the Spanish Riding School, a stallion is continually taught the concept of thoroughness—an exquisite sensitivity to the rider's cues (called aids), communicated to the horse through the seat bones, legs, weight, reins, and occasionally the voice. Just as Xenophon recommended in ancient times, horses and riders at the Spanish Riding School achieve their goals through communication and partnership, never coercion.

ALOIS PODHAJSKY GUIDES A LIPIZZANER THROUGH A CAPRIOLE IN HAND.

For centuries, these beautiful creatures performed exclusively for the eyes of the emperor and his royal coterie, the public catching glimpses of the snow-white coach horses only as they drove by on official imperial and royal business. The cataclysmic Great War, from 1914 to 1918, brought all of that to a close. The monarchs were deposed and their empire dismantled. The school seemed doomed to fall into oblivion—the Austrian public was little interested in preserving the cultural remnants of the fallen empire. No one saw any further purpose for the emperor's stallions. But the riders stuck by their horses, struggling to keep the school alive. Once they lost the patronage of the royal family, the horsemen kept the school running by selling tickets, postcards, and trinkets, and even organizing a "broom fund" to maintain the stables. Performing in public for the first time in the 1920s and 1930s, while Austria was gaining a foothold as a young democracy, the horses soon became the new republic's most visible and beloved symbol, eventually touring other European capitals, where they developed a passionate following. During this time, the Spanish Riding School was a civilian institution, under the direction of the Austrian Ministry of Agriculture. In 1938, when Austria was annexed by Nazi Germany, the school was put under the control of the German Army High Command.

Four years had passed since Podhajsky had taken his post as director of the school. When the Germans offered him the post under the new military leadership, Podhajsky did not hesitate. He was willing to save the horses and the school even if it meant collaborating with the Germans. The Olympian had made a Faustian bargain: He had saved one of Austria's most important cultural institutions, and he had ensured the safety of the horses. But now he answered to the High Command of the German Army, who had sworn allegiance to the führer.

The months of 1942 passed slowly, as the horrors of all-out war intensified, circling the globe. In America, Roosevelt signed Executive Order 9066, which authorized moving Americans of Japanese descent into relocation centers. Nazi leaders met in secret at an event later known as the Wannsee Conference, where they put into place what was called "the final solution": the extermination of the Jews of Europe. In 1934, there were 176,034 Jews in Vienna. By 1941, 130,000 of them had fled the city. Of the 65,000 Viennese Jews who were sent to concentration camps, only about 2,000 survived. Later, when Podhajsky wrote his memoirs, he voiced no opinion about the horrors that visited his city during the war. Like a harnessed horse wearing blinders, he kept his eyes focused on the one task that was entirely his: keeping the horses safe. Right now, that meant figuring out a way to prevent Gustav Rau from moving the Lipizzaner mares and foals out of Austria.

In July 1942, Podhajsky set off for the small village where the Lipizzaner were bred. Since taking over as director, he had made periodic visits to the breeding farm, but this one felt unusually urgent. He needed to see what was happening firsthand. Far from the bustling metropolis of Vienna, the village of Piber looked like a scene from *The Sound of Music*. Milky-white mares and their chestnut, black, or brown foals grazed in pastures that sloped gently, offsetting the blue mountain peaks in the distance. In the spring, the green pastures were studded with wildflowers and laced with sparkling streams. The highest point in the valley was the dome-shaped spire of a red-roofed castle. Piber was first founded as a sanctuary for Cistercian monks whose singing once echoed through the valley's crystal-clear air.

Broodmares and young foals grazed along the Geilbach River in the mares' summer pasture, while the yearling and two- and three-year-old stallions were sent to the upper-mountain meadows, where they galloped freely. The way that Lipizzaner were raised and cared for in their early years was quite particular. While most purebred horses were cosseted in carefully kept stables and neatly manicured paddocks, these future performers at the Spanish Riding School were galloping in herds against the picturesque and rugged background of the Styrian Alps. Here, they developed stamina, balance, and extraordinary strength, and here, too, they enhanced their equine intelligence in their natural habitat—in herds with their age-mates, forming lifelong friendships (and sometimes animosities) that would guide how the stallions were stabled in the Spanish Riding School: Fast friends from their youth stayed together, enemies were kept apart. Podhajsky believed that this carefully monitored environment contributed to the Lipizzaner's unique characteristics. In essence, Rau and Podhajsky were on different sides of the nature-versus-nurture debate. Podhajsky believed that without the special nurture of the Piber Stud Farm, the Lipizzaner would lose something crucial; to Rau, only blood mattered. Conveniently, this allied him with the attitudes in vogue in Nazi Germany.

Podhajsky toured the farm at Piber, conversing with the stud farm director and carefully looking over the stock. He knew each of the mares by name, and the horses would come to him when he called them at pasture. All of them recognized the quiet man with the serious demeanor whose pockets were always stuffed with sugar cubes. If Podhajsky's face was somber in repose, it always lit up with a smile when he conversed softly with the horses—just to look upon him in the company of the Lipizzaner was to understand that these animals were the loves of his life.

Podhajsky shared his worries with the stud farm director at Piber, reiterating the importance of the natural surroundings to the development of the young Lipizzaner, but the stud farm director only parroted his bosses at the German Army High Command, dismissing

LIPIZZANER MARES AND
FOALS GRAZE PEACEFULLY.

Podhajsky's concerns. Podhajsky was left feeling that political jockeying and manipulation were affecting decisions that should be made to benefit the horses, not their minders. After returning to Vienna, Podhajsky sent a letter to Berlin, pleading that the mares from Piber not be moved, as the conditions of climate and terrain were ideal for nurturing these special horses. "If the Lipizzaner strain is to continue to be preserved in the interests of the Spanish Riding School, then at all costs, any experiments which might impair its suitability for the classic style of riding must be prevented." He received no answer. He was unaware that Rau had seen his pleas and scribbled dismissive remarks in the margins. Rau considered Podhajsky's arguments backward and unscientific, totally dismissing the idea that the location or the manner in which an animal was nurtured made any difference.

In early October, unbeknownst to Podhajsky, the Piber staff watched as the entire bloodstock of their stud farm—stallions, mares, and foals—was loaded onto specially designed train cars. Their destination: a much larger stud farm located in the village of Hostau in the western Bohemian region of Czechoslovakia. For the first time ever, the Lipizzaner were leaving Austria. The decision to move the horses had been made by Gustav Rau, having decided on an earlier visit that the methods used at the Piber Stud Farm were antiquated. His plan was to centralize the Lipizzaner from Lipica, several stud farms in Yugoslavia, and Piber into a single location: a spacious, well-maintained farm with plenty of room for expansion. For now, that location would be in the sheltered region of Bohemia that was controlled by Germany and far from the war zone. The long-range plan was to move all of the Lipizzaner back to Lipica—part of Hitler's plan for a thousand-year Reich. By the time the news reached Podhajsky in Vienna, the stables at Piber stood empty.

WHEN PODHAJSKY LEARNED THAT the Lipizzaner mares and foals had been sent out of Austria, he was devastated. In a panic, he immediately petitioned for permission to visit the horses in Hostau, and in early November, he boarded a train bound for Czechoslovakia, a voyage of about a hundred miles. Podhajsky believed that the climate and soil there were ill suited to the breed, in addition to his greater fear of letting the horses out of Austrian control. Having lived through the dissolution of the Austro-Hungarian Empire, Podhajsky had seen the chaos that reigned in the aftermath. What would happen to the Austrian horses if the Germans eventually lost control of their territories? The locals here had neither special loyalty to the Lipizzaner breed nor any connection to the Spanish Riding School. If Hitler's Reich came crashing down like the empire before it, Podhajsky feared that no one here would even attempt to protect the horses. But he could express none of these fears aloud. To suggest that Germany might be defeated was treason.

Arriving on the grounds of Hostau, he found a spacious and well-run establishment and saw that the mares and foals had arrived in good condition. But to his horror, he discovered that Gustav Rau had visited the farm just a few days before and instituted a host of what he considered modernizing changes: that younger mares be covered by stallions, instead of waiting until the mares were more mature; that close relatives be mated to each other; and that Yugoslavian stallions be paired with Austrian mares rather than keeping each strain separate. In Podhajsky's words, "The good doctor was once more in his element, carrying out experiments, but the pity was that this time he was experimenting with the Lipizzaner breed." While he was not in fact a doctor or veterinarian, possessing only an honorary degree, people often called him Dr. Rau in deference to his authority in the matter of horse breeding.

Podhajsky saw the situation all too clearly: Rau and his accomplices had been systematically collecting all of the Lipizzaner scattered in small pockets across the occupied territories. With virtually every pureblood Lipizzaner under his control, Gustav Rau had in mind a grand experiment in which he would utilize the most aggressive breeding strategies. As Podhajsky had discovered, Rau was going to embark on a plan called line breeding, in which close relatives were bred to each other to accentuate certain characteristics in the horses. By mating father with daughter and brother with sister, Rau could try to reshape the Lipizzaner. He now had a free hand to put his theories into practice, with Austria's greatest natural treasure as his guinea pigs.

SHORTLY AFTER HIS RETURN TO VIENNA, Podhajsky arranged to visit the Army High Command in person, determined to continue his fight. He traveled to Berlin, along with sixty-one-year-old Ernst Lindenbauer, who had been chief rider at the Spanish Riding School since 1926. Podhajsky was determined to meet directly with Rau and to present his case. Arriving in Berlin, the two made their way to the Tiergarten and entered the Bendlerstrasse, where the large granite face of the Bendlerblock, headquarters of the German Army High Command, towered forbiddingly over them. Inside, Podhajsky and Lindenbauer were escorted into a large, well-appointed conference room. There, General Curt Schulze, inspector general of the cavalry, had gathered fifteen of his uniformed officers and one single bald, portly civilian: Gustav Rau.

Also sixty-one, General Schulze was a formidable figure in the military equestrian world. A professor of veterinary medicine at the Friedrich Wilhelm University in Berlin, he was appointed head of the German Army's veterinary service in 1939. Under his charge, he had a staggering 1.25 million horses, 125,000 cavalrymen, and 37,000 blacksmiths. The forty-eight veterinary hospitals he supervised treated more than 100,000 horses per day. Yet so important was Rau's Lipizzaner breeding project that the general set aside time to discuss these few hundred remarkable horses. Schulze, who had a peaceable manner, began the meeting by announcing that the military authorities had taken over control of the Lipizzaner stud for the express purpose of furthering the needs of the Spanish Riding School. He then invited Podhajsky to explain his objections to the reforms being made at Hostau.

Podhajsky glanced nervously at Lindenbauer. Aware of his deficiencies as an orator, he'd brought along his experienced senior rider to help him make his case. While renowned as an equestrian, Podhajsky was not known for his particular expertise in breeding horses, and to make matters worse, he was aware that the Germans looked down on him as an Austrian. Unfortunately, Lindenbauer became entirely tongue-tied in such august company and said not a word, only nodding silently while Podhajsky made his argument.

Rau interjected frequently. Unlike Podhajsky, the German was known for his rhetorical skills and his professorial, often bombastic manner.

Podhajsky demanded that mares younger than four years old not be used for breeding. "The Lipizzaner matures slowly," he said.

Rau sprang from a seated position, his face bright red. "Your ideas are antiquated," he said. "There is no evidence that the Lipizzaner matures more slowly than other warm-blooded horses. That is one of those ideas that is repeated parrot-fashion without any truth to it! We plan to expand the stud and rapidly increase the number of horses. To do this, we must breed the younger mares!"

The two men parried back and forth, passionately arguing their positions. The Austrian cautioned that breeding mares too young would

prove disastrous. Podhajsky accused Rau of not knowing how to evaluate young Lipizzaner, citing as proof an ill-considered acquisition—a
yearling purchased by Rau in Yugoslavia that, according to Podhajsky,
grew up to look like a mule.

In the end, General Schulze, in an effort to defuse the dispute,
agreed that Rau should avoid breeding the younger Austrian mares.
But any temporary satisfaction Podhajsky might have felt was soon
dampened when General Schulze told him that the Lipizzaner were to
remain at Hostau. Returning the mares to Piber—or anywhere else in
Austria—was out of the question.

Podhajsky and Lindenbauer returned to Vienna thoroughly de-
jected. Podhajsky knew that Rau was far too dictatorial even to listen
to his recommendations. Back at Hostau, Rau would continue his ex-
perimentation on the Lipizzaner unimpeded.

PODHAJSKY PREPARED TO PLAY his desperate final hand. In just a few
weeks, on November 29, 1942, the Spanish Riding School would be
putting on a gala evening performance to which the high-ranking Nazi
brass were invited, including, of course, Gustav Rau. On this night,
Podhajsky was to debut a spectacular new program: the school quadrille performed with twelve stallions. In these highly choreographed
sequences, the horses moved so close to one another that just a few
inches of error would cause them to fall out of line or collide. Podhajsky had poured his heart and soul into the preparations. Surely if the
German overlords could see the Lipizzaner perform such intricate
moves, they would recognize that the horses had a special purpose and
that this baroque art, almost extinct outside these walls, was worthy of
preservation. Perhaps if Gustav Rau and the other military authorities
could see the stallions in action, they would change their minds about
the wisdom of performing breeding experiments at Hostau. This was
Podhajsky's last chance.

With Podhajsky in the lead, the twelve mounted riders from the
Spanish Riding School entered the hall in single file. With magnificent
precision, they passed between the pair of training pillars adorned with
Nazi flags, then performed a movement called the herringbone, in
which the stallions, still in line, began to move laterally, alternating
right and left like a braiding and unbraiding strand. A moment later,

the horses pulled twelve abreast. In perfect synchrony, each horse stopped as the rider doffed his bicorne hat and saluted the portrait of Charles VI.

Under the portrait, the imperial box—where the emperor and his glittering retinue once were seated—was bristling with men in uniform. Seated among the ranking brass, Gustav Rau looked out over the arena, noting with interest the admirable characteristics of the white Lipizzaner team: They were patient, obedient, and energetic, with broad chests, barrel rib cages, and muscular necks. Podhajsky's mount, Neapolitano Africa, was especially handsome. As the white horses danced to the music, people's cares lifted for a few hours. Podhajsky focused intently on the performance, on telegraphing his thoughts to Africa through his legs and reins, while keeping constant watch on the eleven other members of his team.

The music of Mozart swelled over the loudspeakers as the horses trotted and cantered with the precision of a military marching band. Finally, the horses formed a single line again, halting in the center of the arena in perfect formation, twelve abreast. The only movement was their slightly bobbing heads. The only sound was the trumpeting of their breath.

As the spectacle drew to its rousing conclusion, the spectators applauded the horses enthusiastically. Up in the royal box, uniformed Nazis stood and clapped with evident pleasure, no doubt relishing the fact that the emperor's horses now danced for them. The performance had gone off without a hitch. Podhajsky had achieved his goal of showing off his stallions to the greatest advantage. But he remained uncertain about what lesson Rau might have taken from the flawless performance.

As Podhajsky would later learn, Rau, in his next official report to Berlin, would declare, "There are no high-legged Lipizzaner, there are no flat-ribbed Lipizzaner, there are no bad-tempered Lipizzaner. . . ." Clearly, he was impressed with what he had witnessed in Vienna. And yet Rau seemed to give no value to their performance, attending only to the qualities that they might be able to pass along. "Even a poor driver," he continued, "can get by with them . . . they are well-suited to pulling a dray." Where Podhajsky saw willing, intelligent, almost human animals, Rau coveted only their bloodline and cared only for their utility.

At the end of the performance, the stallions filed out of the riding hall, the tinkling music ended, and the applause seemed to go on and on. For Podhajsky, the applause was bittersweet. As 1942 drew to a close, he walked a narrow rail—pressing the case of his horses but only as far as he dared. Whenever he walked through the aisles of the stables, his friends greeted him with a chorus of neighs, stomping feet, and friendly whickers, and Podhajsky paused, speaking softly to the gentle giants. He knew that even in these turbulent times, the stallions could trust that their steadfast friend would always put their interests first. His own mount, Neapolitano Africa, always seemed to know what he was thinking—in the horse's wise eyes, Podhajsky could read the language of friendship. The control of the Lipizzaner mares and foals had slipped from his grasp, but he vowed to redouble his conviction to protect his stallions.

6.

THE HIDDEN STUD FARM

Alois Podhajsky need not have worried about the welfare of the mares that had left Austria in October 1942. The herd had made the 350-mile trip northwest from Piber to Hostau, Czechoslovakia, without incident, and were settled into the Third Reich's most sheltered stud farm, located in Bohemia, just a few miles from the Bavarian border. Beyond the farm's serene green pastures, golden valleys stretched toward distant mountains crested by dark waves of evergreens. The Böhmerwald, or Bohemian Forest, served as more than a beautiful backdrop for the farm; it formed a natural barrier between Germany to the west and Austria to the south and had withstood invasion and attack for centuries. During the Nazi era, this locale was known as "the Bohemian bastion." Among Germans, it was thought to be the safest place to ride out the war, least likely to be invaded from east or west. It was here that Rau had secreted the Lipizzaner, as well as the finest Arabians from Janów, including Witez. Even in the middle of a war, here, all was deceptively tranquil.

Quiet villages dotted this part of Bohemia, each graced by a Catholic church with an onion-domed spire. Flanking each cluster of tidy whitewashed houses were well-kept farms growing crops that thrived in the region's rich agricultural soil. But in the wake of Hitler's annexation of the area following the Munich Agreement of 1938, its bu-

Military stud-farm in Hostoun Sumava. Horse Farm Hostoun WWII.

Voj. hřebčín v Hostouni na Šumavě. Dvůr Hostouň.

THE NAZI STUD FARM IN HOSTAU.

colic appearance was deceiving. Once a multicultural region where Czechs, Germans, and Jews lived side by side in peace, Bohemia, now called the Sudetenland, had turned into a firm cornerstone of Hitler's Third Reich. When the Nazis annexed the area in September 1939, the local German-speaking population had lined the streets cheering to welcome Hitler's forces. Local Czechs and Jews had either fled or been forcibly evicted. Those who remained had been transported to concentration camps. By 1942, when the first Lipizzaner arrived in Hostau, the local Nazi apparatus held a firm grip on the region, but Czech partisans also operated in the area, finding refuge in the hideaways offered by the Bohemian Forest. Though the border with Bavaria, Germany, was less than fifteen miles to the west, the mountainous barrier made it seem much more remote.

The stud farm at Hostau, located next to the village of the same name, had been known for breeding cavalry horses long before Hitler's time. The most prominent local landowners, the Trauttsmansdorff family, had historically served as imperial equerries for the Habsburg Crown. In addition to the main complex of stables adjacent to the village, there were pastures in three neighboring villages—the entire establishment covered fifteen hundred acres and could accommodate more than a thousand stallions, mares, and foals. All in all, it was more than twice as big as Alfred Vanderbilt's showplace, Sagamore Farms, which Rau had visited in 1938.

Rau had selected this expansive facility to put into motion the most exalted part of his grand plan. Throughout 1942, he had systematically transported all of the purebred Lipizzaner from the stud farms of Italy, Austria, and Yugoslavia to this sheltered location for safekeeping. He had also sent a personal emissary on a mission to purchase purebred Lipizzaner from wealthy noblemen who raised smaller strings of pure-breds for private use. By the end of 1942, Rau had gathered almost every Lipizzaner in the world into a single location.

Austrian-born Hitler's goal, expressed in *Mein Kampf,* was to bring all of the German-speaking peoples of Central Europe, including Austria, into the fold of the Third Reich. Just as Hitler aimed to eliminate "impure strains" and combine the different Germanic groups into a single "Aryan race" of people, so Rau planned to use the science of selective breeding to erase the individual differences characterizing the several strains of purebred Lipizzaner that had emerged since the end of World War I and replace them with a single mold: pure white, imperial, identical, and ideally suited for military use. Like Hitler himself, the horses, once quintessentially Austrian, would be given a distinctly German stamp.

Gustav Rau believed that these intelligent and tractable animals possessed a nearly ideal temperament. But he had a less favorable opinion of the breed's conformation. The Lipizzaner had some very specific breed characteristics: a relatively small stature, a Roman or convex profile (this was less pronounced in some stallion lines than others), a very straight shoulder that resulted in a choppier gait, low withers (the bony prominence at the base of the neck that the saddle rests against), and a short back. All of these qualities were especially well suited to the art of classical riding, which differed from modern riding in many respects, but Gustav Rau was determined to remold the Lipizzaner according to a template that he held in his mind's eye.

Rau's vision of the ideal military horse had been forged in the same crucible that had so affected Alois Podhajsky—World War I. As a young man during the Great War, Rau had served as a cavalry soldier; his abdomen was latticed with battle scars, including a stoma from a lance wound sustained during a mounted charge. Despite evidence of mounting technological change, Rau remained stubbornly antiquated, convinced that vehicles could never replace horses. Instead, he believed that the military horse could be perfected, through selective breeding, to outperform any machine. According to Rau, "The military horse . . . should be noble, but not too forceful, energetic, but not excited." He aimed to breed a horse with endless endurance and an efficient digestive system that could run on little grain. But the cause to which Rau had devoted his life was being threatened by an endless supply of motor vehicles that rattled off Germany's assembly lines, each one identical to the next.

As head of the Polish stud farm administration, Rau had modernized the production of horses, increasing the number of stallions, mares, and foals born in Poland year upon year, and feeding the voracious pipeline of horses to the war. Yet horses—living, breathing animals that require fodder, exercise, nurture, and care—could not be fabricated like nuts and bolts in a factory.

As the war continued to escalate, Rau pedaled ever more furiously, trying to produce a perfect standardized horse. He believed that with aggressive inbreeding, he could rapidly expand the number of Lipizzaner without sacrificing anything in quality; in fact, he believed that the Lipizzaner could be enhanced and changed, elongating the back, increasing the height of the withers, and changing the slope of the shoulder. He had predicted that he could completely change the breed in just three years. Perhaps Rau envisioned hundreds of thousands of purebred Lipizzaner fanning out in formation across the German empire, each as reliable and identical as Germany's BMW automobiles— even better, as they would require neither scarce rubber nor costly gasoline.

WITHOUT ACCESS TO A modern understanding of genetics, Rau's views regarding horse breeding were rudimentary, drawn largely from later discarded nineteenth-century notions of blended inheritance, in which an offspring's traits were supposed to be a fifty-fifty mix of mother and father. For example, a tall father and short mother should produce a child whose height was exactly midway between the two parents' heights. The problem with this theory was that if it were true, then over time, the population would become increasingly homogenous as the blending process evened out outliers. Not only did this not occur, it was precisely the opposite outcome of the highly differentiated forms that resulted according to Darwin's theory of natural selection.

When Darwin devised his theory of evolution, he knew that traits were passed from parent to offspring, though he did not understand quite how. The father of the science of genetic inheritance was Gregor Mendel, an Augustinian friar whose experiments with pea plants, published in 1866, provided the first demonstration of the principles of inheritance. But Mendel's findings were not widely disseminated during his lifetime, and throughout the late nineteenth century, scientists continued to believe that offspring could inherit characteristics acquired by parents from their environment. Lamarckism, named for French scientist Jean Baptiste Lamarck (1744–1829), supposed that children inherited characteristics that had been developed in the parents— for example, giraffes elongated their necks by reaching into high branches for food, and these longer necks then were passed along to their offspring. But later in the nineteenth century, scientists were beginning to question that line of thought. German scientist August Weismann (1834–1914) postulated that there was a substance, which he called the "germ plasm," that could be passed from one generation to the next without changing its essential form, discounting entirely the influence of nurture or environment on inherited traits. He performed an experiment in which he cut the tails off six generations of white mice to prove that the next generation would still be born with tails. While the purpose of Weismann's experiment was scientific and not social, the increasing belief that inherited traits were not mutable or affected by the environment contributed an underpinning to Nazi racial beliefs. Weismann's germ plasm theory seemed to provide a scientific rationale for bigotry, leading some to argue that no matter how assimilated a Jew might appear, every Jewish baby was born with certain immutable (and, in the bigots' view, negative) characteristics.

In his approach to horse breeding, Rau followed Weismann's theory. He believed that purebred horses had an uncorrupted substance that was passed along ancestral lines. This germ plasm was inherently fragile and needed to be protected from corruption from outside influences, such as "mixed blood." Rau wrote, "We have to promote inbreeding of the best bloodlines to get identical germ plasm to prevent corruption and to preserve it." Not understanding the dangers of inbreeding, Rau believed that increasing purity would improve quality.

With a modern understanding of genetic inheritance, animal breeders are now well aware of the problems that can accrue in animals bred too closely—one result is that inherited genetic defects or susceptibility to disease can increase. But these insights were not available to Rau. And so, like a painter working with a palette of colors, Rau tried to fashion the perfect horse from each of a million small equine details— the angle of the shoulder, the set of the eye, the curve of the barrel, as well as elements of temperament that once were considered ineffable and not suitable to manipulation: courage, intelligence, fortitude, and spirit.

To lead this enterprise on the ground, Rau had chosen his personal protégé, forty-six-year-old Czech-born German Hubert Rudofsky. As a civilian, Rudofsky had been considered one of Czechoslovakia's foremost experts on equine breeding. He first attracted Rau's attention when horses bred in this region of Bohemia had made a strong showing in the 1936 Olympics in Berlin.

Now a colonel in the German Army, Rudofsky was over six feet tall, a bachelor known for his dapper manner and immaculate dress. He owed his love of horses to a youthful fascination with mounted dragoons, uhlans, and hussars, whose silver bayonets, shiny knee-high boots, and colorful regimental uniforms had impressed him as they paraded through the world of his childhood. Rudofsky had learned to ride at the age of ten, instructed with great precision by a cavalry squadron commander. And so, when World War I broke out, the seventeen-year-old Rudofsky eagerly enlisted in the Austrian cavalry. At the war's end, he was awarded a silver medal for courage.

In peacetime, Rudofsky was a civil servant who directed stud farms in both the Czech and Slovak regions of the country, where he maintained excellent relationships with his fellow citizens. When the Germans occupied Czechoslovakia, like all other eligible ethnic German men, Rudofsky was called up to serve in the German Wehrmacht. Through the patronage of Count von Trauttmansdorff, a family friend, he joined the 17th Bamberger Rider Regiment, later to become famous when Claus von Stauffenberg and four other members of the regiment plotted to assassinate Hitler on July 20, 1944. Soon after, Rudofsky was pressed into service training carriage drivers at a Wehrmacht training center. A year later, Rau summoned Rudofsky to serve in the stud farm administration of Poland. Rudofsky acquitted himself well, so he was put in charge of what was at the time the largest stud farm in Europe, at Debica, in occupied Poland, which housed more than four hundred mares at its height. Among the horses at Debica, Rau had placed forty-four Lipizzaner mares, as well as two Lipizzaner stallions imported from Yugoslavia, among the few he had kept outside of Hostau.

Hubert Rudofsky was an expert at carriage driving, possessed of an advanced diploma in this complicated art. The ability to drive a four-in-hand is one of the equestrian world's most rarefied skills. Traditionally, four harnessed horses pulling a heavy carriage or coach required two drivers, one to control each pair of reins. During World War I, the demand for ambulance carriages to evacuate wounded soldiers led a German count to develop the four-in-hand driving method known as the Achenbach system, which for the first time allowed a single driver to control all four horses.

"Four-in-hand" refers to the four reins, one for each horse, that a

HUBERT RUDOFSKY DRIVING A FOUR-IN-HAND IN THE 1930S.

driver controls in a single hand—the left. With the right, the driver holds a long carriage whip anchored between the thumb and little finger, freeing up the middle three fingers to control the reins during turns. The whip, with a weighted silver base and braided leather lash, is held erect at a precise angle to avoid accidentally obstructing the view or dislodging the hat of a passenger. Driving a four-in-hand requires no fewer than thirty-one separate pieces of harness equipment. Even more, it requires a deep knowledge of horsemanship. One turn-of-the-century enthusiast's journal put it thus: "To become an expert driver and thorough coachman one should be more or less a lover of horses; indeed a large percentage of the best drivers have been associated with horses the greater part of their lives, have ridden everything from a rocking-horse to a runaway thoroughbred, and had become competent drivers of single horses and pairs long before they essayed the tooling of a four." Only highly trained drivers, such as Rudofsky, had the requisite skill to drive a four-in-hand, an expertise that took no fewer than five years of practice to master. Imperial coaches pulled by matching pairs of Lipizzaner once whisked the members of the Habsburg monarchy around Vienna on official and royal business. With Rudofsky's expertise and Rau's white horses, these same conveyances could be used to display the reach and might of the Third Reich.

IN THE FALL OF 1943, Rudofsky would show off his skills at a grand parade to be held at the stud farm in Debica. The staff of the stud farm had spent weeks preparing the horses for this special occasion. On the day of the parade, a large viewing stand, draped with freshly cut tree boughs and a scarlet swastika banner, filled with Nazi officials and high-ranking German military officers. Lining up along the railings of the grand exhibition fields were beleaguered Polish citizens of the occupied town who had come out to watch the fine horses, hoping for a few hours of distraction.

Rudofsky, splendidly clad in a full dress uniform, oversaw the proceedings and prepared for his turn in the driver's box. He meticulously inspected each horse from top to toe, checking the brass-studded imperial harnesses as he gave hurried last-minute instructions to the grooms.

The parade began with uniformed grooms entering the vast exhibition field on foot, leading a group of fine yearlings. As they circled in front of the viewing stands, a heavy rain started to fall. The horses' hooves churned the wet ground into soupy mud, which flicked up to stain the horses' legs and bellies. Despite the bad weather, the audience did not move. A few people pulled out umbrellas. Most of the officers on the viewing stand seemed impervious to the storm, simply letting the rain soak their wool uniforms and drip off their visored caps.

Rudofsky was focused on the horses, so at first he did not notice that a hubbub was brewing, but soon he heard a commotion. Near the spot where he was preparing horses for their entrance to the field, Gustav Rau was engaged in an increasingly heated conversation with an SS officer. Rau's adjutant, Rudolf Lessing, stood next to him, visibly struggling to maintain his composure. Rudofsky realized that while the Poles had been lining up to watch the horse parade, a regiment of SS soldiers had moved in behind them. The grounds of the stud farm and all of the spectators were now entirely surrounded by armed SS storm troopers.

The SS officer had approached Rau to explain that he had orders to arrest every member of the crowd. All of the Polish men between the ages of eighteen and thirty would be sent to a forced-work camp to manufacture German munitions. The horse parade, which had drawn a large crowd, was simply being used as a trap.

Gustav Rau pulled a pistol from his hip and pointed it directly at the SS officer. "You have no authority here," he said. "This horse farm is under the jurisdiction of the German Army."

Rudofsky watched, scarcely daring to draw a breath. Out on the large exhibition field, the horses continued to prance and dance. The group of officers up on the viewing stand was too far away to hear the altercation.

Rau kept his pistol pointed at the SS officer's heart. Neither man moved until, with a curt nod, the officer stepped back. He agreed to remove his men. Only then did Rau lower his pistol. A few minutes later, the SS regiment withdrew. The assembled crowd never realized what had happened.

When the time came for the grand finale, Rudofsky sat aboard the driver's box of his immaculate carriage, ready to take his turn in the arena. His feet were braced against an angled toe box, which provided the traction needed to control the two pairs of horses. In his white-gloved left hand, he held the four reins; in his right, he balanced the ten-pound whip. His back was ramrod-straight and his face showed no emotion, but as he circled in front of the viewing platform, crowded with smiling, applauding officers and Nazi Party officials, the cold rain dripped down his face like tears.

Just a few weeks later, Rudofsky was admitted to a hospital in Krynica, Poland, suffering from chest pains and severe agitation. The doctors were unable to find any physical cause for his ailments. He had suffered from a heart condition since childhood, but he showed no cardiac symptoms now. Rather, his symptoms appeared to be the result of severe stress. Upon his release from the hospital, Rau, perhaps realizing that this highly skilled horseman could no longer handle the fraught conditions in occupied Poland, sent him back to his home region of Bohemia, where he would assume the job of overseeing the Reich's greatest equine treasures: the Lipizzaner.

Rudofsky returned from Poland to find his home much changed. Hostau, a village of only a few thousand inhabitants, was located just adjacent to his family's home in the seat of a county where the Rudofskys were prominent citizens. The stud farm itself was in tip-top shape, with no luxury spared to care for its precious horses. But the war had fractured and splintered this quiet community. Within Rudofsky's own family, sentiments toward the Third Reich were bitterly divided. His father's first cousin owned the local bank and had person-

RUDOFSKY DRIVING A LIPIZZANER PAIR, POLAND, 1943.

ally bankrolled the departure of at least one family of Jews when the Nazis took over the area in 1939. His younger brother, Waldemar, a physician, had joined the German Army and was stationed at a field hospital in the Ukraine. His younger sister was director of the local Nazi women's organization.

As a young man, Rudofsky had considered himself Austrian; his father had been a personal consultant to the Austro-Hungarian emperor Franz Joseph, but between the end of World War I and the German annexation, young Rudofsky had served the Republic of Czechoslovakia, proud of his role in bringing the republic to prominence in horse breeding on the world stage. Privately, Rudofsky disdained the Nazis. But after 1939, he had donned the Wehrmacht uniform without complaint. In his eyes, he had no choice; the civilian horse-breeding system he worked within had been swallowed whole by the German Army, and his expertise made him a valuable military commodity. But in the eyes of the Czech citizens who had been chased from their homes when Hitler's forces arrived, he and his German-speaking compatriots were traitors. When Rudofsky returned to Bohemia, now "cleansed" of its ethnic minorities, he found his homeland sadly diminished.

Being closer to home did have one advantage for Rudofsky. Though he did not have any children of his own, he had a ten-year-old nephew, Waldemar's son, Ulli, whom he adored as his own child. The angelic-faced altar boy gazed upon his suave uncle with tremendous pride each time the six-foot-tall officer strode into Mass at the Church of St. James in his full cavalry uniform, the heels of his shined high-top boots clicking on the stone floor. The devout Rudofsky carried in his pocket a military card stating that if he were in extremis, he wanted to receive final unction.

Rudofsky made it a point to keep watch on the young boy. When he stopped at his mother's Italianate villa not far from Hostau for dinner, he never failed to quiz young Ulli, a clever and studious boy, on his arithmetic tables. Nobody had heard from the boy's father in quite some time. The adults around the Rudofsky dinner table understood that the doctor might be languishing somewhere in a prisoner-of-war camp, or was perhaps already dead.

———

THE STABLES FULL OF white horses made a powerful impression on young Ulli. In the winter of 1943, soon after his uncle returned home from Poland, Rudofsky arranged for Ulli and his older sister, Susi, to visit the majestic horses at Hostau. Like something out of a fairy tale, a carriage pulled by two snow-white horses appeared in front of the children's house, and a handsome uniformed coachman stepped off the driver's box. His ornate uniform—which looked Polish or Russian—impressed the young children. The driver opened the carriage door and tucked Ulli and Susi into warm blankets sewn together like sleeping bags. The air was crystalline as the Lipizzaner trotted toward Hostau, their hooves ringing against the frozen ground. From inside the snug carriage, the children could see the straight back of the coachman up on his box and the snowy expanses of rolling fields, the Bohemian Forest dark and forbidding in the distance.

WHEN THEY ARRIVED AT Hostau, their uncle greeted them. He took them to the stables so that they could see the white horses up close. Ulli was surprised to discover that when you blew on the white coats of the Lipizzaner, their skin was blue-black underneath. But when his uncle lifted him up onto the bare back of a coal-black horse named Tyrant, the boy was terrified to be up so high and screamed out, "It's hot up here." His uncle, perfectly comfortable around the beautiful animals, laughed and lifted him back down. Returning to their home, once again tucked snugly into the carriage, the children were left with an indelible impression of the seemingly magical horses that had been entrusted to their uncle's care.

RUDOFSKY RAN THE STUD farm at Hostau with unstinting precision. Every morning, his valet laid out his perfectly tailored and pressed uniform and buffed his boots to a high shine. At the stable, grooms had already hitched up his Lipizzaner mares. The silver tip of his braided leather carriage whip shone with the well-polished patina of use. This carriage master who could drive a four-in-hand with such ease had never learned to drive a car, and so his upright, elegant figure with the pair of white horses was a familiar sight all over town. As he pulled up in front of the large structure that served as an administrative building for the stud farm, his stable masters always had a report ready. No detail was to be considered too small to bring to his attention.

The day-to-day routine in Hostau was steeped in centuries-old tradition. Rudofsky's farm followed precepts laid out in a book called *Regulation of the Stud Farm,* written in 1656. Grooms were in charge of the horses' everyday care, feeding, grooming, exercise, and pasturing,

ULLI
RUDOFSKY,
AGE ELEVEN.

a job that lasted from sunup to sunset. A good *Landstallmeister,* or rural stud farm director, would never tolerate a groom who was rough or slapdash with the splendid creatures in his charge. These horses were to be treated with the utmost care and kindness. Rudofsky followed these precepts to the letter.

Every Monday, Rudofsky inspected all the horses. Up and down the long aisles of the stables, grooms fussed with their charges, making sure every detail was perfect, from the tips of the horses' well-formed ears to the very ends of their silky tails. Rudofsky watched attentively as each horse was led from its stall by a groom who then coaxed his charge to prick forward its ears, stand square on all four feet, and make the best possible impression.

Details of each horse were recorded in the voluminous stud farm books: the horse's health, temperament, soundness, and physical characteristics. Pertinent information was passed up the line to Gustav Rau. Rudofsky was a consummate expert in the complex details of stud farm management, but decisions about pairings of mares and stallions remained in the hands of his superior.

During 1944, Alois Podhajsky and his wife, Verena, made three separate trips to Hostau to visit the Lipizzaner mares from Piber. Verena Podhajsky, a friendly woman with curly chin-length hair, would visit the horses in their pastures and socialize with the stud farm's staff. But Podhajsky's relationship with Colonel Rudofsky was chilly. Podhajsky was eager to interfere with Rau's plans, convinced that the Austrian mares should not be mated with the other Lipizzaner, nor be subject to any breeding experiments that would ultimately affect their performance. Rudofsky did not appreciate Podhajsky's desire to meddle in the affairs of the breeding farm; he had no choice but to follow Rau's recommendations. But in the end, it mattered little. The decisions affecting the Lipizzaner breeding program were being made above the heads of both men.

One thing is clear: Rau's plan to increase the number of specially bred Lipizzaner was successful. By 1944, the pastures around Hostau were filled with placid white broodmares with frolicking dark-coated foals at their sides. The first of Rau's new breed of Lipizzaner were being born, though it was too soon to tell what the outcome would be; it would take years to fully evaluate the performance of these close-bred newborns, and several generations before selective mating could substantially alter the offspring. But for now, the German project to reshape Europe's oldest and most refined breed, to place upon it the unmistakable mark of the Third Reich, was continuing unimpeded.

In German, the word *Rasse* means both "race" of people and "breed" of animal. Rau's program at Hostau to produce a pure white race of horses shows parallels with one of Nazi Germany's most infamous "other" breeding projects: the *Lebensborn*. At special "birth clinics," SS officers mated with specially selected women who exhibited quintessential Aryan traits. The babies were baptized in a special SS rite, cradled beneath a symbolic SS dagger while incantations pledged that these Aryan babies would have lifelong allegiance to Nazi beliefs. The horses foaled at Hostau were also given a special rite: They were branded with the letter H, which was pierced through with a dagger. This was the mark of Rau's pure new race of white horse.

7.

PODHAJSKY'S CHOICE

Neapolitano Africa walked along a well-tended lane, his nose extended and his gait relaxed. After a season of rigorous training at the Spanish Riding School, the sensitive stallion had won some well-earned rest. Here, just on the outskirts of Vienna, the horses took long, leisurely strolls in the countryside; like children on a summer holiday, the horses and riders blossomed in the sweetly scented country air. Founded in 1526, the summer stables of the Lipizzaner were located in a spacious park, the Lainzer Tiergarten, a twenty-five-square-acre preserve that long had been a protected hunting ground for noblemen. Even now, wild boar and deer roamed the grounds. In this peaceful setting, the hardworking stallions from the riding school passed their summer holidays, substituting long rides through the countryside for rigorous practice and performance schedules.

As he rode, Podhajsky's mind was far from relaxed, preoccupied as he was with the fate of his stallions. The time was nearing when the school normally returned to the city for the winter season, but this year, no one knew whether that was a good or a bad idea. Since the beginning of 1943, the tide of war had started to turn against the Axis powers. Allied bombers were dropping enormous payloads on German cities, and Podhajsky and others feared that Vienna might be next.

Podhajsky hated to break with tradition. He knew that the stallions' progress in their training relied on an orderly progression. Just as a professional ballet dancer or musician cannot stop practicing, so, too, the stallions required patient sequential training practiced faithfully over months and years. Podhajsky had brought the school stallions to the highest level of performance only by sticking religiously with this highly methodical program of instruction. But 1943 was not shaping up to be an ordinary year; he knew that his first duty was to keep the stallions safe. The problem was that he was not sure how best to protect them from danger. One view was that the school should break with tradition and stay at the Lainzer Tiergarten, open parkland that would be an unlikely target for Allied bombers. But the summer stables at Lainzer were flimsy wooden structures—at least in the city, the walls of the imperial stables were solid and thick. Maybe he was an idealist, but Podhajsky could not believe that the Allies would drop bombs upon Vienna, home of some of the world's most important Baroque treasures. And at a deeper level, Podhajsky could not imagine what message the Lipizzaner's absence would send to the city's beleaguered citizens. The horses were a symbol of Austrian identity. If the horses failed to return, would not the citizens start to lose hope? As steward of one of Vienna's most priceless treasures, Podhajsky felt his duty keenly. After wrestling with the dilemma for some time, Podhajsky decided that the Lipizzaner would return to Vienna as usual. In this way, they could continue training, and if the unthinkable occurred, at least they would have the thick eighteenth-century walls of the Spanish Riding School to shelter them.

But a few months later, in the autumn of '43, back in Vienna, the situation had only grown worse. The tide of the war seemed to be breaking increasingly against the Germans, and the Allied bombers were getting closer every day. Alois Podhajsky stood in his office inside the riding school in the company of a local Wehrmacht commander, holding a letter prominently displaying the insignia of the Third Reich that the commander had just handed to him. The letter was from Baldur von Schirach, *Gauleiter* of Vienna, complaining that not enough care had been taken to ensure the safety of the Lipizzaner. Why had Podhajsky chosen to bring them back to central Vienna? Podhajsky stared at the letter in confusion. Were the Nazis so worried that they believed central Vienna would soon be under siege? And if the bombers did come, would the horses really be safer in the wooden stables at the Lainzer Tiergarten? Podhajsky decided to ignore von Schirach's order for the time being. Mercifully, he would hear no more from the *Gauleiter.*

Despite the grim conditions in the city, within the walls of the riding school, Podhajsky had managed to maintain strict discipline. The horses and riders carried on with their exacting training regimen. Noticing that each of the stallions' performances attracted more visitors, he sensed that after a few hours spent in the magical presence of the horses, people returned home with just a little bit of hope. As the war dragged on and the situation in occupied Vienna became more and more difficult, the white horses reminded people of what the world once was and what it could be again. But each day, the world seemed to grow grimmer—even the stallions could not hold back the dark curtain forever.

On May 24, 1944, Podhajsky waited just outside the entrance to the Winter Riding Hall, mounted on Neapolitano Africa. The two were going to perform a solo routine in front of a large audience. Podhajsky could feel the harnessed energy that radiated from his mount. Wordlessly, he communicated with his stallion, urging him to stay focused—in a moment, the horse would convert all of his natural energy into a brilliantly disciplined performance. Podhajsky's hand on the reins was feather-light; he knew that the slightest change in pressure would telegraph a world of intention to the stallion. When the music cued them, the pair entered the ring. Suddenly, the crowd was silent as Africa's perfectly cadenced footsteps danced to the rhythmical accompaniment of a recorded Viennese waltz.

Tonight, the entire festival hall seemed enchanted. The crowd peering down between the Corinthian columns that lined the arena seemed hardly to breathe. As Podhajsky led his horse through the carefully choreographed sequence of steps, each of Africa's movements burst with energy and purpose. On this night, every stallion and rider seemed to bring something extra to the performance, from the simple maneuvers of the youngest participants to the statuesque pose of the *levade,* in which the stallion sank onto his haunches like a charger in a portrait of Napoleon, to the perfected coordinated school quadrille, the finale, in which twelve stallions moved as one. As the performance came to a close and Podhajsky swept off his bicorne cap in salute, it seemed as if the applause would go on forever, as if the members of the audience did not want this magical moment to end. As the thunder of clapping hands finally faded away, an echo was left in the hall. No one, neither man nor beast, could know that this would be the last time the stallions would perform here for a very long time.

LIPIZZANER PERFORMING AT THE
SPANISH RIDING SCHOOL.

Not two months later, on July 20, 1944, high-ranking members of the German military made a failed attempt to assassinate Hitler. After that, more fanatical Nazi adherents who had little sympathy for the Austrian institution replaced those in Berlin who had been sympathetic to the riding school. After several years of being well treated, Podhajsky suddenly found the school being gutted once again: He was forced to send some of his horses to mounted army units, and his riders who were between the ages of twenty-five and twenty-eight, previously exempt, were called up. By now, military reverses in Russia were driving the Germans back. Not long after, Podhajsky's worst fears were realized. On March 17, American B-17s appeared over Vienna. The bombings had begun.

By the summer of 1944, the white stallions had learned to recognize the air raid signal. One by one, the horses would poke their heads over their half-doors, ready to do their part to speed the evacuation. Soon the footsteps of uniformed grooms would hurry down the wide aisles of the imperial stables. Africa, now eight years old, looked alert for the arrival of his groom, lowering his head to ease the job of putting on his halter. In the next stall, Theo did the same. At the first sound of the air raid signal, Podhajsky would rush to the stables to supervise the transfer of the horses to the Winter Riding School, where the men and animals would wait out the bombing.

Each time a bomb struck, Africa cowered, as if trying to escape the loud explosions coming from above, but neither he nor any of the others panicked or tried to bolt. To Podhajsky, it seemed that Africa and the other school stallions had a peculiar expression on their faces, as if saying, "How incomprehensible humans are!" Ultimately, the responsibility for their safety rested entirely with him, and as the raids grew more frequent, he had to admit that the horses could not stay here, even if their performances helped boost morale. The danger was too great.

Given von Schirach's earlier concern for the stallions' well-being, Podhajsky did not expect any problem getting permission to take the horses to a safer location, but when he met with a German city official, he was told that if the Lipizzaner left the city, people would lose heart. Podhajsky was all too aware of that, yet he did not miss the subtext of threat. At this point in Nazi-occupied Austria, anything that smacked of defeatism was punishable as treason.

And so the Lipizzaner were to dance through the hail of airstrikes, to keep alive the illusion that everything was still okay. As the Germans suffered waves of defeat and the Allies streaked toward them from the west, Podhajsky harbored no illusions. With increasing frustration, he realized that the stallions were to be sacrificed to keep up appearances, the way the orchestra on the *Titanic* had to keep playing the waltz as the ship went down. He would have none of it. Secretly, throughout that fall, he packed up every single belonging of the Spanish Riding School, even having the enormous crystal chandeliers disassembled and boxed up. He found a sympathetic city official who gave him wagons and harnesses. If worse came to worst, he would hitch up his priceless stallions and drive them straight out of the city; on foot, they could make it as far as the Lainzer Tiergarten. But Podhajsky could not stop worrying about the inadequacy of the wooden structures. Sure enough, in the fall of 1944, a bomb partially destroyed one of the summer stables. Had he moved the horses, they would have taken a direct hit. Podhajsky redoubled his efforts, trying to find a safer place farther from the city that could accommodate so many horses.

Finally, he discovered a large estate in Upper Austria that had stables large enough to hold his seventy-five horses. Countess Gertrud Arco auf Valley owned a large castle with spacious stables located in the village of St. Martin. She had room for all of Podhajsky's stallions, and she extended an invitation to him. But an increasingly desperate Podhajsky could not get the authorities to let him leave. No transport was available. All trucks were being used for military purposes. Meanwhile, he received a frantic message from the stud director of the Spanish Riding School's sister school in Budapest; they had evacuated their stables and were on the run with the horses but had nowhere to go. Could they bring their horses to Vienna? It was then that Podhajsky realized just how bad things had gotten—he was trying to get his horses out of Vienna, and somebody else was trying to get theirs in!

One day in January 1945, looking out the window of his office, Podhajsky saw four large furniture moving vans; movers were loading priceless works of art from the National Museum to transport them out of the city for safety. Podhajsky had a thought: Even if his pleas to save the horses were not working, perhaps he could make a case to move the rest of the precious artifacts—saddles, bridles, and artwork— from the school. When he obtained permission to remove the artifacts, he added an additional request: Could he not use some of the extra space on the truck to remove some of the horses to the empty stables in Upper Austria where he had been offered accommodation? Instead of presenting this as the riding school leaving the city, he said that it was just to ease overcrowding at the stables in Vienna. To his relief, the city official agreed. In this way, in January and February, Podhajsky managed to ship small groups of horses to safety, so that by late February 1945, only fifteen stallions and a small number of riders remained. He had fulfilled his obligation to keep the riding school in the city while making sure that a good number of the horses were out of harm's way.

But as February dragged into March, the bombings intensified. On March 7, the Allies crossed the Remagen bridge over the Rhine into eastern Germany. Meanwhile, the Russians were pressing in from the east. Podhajsky then tried to contact the Army High Command in

Berlin, but the phone lines were so badly damaged that he had trouble making contact. Finally, he managed to obtain permission from General Weingert, the cavalry inspector in Berlin, to evacuate the remaining fifteen horses and at last to close down the riding school entirely, although the inspector informed him that it would not be safe to proceed without permission from the *Gauleiter*. Podhajsky was reluctant to approach him. The school was under the direction of the Army High Command. He felt that bringing himself to von Schirach's attention might do more harm than good. But he could not think of any other way forward. He remembered the letter from von Schirach commanding him to keep the horses safe—was that just Nazi business as usual, or was he possibly a lover of horses? Podhajsky steeled himself. He would have to find out.

On the telephone, he was given a chilly reception, but after a three-day wait, he was told that the *Gauleiter* would receive him at his villa. Von Schirach was tall and blond, with a somewhat effeminate face echoing that of his mother, a Philadelphia socialite who had married a German. The former leader of the Hitler Youth sported a brand-new brown uniform, in spite of the fact that he was not a military man. When Podhajsky was finally led into his study, the *Gauleiter* appeared alarmed to see the director of the Spanish Riding School standing in front of him.

"Is the situation with the Lipizzaner under control?" von Schirach quickly asked.

Podhajsky looked at von Schirach, realizing that this gussied-up Nazi had no idea what was going on. The question was absurd. The horses, like the rest of the city, were under siege, their safety in constant jeopardy. Any fool could figure that out. Podhajsky stood tall, demonstrating his well-trained military posture and his implacable calm. This pretender was not going to intimidate him, no matter what kind of titles he had slapped upon him, what uniforms he wore without the dignity of having earned them, or what insignias showed how he had aligned himself with Hitler.

Podhajsky, wasting no time, stated his business. "Due to the danger to the horses posed by the air raids, it is necessary to remove the horses from the city *immediately*."

"If the Lipizzaner are seen leaving the city, it will make the citizens feel as if they are in a hopeless position," the *Gauleiter* countered, appearing even more agitated.

Podhajsky avoided stating the obvious—that the citizens of Vienna were indeed in a hopeless position. The only question now was whether the Russians would invade or the Americans and British would flatten the city with bombs. The citizens could not even pick their poison.

"Besides," the *Gauleiter* added, "the city will be delivered soon. We are just on the verge of unleashing new military measures against the Allies."

"The stallions are irreplaceable. The danger here in the city is too great. They need to be evacuated to a safer location immediately," Podhajsky repeated firmly. He was trying to create the impression that the matter was not open for debate, though he knew that he was entirely at the mercy of the Nazi leader's whim. He was grateful that he had been able to secrete some of the horses out in twos and threes, but even the piecemeal strategy was no longer feasible. Trucks and fuel were now impossible to come by without permission at the highest levels. To remove fifteen stallions from a wartime city under siege would be a grand undertaking; he would never pull it off without the agreement of the man who stood before him.

A long pause ensued while the *Gauleiter* reflected. Podhajsky kept his level gaze upon von Schirach's noncommittal expression, certain that the fate of his stallions hung in the balance. For months, the German authorities had been toying with him—asking him to leave the city, then refusing to grant travel permission.

"It is not easy for me to agree to the evacuation," the *Gauleiter* said. "I have always considered the Spanish Riding School to be Vienna, and with the departure of the Lipizzaner, a piece of Vienna goes from us."

Podhajsky wondered if he should say more or remain quiet while von Schirach deliberated. To stand here, begging before this sham officer—a civilian preening in faux military dress—was becoming unbearable.

The Nazi leader finally spoke. "But I love them too much to leave them in danger any longer . . ."

Podhajsky felt his knees almost buckle in relief, but he responded only with a curt nod. Inside, he felt a deep surge of gratitude toward his stallions. The horses inspired people to love them, even this cold-hearted and brutal Nazi. Effectively, the stallions had won their own freedom.

Now that he had a plan for his own horses, Podhajsky turned his attention to the plight of the horses at the Spanish Riding School in Budapest. While the Vienna stables were hardly an ideal shelter, the thick walls of the building could provide at least some small protection. He sent a wire to the director of the Budapest school, letting him know that the imperial stables would soon be empty if he needed to bring his horses there, explaining that he himself was going to flee with his horses to a safer location in the countryside.

Unfortunately, the twenty-two Hungarian Lipizzaner would never arrive: Confronted by Russian forces while en route to Vienna in March 1945, Red Army soldiers tried to confiscate the horses for war use. Four of them were successfully harnessed and forced to pull a heavy cart transporting arms and ammunition toward Vienna. The remaining eighteen, who were frightened and balked, were shot on the spot. Their carcasses were butchered and fed to the Red Army's hungry soldiers.

The fortunate stallions from Vienna had been granted a reprieve: They were headed to the safer territories of Upper Austria. But Podhajsky knew that his ordeal was far from over. It would be a long, difficult trek to get the horses safely away while air raids bombarded the city daily.

8.

HORSES IN PERIL

In the spring of 1944, while Podhajsky struggled to keep his stallions safe in occupied Vienna, the war was creeping closer to the German-controlled Arabian stud at Janów Podlaski. Once again, Janów's location, just a few miles from Russia, put the farm in close proximity to the fighting. In this eastern part of the country, the Polish resistance was making a ruckus—bombing trains, disrupting German activities in the area. Adding to the danger, the enormous Red Army was on the march from the east. The Polish staff of Janów waited anxiously. Their safety was dependent on the decisions of their German occupiers. In early May, they received orders from Gustav Rau. Nine of Janów's best Arabians would be shipped to Hostau, where, with the careful movements of a chess master, Rau had been strategically moving the very finest horses. Among those chosen by Rau was the most valuable of all of the young stallions—Witez.

In the stable under the tall clock tower, one of Janów's most devoted grooms, Jan Ziniewicz, moved with slow, saddened steps and a heavy heart. He walked from stall to stall, speaking a soft word to each horse as he passed. When he approached Witez, the Polish prince greeted him with a soft nudge. Ziniewicz slipped a halter on four-year-old Witez, then gave his nose an affectionate stroke, tracing a finger over the small white marking on his muzzle. The stallion's thin fluted nostrils quivered and he reached his head forward, pricking his small ears toward the groom. Ziniewicz was just over five feet tall, with the craggy, well-lined face of a man who had spent much of his life outdoors. He had a quiet, sympathetic manner that the horses all responded to. Witez was no exception. Realizing that he had no choice but to follow German orders, Ziniewicz clipped a lead rope to the halter's brass ring, and the stallion willingly followed him out of the stable. Today was the day when Witez would board a train bound for Czechoslovakia.

On the station platform in the nearby village, grooms circled their sleek charges, waiting their turn to board the train. Each Arabian was cosseted in a soft blanket and had all four legs swathed in cotton batting, neatly held in place by flannel bandages. The train's interior had been specially fitted out with plush padding to protect the precious horses on their journey. One by one, each of the nine selected Arabians walked up the ramp. Ziniewicz had been assigned to accompany the horses on their journey. One of the stud farm assistants, a young woman named Liselotte, lingered next to Witez as he was preparing to board. She wondered if she would ever see him again. As the train lurched and started to pull away, Liselotte whispered, "Goodbye, Witez, go with God." The train whistle hooted twice and Witez departed on the Prague-bound train, not knowing that this would be the last time he would ever see his homeland.

Ziniewicz watched out for Witez's well-being during the nine-day train ride, which took them west through Warsaw and Lodz, then south toward Prague. When they finally arrived at Hostau, the groom found familiar faces from Poland—the stud master Rudofsky and the kindly young veterinarian Lessing, both of whom had been frequent visitors at Janów. Still, the familiar faces offered only fleeting comfort: Ziniewicz had to say a hurried goodbye to his horses, then, following orders, turned around to return to Janów, leaving the pride of Poland behind on foreign soil. Back at Janów, Ziniewicz missed the bright eyes that shone from Witez's noble face, which was lit up by the uneven white star splashed across his forehead. The Polish staff of Janów Podlaski could not believe that their treasured horse had slipped from their grasp. Even as conditions in Poland had become more dangerous, at least they could protect and care for their beloved charges in their own home. Now Witez was far away, on a farm in a foreign country controlled by Germans. Nobody knew if Witez would ever return. Now, of Ofir's three greatest sons of 1938, only two remained—Stained Glass and Grand Slam.

Settled at Hostau, Witez fared well. Hay and grain were plentiful, and the stable was roomy and comfortable. Witez and his stablemates, though far from Poland, were well cared for and no longer in immediate danger. The remainder of Rau's thousands of valuable horses, flung across the vast territory of Poland and the Ukraine, including those left behind at Janów, were directly in the path of an oncoming tsunami of warfare. As the Russian Army pushed westward through the Ukraine and Belorussia and into eastern Poland, routing the German Army and recapturing territories it had held, Rau's horse farms fell directly in their path. Already the newly established Lipizzaner stud farm at Debica had been overrun, the horses relocated just in time. All over Rau's empire, anxious horsemen worried and wondered, awaiting any word of instruction. At the stallion depot in Drogomyśl, which sat on the eastern bank of Poland's Vistula River near the Czechoslovakian border, the station master, Brandt, made his wife and children practice harnessing the stallions and loading the carriages. If the Russians approached, he drilled his family, they would need to drive the horses across the Vistula, fording the river if the bridges were blown out. Their destination would be Hostau, over more than 250 miles to the west.

Back at Janów Podlaski, the staff of the stud continued to wait for orders from the occupiers. Frequent skirmishes occurred between the German Wehrmacht and the Soviet partisans operating in the area. In May 1944, a German bomb landed on Janów, partially destroying one of the stallion barns. Fortunately, the horses were out at pasture and none was hurt. Only five years after the near destruction of the stud farm at the hands of the Russians, the staff of Janów stood dazed in front of the smoking ruins of one of their newly rebuilt stables.

In late June, Rau finally announced that the entire farm and all of its livestock would be evacuated. At least this time the horses would not have to flee on foot: Rau had arranged train transport to Sohland, a small city several hundred miles to the west, inside Germany proper. Rau persuaded a retired cavalry officer in Sohland, Colonel von Bonnet, to open his stables to the refugees and take over responsibility for the horses. With any luck, they could ride out the remainder of the war without having to move again. Even aboard trains, the horses would be undertaking a dangerous journey. Polish partisans were operating in strength in the area around Janów and might very well try to blow up the trains as they fled.

Late at night, in the quiet of his home, Andrzej Kristalovich and his wife discussed the plan in anxious whispers. Traveling with their young daughter would be dangerous, and venturing west toward Germany was marching into the jaws of the enemy. But ending up in the hands of the Russians was also terrifying. Hans Fellgiebel, the farm's German director since 1940, had established a good relationship with the Polish staff at Janów. He had protected the many craftsmen, such as farriers and saddle makers, who worked on the farm. In spite of his German uniform, he had earned their trust concerning the horses. In the end, Kristalovich and his wife agreed—his primary duty was to stick with the horses. He had been entrusted to safeguard Poland's national treasure—especially when Stanislaw Pohoski, the farm's former director, suddenly fell ill and died. Kristalovich was now the highest-ranking Pole at Janów.

On July 1, ninety-six of Janów's remaining horses were boarded onto trains. Witez's two half brothers, Stained Glass and Grand Slam, pranced up the gangplanks, and the doors were bolted shut behind them. Trucks loaded with sandbags raced alongside the tracks to protect the trains from those who would try to fire upon them as they fled. In spite of the great risks, the horses left Janów without incident.

Nineteen days later, a second shipment of horses left Janów, also headed for Germany. Just one day later, on July 20, 1944, a dramatic event in the Third Reich had an outsize impact on the fleeing men and horses from Janów: A group of conspirators attempted to assassinate Hitler inside his Wolf's Lair bunker in East Prussia. The purpose of the plot was to assassinate Hitler, seize control of the government, and negotiate more favorable peace terms with the Allies. A bomb exploded, but due to it being slightly misplaced, Hitler suffered only minor injuries.

The July 20 plot had hit close to home for the escapees from Janów. One of the co-conspirators in the plot was Hans Fellgiebel's brother

Erich, who was swiftly caught and executed. A few days later, Hans was arrested and imprisoned in Berlin.

Though Rau's empire was slipping away from him, he struggled to maintain control. The horses he had shipped to Sohland were out of immediate danger, but all was not well. The crowded conditions, the lack of staff, and the scarcity of good-quality food in these borrowed stables had left the beautiful Arabians in pitiful condition. To make matters worse, von Bonnet got daily demands from the German Army to release his men to join the fight, yet he had scarcely enough men to tend to the horses. Conditions kept deteriorating. In January 1945, a bedraggled herd of hundreds of horses with their grooms and handlers appeared at von Bonnet's estate, pleading for shelter. The horses and men had trekked hundreds of miles through ice and snow, abandoning two of Rau's stud farms, Boguslawice and Kozienice, farther to the east. They crowded into the stables where Witez's brothers were kept.

The conditions, already difficult, became deplorable. Colonel von Bonnet was torn apart by demands—he had barely enough men to care for the Arabians, and both space and fodder were growing short. Kristalovich and Ziniewicz did everything they could to help, but von Bonnet's estate had been pushed beyond its capacity. There were too many horses crowded into one place. Just twelve months earlier, these horses had been the best kept in all of Europe, and now their condition was pitiful—cramped stabling, untended hooves, respiratory infection, dull coats. The horses looked like feedlot rejects, not equine royalty.

Finally, Gustav Rau arrived in Sohland to take charge. He decided to whittle down the herd until only the very best remained. With pleading eyes, the bedraggled horses seemed to watch warily as Rau made his rounds. Kristalovich and Ziniewicz had tended to Witez's brothers carefully, currying them until they shone and eking out extra rations of grain: Among the worn-down lot, they looked better than most.

After a ruthless triage, only Rau's selections were allowed to stay at von Bonnet's estate. He instructed the staff to give the rejected horses to locals. As a motley assortment of local farmers and low-ranking soldiers led the formerly magnificent Arabians away, Gustav Rau took great pains to tell the new owners that the horses were being given "as a loan to fighting troops and soldiers, to be returned after the war." One by one, some of Poland's most priceless horses were led down the country lane and disappeared out of sight. None of these Arabians would ever be recovered for Poland. Once again, the two Polish horsemen could only watch as the number of purebreds from Janów diminished.

By February 1945, six months after fleeing Janów, the men began to realize that Sohland was no longer safe. In spite of the lack of sufficient staff and the remaining horses' poor condition, they had no choice but to keep moving west. This time, their destination was a large army remounting station at Torgau, about ninety miles away. Trains could no longer be spared, so just as they had done five years earlier in the opposite direction, they would have to flee on foot. The plan was to head first to Dresden, covering fifteen miles a day, with one night to break the journey, then continue to Torgau after a few days of rest. The stallions would set off first. Kristalovich would follow with the most vulnerable group—the mares and foals.

As they made their way along the narrow, hilly country lanes, an icy rain soaked through their wool coats and blankets and froze in treacherous ruts on the ground. Wind whipped through the men's drenched outer garments, through the horses' manes, and through their dull, heavy winter coats. Mares with swollen bellies trudged along, heavy-footed, their heads hanging and eyes dull. Kristalovich watched the broodmares anxiously; the harsh conditions would affect them first. Soon enough, his worst fears were realized—the stress put some of the mares into labor. Their tiny newborns could not keep up. The men banged on doors, trying to requisition wagons to transport the newborn foals, but the area was so stripped that four-wheeled conveyances were almost impossible to find. By this point, millions of people in the eastern part of Germany's realm were trying to flee in advance of the Russian Army's arrival. Wagons, cars, trucks, gasoline— all were scarce. Most had been seized for the war effort, and whatever was left had been hoarded by civilians to enable their escape.

In this time of misery, no one had sympathy to spare for this downtrodden group of horses and humans from Poland. Kristalovich cradled the wobbly newborns in his arms, sheltering them with his own overcoat; he watched helplessly as the light flickered from their eyes. Still, they had no choice but to keep moving.

When night fell following that bitter first day, they were unable to find shelter. They knocked on doors, beseeching farmers to spare an empty pasture, but found no offers. Finally, von Bonnet and Kristalovich decided they had no choice but to continue riding through the dark of night, hoping to reach Dresden before morning.

Defying their own exhaustion, the lead group of about fifty stallions, including Stained Glass and Grand Slam, covered thirty-five miles in twenty-four hours. They had joined the ranks of more than half a million other refugees fleeing west, toward Dresden—which everyone believed would not be a target of Allied bombs because of its magnificent architecture and significance as a center of art and culture. In Dresden, the train stations were jammed; the Grosser Garten, a spacious garden in the city's center, was crowded with the tents of almost two hundred thousand refugees, and endless columns of wagons, horse-drawn carts, cars, and trucks lumbered toward the city. Bedraggled families, footsore and weary, marched along the roadsides, nursing infants and lending an arm to the elderly. Among this mass, the stallions of Janów marched until they reached the outskirts of the city.

Their timing could not have been worse. As they approached the city on the night of February 13, a Dresden radio announcer interrupted the program: "*Achtung! Achtung!* An attack is coming! Go to your cellars at once!" In the center of Dresden, people hurried underground, but on the city's outskirts, where masses of refugees, including the group from Janów, were milling around, most never received the message. Besides, there was nowhere to hide. Green tracers, called Christmas trees, lit up the sky over the old city. A few moments later, a crushing roar rumbled above.

The stallions squealed in panic, but soon the high-pitched sounds were drowned out by the unceasing roar of planes overhead. In the words of an eyewitness, "It was as if a huge noisy conveyor belt was rolling over us, a noise punctuated with detonations and tremors." Unwittingly, the men had ridden the horses directly into one of the biggest air attacks of the war: the Allied bombing of Dresden, during which 722 heavy bombers from the RAF and 527 from the United States Army Air Forces dropped 3,900 tons of explosives in two waves about three hours apart, resulting in a firestorm that destroyed most of central Dresden.

The entire bowl of the sky turned a violent crimson orange. As flames engulfed the city, the horizon turned fiery orange-white, and a thick cloud of black smoke obscured the sky. The stallions panicked, rearing and lashing out, crazily trying to escape the cacophony and intense heat. People lost their bearings, and the horses, too, wheeling as they pawed and reared, the whites of their eyes flashing and picking up the orange and crimson colors of the bone-shattering explosions. Men and animals fled in all directions, but the hellfire rained down everywhere—there was nowhere to run.

Jan Ziniewicz, strong and wiry but weighing barely 140 pounds, focused every bit of his strength on the two stallions in his charge. Strobing flashes of light revealed a terrifying picture—craters and flames, people on fire, horses rearing and running in all directions, and still the terrifying sound, like a freight train running through the sky. Stained Glass and Grand Slam strained hard against their halters. Their eyes whitened in fear, and their nostrils trumpeted like the gills on a landed fish. Ziniewicz braced himself, holding tight to the two lead lines as the ropes burned painfully through his palms. He wrapped the leads several times around his hands for better traction. In spite of his gloves, the ropes finally stripped the skin off his palms. Sweat beaded up on his brow, but he clenched his teeth and held on. A flash of fire and a singe of burning hair almost blinded him—Grand Slam's tail was on fire. Unable to reach it, Ziniewicz blinked and simply held his breath, waiting for the fire to engulf them, but the flame sputtered out.

Then, all of a sudden, the unholy roar ended. Aside from Grand Slam's singed tail, Ziniewicz and his two horses had made it through the bombing unscathed. But he could not even see half of the group— all around him was a mass of wailing people, charred bodies, and smoking craters.

Kristalovich, traveling with the mares and foals, was half a day behind. When his group arrived along the road just at the city's outskirts, he came upon the charred corpses of seventeen of his beloved stallions and began to weep. At last, he came upon Jan Ziniewicz, whose palms were lacerated with deep rope wounds. Stained Glass and Grand Slam had survived. The two men embraced. Together, they tried to round up the survivors.

The group congregated in the Weisser Hirsch forest just outside the city limits, now flooded with refugees and stricken animals. Some of the surviving animals were too tired and injured to continue on. Von

Bonnet and Kristalovich handed over the wounded horses to an equestrian field hospital, itself on the run, and after only two days of rest, what was left of the group limped on toward the final destination in Torgau, about forty-five miles farther northwest, a journey of three additional days.

When they finally arrived, they found the stables overflowing—not a single stall was available. Eventually, they found refuge in an empty riding hall, and the exhausted men bedded down on the sand right next to their charges.

The next day, Colonel von Bonnet returned to Sohland to evacuate the rest of the horses and personnel from his estate. By then, the Russians were so close to his farm that he could hear them in the distance. Just as he prepared to leave, the local Nazi authority told him that he must stay and fight or "be lined up against the wall and shot." Von Bonnet ignored the *Kreisleiter*'s orders and hurried away, hoping to evacuate some of the horses left behind on the initial trip. But von Bonnet never made it back to the group from Janów. He was captured by the Russians and would die of dysentery in one of their prison camps.

Among the crowded and wretched refugees in Torgau, Kristalovich and Ziniewicz did what they could to care for the remaining horses. They had no time to focus on the heartbreak of their losses, as every waking moment was taken up by caring for the surviving Arabians. In March, the group moved once again, by train, and found shelter still farther west, in Nettlelau, Germany, where they were able to ride out the war. More than two hundred purebred Arabians had fled Janów in January 1944. There were fewer than fifty remaining. Kristalovich and Ziniewicz had no idea what fate had befallen the few prized stallions and mares selected to be sent to Hostau—they could only hope for the best.

THE ESCAPE

The scene down at the Franz Joseph train station was chaotic. Tracks were jammed with unmoored cars. Both of Vienna's other major train stations, the Südbahnhof and Westbahnhof, had been damaged during the air raids, and everyone trying to get out of the city was bottlenecking through the remaining viable egress. In the heart of the chaos stood two unattached train cars carrying a restless cargo: fifteen Lipizzaner stallions from the Spanish Riding School. Their master, Alois Podhajsky, flew around the station imploring every official he could find to hitch those two cars to a locomotive that could transport them out of Vienna.

These were the last fifteen stallions left in Vienna. Among this final group were Podhajsky's two personal mounts, Africa and his barn mate, Pluto, kept there to continue daily training. Rumors swirled that the Russians would arrive within days. Podhajsky felt overwhelmed, afraid he had waited too long to escape with the last of the stallions.

A few hours earlier, two large cargo trucks had pulled up outside the riding school, ready to transport these remaining few horses. Podhajsky watched the stallions walking obediently up the ramps into the trucks, which had been fitted out with simple standing stalls softened with a bed of thick clean straw. When the last stallion was loaded, for the first time in more than three centuries, the imperial stables stood empty and eerily silent.

Once the last of his stallions was safely aboard, including his own precious Africa, Podhajsky hurried through the covered walkway to take a final look inside his beloved riding school. As soon as he stepped indoors, the sounds of the city fell away. The two-foot-thick walls blocked out all the noise. Inside, the hall was dark—several of the windows were papered over with cardboard after shattering during the bombings. The crystal chandeliers were gone; their absence made the riding hall seem more ordinary. Despite his relief that he had found a way to get the horses out of the city, Podhajsky was melancholy. Never in the long history of the riding school had the horses fled the city. Would they ever come back? The future was completely uncertain—hopefully, the horses would live, but the institution might not survive. In spite of these misgivings, as the trucks pulled away, headed for the train station, Podhajsky felt satisfied, on balance. At last, every one of his horses was headed toward safety. His wife, Verena, had packed up a few belongings, and together they would rejoin the horses at the train station.

But several hours had passed since they had arrived at the station, night was closing in, and the stallions remained marooned in their train cars. One official said that he could not let them pass without a permit that Podhajsky could not produce; once that obstacle was cleared away, the locomotive driver refused to hitch up Podhajsky's cars with the jittery cargo—the horse cars were too heavy and would put too much strain on his engine. Podhajsky's relief at having finally secured transport for the rest of the horses turned increasingly to agitation as the two cars sat on the tracks for hour after hour, unmoving.

He begged and cajoled until the locomotive driver finally shrugged and hitched up the cars behind his engine. The grooms rode along with the horses, while Podhajsky, Verena, and several riders boarded a passenger car. By the time the engine pulled out of the station, it was close to midnight. Their route would take them west across Austria, then north toward their final destination, St. Martin im Innkreis, a small town in Upper Austria.

Their progress was agonizingly slow. The train would heave into motion; then, with a lugubrious grinding of gears and a sharp jerk, it would stop unexpectedly. Podhajsky peered anxiously out the train windows, unable to see what was causing the repeated delays, but all he could discern was the inky darkness of the blacked-out countryside. As dawn broke, Podhajsky was shocked by the sign in the station where they had just arrived. Despite traveling all night in fits and starts, they had come only as far as Tulln—normally a half-hour train trip from Vienna.

Podhajsky tried to stay calm and wait out the halt, but finally he went to investigate. To his horror, he discovered that all three of their cars were no longer attached to the locomotive. The conductor had unhitched and pulled the locomotive away without them.

Podhajsky rushed to speak to the stationmaster, who met him with the bland incomprehension of a bureaucrat. He had no knowledge of their train cars. He didn't understand why they were there. He had received no instructions from Vienna. In short, Podhajsky, his wife, the riders, grooms, and fifteen stallions were stranded in unmoored train cars—without even the sheltering walls of the Spanish Riding School to protect them.

The air raid sirens, followed by all-clears, came and went relentlessly, as Podhajsky's pleas were shrugged off by the stationmaster, firm in his opinion that there was nothing he could do, since he had no instructions from Vienna.

A day later, the situation was unchanged. The stallions were restless, unused to being cooped up for long periods of time. Podhajsky was at his wits' end and insisted that the stationmaster put a call through to von Schirach, intimating that the powers would not be happy to know these valuable horses were stuck. He had no idea how the *Gauleiter* would react, but he was so desperate he was willing to take the risk.

When the stationmaster attempted to put the call through, there was no response but a dead line. A series of damaging Allied air raids on Vienna had cut off all communication with the city. Podhajsky continued to threaten consequences if the horses were not allowed to pass. In between his exhortations, he circled back to the train cars, where the horses stood, fidgety but patient, their eyes so trusting—showing a faith in their master that he desperately feared might not be warranted. He fished into his ever-present leather pouch and fed sugar lumps to each stallion, whispering comforting words in a low voice, trying to project a confidence that he did not feel. He lingered next to Africa for an extra moment, thanking him for his patience in this trying situation. The animal's dark eyes were so wise and understanding; even in this most gloomy predicament, the horses endured like stoic old soldiers. Hours of endless waiting and frustration stretched on, time still punctuated by the shrieks of the intermittent air raid signals. Night had turned to morning once again before, at last, the stationmaster signaled to an engine driver to attach the three cars. The locomotive pulled them out of the siding and their journey restarted. Eventually, they made progress as far as Amstetten, about fifty miles west of Vienna.

But when the train pulled into the station and Podhajsky saw the conditions around them, his heart sank. Military transports lined the tracks and anxious people milled around the platforms, certain they were about to become the target of a bombing attack.

The grooms led the horses off the train carriages and out onto the platform to stretch their legs, and to lay down fresh straw in the stalls. People crowded around, mesmerized by these exquisite animals, so revered in Austria that observers recognized them on sight, reminded of a simpler and happier time. Podhajsky tried to take advantage of people's obvious sentiment toward Austria's beloved stallions to persuade the stationmaster that the horses needed to be given priority in the general escape from danger. Either his plea, or the sight of the beautiful horses calmly parading in the chaos at the station, managed to convince the stationmaster that they should be allowed to continue. As the train pulled away from Amstetten, Podhajsky heaved a sigh of relief when he heard the sirens receding in the distance. They had gotten away just in time.

His relief was short-lived. About an hour later, as they approached the train station in Linz, the air raid sirens were already wailing. Shortly before they reached the station, the transport officer jumped up and shouted orders: "Unhook the engine and drive it to safety. Passengers disembark and go directly to the air raid shelters."

The engine, stopping before it reached the station proper, quickly uncoupled and zoomed away. Since bombers targeted the stations, the locomotives were vacated during air raids to prevent them from being hit. However, there was no way to get the horses off the transport that quickly and with nowhere for them to go. Podhajsky watched the people scurrying toward the shelters as the sirens wailed in his ears, but he stood his ground. Instead of joining the throng, he turned and headed toward the car where Pluto and Africa were confined. Ignoring the screech of the air raid signal and the mad gestures of the stationmaster, Podhajsky climbed into the train car with his stallions. Without saying a word, Verena and the grooms loyally followed him.

Even before the bombardment began, they could feel the train car vibrating as the bombers approached. Soon the ground was shaking and the air was filled with deafening booms. Then the car started to buck and shudder as if it were about to be tossed entirely into the air. Podhajsky could see the horses trembling in terror; his own knees were shaking so much he could scarcely stand. Verena clutched tightly to her husband, her eyes seeking his for some sign of reassurance. The firestorm that erupted around them seemed ten times more deafening and shattering than what they had experienced within the walls of the riding school.

Podhajsky watched as Pluto huddled up against Africa. White ringed their eyes, their nostrils flared, and their breath trumpeted in fear. Unable to flee, the horses could only snort or paw the floor. Podhajsky murmured reassurances, but in truth, all of them, equine and human, were terrified. The only comfort was that they were together. Earth-splitting booms ripped through the air, each one seeming like the one that would tear them apart. All Podhajsky could do was hold his wife and try to communicate silently to his horses that even in this terrible moment, he would not desert them.

As he huddled in the train car, surrounded by frightened horses, listening to the explosions, his mind flashed back to his days of combat during the Great War, a dark time in his life that he tried to avoid thinking about. He had fallen in love with a brave seal-brown horse, Neger, his cavalry mount during those years. In the midst of a furious firefight, Neger had galloped off the battlefield, bringing his rider to safety. No sooner had Podhajsky realized that the horse had saved his life than the valiant animal stumbled and fell. Thrown from the saddle but unhurt, Podhajsky saw that the gallant Neger was severely wounded by shrapnel and was dying. He had held on just long enough to transport his rider away from harm. Podhajsky, only eighteen at the time, sat cradling the horse's head in his arms as the light dimmed from his eyes. The horse had saved his life. This unspoken truth lay underneath everything Podhajsky had done since then. He would never underestimate a horse's courage or loyalty.

Now, as the bombs fell like rain from the sky, the fates of Podhajsky and his precious horses, Pluto and Africa and the others, were inextricably intertwined. He had spent the last few months tirelessly trying to ensure their safety, and it had come down to this. For two straight hours, Podhajsky, his wife, the grooms, and the horses crouched in the confines of the train car as the world exploded around them.

When the all-clear sounded, they cowered for a moment longer in silence. Then everything whirred back into motion. Podhajsky felt the bump and jostle as the locomotive hitched up their cars and pulled them the short distance into the Linz station.

Before any of them even had time to breathe a sigh of relief, the sirens ripped through the air again. The stationmaster ran out and shouted to the driver: "Uncouple the trains and draw away from the station! Passengers disembark and go directly to air raid shelters!"

In a frenzy, Podhajsky realized that they were about to be plunged back into the same terror they had just escaped. He begged and pleaded with the stationmaster not to uncouple the locomotive and leave the horses stranded. Here, inside the station proper, the danger of being struck was even greater. The bombers were clearly returning to try to score a direct hit.

Podhajsky felt the boxcars roll forward with a jerk. Disobeying the stationmaster, the engine driver had shown mercy on the horses. He pulled away from the station with the horse cars still attached.

By nightfall, they had escaped two more raids, and the sky was blood red from the burning of so many fires. At last, around midnight, the train pulled off the main line onto the northerly local line that would carry them the rest of the way to their destination. The constant air raid sirens ceased.

Podhajsky, Verena, the grooms, Pluto, Africa, and the thirteen other stallions spent four days together on that train, traveling a total distance of 190 miles before arriving at the small village of St. Martin. The quiet country roads leading away from the station could not have provided a starker contrast to the inferno from which they had escaped. Podhajsky managed a smile as he saw the stallions, just released from their cramped, dirty stalls, sniffing the air and looking around their new surroundings, city mice on a visit to the country. The exhausted group of horses and men walked up the narrow country lane, their arrival greeted by the chirping of birds and lowing of cows in distant pastures. When they arrived at the spacious stables, part of the grand estate of Count Arco auf Valley, Podhajsky hadn't slept in over thirty-six hours. The stallions whinnied greetings, joyous to rediscover their comrades from Vienna after the long separation. At last, the seventy-three stallions of the Spanish Riding School were gathered safely under one roof.

The sounds of guns and falling mortar bombs still echoed in his ears as Podhajsky led Africa and Pluto into their stalls for the night; he took heart from their kindly faces as the horses nuzzled up their treats and circled around their box stalls, taking in the unfamiliar sights and sounds. The new stables were so much less grand than their home in Vienna, yet Podhajsky couldn't help but feel that the horses somehow understood. At least no bombs fell on this isolated hamlet.

By now, Podhajsky knew that the war would end with Germany's defeat. Beyond that, he could not predict the future. The stallions would live, but without the survival of the institutions that supported them—the Spanish Riding School and the stud farm for the mares and foals—Podhajsky would have won the battle only to lose the war.

By March 1945, communications in the German Reich had grown undependable, and news from Hostau, where the mares were stabled, was spotty. Podhajsky had lost all contact with Rau and suspected that his empire had been shattered—and who knew what had become of his horses. The Russians were advancing from the east, with Hostau most likely in their direct path, in which case the mares and foals would be in mortal peril. The Russians had been ruthless in their treatment of the horses—drafting them for war use, shooting the uncooperative ones, and worse yet, slaughtering livestock, including horses, to feed their hungry armies. If the Russians arrived in Hostau, Podhajsky had no doubt that the horses would be lost to Austria and might very well lose their lives. And there was nothing he could do about it. The fate of the mares was completely out of his hands.

Podhajsky was haunted by the image of his beloved stallions grow-ing older in this isolated hamlet like the exiled royalty of a former country, the last representatives of a dying breed. The institution of the Spanish Riding School had endured through centuries, but it was not at all clear that it would survive the last few weeks of the war.

PART TWO

The Americans

It is absurd to ask the gods
for victory
in a cavalry battle
if you do not ride.

—XENOPHON

HANK REED SURVEYS THE 10TH CAVALRY
COLOR GUARD AT FORT LEAVENWORTH,
CIRCA 1940.

10.

MACHINE VERSUS HORSE

Under the wide blue Kansas skies, fifty coal-black chargers lined up at parade rest, resplendent in white bridles that set off their shiny dark coats. Each soldier had curried his charger to a high gloss, daubed blacking on his hooves, and oiled and soaped his mount's tack until it glowed, yet the spit and polish of the men's own neatly creased uniforms showed not a trace of their toil.

At Fort Riley, the army's premier equestrian training center, a hundred-thousand-acre complex in the Flint Hills of northeastern Kansas, an increasing urgency filled the air. Ace equestrian Major Hank Reed and his men were training hard for a war that seemed more and more likely. Just three years ago, Reed had crossed paths with Gustav Rau during the Reich equestrians' visit to Fort Leavenworth. At that time, the young officer was in charge of mounting the ceremonial color guard for the visiting dignitaries. Now the world had changed dramatically. Earlier in the year, Franklin Delano Roosevelt had been sworn in for his third term in office. The United States was still at peace, but the world beyond American shores was aflame. An outright German invasion of Great Britain seemed imminent. On February 9, during a radio speech, Prime Minister Winston Churchill made a direct plea to Roosevelt: "Give us the tools and we'll finish the job." No doubt Churchill was referring to tools constructed with blowtorches, rivets, and steel. He knew that America had the ability to gear up for mass production of ships, tankers, bombers, and armored vehicles, Britain's best hope to compete with the industrial powerhouse of Germany. Still, each part of the armed forces had its specialized job, and in 1941, the United States Cavalry's job was horses.

While Alois Podhajsky was building up the Spanish Riding School in Nazi-occupied Vienna, and Gustav Rau was expanding his network of stud farms in occupied Poland, the United States Cavalry was training its soldiers on horseback. The U.S. Army Remount Service, the U.S. counterpart to Gustav Rau's horse-breeding operations, was increasing breeding and acquisition of warhorses in anticipation of entering the European war. These horses were known as "remounts," because soldiers' horses were so frequently incapacitated or killed that they needed a constant supply of fresh mounts to sustain them. A group of Americans led by cereal magnate W. K. Kellogg had donated a number of priceless Arabian stallions to the war effort, some of which shared distant bloodlines with Witez and his brothers. A short while later, Kellogg made another extraordinary gift to the army—his Pomona, California, ranch. The Kellogg ranch, home to America's finest Arabian horses, had been used often as a backdrop for western movies. The ranch was renamed the Pomona Remount Depot, and it took up the job of breeding horses for the army. As America geared up for war, horses were included in the mix.

The epicenter of mounted cavalry training remained at the force's most prestigious equestrian center, Fort Riley. On August 10, 1941, the men of the 10th Cavalry, one of America's oldest all-African-American cavalry regiments, stood at attention. In the center of the formation, mounted on four white horses, the color guard sat tall in their saddles, holding the flags of their regiment and the American flag upright. The Stars and Stripes stirred in the slight warm breeze that fluttered across the parade grounds. Today was an unusual day for the 10th, who interrupted their rigorous training routines to celebrate. Founded in 1866 to help guard the westward-extending railroad from Native Americans, the 10th, known as the Buffalo Soldiers, had planned a full range of festivities, from a parade to a picnic to a theater performance in the evening. Hank Reed was justifiably proud. After years of being largely ceremonial, his regiment had been swept up in the energy revitalizing the army as world events seemed to be carrying the country toward the inevitability of war.

The mercury was climbing and would reach 102 degrees by the afternoon, the sky was cloudless and pale blue, and the men in their uniforms had no shelter from the sun. The brand-new barracks at Camp Funston, west of the center of Fort Riley, sat in barren rows. Beyond them stretched miles of waving grasslands, and rising in the distance, the sheer walls of the base's distinctive landmark, the Rim Rock, a steep line of cliffs accented by a pale white line of limestone that ran across their length. The Camp Funston area of Fort Riley, originally a staging center for World War I, had been torn down after that war, but with the army swelling in 1941, a new base had been hastily thrown up on the silty plain just four miles west of Fort Riley's central grounds. The Union Pacific Railroad hugged the curve of the bluffs along the Kansas River until it disgorged masses of newly minted recruits at the Junction City station. Here, where a sign near the officers' quarters still commanded them not to shoot buffalo from the window, and where General Custer's house still stood, the Wild West past seemed closer than the problems in Europe and Asia.

Major Hank Reed was operations officer of the 10th Cavalry, a white officer leading an all-black regiment. He had been out west for four years—first at Fort Leavenworth and now Fort Riley. His face had leathered from hours in the bright Kansas sun, but his good nature showed in his open expression and prairie-wide smile.

Hank was born on a gentleman's farm near Richmond, Virginia, son of a wealthy textile merchant. He moved easily in the army's high society, but he was equally at home—probably more so—out on a dusty parade field. Born into a new century on Christmas Day 1900, he had reached his fourth decade still hopeful. His eyes were accustomed to looking out over vast distances between two ears at a gallop, the wind rushing past, whispering that the world was full of possibilities. Hank and his wife, Janice, had no children of their own, which made him only more devoted to his animals, his horses, and, most of all, his men. Sure, it was hard to see how what he did every day would make a difference, but he insisted on perfection, trusting that duty had its own rewards. However, as world events grew tense and more attention turned to the military, Reed knew that he and his squadron were on the sidelines—far from the main event. The real action was happening out at Fort Knox, where the cavalry was experimenting with switching some of its regiments from riding horses to mounting tanks and armored cars.

When Reed entered West Point in 1918, the Great War, the world's first technological conflict, had just come to an end. That war definitively proved that horses were no match for the modern mechanisms of war: machine guns, airpower, and chemical warfare. But on the banks of the Hudson, the cadets spent hours on the parade grounds, honing the techniques of mounted combat that recent history had already proved outmoded. The War Department continued to pour resources into its mounted force, in part because skeptics believed that motorized vehicles would never be as mobile cross-country as horses, but also because the cavalry had a rich ceremonial and sporting tradition that no one wanted to let go of. Between the two wars, the army had invested tremendous resources in its training manual for horsemanship, combing the world for the most advanced and effective horseback-riding techniques. In the 1920s, it sent a young cavalry officer, Harry Chamberlin, to Italy, France, and Russia, where he studied at their cavalry schools, importing from Italy the technique known as the "forward seat," an innovation where the rider, instead of leaning back at a gallop and over jumps, rode in balance with the horse's motion, which led to a great increase in a horse's ability to jump well. Cavalrymen were taught to ride horses in a systematic manner leading to a high degree of uniformity and an easily recognizable style. To be one of the best riders in the American cavalry meant that you were one of the best riders in the world.

Hank Reed was one of this elite cadre. At West Point, his fellow cadets had teased him about his way with women and horses, calling him "a good judge of horses and the fairer sex." On June 13, 1922, the day that Reed graduated, the skies had been a clear sunny blue. As a student, he was average, graduating in the exact middle of his class. His prowess on horseback was where he had won the admiration of his instructors and peers. But as he stood at attention in his gray cadet's uniform, he must have wondered at some level whether the army was a good career choice. Two years after the Armistice, many thought that America did not need a standing army any longer. Nonetheless, Reed was proud of his choice to serve his country. The West Point superintendent, Brigadier General Douglas MacArthur, handed him his diploma, then the newly minted second lieutenant quickly changed into an olive-drab uniform and Sam Browne belt and hurried off to the train station. He and the other young graduates would enjoy a three-month leave before they reported for duty. Reed would be heading for his first assignment with the 8th Cavalry at Fort Bliss, Texas, one of the force's many dusty western outposts—relics from the days of the Indian Wars. His future in a peacetime army promised endless exigencies: training, drills, more training, more drills, preparing for a moment that might never come.

Since that day, Hank Reed had spent a third of all his waking hours on horseback. Reed was the best of the best, a crack rider, an ace. In 1930 and 1931, he showed off his skills at jumping and equitation as a member of the army's Horse Show Team and was an alternate for the 1932 Olympic Equestrian Team. That year, he was also selected to join the elite twelve: the army's Advanced Equitation Course, the most coveted spot for its equestrians—a horsey boot camp designed to create the army's future equestrian leaders. At the beginning of the year, these twelve officers were each assigned four horses to train: a remount army-bred horse that might have arrived bucking and kicking from a nearby ranch and was not even halter-broken; an untrained polo pony; an experienced jumper; and a green, untrained jumper. These twelve officers had no other responsibilities throughout the year. All they did was ride, often eight straight hours in the saddle, Monday through Friday. On weekends, they played polo and participated in jumping competitions. Hank Reed and his companions could train a horse from the ground up to be a polo pony, a competitive jumper, or a steady soldier's mount.

The cavalry's skill in training riders was without equal. They could take one of the greenhorns who arrived at Fort Riley without a whit of riding knowledge and turn him into an experienced soldier who could take a horse off the picket line, fully tack him up, and mount in under ten minutes. He could be taught to gallop at full speed in formation, often ponying another horse (leading a horse while riding) alongside or carrying a flag. He and his fellow soldiers would hurl out cavalry *hooah*s as they slid their horses off steep embankments, flew over fence gates, and soared over ravines. Even with intensive training, men were sometimes hurt or killed. If not hurt too badly, a soldier was required to climb back on his horse. Lessons on fording rivers on horseback included advice on how to hold on to the horse's neck, and to grab the tail if a soldier came unseated in a strong current (a period training film intoned that the latter method was less desirable, as being towed by a horse's tail allowed "no control over the horse"). The cavalry training manual also described how to handle a falling horse: In the split second when he realized he was going down, the rider should "push with the arms and legs at the instant of leaving the horse to clear him as there is not so much danger of being struck by the animal's feet when he struggles to regain his footing." No obstacle should deter the soldier and his mount from their destination. The cavalry's informal motto was "Over, under, and through."

A cavalry soldier was trained to be versatile. He drilled on proper technique for mounting and dismounting, and for riding at the walk, trot, and canter. He knew how to ride in formation in the small confines of an indoor riding hall, following precise commands; he also could function in ceremonial formation on the parade field, or at a fast gallop cross-country, navigating natural obstructions in his path. He knew the name of each part of a horse's anatomy, its ailments and possible remedies. He could handle the kick of an MI rifle while balancing on horseback. A young African-American recruit to the 10th in 1941 at Fort Riley remembered the challenge of taking up riding from scratch, noting that on the first day, three quarters of the men fell off their mounts. He recalled that "you had a ten minute break and you spent eight minutes taking care of your horse and then you had a two minute break for yourself . . . but your horse was important, cause if you didn't take care of him, you didn't get to ride." Men are not born knowing how to ride horses. Equitation, defined by the army as a secure and correct seat that would allow a soldier to "control his horse under the normal conditions in which he is used," was drilled into cavalry recruits with the efficiency of a production line.

Fundamental to the whole process was the relationship between man and horse. Training included instruction in animal-human communication, in areas such as "equestrian tact" and "the moral intelligence of a horse." As described by a journalist from *Life* magazine, "An American cavalry man must know everything an infantry man knows. . . . He must be a bit of a motor mechanic, a good tank and armored car driver, a motorcyclist. Beyond all that he must know how to care for and feed a horse, to love and to cherish it in sickness and in health, till death does them part." This was the doctrine that Hank had been living by for twenty years, and he taught his men to care for and love and cherish their horses. In the twentieth-century American cavalry, morale, camaraderie, and esprit de corps included the four-footed soldiers.

Everything that mattered in Hank Reed's life, outside of his family, revolved around horses. Starting with his days as a cadet, he had lived in a world that could measure everything—honor, kindliness, discipline, sporting spirit, diligence, and, most of all, courage—in equestrian terms. His brain was crammed with the nomenclature of horses: cantle, withers, curb chain, bran mash, fetlock, stock tie, near side, picket line. He knew the aids for a flying lead change, the correct attire for a foxhunt, the thunder of charging by platoon, and the serenity of riding alone on a quiet path, with only his mount's breaths and cadenced footsteps for company. The rhythm of a horse's strides was like music to him—the walk a ballad in four/four time, the trot a rousing two-beat march, the canter a smooth three-beat waltz. Reed knew the scent of fresh straw in the stable, the tickle of a horse's whiskers as it nuzzled up a carrot. He knew that endless moment when a fall was inevitable and then the sudden breathless smack of landing hard on packed dirt. He knew what the end of a day on horseback felt like, salty with sweat, dirt under his fingernails, and a mind whitewashed from all worry. More than anything, Hank Reed understood what was unspoken among all of these horse soldiers. Sunburned, brusque, tough, accustomed to giving and taking orders, they knew that if you live, eat, sleep, and breathe horses for long enough, they become part of you, and your soul is forever altered. Hank walked and talked and moved and stood still like a cavalryman—you'd have known him from an infantryman at a distance of a country mile. This was an art, and Hank Reed, age forty-one, was master of it. The only problem was that it was a dying art.

Throughout the 1920s and '30s, the army cavalry had been immersed in an argument about what to do with the horses: One group, the die-hard horse folk (called "mossbacks" for their resistance to change), argued that the cavalry meant mounted soldiers, and the cavalry and the horse were inseparable. The other group, equally adamant, insisted that the force's traditional tactics—surveillance, reconnais-

REED RIDING TEA KETTLE, 1942.

sance, and mobility—were the hallmarks of cavalry forces, and horses were simply a means to become mobile that could be augmented or replaced with machines such as armored cars and tanks. In 1936, the 7th Brigade of the 1st Cavalry was the first to be mechanized, trading in horses for armor. In some branches of the force, this change was considered heresy; in others, it was thought to be the wave of the future. In the year 1940, the United States produced 4,280,000 cars. The transition from horsepower to motorized vehicles was largely complete in the civilian domain.

In 1939, a new chief of cavalry was appointed. Major General John K. Herr, a mossback, wanted people to choose sides—you were either a tank man or a horse man. Herr's appointment raised eyebrows. He was described in the contemporary press as "a grey horseman, a one-time top-flight polo player who hates the smell of gasoline. Does what he can to brake the trend toward mechanization from horse units." His great brainchild was the mechanized horse unit, in which horses, tanks, and armored cars worked alongside one another. Herr and his fellow mossbacks called the men whose cavalry units had been fully mechanized "cushion pushers."

On April 21, 1941, a handsome cavalry soldier and his charger appeared on the cover of *Life* magazine. Inside, the periodical's photojournalists documented the vigorous training of the recruits—one showed a trooper lying on the ground with several broken bones sustained in a fall. The article opened, "In an age of twenty-five-ton tanks, warfare on horseback seem[s] hopelessly antiquated," but went on to extol the virtues of what was called "horse-mechanized" cavalry. Horse trailers, called portees, could transport up to eight men and eight horses. A trained soldier could get his charger from the stables and load him onto the portee, along with all of his equipment, in only four minutes. From there, the portees would carry the men and horses to the field of battle. In spite of the article's positive spin, the mounted men riding alongside armored vehicles looked absurd.

To a career officer like Hank Reed, it made no difference that opinion was turning away from mounted cavalry. His job was to maintain the level of training and skill that the force demanded. Riding horses took constant practice and drill; caring for the horses was a morning-to-night routine. In addition, skilled craftsmen were needed to tend to the horseshoeing and equipment. Soon, his troops would be traveling by train with their horses to participate in war games. This would be a time to prove the horse's utility even in the era of tanks, armored cars, and jeeps.

ON THE GLORIOUS SUNNY DAY of the 10th Cavalry's seventy-fifth anniversary, after the morning mounted parade, the men were not just ready but champing at the bit as they gathered at Camp Funston's parade ground—known as the "Buffalo Stomp Grounds"—to hear their commanding officer, Colonel Paul R. Davison, give a rousing speech from the dais. The men listened attentively, their faces shaded by broad-brimmed campaign hats. Reed sat nearby with the other officers, intent on his commanding officer's words.

Looking out over the sea of dark faces, the white officer explained to the members of the unit that the regimental standard might soon be flying almost anywhere in the world—Africa, China, Latin America. "That is the reason I've been pouring the training on this regiment," he told the men. "When we fight an enemy, we want to be so tough, so hard and so well-trained that we can talk about it afterwards." The American army in 1941, still segregated along color lines, was struggling to come to terms with the influx of new African-American recruits. While prejudice against them in the army was rampant, the white officers who led this historic black regiment believed in their men's ability to fight. Speaking later about the 10th, Colonel Davison said, "In all my years of service, those in command of the Tenth stand out most clearly. In no other command did I receive more loyal, willing, and instant service than in the Tenth. I had the feeling that if given the job in peace or war we could accomplish anything with the regiment." And yet the men seated here had a double whammy of disadvantages to contend with as the world prepared for war: First, they were horse cavalry; and second, they were African-Americans in a segregated army.

Colonel Davison and Major Hank Reed understood how high the stakes were for these African-American enlisted men. In under a month, they would be participating in the biggest war games ever held on American territory—the event that became known as the Great Louisiana Maneuvers. Horse cavalry would be thrown into a mix that included tanks, armored cars, airplanes, and half-tracks (trucks with two wheels in front and two tracks in back). Not only the mossbacks but also most army officers believed that horses still had an advantage over difficult terrain, and the area set aside for the maneuvers—Louisiana swampland—handily fit that description.

ON MONDAY, SEPTEMBER 15, 1941, low-hanging dark clouds dumped rain over the thirty-four-hundred-square-mile area where the largest group of American military forces ever assembled in one place had gathered. The rain poured down upon the paved roads and the muddy ones, the pine forests and quicksand-filled marshes, the isolated farms and main streets and church steeples of the small parishes, and it rained on 470,000 men, 50,000 wheeled vehicles, and 32,000 horses. Congress had handed over $21 million to support these war games.

All eyes were on the army's technology. The German blitzkrieg of tanks and motorized vehicles supported by airpower was perceived as the greatest potential threat. George Patton would be showing what his armored cavalry forces were capable of. The question on everyone's mind was whether the American army had mechanized sufficiently to put up a fight.

Louisiana was not only the proving ground for America's technology. For Major General John K. Herr's equine-centric cavalry, this was the Battle of Little Bighorn, the horse's last stand, a chance to prove that mounted troops were indispensable even nearly halfway through the twentieth century. For the African-American soldiers of the 10th Cavalry, there was even more at stake. Despite their proud history as valiant warriors from the Indian Wars through the charge up San Juan Hill, the racist, pseudo-scientific eugenic theories that had taken hold in the U.S. Army during the early years of the twentieth century had done these men harm. Especially since 1931, their status as fighters had been constantly degraded, leaving them often without weapons, employed as servants to white officers—grooms, valets, drivers—and stripping them of their historical role as fighting men. Here was their chance to prove their real worth.

The unabated rain turned sandy roads into slick sheets of slippery mud and marshes into swamps. The horses, accustomed to traveling over any terrain, appeared to have an innate advantage. The war game maneuvers were set up with two teams facing off: the Red team under the command of General Walter Krueger, the Blue team under the command of General Ben Lear, each side including armored vehicles, cavalry, infantry, and airpower. The 10th, part of the 4th Brigade of the 2nd Cavalry Division, was assigned to the Blue team. Here, in the lands between the Sabine and Red Rivers, the men in uniform would face water, clay, mud, and hills, as well as chiggers and coral snakes. The cavalry leaders complained that the tanks started out with an unfair advantage, grumbling that horses should be given a head start, since they normally performed reconnaissance, operating by stealth, well in advance of the rest of the troops. But the rules of the war games specified that both mounted and mechanized troops had to start at the same time. The two teams faced off one hundred miles apart, imparting an obvious speed advantage to the motorized vehicles. Still, it seemed possible that the horses might be able to showcase their superior mobility over such tricky terrain.

While the press focused their cameras and comments on the technological might of the armored divisions and air capabilities on display, locals in this sleepy corner of western Louisiana were impressed by the sight of columns of horses thundering down the highways. They also noticed some of the unique difficulties encountered by the horsemen, who crept into local corncribs at night to steal extra rations for their horses.

On the second day of the maneuvers, a camera caught the soldiers of the 10th riding alongside a column of tanks that dominated the center of the road. For a while, it seemed as if the horse really did maintain an advantage: Riding hell for leather through the night in the pouring rain, the mounted soldiers beat their teammates in General George Patton's armored division to the town of Zwolle, where their mission was to prevent the 1st Cavalry from crossing the Sabine River. Tanks were sliding off roads, getting stuck in Louisiana's famous "gumbo" mud, running out of gas—subject to all of the shortcomings of motorized vehicles of the era. The horse showed none of these deficiencies. Among the horse cavalry, rumors were flying—perhaps their stellar performance had earned them an eleventh-hour reprieve from being marginalized.

The games were held from September 15 to 20 and 24 to 28, 1941. In the second maneuver, General Patton switched sides, joining the Red team, where he would assist General Krueger. Patton, a cavalryman himself but an early adopter of armor, took advantage of the fact that the Blue team's General Lear didn't trust armored divisions and liked to rely more heavily on the horses. Patton raced through East Texas with his jeeps, tanks, and armored cars, managing to encircle the Red team and proving that cavalry tactics combined with motorized speed could trump the traditional cavalry's capabilities.

Though this was effectively the last time that the United States mounted cavalry would appear in force, Fort Riley still percolated with new recruits. The presence of such star athletes as Joe Louis and a young Jackie Robinson buoyed the spirits of the African-American community, and even though black soldiers were still discriminated against, a few glimmers of progress became apparent as the Officer Candidate School at Fort Riley grudgingly opened its doors to its first few black soldiers.

For the horse, there was no such glimmer of hope. Even though a few voices still argued in its favor, motorized vehicles had won out. In March 1942, with the stroke of a pen, the War Department eliminated Major General John K. Herr's position as chief of cavalry and deactivated the 2nd Cavalry Division, of which the 10th was a part. Bitter regret surged through the old hands in the cavalry, and of John K. Herr, critics said, "He lost it all." Just one year after the glorious seventy-fifth-anniversary celebration, the 10th Cavalry was disbanded and most of the soldiers were moved into service roles. By 1942, the stables at Fort Riley had been converted into tank barns.

Hank Reed was needed elsewhere. On February 21, 1942, Colonel Davison sent him off with these words of praise: "You have contributed more towards bringing the regiment up to its current level and it has prospered from your loyal and conscientious leadership."

On his last night at Fort Riley, Colonel Reed walked across the base toward home. The night sky formed an inverted bowl above; the glittering Milky Way seemed close enough to touch. Off in the distance, a Union Pacific railroad train chugged past, its lonely whistle piercing the air. Reed was preparing to say goodbye. As for all career army men, his life had been a series of departures, each new phase marked by packing bags and boarding trains. He had watched his country roll past the plate-glass windows of his train cars, trading the green, closed-in East for the wide-open West, the empty plains giving way to eastern cities on the way back. But this time felt different. The cavalry as a mounted unit was finished, and the men he had been commanding for seven years would be broken up to face an uncertain future in an army that did not treat them fairly.

Major Reed was leaving for Camp Forrest in Tullahoma, Tennessee, to join the 633rd Armored Battalion. Starting today, he was a cushion pusher. Reed was no Luddite. He understood the necessity of moving into the armored age—his love for horses had convinced him that the modern battlefield was no place for these amazing animals. But still, his departure from Fort Riley was bittersweet.

The final strains of taps floated out over the base, then faded into the still night air, leaving just cricket sounds in its wake, while Hank Reed said farewell to his last day as a mounted officer.

A HORSELESS COMMANDER

The wire from the War Department summoning Hank Reed to his new command arrived a week shy of his forty-third birthday. One year after the Japanese attack on Pearl Harbor, the army was expanding fast: Reed had been promoted to lieutenant colonel, and for the first time, he would command an entire regiment. Before reporting to Fort Jackson, South Carolina, he was spending Christmas with his extended family in Richmond, Virginia. For Reed the horseman, this trip had a melancholy edge. Until now, he had always traveled with his horses, moving them from base to base. With the frenzy of preparations for war, this was no longer possible. Reed had brought his two polo ponies, Tea Kettle and Skin Quarter, home to his family's farm in Richmond, where they would remain until the war was over. In the cozy stables, Reed went about his stable chores with practiced familiarity as he settled down the two horses for the night. Beyond the smokehouse and the icehouse, the big white barn with a cupola and green wooden doors sat on the crest of a hill overlooking the woods. The two chestnuts followed Hank's movements with their big, soft eyes. The horses had traveled with him from Fort Leavenworth to Fort Riley, then on to Fort Tullahoma, but today was the day Hank Reed was saying goodbye to his horses for the duration. As he stroked their velvety noses and spoke a few soft words to each, he did not know when he would see them again.

Reed noticed how quiet it was here at Stanford Hill, so unlike typical army stables, which were companionable places where men went about their duties with a common purpose. On cavalry bases, men jumped to the familiar strains of the bugle: stable call, which sounded at six-fifteen in the morning, and boots and saddles, which called them to mount up. But here, all was peaceful. Beyond the soft sounds of his horses rustling in their stalls and the crickets chirping, the world was deceptively quiet—the calm before the storm.

After one last lump of sugar, one last pat on the neck, Hank said goodbye to his ponies and walked away from the stable without looking back. The horses watched as he disappeared up the lane; soon the Virginia evening enveloped him. No sounds were left but the soft whispers of hooves rustling in straw and the quiet thud of a man's footsteps as he walked back up the lane toward home.

As the new year of 1943 rang in, all over America, young men and seasoned ones alike, in big cities and small towns, from Arizona to Maine, bade farewell to wives and sweethearts, children and grandparents. Dog lovers patted their faithful friends on the head one last time, a lump forming in their throats at the familiar sound of a tail thumping against the floor. Horsemen proffered an extra sugar lump, feeling the tickle of whiskers on the flat of their hands as they looked into their four-legged friends' inscrutable dark eyes. As 1943 dawned, Bing Crosby's bittersweet "White Christmas" hit number one on the Billboard charts. During 1942, 3.9 million Americans were enlisted in the armed services. By the end of 1943, that number would swell to 9.1 million.

Just after the New Year, Colonel Reed shipped out for Fort Jackson, joining the throng of uniformed men jamming railcars all over the country. Like most of these men, Reed would arrive at a camp that had the helter-skelter look of a work in progress: Crews were busy throwing together barracks, building mess halls, preparing for an influx of new soldiers. The crackling energy of high purpose echoed through every conversation, in each strike of the hammer and slap of the paint-brush. Reed's regiment was in its infancy—so far, just a small group of officers formed a nucleus. One was blue-eyed Captain Jim Pitman, a newlywed with a baby on the way who shared Reed's love of dogs and the outdoors. Another was Major Stephen Benkowsky, an old horse hand from the 2nd's days as a mounted unit. Along with a few others, the small group would grow a regiment from the ground up.

Just eight days later, at ten-thirty A.M. on January 15, 1943, Lieutenant Colonel Reed stepped up on a makeshift podium set in the middle of a grassy parade ground. Decked out in the cavalry's high boots and flared breeches, Reed looked handsome, his hair crisply parted in the middle. Today was the official reactivation of the 2nd Cavalry, one of the army's most celebrated cavalry regiments, which had won glory in some of the most decisive mounted battles of the last century. Unlike the 10th, the 2nd was an all-white regiment. The mounted 2nd had been deactivated just six months earlier, its troops disbursed, its horses given away. Today was both a rebirth and a rechristening, Reed declared. From this day forward, the new 2nd Cavalry would have the word "mechanized" appended to its name. Reed evoked the 2nd's proud 106-year history and its motto, "Always ready." "We must not wait for combat, we must seek it," he said. "We will be as the old Sec-

REED LEADS THE NEWLY MECHANIZED 2ND CAVALRY.

ond in battle—Second to None." The four men in the color guard
stood at attention. Aloft, they held the American flag and the yellow
and brown regimental colors. The banner's twenty-nine streamers,
each representing a major battle, fell in a brilliant cascade.

Though Reed's speech echoed with a deep commitment, if he felt
some doubt that day, it would certainly be understandable. For twenty
years, Reed had honed his leadership skills on the army's polo fields
and jumping courses. Now he would be put to an entirely different
kind of test. Within a few weeks, civilians from the four corners of the
United States would come streaming into Fort Jackson. They would
look to the lieutenant colonel to be everything—father figure, mayor,
judge, minister, and physician. He would mediate disputes and mete
out punishment; he would provide for material and spiritual needs. As
he spoke, Hank felt the mantle of responsibility firmly settle on his
shoulders. For the foreseeable future, Hank Reed, whose hands were
accustomed to gripping leather reins, a polo mallet, or a riding crop,
would hold something infinitely more precious: the destiny of the
men he had been entrusted to lead, and the fears, hopes, and prayers of
the loved ones who were left behind.

The reactivation ceremony didn't last long. By eleven-thirty, the
whole shebang was over and Reed was back at work. By January 22,
the new recruits, called "fillers" by the regulars, started to pour onto
the base. Soon, they were arriving twenty-four hours a day, to be inducted by day and night shifts in continual operation. Down at the
train station, where a sergeant met the greenhorns as they debarked in
batches of four or five, a photographer caught one such group. The
young men wore double-breasted suits and felt fedoras—sent off by
their families in their Sunday best—but often the suits were threadbare
and carefully mended, suits for farm boys whose parents still felt the
pinch from the decade of the Great Depression. Their clothes were
dusty, their shoes scuffed, and most carried a single battered leather
valise, just large enough for a few personal possessions. They fell into
line behind a sergeant and marched out of the train station, beginning
to feel how different their lives were soon to become.

The front gate signaled to these recruits that they were entering a
different world. The sign, "Fort Jackson" spelled out in big white letters and propped up with stilts like the famous Hollywood sign, rose
above the manned front gate where uniformed guards watched the

RECRUITS BEING SWORN IN AT FORT JACKSON.

newcomers take their last few steps as civilians. Inside, the young men got a passing look at the officers' quarters, neat white A-frames with green roofs and screened porches, as they lined up in front of a whitewashed clapboard building to take the oath officially inducting them into the U.S. Army. Captured on film by a Signal Corps photographer, their faces are a study in contrasts: "I do solemnly swear or affirm . . ." One holds his right hand extra-high, one looks eager, one quizzical, one shy. Each of them has left loved ones behind. None of them knows exactly where he is headed or when he might be going home. "I will support the Constitution of the United States . . ." One young man's wrists protrude from his too-small suit, one has a pronounced widow's peak, one clutches an overcoat and fedora in his left hand. The men are named Homer and Guido, they are from cities and small towns, sons of farmers and streetcar drivers, all feeling equally unsettled.

Once inducted, the men quickly learned to stand in line—first to receive regulation clothing and a duffel bag, then tent poles and cotton ticking mattresses. If they had wondered what the army would be like, they soon became accustomed to the new world they had entered, where sergeants watched their every move and where good was almost never good enough. Some of the recruits were so young, they looked as if they hadn't been shaving for long—one of these young men, seventeen-year-old Jim O'Leary of Chicago, soon caught Hank Reed's eye. The young Irishman had a tousled mop of dark hair and a face that was all smile. While some of the other recruits were grumpy or shy, O'Leary seemed to know everyone by name and had a friendly word for all of them. The new recruit had lost his father at a young age and later rebuilt his mother's house with his own hands after it burned to the ground. Reed tapped O'Leary to be his personal driver. Everyone in the 2nd Cavalry saw Lieutenant Colonel Reed as a father figure, but between O'Leary and Reed there was a special affection—the fatherless boy was determined to look out for his commander from that moment on.

THE STREETS OF COLUMBIA, SOUTH CAROLINA, twelve miles west of Fort Jackson, were filled with soldiers. Their soundtrack was the brassy gliding trombone sound of Glenn Miller's "A String of Pearls." Their signature was dancing up close in crowded dance halls with restless girls who went from being strangers to intimates in the blink of an eye. The scent was Lucky Strikes, Chantilly perfume, and sweat mingling in South Carolina's heavy, humid air. These temporary young couples flocked to the base movie theater, a big white barn of a building, to snuggle in the dark while taking in the great war movies of 1943: *Casablanca, Destination Tokyo,* and *For Whom the Bell Tolls.* They all knew that they were teetering on a high wire—out there was the war, and that was where all of the young men were headed. The home front was going to empty out, and all of the young women would be left behind.

Among this mass of soldiers, clad in his neatly pressed army uniform and peaked cap, First Lieutenant Tom Stewart stood out from the other officers only for his well-mannered reserve. He was a bit older than some of the other new recruits, already a law school graduate. He was prepared to do his duty for his country, those who knew him well would attest to that, yet Tom Stewart was more of a lover than a fighter. Dark-haired, not tall but well put together, Tom looked strong, though he bore his strength with a gentle manner. He was the oldest of the five Stewart children, a proud Scots-Irish clan with deep roots in their Winchester, Tennessee, hometown. Tom was protective of his younger sister Betty Ann, walking her to school every morning. She in turn worshipped her handsome, soft-spoken older brother.

Tom had taken a shine to one of Betty Ann's friends, but the beautiful girl was several years Tom's senior and paid no attention to the besotted boy who kept shyly to himself as they walked to school. The young belle married not long after high school graduation to a more appropriately aged suitor. On the day of the wedding, Tom sent her two single red roses and asked that she wear one petal in each shoe as she walked up the aisle. Tom cloaked himself in a mantle of reserve, but beneath the quiet exterior ran a deep well of passion. He loved to read—his favorite book was Joseph Conrad's *Heart of Darkness*. His nickname was "the little minister," because he was so devout. One day, Tom came home from school and went upstairs to his room without saying a word. A few minutes later, his suspicious mother caught him slipping something into his chest of drawers. When she asked what it was, he blushed and stammered before showing her what he had hidden: two trophies from an athletic contest at school. It just wasn't in him to brag about his own achievements.

When he enlisted in 1941, Tom Stewart was twenty-seven years old. His father, big Tom, had gained notoriety when he served as prosecutor during the famed Scopes monkey trial, and later, in 1939, was elected to the U.S. Senate. By any measure, Tom was a young man of privilege. But World War II was a time of unprecedented solidarity in the United States, and servicemen enlisted from every walk of life, including the sons of senators. Tom was assigned to Lieutenant Colonel Reed's headquarters troop as an intelligence officer and would soon become someone his commander could count on for important tasks. But in January 1943, Tom was a green officer, following orders and trying to learn his job.

As time passed, this scraggy group of recruits lost their newness. Their days were filled with calisthenics, training on strategy, and long hikes. Their fitness improved, their bodies got harder, and the men learned to pull together as a team. On May 25, 1943, it was humid and raining and the roads were muddy and boggy when the men set out on their first hundred-mile hike. By the end of that day, the medics were getting plenty of practice treating blisters and sore feet. The soldiers pitched their tents and fell into them, muttering and cursing their superiors. On the third day, the troops were awakened at three A.M. for a forced march: ten straight hours of hiking that traversed twenty-seven miles. Reed, recently promoted to colonel, covered every step of the march alongside them. When the men finally reached their destination—Folly Beach in South Carolina—Reed had a surprise: The regiment's brass band accompanied the men on their last mile. As the recruits caught sight of the ocean in the distance, they broke out into whoops of celebration. Sweaty, blistered, grimy, and undaunted, the men of the 2nd Cavalry had turned into soldiers. For the next nine months, the men continued to train and participate in maneuvers until all traces of their inexperience had been replaced by an easy sense of teamwork. For a while, it had seemed as if the training would last forever, but on March 9, 1944, Hank Reed received an official letter from the War Department. The 2nd Cavalry Group was shipping out.

ON MARCH 20, 1944, a small group of hand-selected officers set sail from New York Harbor on the *Queen Mary,* members of the 2nd Cavalry advance team selected to help with logistics overseas. Among the advance group, leaning over the deck rails and watching the Statue of Liberty slide past the ship and then recede from sight, was the quiet Tennessean with the soulful eyes—Tom Stewart. Hank Reed had entrusted the young captain to lead the way.

A few weeks later, Reed and the rest of the men boarded the *Mauretania* for their own transatlantic trip. A high-speed liner, the ship did not travel in convoy but zigzagged across the Atlantic on its own course. On April 30, the ship arrived in Liverpool, where the men were greeted by the welcome sight of Red Cross girls with donuts. The soldiers walked across the city carrying their barracks bags, then boarded blacked-out trains. They caught their first glimpses of the English countryside by moonlight. At an anonymous rural station, truck convoys picked them up, and shortly after, they arrived at their destination: Camp Bewdley, Number 1, near the village of Stourport-on-Severn in North Worcestershire. Hank Reed settled into his quarters, pleased with the work that Tom Stewart and the rest of his advance team had done to prepare for their arrival. There was no time to waste. Tomorrow, Reed would need to see that training continued without interruption. But he was already feeling proud that what once was a group of unfamiliar faces, gathered from all over the country, had begun to feel like a family.

AMERICA'S FIGHTIN'EST GENERAL

On May 31, 1944, a restless crowd of more than three thousand American soldiers waited for the big moment. The tall trees lining the roads into Camp Bewdley were swaying gently in a breeze that stirred across the West Midlands. The air was bright and fresh, and on a field facing the camp, a farmer and his horse methodically tilled the soil, row after row. Atop a nearby hill, a group of local boys gathered, waiting to see the show. Hank Reed, now a full colonel, sat on a platform with a dozen other XII Corps commanders watching long columns of troops march down the hill by company, counting cadence, then turn left up the rise into a roped-off field. This was the first time that the entire camp had turned out en masse. The young soldiers were still unused to being so far from home. Most had arrived only weeks or days before. But today, they marched with a distinct sense of purpose.

From Reed's vantage point, the hillside soon became a solid mass of uniformed men, each with an expectant look on his face. To keep order in the large crowd, military policemen wearing white belts, leggings, and white-banded helmets swarmed everywhere, efficient and unsmiling, directing each company to its place on the grassy embankment. The sounds of the men marching in, sitting down, and murmuring to one another were not loud enough to drown out the birdsong that

Reed could hear in the distance. Soon, men lit cigarettes and settled down to wait.

After a few minutes, the bright sound of brass horns filled the air when a band situated next to the waiting speaker's platform struck up a rousing march. The PA system crackled as a nervous-looking sergeant tapped a waiting microphone several times. Then a captain stepped up to the microphone and said, "When the general arrives, the band will play the General's March, and you will all stand."

A moment later, a soldier stationed near the road turned and started to wave as a jeep full of uniformed MPs roared up the road. Behind it zoomed a long black car, blindingly shiny in the bright sunlight.

In May 1944, the number of Allied troops and armaments stockpiled in England was staggering. Millions of soldiers needed to be supplied with uniforms, weapons, ammunition, food, and medical supplies. In depots across England, cow pastures had been hastily converted into military parking lots where jeeps, planes, tanks, and artillery were lined up in long rows. Pundits joked that the island was so overloaded that only the silver barrage balloons kept it afloat. An estimated five million tons of equipment awaited shipment east across the English Channel. All of this man and machine power would have to be carried across the water by a vast array of amphibious craft. The buildup had started more than five years earlier; in the words of Eisenhower, it seemed as if the entire United Kingdom had been transformed into a giant military base. In Berlin, Hitler was aware of this massive Allied buildup and had begun a large-scale fortification project along the coast of northwest Europe. The only question was where and when the Allies would strike.

In May 1944, while the men in Janów Podlaski, Poland, were preparing to flee with the Arabians, and the white stallions of Vienna were putting on their last wartime performance, Colonel Reed and his men were enjoying the mild spring afternoon at Camp Bewdley while awaiting a visit from the commanding general of the Third Army.

The door to the black car swung open, and out stepped General George S. Patton, now secretly in England, where he was participating in a mock mission to confuse the Germans about the Allied invasion. Resplendent in high brown cavalry field boots and a gleaming helmet, he walked briskly down the hillside toward the ten-man guard of honor, who stood at attention. Patton passed slowly in front of them, looking each soldier up and down and then peering into each man's face. From there, he walked straight up onto the platform.

The corps chaplain stepped up to the microphone to give the invocation, asking for divine guidance so that the Third Army might help speed victory to an enslaved Europe. Next to speak was Lieutenant General William H. Simpson. "We are here," he said, "to listen to the words of a great man, a man who will lead you all into whatever you may face with heroism, ability, and foresight. A man who has proven himself amid shot and shell." Most of these soldiers were awestruck, having never seen the famous commander in person, but this was not the case for Patton's fellow cavalryman Hank Reed, who had been acquainted with him for many years. Since the invasion of North Africa and Sicily, in which the general had played a starring role, George Patton's name had been familiar in every American household. But Reed had known him as a rough-and-tumble polo player possessed of a foul mouth and a fierce competitive spirit.

Though Patton was eighteen years Reed's senior, the two officers shared a strong tie. Each had been a member of the prestigious War Department polo team, Patton in the 1920s and Reed in the '30s. Patton's ferocity on the polo field was an army legend. He seemed to go to war every time he galloped out onto the pitch. Even among tough competitors, the general was renowned for the particular bellicosity with which he approached the game. Once, while playing at the Myopia Hunt in Massachussetts, he was hit so badly in the head with a mallet that blood started streaming down his forehead. Patton wrapped a bandage around his head, shoved his helmet back on top of it, and continued to play. Another time, he fell so hard that he sustained a severe concussion. His daughter, Ruth Ellen, who was watching the match, knew something was terribly wrong because it was the first time she had ever seen him let go of the reins when he fell off a horse.

Patton, like many others in the army, had believed that in peacetime, when men had no chance to experience combat firsthand, the horseback battles played on the polo field were the best way to train a man for combat. If Patton's theory was right, then the ace polo player

Hank Reed was among the best-prepared soldiers at Camp Bewdley that day. None of the 2nd Cavalry men had seen real combat before, including their leader, Colonel Reed.

The general approached the microphone and looked out over the great mass of soldiers standing at attention on the hillside. "Be seated," he said. His amplified voice echoed out across the hillside, high and clear. His tone was firm and commanding. In an undulating wave, the men sank back down onto the grass.

"Men, this stuff we hear about America wanting to stay out of the war, not wanting to fight, is a crock of bullshit! Americans love to fight—traditionally. All real Americans love the sting and clash of battle. When you were kids you all admired the champion marble player, the fastest runner, the big league ball players, the toughest boxers. Americans love a winner and will not tolerate a loser. Americans play to win—all the time . . ."

Up on the hillside, the men of the 2nd Cavalry listened intently. All of them knew that General Patton was the one who got called in when the going got tough. Indeed, the general then strictly admonished the crowd that his presence in Bewdley was to be kept top-secret. Nobody knew exactly what was coming next; they just knew that they would be part of something bigger than all of them.

From Patton's vantage point up on the platform, the assembled men of the Third Army looked like an enormous sea of humanity gathered with a common purpose. Despite the uniforms that made them resemble one another, every man sitting there that day had his own life story, his own pathway that had brought him to that place. Born in 1915, blue-eyed Jim Pitman was one such soldier. He had the face of a sprite, all upturned angles, quick to smile, his smooth skin radiating youth. Hank Reed had had twenty years to prepare for this moment; Jim Pitman had just four. Graduating from West Point in 1940, he joined an army gearing up for war and had been swept right into the heart of it.

Major Pitman hadn't seen his wife and child in over six weeks. He didn't have much to remember them by, just the mementos most men carried—a creased letter, read until memorized, and a couple of photographs. But he'd never forget the moment he said goodbye to his wife and baby son, only two months old. How many milestones would

Pitman miss while he was away? The first birthday? The first step? The first word? His tiny son would not even remember him when he returned. His wife, Tee, so beautiful, had seemed so fragile when he looked at her the last time. How would she hold up without him? He pictured her in their little house in Columbia, South Carolina, washing dishes in the kitchen, or sitting with the baby while the radio played in the background, or sometimes he remembered her face as she smiled and looked up when he returned home from a long day. He thought of his golden cocker spaniel jumping up and licking his hand to greet him. He remembered the moment he had taken his saber from West Point and tucked it away in the little cupboard behind the kitchen. On their wedding day, they had used it to slice their cake. Someday, he would pass that saber along to his son—and maybe his son would follow him into the service.

All of these flitting thoughts did not distract Pitman from the subject at hand. Since the days of his boyhood near Mount Holly, New Jersey, he had always wanted to be a soldier. Jim and his younger brother, Don, spent hours with their father, out hunting pheasant and quail in the area around their home. He loved dogs and especially prized their bird dogs. Before he ever entered West Point, he was a crack shot with a rifle. At West Point, he had learned to ride horseback, played some polo, and excelled at tennis. He was respected and well liked because he was serious but friendly—a man you could count on. Most of his fellow 2nd Cavalry officers had many years on him, but Major Pitman's face was calm and his blue eyes steady as he focused on Patton, whose high-pitched, somewhat nasal tone was amplified over the tinny loudspeaker.

"You are not going to die," Patton exhorted the men. "Only two percent of you here, in a major battle, would die. Death must not be feared. Every man is frightened at first in battle. If he says he isn't, he's a goddamn liar." Every man on that hillside was asking himself the same question: How would he react when his moment came? Not just would he be killed but, more important, would he be brave enough? Here on the hillside, it was all narrowing down to the essence: one group, one task, and one goal.

Patton continued with his speech, hurling out examples of what he once called "eloquent profanity." According to Patton, "An army

JIM PITMAN
WITH HIS
WIFE, TEE,
IN FRONT OF
THEIR
HOUSE IN
COLUMBIA,
SOUTH
CAROLINA.

without profanity couldn't fight its way out of a piss-soaked paper bag." True to style, Patton peppered every sentence with colorful epithets, giving it to them "double-dirty," as he called it.

"We are advancing constantly and we are not interested in holding on to anything, except the enemy's balls," Patton said. By now, the crowd was stirred up and laughing appreciatively. But there was a serious message within. Pitman recognized the cavalry rhetoric in Patton's speech. His admonitions to keep moving, over, under, or through, were just what the young major's commanders had shouted at him as he galloped in formation across the plains of Fort Riley during his cavalry horsemanship training back in '42.

Finally, Patton paused and, gripping the microphone, cast his gaze out over the assembled men. "Remember this," he said. "Thank God that at least thirty years from now, when you are sitting around the fireside with your grandson on your knee, and he asks what you did in the great World War II, you won't say, 'I shoveled shit in Louisiana.' " En masse, the crowd of soldiers erupted in raucous laughter. "No, sir, you can look him straight in the eye and say, 'Son, your granddaddy rode with the Great Third Army and a son of a goddamned bitch named Georgie Patton!" The sounds of guffawing, thigh slapping, and cheers rang up from the assembled soldiers. "Old Blood and Guts" had scored well with the men.

Just six days later, on June 6, 1944—D-day—the invasion of France began. The men of the 2nd Cavalry were as surprised by the magnitude of the operation as any civilian when they saw the skies jammed with fighters and bombers heading for the south coast of England and on to France. That day, Pitman understood that all of his past years of training were about to be put to the test. But he and his fellow cavalrymen had little time for reflection as they waited their turn to ship out for France. The next six weeks were a frenzy of preparation and movement: The 2nd Cavalry underwent introduction to new kinds of weapons, built and memorized relief maps, helped unload wounded German prisoners, and took classes in French and German. One day, they got their marching orders. They were headed for the Continent.

On the morning of July 16, Jim Pitman caught his first view of the gray waters of the English Channel when he arrived in the town of Broadmayne, on the coast. The next few hours were filled with an endless series of details: The men camouflaged their tanks, half-tracks, and jeeps, then reported to the billeting area to fill out forms. Each man received two hundred French francs (the equivalent of four dollars) before moving to the port of embarkation at Portland. On July 20, they boarded the transport ships called LSTs (or landing ships, tank), large vessels that had been specially designed to transport both troops and vehicles across the Channel—each LST's bow flipped down to form a landing ramp for debarkation of equipment directly onto the beach. Once aboard, the men first lashed down all of the vehicles and then settled themselves inside their cabins. At five A.M., their convoy set sail.

The convoy's thirty-one ships made a stately procession across the English Channel, escorted by U.S. Navy destroyers and corvettes. Three hundred feet above, the sky was dotted with silver barrage balloons, one anchored to each LST, that made a zipping sound as they tugged at their steel cables. From time to time, they passed through ghostly banks of fog, but mostly, the sea was calm. Inside Jim Pitman's landing ship, the atmosphere was jittery, a heady mixture of dread and anticipation. Jim and the other men ate and drank heartily, not knowing when they would see their next hot meal. The crossing was smooth, and most of the men were feeling pretty good—at least physically. But Pitman was summoned when the commanding officer on board, Major Stephen Benkowsky, started to feel sick. What seemed like a simple upset stomach soon developed into sharp pain, nausea, and fever.

By eight P.M., the convoy had sailed about sixty-five miles, and dropped anchor just off Utah Beach, north of Sainte-Mère-Église, France. They were now surrounded by hundreds of other craft, each flying a silver barrage balloon. The plan was to prepare to disembark at two A.M.

Inside the ship, Benkowsky's condition was worsening, and within a couple of hours, it was clearly serious. The doctor diagnosed a ruptured appendix. Benkowsky needed to be evacuated off the ship; he required an immediate operation or his life was at risk. But at eleven P.M., red flares shot up through the fog, giving the clouds a lurid hue. Ships anchored nearby, off Omaha Beach, had detected enemy aircraft in the vicinity; quickly, a smoke screen was laid down to camouflage the ships. The convoy was under threat of imminent attack. On board, Benkowsky's fever rose, and his pain was worsening. But now evacuation off the ship was impossible. With few options available, the ship's doctor made a split-second call: He was going to operate. In a bank of fog, with the red flares flashing overhead, he improvised a surgical field on the ship's dining room table and, with a steady hand on the scalpel, tried to save Benkowsky's life.

Just a few hours earlier, Jim Pitman had been second in command. Now he had taken over as leader of the 42nd Squadron of the 2nd Cavalry, 120 men. By two A.M. the alert had ended, and Benkowsky was stable. The 2nd Cavalry was cleared to proceed with debarkation. When they landed, Pitman's first official duty was to dispatch the recovering Benkowsky to the medics.

The English Channel was at Pitman's back; in front of him stretched the continent of Europe. Somewhere, thousands of miles away, his beautiful young bride, Tee, was sitting in a rocking chair with their baby, James, the radio most likely playing a Glenn Miller song in the background, the tranquil streets of America outside her window. Baby James might be sleeping contentedly, his eyes fluttering gently, his small body carefully wrapped in clean blankets, with no idea that his father was stepping boldly toward an uncertain future, driven by his sense of duty, honor, and courage. As Pitman's feet touched the sandy soil of France for the first time, the newly anointed commander of the 42nd Squadron would have had two goals in mind: to accomplish the aims of his commanding officer, Colonel Reed, and to make his son proud.

TWO HANDS AND
A PURPLE HEART

In the autumn of 1944, as Alois Podhajsky was struggling to decide whether he should evacuate the remaining Lipizzaner from the Spanish Riding School in Vienna, Hank Reed was fighting his way across the Aube region of northeastern France. While some unit leaders commanded from far behind the action, Reed stayed close to his men. Today, he was en route to survey his troop positions. His driver, Jim O'Leary, was at the wheel, and a corporal sat in the front passenger seat, manning a .30-caliber machine gun. Reed had asked one of his senior officers to take him to view their command post; however, the officer, Captain Andrews, had misunderstood. Thinking that his CO wanted to observe the enemy position, Andrews instructed O'Leary to turn north off the main road and proceed along a smaller country lane. German strength in the area was unknown, so a single platoon of Reed's men had headed this way on a scouting mission a few hours earlier. The road they traveled along first led through a patchwork quilt of well-tilled fields and scattered farmhouses, then plunged into heavy woods as it climbed a small hill. About a mile southeast of a small village called Marcilly-le-Hayer, the road suddenly emerged from the forest, so that Reed could see a wide valley spread out before them. In the distance, the stone buildings of the village clustered along the banks of a small stream. O'Leary pulled off the road onto high ground, and Reed and Captain Andrews got out, pulled out binoculars, and surveyed the scene in front of them. Reed quickly realized that there had been a miscommunication—Andrews had brought them closer to the German position, not the American one.

The mission of the 2nd Cavalry was reconnaissance—operating out in front of the rest of the troops, often behind enemy lines. Their job was to be Patton's eyes and ears, to find out where German forces were located. Highly mobile, they were only lightly armed, and operating at the vanguard often led them directly into trouble.

Today, as Reed surveyed the valley through his field glasses, he could see that one of their own vehicles, an armored car that had been sent out on patrol, was stuck about halfway up the hill below them, about a thousand yards from the outskirts of the village.

A sixth sense told Reed that something was amiss. Noting their exposed position, he turned to Andrews and said, "Don't you think we are being a little too brave?"

The men flung themselves onto the dirt, and none too soon. In the same instant, they saw a German panzer grenadier unit, recognizable by their black uniforms, leave the town in formation and march up the hill toward the stranded armored car. Hank Reed slowly raised his sniper rifle and fired, dropping a German soldier with his first shot. Down the hill, O'Leary opened fire with the machine gun. As a battery of shots ricocheted around him, Reed shouted to the machine gunner to move away and get a different angle. Vastly outnumbered by the thirty to thirty-five panzer grenadiers, the four men kept shooting; they could see that all of the German soldiers had clapped on their helmets. A moment later, the stranded armored car broke free and spun around, unloading its guns at the Germans.

In the hail of bullets, O'Leary crawled from the jeep to Reed's position, his face improbably cheerful given the circumstances. "Sir, the commanding general of the Twelfth Corps has just radioed for the colonel to report to his command post immediately."

Without missing a beat, Reed said, "Tell him I'd be happy to if he could just get these panzer people out of my hair." He smoothly looked through the sights on his rifle, got a bead, and pulled the trigger.

A few moments later, reinforcements arrived and the Germans retreated back into the town. Brushing off his uniform, Reed climbed back into the jeep and continued on to the command post. Among his men, their CO was fast becoming a legend.

———

FOR THE AVERAGE SOLDIER in Reed's 2nd Cavalry, the combat experience was made up of long stretches of tedium and discomfort interspersed with fiery bursts of action. Tension was their constant companion—that and the mud clogging their vehicle tires, and the canned meat and cheese, crackers, and malted milk balls from their K rations. In November 1944, Francis Herron, writing in *Warweek*, called the soldiers of the 2nd Cavalry "the loneliest men in the world." Consistently operating behind enemy lines, they were dubbed "the ghosts" by the German forces because they often seemed to materialize out of nowhere. An officer from the 2nd Cavalry said, "On one occasion we took 500 prisoners in one week, killed I don't know how many [others], shot more than 30 vehicles to pieces, and nine-tenths of the fighting came as a result of stumbling into it." By late August, they had traveled close to three hundred hard-fought miles since landing on the beaches of Normandy.

FROM THE PERSPECTIVE OF the cavalrymen under Reed's command, the war was fought at the micro level, a struggle for each hillock and river crossing, each bridge and fork in the road. In the words of one captain, "You can take it from me, it doesn't take long to find out how to get close to Mother Earth when the business end of a machine gun is pointed your way. Your throat becomes dry, the palms of your hands clammy and suddenly you are aware of every little contour of the terrain in front of you. A small knoll, insignificant to the casual view, assumes the protective importance of a mountain."

As commander of the entire 2nd Cavalry Group, with its two main units, the 42nd and 2nd squadrons, Hank Reed had the job of seeing the bigger picture. Each squadron had its own headquarters troop as well as six troops, lettered A through F, and each of these troops was made up of about twenty soldiers, along with tanks, guns, armored cars, half-tracks, and jeeps. In addition, Reed traveled with the Headquarters Troop, which included intelligence, medical, and supply officers. A group of specialized interrogators also moved with the 2nd. Altogether, more than four hundred men were under Reed's command. The cavalry was mounted on motorized vehicles, but keeping these mechanized steeds running was a constant job. They rumbled across France on country lanes where some days the mud was as formidable a foe as the enemy guns. The soldiers' language was still full of the colorful metaphors of the former mounted forces. They spoke of mounting and dismounting their bucking jeeps, and crossed country at a high gallop.

The American cavalry was fully mechanized, but not so the Germans. Reed and his men had to face the reality of aiming their guns at horses on the field of battle, and as they crossed France on their four-wheeled stallions, they sometimes witnessed or were involved in situations when horses were brutally caught in the cross fire. One such incident occurred on August 23, near the village of Montargis, twenty miles west of Marcilly-le-Hayer. When Hank Reed's men stumbled across a column of sixty horse-drawn German vehicles moving west into American-held territory, the colonel had no choice but to order his men to destroy the column. Reed and his men saw plenty of horses wounded and suffering—but all of them belonged to the Germans, and as a matter of principle, the 2nd's first duty was to save men's lives and win the war. However, the haunting images of fallen horses stuck with the men long after they had moved on.

Though Reed's "horses" were powered by gasoline instead of hay, the philosophy that drove their mission was unchanged from their mounted days. In the words of cavalry historian George F. Hoffman, "It was never a cavalry mission to stand and fight for an extended period at a single time. Hit and run, move fast, search out and surprise the enemy, ambush if possible, outflank him, confuse him, then hit and withdraw."

As the Third Army maintained a breakneck pace while moving east across France, Reed's command post moved frequently, keeping up with their position at the vanguard of the American front. Between August and September 1944, he moved forty times. Usually, Reed relocated either early in the morning or in the late afternoon, first sending out an advanced squad to select the site. It was not uncommon to move twice in one day. Between camps, Reed led his command from a jeep strategically positioned in a gully or grove. Always in danger of a surprise encounter with the enemy, Sergeant O'Leary drove like Disney's Goofy—hunched forward with his elbows stuck out to the sides, ready to press the gas.

———

IN THE CHILL EARLY morning of September 18, 1944, no danger was readily apparent. The 2nd Cavalry was scattered to the west, south, and east of a midsize French town, Lunéville, situated at the confluence of the Meurthe and Vezouze Rivers. The 42nd Squadron had captured the town the previous day. Not anticipating any trouble, most of the 2nd Cavalry had already moved farther east, leaving only Pitman's lightly armed squadron to guard the town. The first sign that something was amiss came just before dawn, when Reed received word that one of Pitman's platoons, out on patrol, had stumbled across a small group of approaching German tanks. A short while later, Pitman's radio crackled with more bad news—a second patrol had encountered powerful German panzers. Pitman quickly relayed these reports to Reed, who was bivouacked about twenty miles away.

As repeated tank sightings came in over his radio, Reed began to suspect that the Germans were massing a full tank battalion to try to reconquer the town of Lunéville. Reed knew that Pitman's squadron was not large or well armed enough to take on a tank battalion alone, and sure enough, just after eight in the morning, Pitman urgently radioed Reed to report that some of his vehicles had been disabled by tank fire. Pitman requested immediate reinforcements, but Reed had only bad news in reply. It would take several hours, at least, before reinforcements would arrive. It would be up to Pitman's small, badly outgunned force to delay the German advance—at least long enough for Reed to retreat back into the town along a different route.

Though Reed was concerned, he had tremendous faith in the young major's leadership. Just two weeks earlier, Pitman had demonstrated his courage when he acted as an emissary to a German general— traveling blindfolded in an enemy jeep, through barbed wire and reinforcements, to the enemy headquarters, bearing a letter from Reed demanding that the Germans surrender their position. The Germans had refused the American's offer, but Pitman had been returned unharmed.

Reed did not underestimate the difficulty of what he was asking of Pitman, but he also knew that the major was a man he could count on. The two had served together since the beginning, at Fort Jackson. He could picture Pitman's bright blue eyes peering out from under his helmet. Reed told his major that the 42nd Squadron would have to fight alone.

Jim Pitman got the message loud and clear. Colonel Reed was telling him to hold at all costs, and he took his CO at his word, perhaps bearing in mind one of his favorite maxims, from the poet John Dryden: "Presence of mind, and courage in distress, / Are more than armies to procure success." Trained to perform under duress, Pitman tried to prioritize—giving orders, evacuating the wounded, firing his own weapon, aware that each individual choice had life and death consequences. He blinked back the smoke, shut out the roaring gunfire around him, and ignored the hammering sound of his own heart in his ears as he made split-second decisions and shouted orders to his men.

As Pitman's squadron valiantly delayed the more powerful German force, Reed's headquarters group, under heavy shelling, retreated back into the town proper so that Reed could set up a command post. He radioed the coordinates of a meeting place to Pitman, ordering that the major meet him for a face-to-face report. About an hour later, Reed and Pitman arrived at the meeting point at almost the same moment. Reed, who was emerging from his armored vehicle when the major arrived, got a quick glimpse of Pitman's face, which was shadowed by dirt and fatigue. Just as Pitman stepped toward his commander, a tremendous explosion rent the air as a mortar shell exploded. In a single moment, every photograph of this young father with his wife and baby son became the last.

At that same instant, a searing pain pierced Reed's right hand and left thigh. The last thing Reed saw was Pitman's body crumpling to the ground in front of him before he, too, collapsed into unconsciousness. For a moment, all was chaos. Jim O'Leary picked his way across the cratered road, grabbed his commander, and pulled him to safety. Another soldier carried Pitman to an ambulance, but he was already gone.

Pitman dead and Reed injured—word spread like lightning. The men climbed down from second-story windows and came out from behind sheltering walls, quickly gathering around their wounded leader to form a protective shield. In the half-light, the men's expressions were grim. They'd been out here long enough to learn how to shrug things off. But as they gathered around Reed, using their own bodies as shields to protect him from further fire, tears cut traces across the soldiers' dirt-caked faces.

Pitman would never learn that his delaying tactic had saved the day. As the daylight waned on September 18, the men of the 42nd Squadron had lost most of their vehicles and were surrounded on all sides. An American reconnaissance plane flying overhead radioed them that a single road through the woods remained open. So many of their vehicles had been destroyed that the men had to hitch rides on those remaining, hanging off the sides wherever they could grab a toehold. Each time a shell hit, the beleaguered men dove off and hit the ground, then scrambled along the road on foot, catching up and remounting when the shelling stopped. By the end of the day, five men had fallen, but the 2nd Cavalry had prevailed, and the town of Lunéville remained in American hands.

REED WAS SENT TO PARIS for surgery and recuperation. He was going to recover, but he would never regain full use of his right hand. His polo-playing days were behind him. But when visitors came to see him, Reed said nothing at all about himself—just asked after his men, in particular wanting to know how the other wounded cavalrymen were faring. Forever after, Reed would carry the shadow of Jim Pitman's face in his memory, along with all of the other fallen men in his command.

By December 1944, he was back with his men in Luxembourg, having turned down a desk job and promotion far from the danger of the front lines. Colonel Reed would celebrate his forty-fourth birthday, December 25, back at the reins of the 2nd Cavalry.

From Third Army Headquarters came General Patton's greeting:

> To each officer and soldier in the Third United States Army, I wish a Merry Christmas. I have full confidence in your courage, devotion to duty, and skill in battle. We march in our might to complete victory. May God's blessings rest upon each of you on this Christmas Day.

On that Christmas Day, all was quiet as drifts of snow piled up around their tents and road-scarred vehicles. Out of the blue, a single piece of shrapnel fell on the command post, piercing one of their maps, but otherwise, the day passed peacefully while the men enjoyed their Red Cross Yule packages and letters from their loved ones.

Back at Stanford Hill, Reed's wife, Janice, and their family gathered around the large mahogany table. Down at the barn, Tea Kettle and Skin Quarter gazed out over winter-brown fields whitened with frost, stamping their feet as their nostrils made plumes of white steam in the air. In homes all over America, holiday tables were set with one less place. James Hudson Pitman, only fourteen months old, celebrated his second Christmas with his mother, a young widow now shadowed by grief. Though James would never know his father, the boy would later take pride in the knowledge that his regiment would be the only one in Europe ever to fight off an entire German tank division.

Reed and his men, camped in the bleak midwinter, must have wondered right then what their purpose was—but the 2nd Cavalry's greatest days were still to come. As they continued their way east, the winter would thaw, and the Germans would get pushed back. By April 1945, Reed's 2nd Cavalry would have covered more territory, killed more enemy soldiers, captured more prisoners, and suffered fewer casualties than any other regiment of comparable size in the European theater. The snow would melt, the Germans would fight their last battles, and the 2nd Cavalry would be offered the chance to embark on their most exhilarating adventure. But right now, Christmas 1944, they were grateful to pass a silent night.

PART THREE

The Mission

A good solution applied
with vigor now is better
than a perfect solution applied
ten minutes later.

—GEORGE SMITH PATTON

PUREBREDS LED BY POWS IN NAZI PARADE.

ARMIES CLOSING IN

BOHEMIA, CZECHOSLOVAKIA,

LATE APRIL 1945

Four months had passed since the bleak Christmas of 1944. As April 1945 drew to a close, massive Russian and American forces marched toward each other from east and west, the gap between them shrinking daily. Between the two fronts, Germany was crumbling, its infrastructure in tatters. Trapped in an ever shrinking wedge, millions of refugees tried to stay out of danger. Desperate horsemen who lived in areas affected by fighting were trying to flee to safer areas. Thus far, the Lipizzaner stallions in Austria and the mares in Hostau had not been affected, but in the chaos of the Third Reich's near collapse, the displaced Lipizzaner had never been in greater danger.

Along a country lane, near the village of St. Martin in Upper Austria, Alois Podhajsky sat astride Neapolitano Africa, eyes trained on his horse's sensitive ears. He and the other riders from the Spanish Riding School had taken the stallions for their daily exercise. In a loose formation, eight riders followed, similarly mounted on white Lipizzaner. The ground beneath Africa's hooves was spongy and muddy; pockets of snow clung to the earth. His opalescent coat shone brightly against the bare brown branches just starting to green up for spring. Podhajsky was engaged in a wordless conversation with his mount as his seat, legs, and reins picked up clues to his horse's emotions. Podhajsky's face was serene, and his posture in the saddle appeared just as erect as it had nine years earlier, when he had ridden across the stadium at the Olympics in Berlin, but he rapidly scanned the woods that lined the road, then glanced back at Africa's tapered white ears. Sometimes his horse heard the approach of the dive-bombers before his own ears could pick up the sound.

Africa's ear flicked twice, and Podhajsky felt the stallion tense slightly underneath him. Podhajsky raised his hand, signaling his fellow riders to take shelter with him under a small copse of trees, though the horses, with their bright white coats, would be easily visible from the air. Under his seat bones and between his legs, Podhajsky felt Africa coil up, ready to spring from danger; but the obedient stallion, trusting his rider implicitly, stood perfectly still. Overhead, the drone of an airplane became audible, buzzing louder and louder until it seemed to hang directly overhead, then fading to a rasp in the distance. No one said a word. When the danger had passed, Podhajsky rode back into the open, and the riders silently followed. Each time this happened, Podhajsky wondered about the wisdom of exercising the stallions out in the open, but what choice did he have? The high-spirited animals, used to daily training, could not stay cooped up in the small stables that had become their temporary home, and the indoor riding hall was so cramped that it could accommodate only two or three horses at a time.

Podhajsky and his riders were lodged in the Arco Castle in St. Martin, where they had taken refuge after fleeing Vienna in March. They were not its only inhabitants; it was packed with other German refugees who had fled the Reich's eastern territories. Their rooms in the former servants' wing were humble, but Podhajsky knew that they were fortunate. The village was full to the bursting point with Russian and Polish prisoners of war who had been brought in to work on the local farms. Misery, deprivation, and anger ruled in the small town. The POWs were restless and volatile, waiting for the war's end to bring their liberation. Local Austrians were locked into a paralyzing apathy— certain the war was almost over but fearful of what the future might hold. Podhajsky understood that to these suffering people, the fate of the white stallions was unimportant. Some of the refugees even said aloud that they didn't care about the horses and thought they should be slaughtered to add to the meager food supply.

Foremost in everyone's mind was the fear of which occupying force would arrive first—the Russians, who had already seized Vienna, or the Americans, who were fanning out across Germany and were less than a hundred miles away. As Podhajsky described it, "What was happening at the Front concerned us most deeply, for on the advances of the separate armies to occupy Germany hung our fate."

One day late that same month, Podhajsky was surprised to find a visitor who had come all the way from Berlin to visit the horses. It was General Erich Weingart, chief of riding and driving in the German Army's High Command, the same individual who had given Podhajsky permission to evacuate the stallions from Vienna if the Nazis agreed.

The general walked through the stables slowly, stopping to look at each of the horses in turn. The tour was suffused with a feeling of melancholy, as if Weingart seemed to know that he was seeing these horses for the last time.

As the two men walked in the gardens before dinner, Podhajsky confided his fears: His riders, during German occupation, had worn the Wehrmacht uniform. He was afraid they would be separated from the horses, seized as prisoners of war. Already, each rider was responsible for ten horses. If the riders were taken away, no one would be left to safeguard them. But the general reassured him; the Americans would arrive in their area before the Russians, he said. "You will succeed in putting these soldiers as deeply under the spell of your white horses as you have always managed to do with me."

General Weingart continued, "I am going back once more to my superiors . . . and I will have a document drawn up for you, duly signed and sealed and to be put into immediate effect, removing the Spanish Riding School from the command of the army and declaring it once more a civil riding school as it was before 1938. Perhaps this document may help you cope with the transition period more easily. For me, this final service to the Spanish Riding School will be the last good deed of my life."

The general parted emotionally with Podhajsky that day, assuring him that he would return with the promised document in a few days. Less than a week later, the Arco Castle refugees could hear the sound of artillery fire in the distance, heralding the Americans' approach. Grimly, Podhajsky realized that whatever happened next would be unpredictable and dangerous. Only later would he learn that General

Weingart's car had been found on the banks of Lake Chiemsee. The German had returned to Bavaria and taken his own life.

Trying not to draw attention to himself, Podhajsky began to prepare for the end: He hid some of their most valuable equipment behind a bricked-up partition inside the castle and stashed away civilian clothes so that his riders might not be noticed among the other refugees and evade being taken as prisoners of war. He knew that everything he had done so far to safeguard the horses could easily be swept away in these final days of conflict.

The riders took turns standing armed guard at the stables. If the Nazi holdouts chose to fight when the American tanks arrived, the animals might be caught in the cross fire. If Podhajsky and his riders appeared too eager to surrender, they might be shot as traitors. As their tense vigil continued, Podhajsky carefully rationed the remaining grain: He had been getting extra feed from Hostau, but now he received nothing—neither feed nor word of the mares and foals. He feared the worst.

ABOUT A HUNDRED MILES due south of St. Martin, the stud farm at Hostau was now cut off from the rest of the German Reich due to a breakdown in communications. It appeared eerily untouched by the ravages of war. In the well-kept stallion barn, Witez, plump and sleek, peered over the half-door of his stall. His warm, throaty whinny greeted the grooms as they passed. He raised his head and his ears flicked forward at the sight of veterinarian Rudolf Lessing hurrying through the stables, intent on his duties. But Lessing did not tarry in the stallion barn. Late April was foaling season, and most of his attention was focused on the broodmares.

In the long barn with the wide foaling stalls, Lessing quietly observed the mares, noting the condition of each. He was attentive to indications that a mare would foal soon; he looked out for signs of restlessness and examined their teats for waxing, a signal that delivery was imminent. If a mare went into labor, he would be called to stand by day or night, no matter the time, and the mares tended to give birth during the hours of darkness. He carefully looked over Madera, one of the Lipizzaner broodmares from Piber, whose sweet disposition shone in her soft brown eyes, and he noted that her udders were starting to fill. She would give birth within the next few days.

Next, Lessing checked on those who were already nursing their pitch-black, wobbly-legged charges. Having for years spent most of his waking hours among horses, he could read their thoughts and understand their expressions. Sometimes when he saw the trusting way they responded to him, especially the mares, heavily pregnant or with newborns by their sides, his heart ached. The horses were at their most defenseless during foaling season. Even here in Bohemia, one of the most sheltered places to ride out the war, no one could ignore the ominous atmosphere lurking below the surface calm. Lessing kept his mind on the work at hand, but the impending danger was never far from his thoughts.

News arrived in tattered rumors and panicked whispers. The official German radio still extolled the soon-to-be triumph of Hitler's Reich. But late at night, as Lessing and his wife leaned toward a clandestine radio tuned to an Allied station, he surmised the truth: The tide of war had turned against the Nazis, and the Russians were advancing rapidly west toward their position. Like many of his countrymen, Lessing believed that the war would end soon in German defeat; but for civilians even to express such a thought out loud was punishable as treason.

German-speaking civilians, fleeing from intense fighting farther east and fearful that the Russians and Czechs would show no mercy at the end of the war, poured into town, trying to make it across the border into Germany. A few lucky ones had cars or trucks; most had overloaded wagons pulled by worn-out horses; the most pitiful walked, carrying bundles or young children in their arms. The veterinarian lent a hand whenever he could to help the worn-out animals; he treated cracked hooves and skin excoriated by harnesses rubbing on starved bodies. Some of the horses had infected pustules on their withers where stiff leather had rubbed them raw.

Even here on the stud farm, the once orderly pastures were now teeming with extra stock. In mid-March 1945, one of Rau's stud farm directors had straggled into town, accompanied by a White Russian duke seeking shelter for his herd of sturdy Kabardins and rugged Panje ponies, bred on the Russian steppes. They had fled nearly four hun-

REFUGEES ENTERING HOSTAU, MARCH 1945.

dred miles, from one of the Rau-run stud farms in central Poland, to find refuge in Hostau. Lessing knew that this group was better prepared than other fleeing horsemen—the Cossack horses were bred to be hardy and to subsist on sparse rations, and the Cossack equestrians were skilled outriders, experienced in herding horses overland. Lessing and his colleagues could only imagine the fates of the rest of the horses he had tended in the eastern part of Rau's empire—they were not likely to move on foot so easily. The farm had also completely lost touch with Alois Podhajsky and the white stallions of Vienna. None of them knew if the historic riding school was still standing. Lessing feared for himself, for his family, and most of all for the swollen-bellied mares and tiny newborn foals who trusted him to keep them safe.

COLONEL HUBERT RUDOFSKY'S TALL leather boots, polished to a high shine, clicked across the cobblestone floors of the stable at Hostau as he scanned the area with his exacting eye. Every detail of the stud farm director's Wehrmacht uniform was turned out to perfection. Next to Rudofsky but half a head shorter stood Luftwaffe colonel Walter Hölters. Roughly the same age as Rudofsky, around fifty, he sported a narrow Hitler-style mustache. Both men were examining the gray

Arabian Lotnik, one of the imports from Janów. Lotnik's groom clicked his tongue softly, coaxing his charge to prick his ears forward to appear at best advantage. A tasseled gold-threaded Arabian head-dress set off the stallion's beautiful dished face and luminous dark eyes. Rudofsky proudly pointed out the gray's exceptional characteristics: the large eyes, short back, clean straight legs, and exquisitely fine fluted nostrils. Rau especially prized this stallion, finding him suitable for interbreeding with the Lipizzaner mares because of his light color and "pure blood." Hölters listened attentively to Rudofsky's lecture, aware that the stud farm master of Hostau was known to be one of the Reich's foremost horse-breeding experts.

Hölters had not explained to Rudofsky exactly what his business was in the area. Rudofsky trusted the man's bona fides as a horse lover but did not press too hard to find out his true intentions. He had found that sticking to horse talk was a lot safer than wading into murkier political waters.

When Rudofsky's presentation of the horse was over, the visitor signaled that he wished to speak to Rudofsky alone. As the two men strolled toward the pastures, out of earshot of curious grooms, the officer whispered nervously to Rudofsky that he had important informa-

HUBERT RUDOFSKY WITH LOTNIK AND
ANOTHER ARABIAN AT HOSTAU.

tion to share. "Vienna has already fallen to the Russians," he said. "The Red Army is just outside Pilsen, less than forty miles away. They will be here before you know it."

Rudofsky absorbed this news with shock. Pilsen was the nearest large town to the east; if what the officer said was true, the Russian conquerors would be upon them in a matter of days—possibly even hours.

"I've spent time on the Eastern Front," Hölters continued. "The Russians care nothing for horses—they will slaughter them on the spot and fry them up as steaks to feed their hungry troops. You are in the greatest danger, and you must act now to save them."

Rudofsky scrutinized the officer's face. What solution could this man possibly suggest that he himself hadn't already thought of and ruled out? Even over and above his direct order to stay put, moving the horses on short order would be impossible. It was the middle of foaling season. They had no trucks to transport them, no gasoline, and no orders to leave. Until now, Hostau itself had been the refuge. The Russian duke and his entourage had made it to Hostau; others might well be headed in their direction. Where could be safer than here?

Rudofsky knew enough to understand that Hölters's alarm was justified. Examples abounded of valuable horses destroyed during these last few chaotic months of advance and retreat. Trakhenen, Germany's famed "city of horses," had seen a mass exodus of all of its equine inhabitants. The owners and breeders of the famed Trakhener cavalry horses, close to eight thousand in number, had fled across the frozen Vistula River while being strafed by Russian bombers. Germany's greatest Thoroughbred racehorse, Alchimist, was shot to death on April 15, 1945, after Russian soldiers tried to seize him and the stallion refused to load onto their truck. Rudofsky could not know the precise fate of all the horses in Rau's eastern empire, but he suspected that many of them were scattered or dead. Just a week previously, he had contacted Berlin, asking what to do should the stud farm be in danger of being overrun, and received only the curt reply: "Stay put, at all costs."

Rudofsky listened intently, desperately hoping that this officer could suggest a better solution. But when Hölters spoke, he was undone. "You must make contact with the Americans. They are not far—just over the border to Bavaria. Perhaps you can deliver the horses to them. It's your only hope."

The Americans? Rudofsky made use of his military background to maintain a neutral expression, but behind his dignified facade, he was shocked to the core. This officer, a stranger to him, was suggesting what Rudofsky had not imagined in his wildest dreams. It was unthinkable, preposterous, it bordered on the insane—he was advising Rudofsky to commit an act of high treason! Rudofsky silently ticked through the possibilities. Perhaps the officer had been sent specifically to test his loyalties, laying out a trap for him to stumble into? Even more terrifying, perhaps he spoke the truth. If their best hope was to surrender to the Americans, then clearly, all other avenues had been exhausted. One thing was certain: Rudofsky had sensed that this man's enthusiasm for the horses was real, his erudition about the Lipizzaner and the Spanish Riding School authentic. Without speaking, Rudofsky ended the taut pause with a curt nod of assent.

After instructing Rudofsky to await further communication, Hölters got back into his car and drove away. Rudofsky would never see the short colonel with the Hitler mustache again.

AFTER HÖLTERS'S DEPARTURE, RUDOFSKY was thrown into a chasm of indecision. He understood that the horses were in danger and that a catastrophe was imminent, but he remained deeply uncertain whether he should take the Luftwaffe colonel's advice. He wondered if he had been set up and was about to be double-crossed, then mulled over what the Americans might do if approached. Of all the horsemen in the Reich, Rudofsky had been selected to be in charge of these, their most precious horses. He was responsible for their safety. There was no easy solution to the problem, and he had precious little time to consider his options—if he spent too long thinking, it would be too late to act.

Just shy of his forty-eighth birthday, Rudofsky had been born into a place and time that quickly taught a hard truth: Republics and empires, dictators and presidents, came and went, ruthlessly demanding loyalty but constantly being overturned. Throughout almost forty straight years of upheaval, Rudofsky had kept his mind on horses and blended in like a chameleon with his surroundings. His loyalties lay close to home: to his ailing mother, his niece and nephew, to the Catholic parish where generations of Rudofskys had been baptized, married, and buried, and of course, to the animals entrusted to his care. Horses had been here before Hitler's Third Reich arrived, and horses would be here, he believed, after Hitler was gone. Rudofsky was deeply reluctant to flee with the horses—not because he didn't care about their well-being. Nothing was more important to him. But where, he wondered, could he protect them better than here in Hostau, where he was a highly respected member of the community? The safest thing for the horses, in Rudofsky's opinion, was for them to remain at the farm.

WEARY AND BATTLE-WORN, HANK REED and the 2nd Cavalry had been fighting their way eastward for four months since Christmas 1944. On March 19, they had crossed the Rhine, and since then, they had been rapidly leapfrogging across Germany. The fighting was sporadic but ugly, with fanatical Germans digging in, willing to battle the Americans to the death. Colonel Reed and his men had penetrated so far into Germany that the Czechoslovakian border was just a few kilometers away. Right over that border, unbeknownst to them, lay the still peaceful village of Hostau.

Two hundred and ninety-five days. That was how many times the sun had risen and set since the day Reed and his men first set foot in France. The impress of each day was etched across Reed's windburned face, written in his hooded gaze and somber expression. Everyone was predicting German defeat any day, but even as they marched closer to the end of the war, Reed was losing men from his ranks almost daily— shot by snipers, burned alive by mortar fire, rained on by lava-hot shrapnel, and blasted by cannon. It always hurt to lose a man, but somehow, the closer the end seemed, the more each loss counted. He could see the prospect of home flickering in the back of his men's eyes with each mile covered and each new town captured. Every day, the after-action reports totaled the losses, adding new numbers to the columns of emptied boots. He had to try not to think about the mothers and sweethearts at home—the ones reading in the newspapers that the war was almost over, the ones who were allowing themselves to believe that surely their loved one was going to make it home alive.

The late-April sun shone down on all of them: on Podhajsky, who knew that the next few days would most likely decide his stallions' fate; on Lessing, who nursed the mares and foals, wondering what would become of them; on Rudofsky, a man who had been thrust unwillingly into the most momentous decision of his life; and on Hank Reed, a man who loved horses, who had no idea he was about to be given the chance of a lifetime. The sun also shone upon the horses— reflecting glints of sunlight on the backs of the white stallions in St. Martin, and the broodmares in Hostau, and Witez's blood bay coat, which shone like burnished bronze. The next few days would determine the fate of all of them, men and horses alike, encircled by warring nations pointing the world's most powerful guns in their direction.

THE PHOTOGRAPHS

Hank Reed stood inside a rustic farmhouse just on the outskirts of the Bavarian village of Vohenstraus, in southern Germany. Outside the window, he could see pockmarked buildings with caved-in walls, destruction wrought by a brief burst of shelling as the American tanks rolled into town two days earlier.

Reed had just received an important communication. A German Luftwaffe intelligence group had been fleeing Berlin, desperate to escape before the Russians took over the capital. When they ran out of gas, they holed up at a remote former hunting lodge in the Bohemian Forest—an area so deeply wooded that the trees created a nearly impregnable natural barrier. The group was made up of high-ranking officers known to be traveling with important documents. They were calling themselves a "meteorological group" as a front for their espionage activities and were believed to be transporting highly classified photographs and maps documenting the location of Russian airfields and industry in the east. For now, the Russians were among America's allies, but some were already looking toward the need for strategic information in the postwar world. Reed's commander at XII Corps headquarters made it clear that the capture of this group was a high-priority mission.

Reed summoned Captain Ferdinand Sperl, a valuable POW interrogator who was fluent in German and had some familiarity with the local area. Sperl was known as a wit with a fondness for practical jokes—one of his prized stunts was filling his canteen with wine or cognac, then submersing a water-filled condom inside the canteen's lip so that he could evade detection in case of surprise inspection. But behind his fun-loving demeanor, Sperl was highly intelligent and a skilled linguist. Reed relied on Sperl to handle missions requiring sophisticated language skills and diplomatic tact.

Sperl, who was born in Switzerland, was commanding officer of the group of interrogators who moved with 2nd Cavalry headquarters. Among them, the six men spoke nine languages and traveled together in a jeep affectionately known as "Chez Stubby." When they set up camp, it was always far enough from headquarters that the POWs being interrogated there couldn't see the colonel's encampment, but near enough that they were within the sentry's perimeter.

Reed had a map spread out on the table. He showed Sperl a location just over the Czechoslovakian border, a few miles away—a hunting lodge called Dianahof.

"There are about twenty men hiding up there, fleeing Berlin," Reed said. "We need to capture them and, most importantly, keep their documents intact."

FERDINAND SPERL WITH HIS JEEP,
NICKNAMED "CHEZ STUBBY."

It was a dangerous mission, but Reed explained that Sperl had a powerful bargaining chip. Because these were high-value captures, they would be sent directly to France for interrogation by the Americans rather than being held as ordinary prisoners of war. This should prove a strong incentive for the men to surrender.

Figure it out, Reed told Sperl. Sperl named the mission Operation Sauerkraut.

THE NEXT DAY, APRIL 26, around noon, before Sperl had finished making his plans, a motorcar slowly approached a 2nd Cavalry headquarters checkpoint with a white flag fluttering from its antenna. The car was transporting an officer of the German Luftwaffe. He looked to be about fifty, short, with a narrow mustache. The German demanded an interview with the commanding officer, claiming that he had "urgent information." Sperl hurried over to see what was causing the commotion. Nobody got to Colonel Reed without speaking to him first.

Sperl had the officer escorted to his interrogation tent, then looked him over with a practiced eye. He particularly noted the German's distinctive small mustache; the man had an oval face and sported a pince-nez, which gave him a scholarly look. Sperl was born people-smart, and his training as an interrogator had only sharpened his skills. A hotelier by trade before his stint in the army, he had worked in some of the world's grandest hotels. His "field office" was a lot more humble— just a dusty blackout tent, a standard-issue portable field desk and chairs, and a manual typewriter painted in camouflage colors.

Sperl gestured for the man to be seated. "What brings you here?" he asked. His German was Swiss-accented, but his demeanor, friendly with a hint of swagger, was one hundred percent American.

"I come here on urgent business," the officer said. "I need to speak with the commanding officer." His manner was proud as he held himself stiffly before the Swiss-American captain.

Sperl's face was open, and though his expression was mild, it was clear that he meant business. He started with simple questions. "Name and rank?"

"Oberst Walter H.," the German replied.

Oberst was a military rank equivalent to colonel, Sperl knew, but he asked again for the officer's full name.

"Walter H.," the colonel repeated.

Sperl was familiar with this tactic. Intelligence officers who were negotiating refused to give their surnames.

"I need to speak to the commanding officer. I come with urgent information," the man repeated.

Sperl flipped open the officer's seized wallet, looking for clues to his identity. Not surprisingly, the officer had removed any form of identification before presenting it to the Americans.

But the wallet was not entirely empty. Sperl saw the serrated edges of some photographs and slid them out. He was expecting mementos— usually, people carried heartbreakingly well-worn pictures of wives or children, and sometimes these keepsakes offered clues to their bearer's identity, or a window for an interrogator to forge a bond.

But Sperl was surprised. Instead of family members, he was looking at two photographs of beautiful white horses. The officer was watching the American expectantly; Sperl could tell right away that these pictures mattered a lot to this man. It was his job to learn the reason.

"Why do you have these pictures?" Sperl asked bluntly.

"I want to speak to the commanding officer," the German replied.

"Why do you have these pictures?" Sperl repeated. He made an effort to keep his tone friendly.

The officer hesitated, obviously weighing whether he should tell his tale to the captain or continue to insist that he be taken to his superior. "I took these photographs just a few days ago. Not far from here, in a village called Hostau, there is an old imperial horse-breeding station . . ."

Sperl nodded for the man to go on.

"In this location, some of the most valuable horses in the world are being sheltered."

Sperl appraised the man carefully. The officer wore a German Air Force uniform, not cavalry; there was no obvious connection to horses. "Did you come here from Hostau? Is that where you are stationed?"

"No," the officer replied.

"Then why are you concerning yourself with this matter?"

A half-smile crossed the colonel's face. "I'm a lover of horses," he said.

"So, you are not stationed at Hostau, but you are a horse fancier . . ." Sperl leaned in, peering at the officer's face. "And who are you, *exactly*?" Sperl elicited confidences with the easy air of a maître d' chatting up a guest.

The officer's answer was clearly well rehearsed. "I'm a meteorologist, part of a meteorological group recently evacuated from Berlin."

A meteorological group recently evacuated from Berlin? Sperl carefully kept his face neutral as a bell rang in his head. This Colonel H., the horse fancier, was also a spy. And not just any spy—one of the exact spies he was looking for.

Sperl looked straight into the officer's eyes. He knew this playbook well.

"You're not telling the truth," Sperl said. "You're not a meteorologist. You're part of a Luftwaffe intelligence group. You're staying at a hunting lodge called Dianahof not far from here. You were fleeing Berlin when you ran out of gas."

The colonel's eyes widened in surprise, but he betrayed no emotion. "I need to speak to your commanding officer," he repeated.

Sperl held firm. "Explain why you have pictures of horses."

The officer, perhaps realizing that he would not get to the commander if he did not first cooperate with Sperl, started to explain.

"These are no ordinary horses. They are royal Lipizzaner from Vienna. The German Army sent them to Hostau for safekeeping. Now they are in danger of being captured by the advancing Russian Army. I want to speak to your commanding officer to see if he can help." In spite of his formal military bearing, the officer became visibly emotional when he spoke of the horses.

Taking the two photographs, Sperl went looking for Colonel Reed. He had a hunch that his CO was going to find this new development very interesting indeed. The German had no idea just how lucky he was. In April 1945, of all the American army commanders in Europe, only a handful were passionate horsemen. Hank Reed had arrived in Europe at the head of a horseless cavalry, but when it came time to choose the code name for his regiment, he came up with one that revealed what was deep in his heart: Thoroughbred.

WHEN SPERL SHOWED REED the two photographs, his CO reacted with utter surprise. The last thing he expected to see out here was beautiful purebred horses. Since the war started, he'd seen enough sorry specimens to last him a lifetime—horses hitched to artillery wagons, half-starved horses pulling heavy loads, horses with bullet holes in them, their fly-speckled carcasses lying by the side of the road. At this late and desperate stage of the fighting, starving refugees hacked meat directly from exhausted horses the moment they dropped. This was supposed to be the first fully mechanized war, but in fact, that was true only of the Americans. The Germans and the Russians were still using horses for supply trains and other heavy-duty work. But Reed saw immediately that the animals in these photos were no ordinary plugs.

He scrutinized a photo that showed a handler holding a snow-white horse, its delicate features set off by a ceremonial halter embellished with woven tassels. Two German officers looked on admiringly against a backdrop of well-kept white stables. When a layman looks at a horse, he will see the obvious things like size and color, but when a horseman looks at a horse, a million tiny details catch his notice. Reed saw the animal's perfectly formed legs, his well-formed face and small tapered ears. The horse's coat shone with good health, a brilliant pearl; his eyes peered soulfully toward the camera. Appearing untouched by the ravages of hunger and war raging around him, this equine was clearly so precious that men in uniform paused to gaze and take photographs: a specimen so rare that a uniformed officer would come under a flag of peace to beg that the horse be saved.

With Sperl acting as interpreter, Reed explained to the German that the Americans might be willing to help find an escape route for the horses. Next, he laid out his terms. The intelligence group must surrender with all of their documents. If they met Reed's demands, they would be kept together and transported directly for interrogation at European Theater Operations headquarters. There, they would not be treated as prisoners of war, although they would be restricted in their movements. They would work with the Allies only in regard to their intelligence about Russia, which meant that they would not be committing treason. If the plan went off as promised, then Reed gave his word: He would do his best to bring the horses in Hostau to safety.

The officer agreed with a crisp nod. He would bring Sperl to Dianahof under a white flag to arrange the terms of surrender. He then explained the German defenses that they would encounter along the way. There were only a few checkpoints between the American headquarters and the hunting lodge where his group was located, and for these he knew the passwords. The German colonel made no absolute guarantees. He did not know if there were any SS forces in the woods, and there might also be bands of Czech partisans carrying out small-scale attacks on German targets.

Reed asked about the quantity and location of the documents. The German colonel explained that the group had maps and aerial photographs buried in crates on the grounds of the lodge. Reed and Sperl exchanged a look of triumph when the German explained that the hidden documents would fill an entire truck—a yield of unprecedented proportions. That is, if they were able to pull it off, and if this officer could be trusted.

WAITING UNTIL DUSK so the darkness would make them less conspicuous, Sperl set off with the German officer toward Dianahof. Colonel "Walter H." had said the unit was prepared to surrender, but Sperl knew that any situation of this kind was unpredictable. When he ventured out alone with the German, he put himself at considerable risk.

The road wound upward through ever deepening pine forests, and darkness fell over them like a thick wool blanket. Sperl pulled his overcoat tighter around him as the jeep bumped and jarred over the rutted country road. He kept an eye on the man who was now his guide. The forest was spooky and mostly quiet until they came across a roadblock manned by German sentries. The guards pulled out their rifles and fired shots into the air, splitting the silence.

Sperl waited, rigid, as the colonel spoke the passwords. His life and safety were at the mercy of an enemy officer he'd first laid eyes on only earlier that day. Sperl kept his face neutral as he stared down the muzzles pointed directly at his face, hoping that the sentries believed he was the colonel's prisoner and not an American spy. After a long, tense moment, the guards lifted their guns and let them pass.

When they arrived, it was almost dark, but Sperl could make out the large marble statue of Diana, goddess of the hunt, in front of a boxlike three-story stucco manor house that glowed white in the darkness. This remote location, with a house prettily situated on top of a three-sided hill, had once been the staging ground for a count's private stag-hunting parties and summer soirées for noblemen. But once inside, Sperl saw that there were no longer any signs of gaiety here. In the place of noblemen on a summer retreat, there were two dozen Luftwaffe officers who knew that their war was coming to an end.

Saying that he wanted to speak to his men alone, the Luftwaffe officer escorted Sperl into an antechamber to wait. After leaving him there for what seemed like a long while, the colonel returned and motioned for him to enter a large conference room. Ringing the table were more than twenty officers and men, as well as several enlisted women. Sperl stared into the impassive faces around the table and, as clearly as possible, laid out Reed's terms. When he had finished, his words were greeted with stony silence.

The group's commander asked Sperl to retire once more. This time the wait was much shorter. The colonel came back a moment later and announced their decision: The Germans would surrender themselves and all of their documents to the Americans. They had only one request: They wanted a small mock firefight to make it look as if they hadn't surrendered voluntarily.

Sperl instructed them to dig up the crates filled with the documents and have them ready to load in the morning. The Americans would return at dawn the next day. The German officers were edgy, knowing that surrendering, even this late in the war, could be fraught with risks: If an SS detachment, Hitler's loyal diehards, got wind of the plan, they would shoot the officers rather than allow them to surrender. And so close to the border, Czech partisans might be lurking, their behavior hard to predict. The plan was to stage a sham fight, but all of the men, Sperl included, had seen enough to know that the line between a mock fight and a real one was razor-thin. If the mission succeeded, it would be a major coup—to capture an entire high-ranking German intelligence group with all of its documents. Nobody said a word about horses.

BETWEEN THE WORK OF PREPARING the convoy—two tanks, two armored cars, two trucks, and some jeeps—and the tension in the air, Sperl hardly managed to sleep that night. As soon as dawn broke, the Americans headed out. The night before, Sperl and his escort had traveled under cover of darkness, but now the sun was rising, and the noise of their vehicles rumbling over the roads echoed through the trees, giving an enemy plenty of time to prepare an ambush.

As the convoy lumbered up the mountain road, a brief volley of gunshots started ricocheting through the trees. Sperl could not tell who was firing at them or whether an SS unit, hell-bent on self-destruction, might be around the next corner. As he tried to stay focused, his mind was flooded with a million possibilities—none of them good. If they were caught in a gunfight, whose side would his German escorts be on? His ears strained to pick out menacing sounds above the loud rumbling of their vehicles. But Sperl heard nothing beyond the vehicle noises. When they arrived at the checkpoints, they found them unmanned. Before long, they reached the hunting lodge.

Reflecting in the slanting rays of dawn sunlight, Dianahof was imposing, with peaked slate roofs and rows of tall windows glinting like peering eyes. The statue of Diana gazed serenely over the group of German officers assembled next to their mountainous stacks of wooden crates, all filled with valuable classified documents.

The German colonel was nattily attired in full uniform, his pince-nez glinting in the morning light. His demeanor was excessively formal as he surrendered to the Americans. He proudly declared that he had been a World War I fighter pilot in the infamous Immelmann squadron. For the first time, he gave his real name: Walter Hölters. He oversaw the loading of the documents onto the German trucks. The entire enterprise took only a few minutes.

When the documents were secured, the convoy headed down the hill toward the German border, leaving behind a tank and an armored car. As soon as Sperl rounded a bend and was a safe distance away, he heard the American tank bombarding the now empty lodge, quickly followed by machine-gun chatter to create the impression of cross fire. Sperl hoped that this decoy would distract anyone who was waiting in the woods to ambush them. From his vantage point, he could see billows of smoke curling up from the burning lodge. Once the noise of the fake skirmish subsided, Sperl and his prisoners found themselves alone on the mountain road with only the sounds of their trucks and jeeps to break the silence. Sperl heaved a sigh of relief. He radioed ahead to Colonel Reed at headquarters: Prepare for the arrival of the captives.

BACK AT HEADQUARTERS, REED invited Hölters to share a meal and pressed him for more information about the horses. Where exactly were they located? Who was guarding them? How many were there? What breeds? How many people on the staff? What about the presence of Allied prisoners of war?

Hank Reed and Walter Hölters couldn't have looked more dissimilar. Reed, the handsome American with the wide smile and friendly gaze, had been out in the field for months. His weathered face was lined with exhaustion; his green soldier's fatigues were faded and worn. Walter Hölters wore a fresh uniform studded with ribbons and shiny brass. All around them, brutality, chaos, and bloodshed ruled the day. Still, between them, there was a scrap of understanding tied to their mutual regard for horses.

One thing was certain—the German was eager to help Reed figure out a plan to safeguard the animals. Colonel Hölters had spent his war years working as a spy, and the plot that he and Reed came up with was worthy of an espionage novel. First, on two sheets of lined paper, Hölters penned a note to Hubert Rudofsky, chief of the stud farm at Hostau, whom he had met a few days earlier.

Hölters sent his personal valet off on a bicycle carrying the note with instructions to take it to a forester's house deep in the woods, about halfway between Hostau and the American lines. The forester would then carry the note the rest of the way.

The plan was in place. The message from Hölters did not mention the Americans but gave instructions to Rudofsky about how to contact him regarding a possible escape route for the Lipizzaner. Reed told his sentries to be on the lookout for a German soldier crossing over enemy lines, wanting to talk about horses.

Now there was nothing to do but wait.

THE PLAN

Rudolf Lessing hurried toward Rudofsky's office, where he had been summoned to see his commander. The call could mean anything— a horse with colic, a malpositioned foal, or any one of the countless problems that cropped up in the course of an average day. When Lessing entered Rudofsky's office, the commander's face was grave, and he held a letter in his hand.

Lessing listened thoughtfully as Rudofsky revealed the secret purpose of Hölters's recent visit to Hostau; the colonel had urged him to consider evacuating the horses, but Rudofsky had been reluctant, believing that they would be safer staying put. But he had reconsidered. Hölters had seemed adamant that fleeing would be safer, and after much agonizing reflection, Rudofsky had decided he was right.

Rudofsky waved the letter toward Lessing. Just now a messenger had brought a note from Hölters promising an escape route for the horses. There were only two caveats: The plan was secret—and dangerous.

"An escape route?" Lessing asked. "But how? When?" He was thinking about the broodmares, some nearly ready to foal, others with tiny offspring at their side.

But the urgency on Rudofsky's face was unmistakable. They needed to take immediate action. Lessing was to ride horseback into the thick forest that ran along both sides of the German-Czechoslovakian border and locate a forester's house where he would make contact with Colonel Hölters. To avoid raising suspicion, Rudofsky would remain on the farm. Lessing should take along a groom riding a second horse in case he needed to bring back a negotiator. They could trust no one. A wrong word or action, no matter how innocent, could lead to the most serious consequences.

His head spinning with a million unanswered questions, Lessing nodded curtly in agreement and left immediately for the stables.

In the close quarters of the stall, he spoke softly to his Thoroughbred, Indigo, as he hoisted the saddle on the horse's back and tightened the girth. Indigo—so named because his coat was so black it appeared almost blue—had started out life as a racehorse, and back in more peaceful times, he had been a frequent winner. These days, he had a far humbler task: carrying the veterinarian to house calls at neighboring farms. Today, Lessing would trust Indigo to carry him up a mountain path deep into the forest—likely the most important ride of his life.

Lessing and the groom set off at a brisk trot. Lessing rode as if in a hurry, his straight back inclined forward, his heels sunk down. Indigo

LESSING RIDING INDIGO.

stretched his nose out, his long strides quickly covering ground. Alongside him, in sharp contrast to his pitch-black companion, was a white Yugoslavian Lipizzaner stallion whose snow-white mane floated from his powerful arched crest and high-set tail billowed behind him like clean sheets on a line.

As a veterinarian, Lessing often crossed the rolling countryside on horseback. The farm at Hostau, over fifteen hundred acres of pasture, all told, had several ancillary stations, and when Lessing wasn't caring for the horses of Hostau, he took calls for private owners. He had clocked many miles in the saddle on these lands, and he was at ease in the fields and country lanes. But Lessing knew that this ride was different. He was taking a great risk that might end badly. Trying not to think about his wife and daughters, who lived with him in an apartment on the farm and did not know anything unusual was afoot, he willed himself to keep his wits about him.

As they got closer to the edge of the forest, Lessing's anxiety started to abate. Taking action felt better than the previous weeks of uncertainty and waiting. They reached the forest's edge and entered its shaded pathways. Dark-coated Indigo was swallowed up in the black shadows, while the Lipizzaner at his side glowed like a pale moon. At last, the pair came to the designated forester's lodge deep in the woods. They approached cautiously, unsure what they would find there.

The forester was at home. Lessing inquired as to the whereabouts of the German colonel, but the man explained that Colonel Hölters had departed, and furthermore, he believed that he might be in American captivity. The forester offered the use of his stables and his motorcycle should Lessing wish to proceed in his search, but warned the veterinarian that he might run into American patrols if he ventured much farther. Unprepared for this news, Lessing pondered his options. Perhaps the smartest choice was to turn around. But Rudofsky had told him to make contact with Colonel Hölters. If he returned to Hostau, then what? They had no backup plan.

Lessing decided to leave the horses with the groom in the safety of the forester's stable and proceed on the borrowed motorcycle. It was late afternoon, and getting cold. Deep in the forest, the shadows gathered fast. The sound of the motorcycle's engine battered his ears like gunfire.

—

"Hands up!" American soldiers toting machine guns suddenly blocked his path.

Lessing cut the motor and froze. He searched his mind for English words, but his tongue was heavy, his mind blank. The American soldiers stared at him, guns pointed directly at his chest. Lessing raised his hands over his head. Haltingly, expecting them to doubt him, he explained that he was a veterinarian from a nearby horse-breeding farm, but the GIs seemed unsurprised to find him there. Fear and wild thoughts started banging around his brain. He knew nothing of Americans except that they were enemies, and now he was their prisoner.

The sentries signaled to him to proceed up the road on foot. A little ahead, they came to a waiting American jeep and told Lessing to climb aboard. Now he learned his destination: He was being taken to speak to their commander at regimental headquarters.

As the jeep rattled up the road, Lessing tried to remind himself that he was doing this for the sake of the horses. He wasn't sure what it might mean for him—a prison camp? Worse? They covered the short distance to 2nd Cavalry headquarters in no time. Before he had time to reflect upon his situation, he was standing face-to-face with an American colonel. Lessing made a split-second decision. Even though he had not been expecting to meet American soldiers, why not press the horses' case to his captors? He figured he had nothing to lose.

So far, the plan had worked. Here before Reed stood a young German veterinary officer. The man was good-looking and built like a rider, with a slender torso and long, thin legs. He was several inches taller than Reed, and over a decade younger, and clearly terrified. Fortunately, the German was able to communicate in English. Reed listened as the man carefully chose his words, explaining about the nearby remount depot and the valuable horses hidden there.

Wanting to set the young officer at ease, Reed quickly explained that he was aware of the horses in Hostau and understood they were in immediate danger. Lessing was surprised to learn that the Americans already knew about the horses, but he didn't let on. Instead, he pretended that he had come to the Americans with the express purpose of asking for their help. He could only hope that his action would meet with Rudofsky's approval.

"The horses are in danger," Lessing said. "That is why I've come."

Reed assured the young officer that he had a plan: The German staff of the stud farm needed to transport the horses over the border. From there, the Americans would ensure their safety.

Perhaps Reed could see the crushing disappointment in the eyes of the veterinarian. Lessing was keenly aware that he did not have permission from Rudofsky to open a negotiation with the Americans, yet here was an opportunity that could not be missed. Hesitant but determined, Lessing began to slowly explain why Reed's proposal would never work. It was foaling season on the farm. Many of the mares had recently given birth or were just about to. They couldn't travel that distance on such short notice; the mares and foals could never walk that far, and they didn't have enough men or trucks, not to mention gasoline, to ship the horses—besides, there were so many horses at Hostau, several hundred, most of them snow-white in color. How could they possibly escape without notice? Lessing tried to be both calm and forceful as he explained what needed to be done. The American army needed to occupy Hostau.

Lessing hastened to explain that he was certain that his commander, Colonel Rudofsky, would agree to surrender the depot. The veterinarian sounded more confident than he felt. Rudofsky had made no such promise.

"Regardless of what you decide," Lessing finished, "I do not have the authority to make this decision. Give me an American officer. The officer should come with me and speak with my superior." Lessing mentioned the two horses in the forester's lodge and said that the American officer could ride back with him easily.

Reed gave no sign of what he was thinking, but he knew something that Lessing did not. Commanding officer though he was, Reed did not have permission to take his troops across the border to Czechoslovakia. In February, at the Yalta Conference, Roosevelt and Churchill had agreed with Stalin that everything east of the border with Germany proper would henceforth be under Russian control. As of April 21, a restraining line had been drawn along the border of Czechoslovakia. American troops were forbidden from advancing past this line in force. The continuing cold, the muddy roads, and the snow in the mountains hampered movement, but the 2nd Cavalry, along with the 90th Infantry, stood ready to enter Czechoslovakia as soon as they received orders. However, for the time being, they had advanced as close to the border as they were allowed to go. The horses might be tantalizingly close, but at the same time, they were heartbreakingly out of reach.

Reed considered his options. Could he risk lives and manpower on a crazy mission to save a group of horses? Putting men at risk was never an easy decision. But abandoning the horses just didn't feel right to him. He could not easily forget the cavalry lesson instilled into him for over twenty years: Horses should always be treated well.

He ticked through a mental list of what would be needed—men and firepower to be assembled on a moment's notice. The 2nd never stayed in one place for long; in a matter of days or even hours, he'd be getting orders to move on to another assignment. If he sent an officer to negotiate, the man would have to sneak across the border right under the noses of the enemy, and if he got caught, he'd have to keep what he was up to a secret—perhaps even under torture. Sober minds could certainly call Reed deluded or foolish for even contemplating this maneuver.

The more Reed thought about it, the more he realized there was just one man in the army who might be crazy enough to agree to a scheme like this: the man who had said of the cavalryman, "You must be: a horse master; a scholar; a high minded gentleman; a cold blooded hero; a hot blooded savage. At one and the same time, you must be a wise man and a fool." The man who might be just enough of a wise man and a fool to agree to this plan was Hank's old polo buddy and mentor: the commander in chief of the Third Army, General George S. Patton.

DRESSED UP AS
A PLENIPOTENTIARY

Colonel Reed knew that there was little time to waste—at this point, only a matter of miles separated them from the rapidly advancing Russian front. If this mission was going to succeed at all, it had to happen fast, before somebody besides Patton got wind of it and had the good sense to tell them to knock it off.

Reed needed the right man to accompany Rudolf Lessing back to Hostau. The veterinarian said that he needed a field-grade officer, a major or higher. Well, there was no way Reed could agree to that. It was far too dangerous to send an officer of that rank on this fool's mission. The German had cut through the woods to get there, and they'd need to send someone back the same way. Reed needed somebody who could ride horseback, someone smart and with enough panache to make himself believable as an emissary, somebody whom he trusted. And he knew just the man for the job: Tennessee-born Tom Stewart. Captain Stewart was never one to run off at the mouth; he could understand some German, so he wouldn't be completely lost; and as a senator's son, he had a composed, confident air. Most important, Stewart had grown up around horses in his native Tennessee and could undertake a cross-country ride without difficulty.

TOM STEWART
IN FRANCE.

TOM STEWART HAD BEEN planning to see something miraculous that day. He and some of the fellows were going to pay a visit to a local village, Konnersreuth, where people claimed that a Bavarian woman showed the miracle of stigmata—marks on her body that mirrored those where Jesus was hung on the cross: on the soles of the feet, palms, and forehead. The woman, Therese Neumann, had been cured of partial paralysis while in her twenties. Now she wore bloody bandages on her hands, head, and feet from wounds that supposedly never healed, and was said to subsist entirely without water or food, consuming only the consecrated host at Mass once a week. Konnersreuth was near their headquarters, not far from the Czechoslovakian border. Some of the men were curious to see her—Stewart was not Catholic, but he was the grandson of a Methodist minister, and he had always been devout.

Tom Stewart had been setting up camp, dismantling camp, and moving on almost every day for months on end. His face was battle-weary, his uniform frayed, his combat boots scuffed from miles of trails. Although he was outwardly reserved, beneath Stewart's calm demeanor and dutiful behavior lurked a deep well of suppressed emotion. One harrowing day while the 2nd was fighting across France, Stewart received an urgent order to relocate his men, since a dive-bombing raid was imminent. One of the soldiers refused to comply, insisting that leaving their secure spot behind the hedgerows would not be safe. While the rest of the men hurried to follow his order, Stewart ran back to demand that the recalcitrant soldier get a move on. At that exact moment, a dive-bomber unleashed its fiery payload. In a flash of searing fire, all five men who had willingly followed Stewart's orders were killed on the spot—only he and the noncompliant soldier survived. Stewart had struggled since then to make sense of what had happened. So far, he'd come up short. He was a brave soldier, and he served without hesitation or question, but because of that day, he had retreated deeper into himself. As they prepared to visit the miraculous peasant of Konnersreuth, Stewart, understandably, was looking for some kind of blessing or sign.

But Stewart never got the chance to visit the woman marked by stigmata. Instead, he was ordered to return to 42nd Squadron headquarters at once. The fellows would have to go without him.

Colonel Hargis, commander of the 42nd, was waiting for him with a glum expression. "Colonel Reed wants to borrow you for a special mission," he said. Accustomed to following orders, Stewart did not ask what kind of task he was wanted for. Ignoring Hargis's bleakness, he hurried off to report to Reed.

Stewart arrived just in time to see Hank Reed and a sergeant getting out of the vehicle that held the colonel's radio. Stewart didn't know at the time that Reed had just received a message from Patton, commander of the Third Army. Reed told Stewart to go inside, that he would join him shortly.

Inside headquarters stood several American officers, including Sperl, whose bravery that morning with the capture of Walter Hölters had started the whole chain of events. With them was a young German officer who was introduced as Rudolf Lessing. The German spoke passable English with a clipped accent. His manner was polite and formal, but he was clearly ill at ease. When Stewart arrived, the German was talking about a place called Hostau, explaining to the Americans that most of the staff there were prisoners of war—primarily Yugoslavs and Poles—who were planning to flee to France in advance of the Russian Army. Dropped into the middle of the conversation, Stewart wasn't quite sure what was going on, but Reed soon came back inside and brought him up to date. Just on the other side of the border was a collection of horses like no other in the world, and their lives were in danger. Reed had decided to see if he could help evacuate the horses to a safer location. This German officer was an emissary from the stud farm who had come to try to negotiate terms. Stewart was going to ride with Lessing behind enemy lines—and when Colonel Reed said "ride," he meant on horseback. The object was to negotiate the peaceful surrender of the horse depot.

After three years in the cavalry, Stewart was an old hand, but this was the most improbable mission he'd ever encountered. Far from being flattered at the thought of being chosen, Stewart, in his typical self-effacing way, figured he'd been picked because everybody else was too important to risk. He thought of his buddies en route to see the blessed peasant of Konnersreuth, half-wishing he could go with them.

Before Stewart had much chance to think it over, his CO launched into a quick lesson in how to negotiate with a German general. At the same time, he set Sperl to work penning copies of notes in German and English, explaining that Captain Tom Stewart was an emissary from Colonel Reed.

"Be careful," Reed cautioned. "If you give any sign that you understand German, the results may be fatal." Reed knew that the Germans might speak freely in front of Stewart, giving out secret information in the belief that he didn't understand. If the Germans realized that he had learned something confidential, they would take him prisoner—or perhaps execute him on the spot.

Stewart nodded. He understood the risk.

When Sperl handed him the notes, Stewart scanned the text and immediately objected. "The note says 'emissary,'" he said. "Doesn't that make me sound too much like a spy?"

Sperl and the others burst out laughing. "Well . . . ?" Sperl said. "Sneaking across enemy lines on horseback to negotiate with the enemy? What else would you call it?"

Stewart shrugged. They had a point. All joking aside, he knew that this was a dangerous mission. Stewart still remembered when Jim Pitman had volunteered to travel blindfolded to a German-held château to negotiate with the enemy. Pitman never backed down from anything. Seven months had passed since that fatal morning in Lunéville, but the guys still thought about him every day. Stewart wasn't the first person asked to take a risk out here—every man stepped up when his time came.

Stewart scanned Lessing's guarded Teutonic face, looking for a sign that he could trust the man. But the German was reserved, correct, and silent. No sign was forthcoming. Stewart would have to take this one on faith.

In addition to the three pass notes, Ferdinand Sperl typed up another fake document in the highest-sounding German he could muster. Lacking proper stationery, Sperl tore a page out of the front of a book, neatly trimmed its ragged edge, and rolled it into his manual typewriter. The letter designated Tom Stewart as a plenipotentiary, an officer of sufficient rank to accept the surrender of the station. To this document, someone added the flourish of General Patton's forged signature.

When all was ready, Reed made a firm pronouncement. "Captain Stewart must be returned *safely* behind American lines within twenty-four hours."

Lessing nodded his assent.

"If he fails to return by the deadline, American troops will advance on Hostau, guns blazing."

All three men understood what this meant. In a firefight for Hostau, the horses would be the losers.

The moment the preparations were completed, the two men returned to the 42nd Squadron, bivouacked a few miles away, where they would prepare for their departure. As Reed bade them goodbye, he didn't say much, but Stewart could read his commander's expression. This mission mattered to him—he wanted to save the horses. All over Europe, there were men whose express job was to protect cultural artifacts and recover stolen art. At the highest level, the American military was aware that even in the darkest times, care must be taken to protect irreplaceable cultural treasures. But the horses, equally beloved, equally treasured, infinitely precious because they were living things, did not have the same official protection afforded to museum pieces. Reed knew that no edict from the U.S. government would ever officially sanction his actions. He understood that saving these irreplaceable beasts was a choice he had to make, and a choice that came with exposing his soldiers to risk. In short, Hank Reed was trusting his gut.

By the time Stewart and Lessing arrived back at headquarters, the barracks was abuzz with the news: Captain Stewart was going to meet with a German general! His buddies pitched in, trying to help him get outfitted for this completely unexpected development. Someone produced a jacket—a bit too big, but it would have to do—and someone else handed him an overseas cap. Lessing was dressed to ride in his high black boots. Stewart would have to make do with his combat boots. Ready to leave in officer's disguise, his plenipotentiary document stowed safely on his person, he was stopped by the commander of the 42nd Squadron, Colonel Hargis.

"You don't have to go," Hargis said in a serious tone, no doubt thinking it was foolhardy for a senator's son to be undertaking such a dangerous mission. Not the most encouraging words to embark with. Stewart had already given his promise to Hank Reed, and he was not a man to back out on his word.

It was already nearing dusk when Stewart set off with Rudolf Lessing, armed only with his rudimentary knowledge of German, his impromptu documents, his pluck, and Lessing's sworn oath that Captain Stewart would be returned unharmed to regimental headquarters no later than noon the following day.

Stewart and Lessing walked a short distance to retrieve the forester's motorcycle and rode tandem up the road. By then it was dark, and to avoid drawing attention, they illuminated their path with only a pinpoint light. Soon they heard an airplane rumbling overhead. Lessing cut the motor and turned off the light.

"Don't worry, that's one of ours, Bed Check Charlie," Stewart said. "You can pay him no mind."

"That won't stop him from shooting," Lessing said.

Stewart chuckled. That was true indeed.

In the forester's stable, Tom Stewart got his first look at the Lipizzaner stallion he would be riding. He had a well-formed head with a concave profile and a proud gleam in his soft, dark eyes. Stewart approached quietly, placing his hand gently on the animal's shoulder while murmuring a greeting. The stallion turned his head and gazed quizzically at the stranger. Lessing explained that this horse was born at the royal Yugoslavian stud farm and once was King Peter's favorite mount.

The groom had long since headed back to Hostau on foot. Lessing watched as Stewart checked the bridle and then tightened the girth. Stewart gathered the reins in one hand, put his left hand on the horse's powerful crest, and, standing on the horse's left side, put a foot in the stirrup, preparing to swing up into the saddle, each step in the correct manner of a practiced horseman. But once Stewart put his weight in the stirrup, the stallion became antsy, jigging in place. If the horse bolted when he was only half-mounted, Stewart was in danger of getting entangled and dragged. Lessing said nothing but watched with concern. The horse always tested new riders, and the German wondered if this cowboy was up to the task. To Lessing's relief, Stewart decided to forgo using the stirrup; he grabbed a handful of the stallion's mane and vaulted neatly onto the horse's back. Once settled in the saddle, he leaned over to give the stallion a pat on the neck, grinned at Lessing and winked, and the two set off.

Lessing was in a hurry. It was already dark, and the pair had more than fifteen kilometers to cover. Rudofsky would be wondering where he was, and already the clock was ticking on Stewart's deadline to return to the Americans.

The trail was narrow and threaded through mountainous forests. During daylight, it had not seemed menacing, but now it was difficult to see what lay before them. A ribbon of moonlight snaking through the trees helped illuminate their path, but the way was still shadowy and rife with potential traps. The Bohemian Forest had been a wild area for centuries, populated only by hearty dwellers who made their living from glassblowing, lace-making, and forestry. There was always the possibility of wild lynx lurking in the dark shadows. And more frightening than predatory animals, men with guns might be peering at them from hideouts among the trees. But for now, they heard nothing but the rustling of pine needles and the horses' hoofbeats.

Before they had gone far, Stewart's horse tripped on a hidden log, head and neck plunging as he struggled to maintain equilibrium. Lessing watched in horror as Stewart lost his balance at the sudden movement and toppled onto the ground. If the American or his horse had been injured, it would likely mean the end of their mission. But to his relief, Tom Stewart grinned, shrugged, and clambered right back onto the stately Lipizzaner's back, none the worse for wear. Soon they were on their way again. Stewart appeared relaxed in the saddle and held the reins in one hand, western-style. Lessing still watched him warily, wondering if the American was adept enough to handle this nighttime ride on such a high-strung animal.

Eventually, they reached a barricade of brush across the road. On one side was a steep hill of rock; on the other side, a drop-off. Stewart asked if the barrier was mined, and when Lessing said no, Stewart walked his horse right up to it, looked it over, and then circled back around. Suddenly, he whizzed past Lessing at a brisk canter, heading straight for the barrier, up and forward in his stirrups in a well-trained jumping position.

"That horse doesn't jump," Lessing called out. But Stewart was already airborne, maintaining his erect and balanced forward seat. Rudolf shrugged, then proceeded to dismount and lead Indigo around the barrier on a narrow path that Stewart hadn't noticed.

"So that's how you were supposed to do it," Stewart said, evidently much amused.

The rest of the ride proceeded uneventfully. By the time they reached Hostau, it was two o'clock in the morning. The small town's streets were eerily silent. Lessing took Stewart straight to his own apartment, but when he arrived, he found the farm's other veterinarian, Wolfgang Kroll, on vigil outside his door, a machine gun slung across his lap.

Tom Stewart, staring at the gun-toting soldier, could not have been more isolated at that moment—more than ten miles deep into Czechoslovakia, he may well have been farther east than any free American soldier that night. But Stewart was even more alone than he knew. What Reed had not shared with the young captain before sending him off on this nighttime journey was the substance of the message he had received from Patton on the jeep's radio just as Stewart and Lessing were arriving to speak to him. Reed did not share the whole of what Patton had said with anyone—he kept that burden to himself. The general had told Reed to go ahead, but had added that if Reed acted on this decision to risk the lives of men to rescue horses, he was on his own.

Should the mission fail—if his men were lost, captured, or killed—Reed should say that the confused cavalrymen got lost behind enemy lines. Reed should know for certain that if the mission went awry, Patton would take no public responsibility for the decision.

Now Tom Stewart, alone and miles behind enemy lines, was listening to the rapid-fire discussion between the two German veterinarians with increasing alarm. During Lessing's brief absence, much had changed—and an edict had been issued. Bringing an American to the farm would be regarded as an act of treason.

CHANGE OF HEART

No Americans! Lessing quickly heeded Wolfgang Kroll's whispered warning: He pushed Stewart through the door of his apartment, alerting his wife in hushed tones to keep the American captain well hidden. Lessing's wife did not ask questions but immediately filled her husband in on what had transpired in his absence, whispering so as not to wake their sleeping girls. Then she quickly busied herself making hot coffee for the bone-chilled and saddle-weary Stewart while Lessing headed back to the barn to put up the horses.

Kroll accompanied Lessing, relating further details. Colonel Rudofsky had been in favor of this secret negotiation with the Americans, but in Lessing's absence, militia leader General Schulze had come into town in a big Mercedes, accompanied by his Volkssturm troops—a ragtag band of citizen soldiers consisting mostly of teenage boys. Schulze planned to set up a last-ditch German defense using Hostau as his base, and he was now the ranking officer.

Lessing wondered how to interpret Kroll's news. His fellow veterinarian was not formally a part of the Hostau staff. He had arrived just six weeks earlier, accompanying the White Russian refugees; he had a dramatic air and a reputation for telling tall tales—of his exploits fighting with partisans in Yugoslavia and training camels in the desert in North Africa. But this time, Lessing could see that he was deadly serious. In a few short hours, the situation had deteriorated from fragile to downright precarious.

As soon as Lessing had settled the horses, he rushed off to the big house to find Rudofsky. Although it was the middle of the night, the stud farm director was waiting for him. Rudofsky confirmed that General Schulze was now the highest-ranking officer at Hostau and was dead set against surrender.

Lessing looked at his commandant in disbelief. Unspoken between the two men was the obvious fact that any attempt at defense against either the Russians or the Americans would end in a brutal defeat and would put the horses directly in the line of fire.

"My hands are tied," Rudofsky said. "If I try to negotiate with the Americans, or let on that one of them is here, then all three of us risk being shot for treason."

In the past twelve hours, Lessing had ridden more than thirty miles, been held at gunpoint by the Americans, escorted an American captain through woods studded with pockets of SS snipers, and now here he stood at a complete impasse. Weary but not daunted, he tried to keep his head.

As the two men talked urgently, neither could know exactly how close they were to the end. On Hitler's birthday just a week earlier, the entire town had come out in the pouring rain to "celebrate," lining the streets to watch the Lipizzaner in their fine harnesses on parade. On that day, in his speech to the party faithful, Hitler's Reich minister of propaganda, Joseph Goebbels, had made a clear case for how Germans were supposed to face impending defeat: "Our misfortune has made us mature, but not robbed us of our character. Germany is still the land of loyalty. It will celebrate its greatest triumphs in the midst of danger. Never will history record that in these days a people deserted its führer or a führer deserted his people. And that is victory."

But Goebbels was dead wrong. The führer would indeed desert his people. Lessing and Stewart arrived at Hostau on April 28. In just two days, Hitler would commit suicide in his bunker, leaving the body of his terrible empire gasping for its final breaths. Even now, communication from Berlin was uncoordinated and sporadic, and panicky regional authorities were unsure where to turn. Everyone was improvising.

A mere twenty-four hours before, Rudofsky and Lessing had a viable plan—surrender was necessary to defend the horses. But if the Americans had to fight their way in, the horses' safety could not be guaranteed. If they waited and did nothing, the Russians would arrive in a matter of days anyway. Exhausted and frustrated, Lessing returned to his apartment, filling Stewart in on the near-hopeless situation as the two shared a late-night meal.

MOONLIGHT GLEAMED OVER THE STABLES; the coats of the white Lipizzaner glowed softly in the light. Somewhere in the barn, the broodmare Madera dozed, her rest interrupted by the wobbly newborn foal nudging her belly, looking for milk. Witez was watchful, pacing in his stall, exquisitely sensitive to any tension in the air. Indigo munched on his hay, tired from his long romp through the woods. The stables were peaceful, the nighttime hush of swishing tails and hooves on straw no different than any other night, but the war was about to overrun Hostau. This peace would soon be violently shattered.

When Lessing left the American headquarters with the congenial American riding alongside, the triplicate notes in his breast pocket had promised protection, but now he pondered—protection from whom, from what? The moment he had set off toward the unknown on horseback, a fundamental certainty had shifted. Who were his allies now? he wondered. The answer, he realized, was anyone who wanted to help the horses. The only things that stood between these animals and their annihilation were the choices he was about to make.

Lessing didn't sleep at all that night. At the cock's first crow, he went to speak to the new ranking officer at Hostau: General Schulze. But when he entered Schulze's presence, he did not have a chance to open his mouth before the red-faced commander started screaming at him. "How is it that you are negotiating with Americans?"

Lessing felt a dread chill creep through him as he realized that the general had somehow gotten wind of his trip across the border.

"How dare you deceive the Germans?" Schulze continued. "What right had you to do that?"

Lessing said nothing.

"I'm going to have you shot! You must be crazy!"

Lessing could see from the furious officer's face that he was not going to consider a compromise no matter how many lives were destroyed in the process.

General Schulze was not alone in his fanatical fight-to-the-death plans. Residents of Hostau could already hear the drone of the American trucks starting to patrol near the Bohemian border, and the rumors they exchanged had placed the Russians not over a day or two's trek away. The idea of fighting on when defeat was inevitable seems, looking back, to be illogically self-destructive, but General Schulze's attitude was not unusual. According to historian Ian Kershaw, "Whatever their varying attitudes towards Hitler and National Socialism, from fanatical commitment to little more than contempt—no general, and the same applied to the vast majority of the rank and file in their command, wanted to see Germany defeated, least of all, to be subjugated by the Bolsheviks."

Lessing felt his horror at the general's suicidal stance turn first into anger, then into resolve. The veterinarian was only twenty-eight, and he had a lot more experience dealing with supposedly dumb beasts than with certifiably crazy, angry generals, but Lessing decided that even in the face of a death threat, it was time to speak his mind. He was all too aware that a clock was ticking up at American headquarters, and if Stewart didn't reappear on schedule, American guns would be pointing straight at the stables.

"Sir, discipline, obedience—all that is orderly and honorable. However, at Hostau, we are, first and foremost, here to maintain the horses. And it is thus our first duty to do everything in our powers to save them. We don't care about who wins the war on April twenty-seventh or twenty-eighth, because we should have won years ago. Now it is too late."

Lessing waited, expecting the general to explode again. But to his surprise, Schulze responded in a calmer voice—he had decided to pass the buck. He couldn't make a decision on this matter with the Americans. Lessing would have to go find his superior officer, the brigade commander, to ask for permission. With that, the general dismissed him with a wave of his hand.

Lessing glanced anxiously at the clock and explained to the general that there was no time. Colonel Reed had made it clear: If the American had not been returned unharmed by noon on April 27, they would take "repressive measures" against Hostau.

"I will not let the American leave again. He stays!" the general said. "He's my POW."

As the morning haze cleared, the rising sun crept across the small village, illuminating the spire of St. James Church, then casting its golden rays across the long white rows of stables where the horses were munching contentedly on their morning's ration of oats. The rays illuminated flecks of gold and silver in their coats as it passed over each one. Though the scene was still tranquil, it was clear to Lessing that something had to be done—and fast.

LESSING TAKES CHARGE

At first light, Stewart, Lessing, and Kroll set off on horseback to locate someone in the local Nazi bureaucracy who could communicate with the brigade commander. Approaching the Nazis with an American in tow, pleading for permission to surrender the horses—it was impossible to imagine what kind of reaction they would receive. But each knew all too well that Nazi justice was often simply delivered by bullet.

As they rode through the stud farm's broad front gates, the village of Hostau appeared deceptively serene. The cobblestoned streets were lined with small whitewashed houses surrounded by carefully tended gardens. Evergreen forests the color of thunderclouds rose up the crest of distant hills in waves. The horses' hooves clattered against the rounded, uneven stones. As the men rode along, they agreed on an emergency hand signal: If any one of them gave the sign, each would bolt for the hills at a fast gallop and try to make it to the forest's edge.

Soon, they arrived at a company command post located in a small house. Two soldiers guarded the door. Lessing approached on horseback, but his two companions stayed back, keeping the American hidden from view. Several uniformed men emerged from the house. Kroll looked startled and frantically flashed the emergency sign. Stewart's heart skipped a beat, but he stayed put, watching as Lessing dismounted.

Even from a distance, Stewart could see the tension in the encounter. He glanced back at Kroll, who continued to flash the signal. But Stewart did not move. Taking off at a gallop would blow their cover, and Lessing, now dismounted, would be stranded, unable to join in their escape. And if the Nazis spotted Stewart's American uniform as he fled, Lessing would be immediately branded as a spy—most likely summarily executed before Kroll and Stewart had made it out of earshot.

So rather than turning to flee, Stewart rode directly up to the assembled group in front of the house. A large man walked up and grasped the bridle of Stewart's mount. It was the local *Gauleiter,* the ruling Nazi Party official, grinning, in Stewart's words, "like the cat had gotten into the cream." Squaring his shoulders and raising his chin, Stewart vaulted gracefully off the grand Lipizzaner stallion, and without even glancing at the Nazi boss, he tossed the reins at him as if the *Gauleiter* were a mere groom. After a tense pause, Lessing resumed speaking in a quiet but insistent voice, explaining that the men were seeking an audience with the brigade commander and needed permission to go to his headquarters. Stewart looked on, feet spread wide and arms folded. The *Gauleiter* hesitated, then grunted his assent. He told Lessing that the brigade commander was *Generalmajor* Weissenberger, and that his headquarters were located in the town of Klattau, about twenty-five miles to the southeast.

Glancing at their watches, Stewart and Lessing realized their predicament. They had no chance to go all the way to Klattau and back and make Stewart's noon deadline. To solve this problem, Kroll offered to leave immediately on Indigo to let the Americans know that Stewart would be delayed, promising that after transmitting the message, he would ride the horse back to the forester's house to wait for Lessing's return. Lessing and Stewart then galloped back to the stud farm, where they swapped the horses for Lessing's motorcycle. Stewart, hastily disguised in a German raincoat and field cap, climbed into the motorcycle's sidecar, and the pair zoomed off to *Generalmajor* Weisenberger's headquarters in Klattau, where they were ushered inside.

Seated at a bare table was a small man in a Wehrmacht uniform. Flanking him, two pairs of well-dressed German officers wore formal expressions that masked their emotions. Any one of these officers might be a fanatic Nazi who could denounce Lessing as a collaborator and seize Stewart as a prisoner of war.

Stewart looked straight into the eyes of the *Generalmajor*. The moment to make his case had arrived.

As Stewart spoke, Lessing translated. He offered greetings from General Patton and Colonel Reed before fishing in his pocket for the now crumpled letter of introduction, which he smoothed out on the table with a confident flourish. "The Americans wish to assist you in evacuating the horses safely back across the border to Bavaria," he said.

A long pause followed as Weissenberger scrutinized the note. After his perusal was completed, the assembled officers began to speak to one another in rapid-fire German that Stewart could hardly follow, but he had a sinking feeling that the "slant of the wind," as he later phrased it, was not in their favor. The men appeared angry and agitated and couldn't seem to come to an agreement.

Lessing listened with increasing dismay as the officers argued. Speaking up for the first time, he explained that General Schulze had approved a plan and that the American captain had to be returned behind their lines no later than noon. All they needed was permission.

After a few long, tense moments, the *Generalmajor* gestured for Stewart to be seated.

"The Americans' goal is to safeguard the horses and to preserve human life," Stewart said.

Rather than reply, Weissenberger turned to Lessing in fury. "You never should have acted independently to cross enemy lines. The war is not even over! What you did is very risky!"

Lessing's face revealed nothing, but his blood was boiling. Even with the Americans massed on the border and the Russians rapidly beating a path to their door, these men could not face the truth. But they weren't betting on this young man's determination. Lessing thought of his wife, who had hidden the American officer in their apartment the previous night, even though she was well aware of the risks. He thought of his daughter, Karen, who bore no blame for being born into this topsy-turvy world. He saw the square shoulders of the American soldier sitting in front of him who had traveled thousands of miles to try to help extricate them from this horrible mess that was not of his own making. Then Lessing turned his mind to the horses. He could imagine each of them: the eagle eyes of the Arabian Witez; the soft maternal gaze of the white broodmare Madera, turning her head to watch her young foal venturing a few steps farther into the pasture;

the lively expression of King Peter's stallion; and the forbearance of his own black Thoroughbred, Indigo, once a glamorous racehorse, who now served so faithfully.

Lessing was not going to let down the people who relied on him or give up on his precious horses without a fight. Perhaps sensing something of the veterinarian's strength, the *Generalmajor* stood up to face him. When Lessing spoke, his words were disdainful and direct. "Oh, really? The war is not over? 'Berlin stays German. Vienna will be German again.' This is what we hear on the radio, but do you really believe this?"

The words tumbled out of him. If his superiors didn't like what they were hearing, they could have him arrested and thrown into a prison camp or, even worse, end his life with a swiftly administered bullet to the head. Lessing knew this, but he kept talking. "I fell for beautiful phrases like that for fourteen years. I have had enough. What we are doing here is madness. Should we push this mania even further so that we can destroy even those things in the end which were able to stay in one piece through all of this?"

A taut silence hung in the air until Weissenberger made an apathetic gesture and fell back into his chair. "Okay, fine. Do whatever you want."

Lessing insisted that Weissenberger write a letter stating his agreement. The *Generalmajor* stood, flanked by two of his henchmen, and exited the room.

A moment later, two of the colonels returned. One hastily scribbled a note, then shoved it across the table to Lessing:

Herr General Schulze,

I have taken it as my duty to allow the veterinary officer and the American captain to cross over enemy lines. However, the negotiation of Hostau stud farm cannot be determined by me and will thus require these men to return to Hostau.

APRIL 27, 13:40

Before the men could change their minds, Lessing folded the paper and tucked it in his pocket, and he and Stewart hurried outside. Back on the motorcycle, the men roared to the stud farm to transmit the message to Rudofsky.

Once at Hostau, Lessing showed Rudofsky the note, and then, with no time to make the cross-country ride to the Americans on horseback, Lessing and Stewart climbed on the motorcycle and sped back toward the forester's lodge. From there, Lessing would meet Kroll, and Stewart would continue alone back across American lines.

It was already late afternoon when they reached the forester's lodge. At first, the house appeared deserted until, with an explosion of snapping branches, five men leaped out from behind the house, surrounding them. Stewart and Lessing froze until Lessing recognized them—it was a local Nazi and several of his thuggish cronies. Someone had tipped them off that Stewart and Lessing were coming this way.

Stewart stood his ground as if daring them to come a step closer. Lessing, too, was past the point of fear.

"I have a letter from the general!" Lessing said. "Move aside and let the American pass!" The sight of the general's missive appeared to cow the men; they soon slunk back into the woods. From here, the two parted company. Stewart continued on foot, and Lessing, finding Indigo alone in the stable, waited for Kroll's return.

Stewart walked up the forest path until he spotted the welcome sight of an American sentry. He climbed aboard a waiting jeep and headed toward headquarters. When he arrived, he found Wolfgang Kroll playing cards with the American soldiers and entertaining them with tales of his crazy exploits. Reed was quite relieved to see the senator's son return in one piece.

When Stewart had not appeared by the promised noon deadline, Colonel Reed had started to set up a task force to rescue him. When Kroll arrived, they detained him while awaiting Stewart's safe return. With the captain now safely in their midst, Reed had radioed General Patton for permission to send the task force to capture the stud farm at Hostau. He had received Patton's terse reply: "Get them. Make it fast." Even though Patton's mighty Third Army was poised on the border of Czechoslovakia, ready to make its final push if called upon, it had no orders to advance yet. Task Force Stewart would be making its eastern foray alone. On April 28, 1945, General Patton confided to his diary, "Personally, I cannot see that there is very much more glory in this war." Clearly, Patton did not yet see the glory of what was about to unfold.

———

LESSING WAITED FOR KROLL for several hours at the forester's house, but at last he mounted Indigo and headed toward home. By the time he was nearing Hostau, the pink rays of dawn were illuminating the sky. As the trail he was riding along neared a large manor house, he caught sight of the baron of the manor, whose horses he sometimes cared for. The gentleman waved him down and, perhaps noticing that Lessing looked exhausted, offered him a bite to eat.

Lessing, who hadn't slept in over thirty hours, had not been aware of his own fatigue until he heard the kindly offer. Suddenly, he felt like he was going to fall off his horse. He decided to stop for a moment, and he was grateful for the bowl of hot soup that was placed before him. But before Lessing had a chance to finish the meal, the phone rang. The baron quickly relayed the news. American forces were rolling toward the village; right now they were just a few miles outside of Hostau.

Forgetting his fatigue and hunger, Lessing jumped back onto Indigo. He still had a mile and a half to cover between the baron's villa and Hostau. If he did not arrive in time with the message that the Americans were on their way, General Schulze might start firing on them, and the Americans would enter Hostau with guns ablaze. Lessing urged Indigo into a gallop and headed back down toward the village as fast as his horse would carry him.

20.

THE TANKS ARE COMING

The morning after his safe return, Stewart was mounted up again—this time in a jeep, in command of a hastily assembled task force of about seventy men from the 42nd Squadron of the 2nd Cavalry. Accompanied by two tanks and two assault guns, they were headed over the border into Czechoslovakia, though only the officers knew their precise mission. The rest of the soldiers had been told only that their objective was to take control of a specific location—nothing about the horses hidden there. During their negotiations, the Germans had promised Stewart that their troops would not defend the stud farm but had not guaranteed them safe passage. The Americans would have to fight off any resistance encountered on the way there. As Stewart ventured across the border into Czechoslovakia, he and his men were on high alert.

The cavalrymen of the 2nd had no way to predict the strength of the German forces in this unconquered area that lay to the east. For weeks, they had been hearing about the "last redoubt," where the Germans were rumored to be gathered in strength to dig in and fight to the end. For over a week, the entire Third Army had been champing at the bit, prepared to advance into Czechoslovakia and crush whatever was left of the opposition, if given the order. But for now, that mighty army remained behind them. On April 28, as the small task force headed out, they were supremely aware that they were operating be-hind enemy lines with little reinforcement. Unknown to Stewart and his men, the German Seventh Army, quartered in nearby Klattau, near Pilsen—about sixty miles to the east of the American location—was so low on fuel that they were mostly immobilized, unable to move their armor en masse. Instead, they were concentrating their energy on putting up mined roadblocks, increasing the danger that the Ameri-cans could be hit by lethal sniper fire.

REED HAD DIVIDED THE TASK FORCE into three parts. The men of Troop A, commanded by Stewart, would approach Hostau from the north, crossing through the town of Weissensulz. Meanwhile, Troop F had set off due east toward Hostau, following the more direct route that Stewart had ridden on horseback. A third group—the men of Troop C—were also in the vicinity, under orders to look for a large group of POWs reported to be in the area.

Stewart's convoy of tanks, armored cars, assault guns, and jeeps proceeded slowly, on constant lookout for resistance. Small bands of roving Germans were scattered throughout the area. Some were fight-to-the-death SS snipers. But many were defectors looking to steal gas and provisions so they could flee to Germany in advance of the Rus-sians. One thing was certain: Anyone Stewart's men came across out here would not be a friendly face.

Shortly after they crossed the border into Czechoslovakia, they faced a brief flurry of gunfire. Returning fire with their machine guns, they quickly subdued the inferior force. Stewart had a funny feeling that the same officers who had given their word to him the day before were now shooting at him; he was not surprised when he found Colo-nel Trost, the man who had signed his letter of safe passage just a day before, among the wounded. The opposition quelled, Stewart and his men continued slowly toward Hostau.

IN THE MEANTIME, AT HOSTAU, Hubert Rudofsky could hear the American tanks approaching. From time to time, a sparse scattering of gunfire echoed in the distance. People on the farm were milling around anxiously—some grenades had exploded in the pastures, spooking the horses though doing no damage. General Schulze, whose arrival the previous day had thrown the farm into turmoil, seemed to have little control over his ill-assorted troops: nervous-looking boys too young to be in uniform who scurried around with no apparent purpose. Rudofsky, afraid of the pandemonium that would take hold at any sign of approaching American troops, stood watch in front of the stables. He scanned the horizon, hoping that Lessing would return soon.

It was then that Rudofsky saw General Schulze, clearly agitated, hurrying toward his large Mercedes. Behind him trailed anxious-looking lackeys loaded down with suitcases. Rudofsky watched with relief as Schulze climbed into his chauffeur-driven car while his servants piled the luggage into the trunk. A moment later, the Mercedes careened out the farm's front gates. Soon after, the general's ragged militia with their horse-drawn artillery started filing out of town. The teenage Volkssturm fighters looked giddy, relieved that they would not have to fight. Just then, Rudofsky saw Lessing and Indigo tearing over the crest of the hill. Arriving at the stud farm a moment later, the veterinarian recounted breathlessly that American tanks were just a few miles away. By then, the general was already gone, leaving nothing but a plume of dust behind him.

Rudofsky's thoughts strayed to his family in Bischofteinitz, eight miles to the east and still firmly under Nazi control. In the past few days, the Hitler Youth and Volkssturm militia had started throwing up roadblocks all around the town, preparing to mount a final defense. One of the barriers was on the bridge directly across from his brother's house—from its windows, the family could see militia members hiding behind the castle walls and between tombstones in the cemetery. Just last week, Rudofsky had seen his nephew camped behind a bunker with a gun in hand. Ulli, a slight towheaded boy with a bright face, was by now a few days shy of ten. Rudofsky had taken the gun from his nephew's hands and told him, "This is no business for you." He hoped that the boy had the sense to keep himself out of trouble.

Honor-bound to remain with the horses, Rudofsky pushed his personal concerns out of his mind as he waited for the Americans to arrive. He knew nothing of the approaching enemy except what he'd heard over clandestine radio broadcasts. These unknown men would soon hold the horses' destiny in their hands—and Rudofsky had no way of knowing what they would choose to do with them. The weight of his responsibility hung heavily upon him. Hubert Rudofsky, Austrian by birth, would go down in history as the man who gave away the emperor's horses. He had chosen to put their safety first. Only time would tell if he had made the right decision.

Down in the stables, the horses could almost certainly hear the distant rumble of approaching tanks, but they would have had no way of knowing that today would mark yet another turning point in their lives. Madera, Witez, Favory Slavonia, the Lipizzaner stallion from Croatia—every horse living at Hostau had come from somewhere else. The atmosphere in the stable was restless; the horses could sense tension and fear in the air.

Hastily, Rudofsky pulled down the portrait of Hitler and hid anything with a Nazi insignia. Together, he and Lessing hung white bedsheets out the windows. Grasping another white sheet between them, they strode out the farm's front gates and started up the road that swung through the center of town, heading to meet their conquerors.

THE MEN OF F TROOP were retracing Stewart and Lessing's path through the woods, the most direct route to Hostau. In command of one platoon was one of Reed's most reliable men, Captain William Donald "Quin" Quinlivan, a career soldier in the old horse cavalry who had enlisted at seventeen after running away from home and lying about his age. A strong leader, he was eventually promoted into the officer corps. As the streaks of dawn barely illuminated a heavy gray sky, Quinlivan headed out toward Hostau, knowing full well that the woods would give sharpshooters ample places to hide. Stewart and Lessing had passed through the woods unscathed, but on horseback, they had been able to travel quietly. The captain's noisy motorized procession made his men easy targets. Quinlivan had a soft core and a tough demeanor—he adored all animals, but he knew how to ride herd on his men. Before they had set off, Quinlivan had overheard some grumbling about their mission; everyone knew the war was almost over and nobody wanted to get himself killed now, with an end finally in sight.

Quinlivan also had his own concerns, but he kept them to himself. As they rattled along under the low morning sky, he was thinking about his family back home. He had grown up in a devout Catholic

family in the rough-and-tumble Mississippi River town of East
Dubuque, Illinois, otherwise known as "Sin City." His mother, Ma-
donna, already had one gold star hanging in her window. Her oldest
son, Quinlivan's big brother Bert, had been killed in a training mission
over Nova Scotia in 1940. Quinlivan didn't want his mother *ever* to receive another telegram from the War Department. He hated to think
how she would feel if she found out she'd lost him over some damn
fool mission to rescue a bunch of horses.

As their vehicles rumbled through the forest, Lieutenant Quinlivan
stayed on high alert, snapping to attention at the slightest movement or
sound. He peered through the trees that lined the road, aware how easy
it would be for enemy soldiers to hide in the dense foliage. But the forest around them remained dark and still. Soon, they were blinking in
bright sunlight as they emerged from the woods. They passed through
several small villages, their whitewashed facades brightened by flowers
blooming in window boxes. Not a soul was on the streets. After traveling a few miles, the troop crested a hill. Spread out below them was
the village of Hostau. Quinlivan could see its most visible feature, the
Church of St. James, its onion-shaped spire pointing up toward the heav-
ens. Adjacent to the village was the horse farm with its rows of white
stables and neatly fenced pastures. Groups of white horses were scattered
across the fields, some with coal-black foals at their side. At the sound of
the approaching troops, they spun and tore off at a gallop, seeming to
float upon the wind. Quinlivan sucked in his breath with appreciation.
Cautiously, if not quietly, F Troop proceeded down the hill.

WHILE QUINLIVAN'S MEN WERE arriving in Hostau, Stewart and Troop
A were still en route. After an initial burst of resistance, the task force
had proceeded unhindered. But now they sat at a village crossroads,
poring over their maps. This village was not Weissensulz, the one they
were expecting from their maps. Forced to double back after an apparent wrong turn, Stewart's A Troop would not make it to Hostau for
several more hours.

QUINLIVAN AND F TROOP were already rolling up to the edge of town.
It was here that they came upon two Germans in full dress uniform: a

tall man with round spectacles and a proud, guarded face—Hubert Rudofsky—and a slim veterinary officer—Rudolf Lessing. Between them, they held a white bedsheet.

A moment later, the Americans drove through the gates that led into the horse farm. Hubert Rudofsky gave the order: The German flag came down. The Stars and Stripes shimmied up the flagpole and began to flutter in the wind. Hubert Rudofsky and Rudolf Lessing surrendered their hand-wrought ceremonial swords.

Hitler's secret super stud farm was under American rule.

THE FALLEN

Only twenty-four hours after Tom Stewart had spent the night huddled in a chair in Lessing's apartment, he became the new commanding officer of the village of Hostau. Horses gazed serenely at the men in green fatigues and combat boots as the soldiers moved quickly around the farm's perimeters, establishing checkpoints, inspecting for enemy elements, and creating drops to collect weapons. Most of the grooms at Hostau were prisoners of war—Russians, Poles, and Yugoslavs as well as a smattering of other Allies. With the coming of the Americans, they would soon be sent back to their ranks.

Stewart had orders from Reed to secure the perimeters around the farm's three outlying locations. He headed out in his jeep, bringing Lessing along. The two rattled over the roads between Hostau and Zwirschen, an outlying village a few kilometers away where the stud farm had additional pastures and stables. The countryside was quiet, but from time to time, small children approached calling out requests for chocolate, closely followed by their worried mothers, scolding the children to stay away.

When Stewart and Lessing arrived at the stables in Zwirschen, they found a state of near insurrection. A Russian groom stood waiting near the road. The man was six feet five, built like a brick, and wore a menacing expression. Stewart quickly sized up the situation. The Russian and the other prisoners of war who had been conscripted to take care of the horses had rebelled, certain that German defeat was imminent. Now the pair from Hostau confronted a chaotic situation: Each Russian groom had several stolen wristwatches on his arms, and the local people cowered in fear of the newly freed prisoners.

Just beyond in the pastures, horses grazed peacefully, each worth a fortune on the open market. These Russians, already emboldened enough to pilfer watches, would no doubt be quick to steal the much more valuable horses—if they didn't sell them first for the value of their meat, or to passing refugees heading west who would happily hand over jewels and other heirlooms for a horse to pull their wagon.

The hulking Russian who had assumed the role of leader of the group started toward Stewart, his face contorted into a threatening frown. If the groom understood that he and the American were allies, it was not evident from his expression.

Stewart knew that he needed to get the upper hand immediately. He gestured to Lessing to hang back. Although Lessing was tall, the big man looked as if he could knock both of them over in a single blow.

"Give back the watches," Stewart demanded, his voice showing no sign of fear.

The Russian stepped forward. Stewart held his ground. The air crackled with the electricity of direct confrontation.

"Give back the watches! Now!" Stewart commanded. Lessing hastily translated.

The Russian just sneered and shook his head, pulling himself up to his full height—he was half a head taller than Stewart and twice as broad, his arms muscled and his hands callused from the hard work of wielding a pitchfork on the farm.

Lessing waited almost without breathing. He expected Stewart to walk away and let the Russians keep their spoils. What difference would it make to the American? The Germans were the defeated enemy; why would an American step in to defend them?

Instead, Tom Stewart leaped at the Russian's neck; he was a blur of movement as he punched the hulk in the face with a full fist, then grabbed him, turned him around, and kicked him in the pants.

The giant toppled over into the dirt.

A moment later, the shocked Russians handed over all of the watches, which Stewart returned to the astonished onlookers. Soon, the Americans had set up regular patrols and sentries around the stables and pastures of Zwirschen, and order was restored.

LATE THAT SAME AFTERNOON, Hank Reed rode through the main street of Hostau in the passenger seat of his battered green jeep. Along the narrow thoroughfare, white flags fluttered from every window, and people called out and waved as he passed, creating a festive air. Jim O'Leary steered the vehicle through the main gates of Hostau and pulled up in front of the farm's stately headquarters. After 281 days of battle, Hank Reed had arrived back where he'd started—among horses. Stewart and Quinlivan greeted Reed and brought him to review the farm's military staff, now held as American prisoners of war.

Colonel Rudofsky stood at the head of the line. He studied the American commander's face, wondering what kind of man he was about to encounter. As the colonel approached, Rudofsky noted that Reed was a good deal shorter than he was but seemed taller some-how—he walked with American swagger, as if he had just stepped off a movie screen. Rudofsky was surprised that the man's manner was friendly yet respectful. He noted no hint of scorn in the colonel's de-meanor.

Reed walked down the line of conquered officers, offering a ciga-rette to each of the men to set them at ease. Only Rudofsky declined. Reed could not help but notice the high color on the German com-mander's cheeks and the sheen of sweat on his brow. He had already made the acquaintance of the two German veterinarians, but here be-fore him was the Czech-born head of the German stud farm. The man's extreme discomfort was hard to miss.

The first order of business was to tour the farms. Reed offered Ru-dofsky a seat in his jeep, hoisting himself into the back, where he bal-anced on some boxes. If he noticed the German's look of surprise to be offered a place up front, Reed graciously paid it no heed. O'Leary took them all the way around the perimeters of the stud farm and as far as the outlying pastures where Stewart had stemmed the insurrection earlier that day. Everything was in order. In the fields, white mares grazed peacefully, while their dark-coated foals cavorted at their sides.

The next order of business was a tour of the stables. Sperl translated as Rudofsky gave detailed information about the farm's operations.

RUDOFSKY AND REED SURVEY THE
CAPTURED HORSES IN HOSTAU.

Reed encouraged the enlisted men to come along and have a look. The colonel's enthusiasm for the horses was unmistakable, and it soon rubbed off on the rest of the group.

One young private, as he stood gazing at the mares, remarked, "These horses look pregnant, sir."

Colonel Reed turned to the young man with a chuckle and said, "Where do you come from, Private?"

The young Italian-American replied proudly, "The Bronx."

The colonel smiled. "Where I come from, we call it 'in foal.'"

When the tour of the grounds and pastures was finished, it was time for the presentation of Hostau's finest jewels, the stallions. When Witez was led from the stable, his shiny coat created a halo of light around him. He danced at the end of his lead shank, sinews snapping beneath his taut skin. His tapered ears flicked back and forth; his dark eyes seemed to contain infinite depths; and his hooves seemed almost to float above the ground. Reed drank in the sight of this flawless animal, from the arched crest of his neck, to the straight shafts of his cannon bones, to the high set of his silky tail. Witez's bright expression spoke to something deep inside this hard-bitten soldier.

Satisfied that the stud farm was secured, Reed left Stewart with a small task force made up of several platoons of soldiers, and instructions to Rudofsky, Lessing, and Kroll to continue operations as usual, now under Stewart's command. Reed then headed back to his headquarters.

THE NEXT DAY PASSED peacefully enough, but just after dawn on April 30, Stewart's radio crackled with ominous news. An early-morning American patrol that had come upon a manned German road-block that had been hastily assembled overnight, blocking their route of retreat back into Germany. Stewart quickly organized some of his men to head out to a small town called Rosendorf, near the edge of the forest.

Meanwhile, out in the field near Rosendorf, several miles from Hostau, the American patrol that had encountered the roadblock came under fire from the German soldiers sheltered behind it. Wiping them out with a swift barrage of machine-gun fire, the American soldiers set their sights on a small house close by. It appeared unoccupied but might harbor snipers inside. The sergeant in charge wanted to occupy the house—from that vantage point, the Americans could provide cover while the rest of the patrol maneuvered around the barricade—so he sent one of his men, Private Manz, to see if it was safe to enter.

Raymond Manz was still a few days shy of his twentieth birthday. A tall boy who wore size-thirteen shoes, he had been in the army since graduating from Detroit's Southeastern High School in July 1943. When he posed for his enlistment portrait, his face was round and boyish; his military cap looked too big for his head. Almost two years later, as he clutched his gun and prepared to advance, he had grown into himself: a broad-shouldered, athletic-looking young man with curly brown hair and a sweet, diffident smile. Manz had already fought his way across the hedgerows of France and through the Battle of the Bulge. As he prepared to follow orders, the young private had no way of knowing that today, April 30, 1945, would mark a fateful turning point in the war. By the end of this day, Hitler would take his own life. In forty-eight hours, the Germans would surrender Berlin to the Russians. Allied victory in Europe was one week away. Manz and all of the men of the 2nd Cavalry stood so close to the end of the fight that they could almost reach out and touch it.

But the young private was not thinking about that. Firing his gun, he advanced rapidly toward the house. Within seconds, return fire sprayed from the windows. Manz took a hit in the shoulder and stumbled a reeling half-step back but did not fall. Pressing forward again, he blasted the house with a barrage of gunfire, providing cover so the rest of the platoon could overrun the barrier. A second shot hit Manz in the head.

By the time his buddies were able to get to him, he was already dead. Raymond Manz would never turn twenty. He had died moving toward the enemy, falling dead without ever taking a step back.

Around the same time, back at Hostau, Tom Stewart got word from his forward patrols that the group of Germans who had fired on them on the way to the stud farm had reassembled into an organized force and were advancing on the farm itself. Stewart was guarding the horses with a skeleton crew and did not have a reliable estimate of how large the attacking force might be. Stewart and Quinlivan assembled their small group in an attempt to push the advancing Germans as far away from the horses as possible. To strengthen his numbers, Stewart drafted some of the released POWs, including a Palestinian and a Maori from New Zealand still wearing their POW garb, to join with the Americans. Together they succeeded in keeping the attackers safely beyond the pasture's perimeters. The battle raged for five hours, until the Germans retreated back into the woods and moments later came pouring out between the trees, carrying white flags. Stewart and Quinlivan had defeated the last bits of German resistance.

ON THE MORNING OF Monday, April 30, while Tom Stewart was fighting off the attackers, Hank Reed was in Schwarzenfeld, about eighty kilometers southwest of Hostau. Spring seemed distant as leaden skies dropped occasional snow flurries on the distinguished men assembled there. Colonel Reed and three other officers of the XII Corps, to which the 2nd Cavalry belonged, were being honored with the French Legion of Honor and the Croix de Guerre. The XII Corps command post was awash with important visitors. The day before, General Patton had visited XII Corps headquarters and told their commander, Lieutenant General Stafford LeRoy "Red" Irwin, that the war might be over in the next day or two. While no trace remains of the conversations between Red Irwin, Hank Reed, and General Patton regarding the horses at Hostau, all three knew that Stewart's task force had captured the depot full of valuable horses. They understood that holding the stud farm in Czechoslovakia was only the first step toward getting the horses to safety. Reed stood at attention, eyes forward, as the heavy French sword tapped his shoulder. He was eager to get this over with, impatient to return to his men and their captured prize.

By late afternoon of that day, Reed was back at Hostau, pleased with the work that Stewart had done in his absence. Just like everyone else in the Third Army, Reed had learned many bleak things about the human race over the past twelve months. He had heard about the atrocities that the army had uncovered when they liberated Dachau— the horrors of train cars filled with half-rotted bodies, and the scores of prisoners, as weak and emaciated as scarecrows. But somehow he had been spared seeing those particular evils firsthand and instead had been given the task of freeing such beautiful horses. It was an unlikely and astonishing stroke of grace.

The war had destroyed many things, but one of the worst casualties was the loss of hope for a peaceful world. Yet every man who saw these horses at Hostau ended up with a smile on his face and an image in his mind of a world less troubled than the one in which he currently dwelled. That day, Hank Reed knew that for all of the sadness and loss and pain he had seen, he would accomplish at least one positive thing: Lovely and unbloodied, these horses were going to gallop safely into the postwar world.

22.

THE AMERICANS

While Hank Reed's convoys headed toward Hostau to rescue the horses, two hundred kilometers away, in Austria, Alois Podhajsky listened to the distant sounds of gunfire, certain that the village of St. Martin would be captured within hours. The situation on the ground was volatile. All of his hard work to save the stallions might be lost as these final hours played out. Since communication with Hostau had broken down over the last few weeks, he had been concerned about the safety of the broodmares, but at the moment, he was so preoccupied with the white stallions that he had no time to worry about any of the others. Shortly after Podhajsky had received the final visit from General Weingart—who had since committed suicide—a missive labeled "Most Secret" had arrived: his final military order. He had been appointed commandant of the defense sector St. Martin. His job was to defend the village for Germany. Podhajsky vowed to himself that he would indeed *defend* St. Martin—by doing everything he could to aid a rapid surrender and to minimize violence and bloodshed. But he was aware that not everyone was in accordance with his aims. During the occupation, the local Nazi Party leaders had terrorized the villagers, and with Germany's impending defeat, the remaining Germans and Austrian collaborators would be left to the mercy of those they had mistreated. Fearful of the future, the collaborators had every reason to cling to their dying empire.

Night was falling, and the sounds of fighting, still distant and intermittent, had ceased for the time being. Podhajsky was walking across the grounds of the castle when the mayor of the town appeared, asking for orders to muster up the Volkssturm to fight the Americans. This was precisely what Podhajsky was determined to avoid at all costs. If anyone tried to defend the village, the Americans would come in shooting, and both the civilians and the horses would be imperiled. But as the designated head of the defense sector, Podhajsky could not let on that he had no intention of fighting back—if he showed his cards, he might soon be lying in a ditch with a bullet between his eyes, unable to do anything further to protect his precious stallions.

So Podhajsky had to make the local Nazis think he was playing along. Right now, the mayor stood before him, awaiting the colonel's orders. Podhajsky realized that he had to distract the militia, giving them something to do besides fighting back. Thinking quickly, he devised a scheme to divert the mayor's attention. The mayor would want to protect his own business—a local butcher shop—so the colonel told him to divide up the Volkssturm troops and station them in front of the town's local shops to prevent looting. The mayor, in eager agreement, hurried away to put Podhajsky's plan into motion. Soon after, when a militia first lieutenant presented for orders, Podhajsky directed him to a closed school near the far end of the village, hoping to keep his men far away from the Americans' approach.

Next, two Nazi Party officials appeared. Podhajsky was startled that the men—known bullies who were feared throughout the area—appeared pale and shaken. They had orders, they said, from the *Kreisleiter*—the regional Nazi authority and a known thug—to block all of the roads around the town. They wanted Podhajsky to order the troops to put up barricades. Podhajsky knew how dangerous that would be. The Americans were known to double their firepower if they met any resistance entering a town, and they would certainly do so in this case. If they unleashed their powerful tanks directly upon the barriers, the village would be severely damaged or destroyed, and civilians would be killed. Buying time, he told them to post guards at checkpoints but to leave the roads open.

"But I have orders to close them," one of them stammered. "The *Kreisleiter* himself is on his way to St. Martin for an inspection!"

"He said any insubordination would be severely punished," the other nervously added. The men appeared to be aware how difficult this would be, yet equally terrified not to follow their Nazi boss's orders.

Podhajsky tried to calm them down. "I've given you my orders. If any problems occur, I will speak to the *Kreisleiter* myself." The two local Nazi officials scurried away as Podhajsky thought, *Good riddance.* He remained on high alert, but for the moment, the roads remained open and a tense calm prevailed.

Alois Podhajsky had donned the uniform of the German Wehrmacht in 1938. Back then, he had been one of the top equestrian competitors in the world. When he assumed leadership of the Spanish Riding School of Vienna, he had pledged to use his prestige to safeguard his homeland's premier equestrian institution. Nearly seven years had passed, years of constant compromise—and yet the success of his mission was not ensured. In the next few hours or days, the ultimate measure of himself as a soldier and as a man would be decided. Would he succeed in saving the horses for Austria? How would history regard his many compromises? Through all of this, it was his stallions, Pluto and Africa and all of the others, that had served as his guidepost. Podhajsky unbuttoned his German uniform jacket and slipped out of his pants. In their place, he pulled on civilian clothing. Hastily bundling up the uniform, he hid it. An unnatural silence hung over the village. There was nothing to do but wait.

THE CALM DID NOT LAST. Half an hour later, Podhajsky's phone rang. It was one of the two local party officials, seeming even more agitated, begging him to come explain why the roads were not barricaded. The *Kreisleiter* would arrive at any moment. Podhajsky looked down at his clothing in panic. He had no time to change back into uniform. Instead, he pulled a military greatcoat over his clothes, hoping that no one would notice. Into his waistband, he tucked a pistol. Swallowing hard, he strode out into the night.

When Podhajsky entered their office, the local Nazi leaders, pale and anxious, greeted him in stony silence. The door banged open, and the *Kreisleiter* and two armed SS men burst into the room, breaking the silence with a cry of "Heil Hitler."

"Have the barriers been put up yet?" the *Kreisleiter* shouted.

Like a fish gaping for air, the senior official opened his mouth, but no words came out.

Podhajsky spoke instead, careful to keep his voice even. "No, the barriers have not been put up yet. Otherwise your car would not have been able to get in here."

"Why were my orders not carried out?" The *Kreisleiter*'s face was flushed with anger.

The room bristled with tension. The *Kreisleiter*, flanked by his two heavily armed henchmen, stared at Podhajsky. The colonel calmly met his gaze. Everyone else in the room shrank back, wondering what was going to happen next.

Podhajsky felt the cool stock of his pistol and decided he would not go down without a fight. His mind spun through the possibilities. He knew he was one hair trigger away from being shot and made an example of. If that happened, who would protect his horses? He steadied himself, imagining the faces of his beloved Pluto and Africa.

In the calmest voice he could summon, Podhajsky said, "When our troops brought the advance of the Americans to a halt, as indicated by the fact that the sounds of firing ceased, I did not consider that any useful purpose would be served by closing the streets, since this might hinder the freedom of movement of our own soldiers. But I have had the barriers manned by the Volkssturm, and made the necessary arrangements for them to be closed in the shortest possible time when I give the order."

The *Kreisleiter* said nothing but appeared to be thinking. Podhajsky waited, hoping that his bluff would work.

The SS officers rested their hands on their guns, ready to spring into action if their leader appeared dissatisfied. But the *Kreisleiter* seemed to accept Podhajsky's explanation. "Then everything is in good order," he said.

He spun on his heel and summoned his two SS lackeys, who shouted threats at the local leaders as they strode out the door and into the night. They boarded their shiny black car and, with Nazi flags fluttering, drove off to check on the next village, apparently satisfied that Colonel Podhajsky would defend this one to the death.

Free of the Nazis at last, Podhajsky hurried back to the stables to see that the horses were safe. As he got closer, his heart started beating faster, and he broke into a run. Shouts and jeers filled the air. An unruly crowd of men had surrounded the barn. Podhajsky fought through the crowd to see what the commotion was about. As he reached the doors, he realized that the men were looting cigarettes from a storeroom above the stables. Waving a pistol, Podhajsky forced the men back and then called in some of the Volkssturm soldiers to distribute the loot. He hoped this would draw the crowd away from the stables.

All night, German troops and individual soldiers passed through town on their way to other places, but by the morning, the village was quiet. Around lunchtime, one of his riders came racing in: The Americans were almost here.

At Podhajsky's signal, his riders shed their uniforms and donned civilian clothes. Verena took the cast-off uniforms and hid them in one of the castle's large drawing rooms. He instructed his riders to hand over their weapons, then quickly retreat to the stables and stay out of sight.

Podhajsky soon joined them, eager to keep watch over the horses. During the next few hours, a maelstrom swirled outside. American soldiers rounded up Germans in uniform while freed prisoners of war started to riot and loot. Podhajsky and his riders prepared to take action if necessary, but the ruckus stayed outside the closed stable doors. In their stalls, Africa, Pluto, and the other stallions raised their heads and flicked a quizzical ear whenever the shouting and hubbub echoed through the walls. By the end of the day, the American troops had restored order. All was calm again.

At long last, the bitter days of Nazi domination had ended. But safety still was not assured for the beleaguered horses. The Americans had taken over an area that was on the brink of chaos, teeming with refugees and POWs, displaced people who needed aid, and Nazis trying to escape detection. Among the multitude of problems, how was Podhajsky going to convince these Americans that the horses were important?

The next day, the roads into the village of St. Martin were clogged with rumbling American vehicles and important-looking soldiers bustling around. Word was circulating around the village—the American brigadier general William A. Collier of the XX Corps would be arriving soon to set up headquarters in the castle. Before long, a motorcade rolled into town, and the general disembarked with his entourage. Knowing that he needed the Americans' protection, Podhajsky hurried up to introduce himself. *The horses!* Podhajsky tried to explain, but the general wasn't listening. He rushed past, preoccupied with organizing housing for his staff's occupation. In a moment, he was out of sight.

THE GENERALS

Crushed by the general's reception, Podhajsky returned to the stables filled with a deep sense of dread. The animals were no longer in immediate physical danger, but they had been cast adrift—the school and its horses belonged to no one, yet their need for food and care had not diminished.

The decision to leave Vienna had been gut-wrenching, the moments when Podhajsky had put his stallions at risk some of the most terrifying of his life. Now the sheer horror of bombs raining down on his family and his charges was behind him. The riders acted grateful for Podhajsky's leadership; they kept to a grueling pace, trying to keep up with the demands of having so many horses to exercise, and they did so while separated from their own families and homes. Everyone seemed to believe that Podhajsky had done it—saved the Spanish Riding School.

Podhajsky knew that the truth was more complicated. The horses and riders had survived the war, but the institution that they embodied had never been more at risk. He had had no news of the fate of the mares at Hostau—isolated in St. Martin, he was not yet aware of the American colonel's capture of the stud farm—nor did he know whether the elegant riding hall on the Michaelerplatz had survived.

But his most immediate concern was whom to ask to procure more food and grain for the horses.

For months before the evacuation, Podhajsky had been careful to stockpile food, reducing the horses' rations slightly and requesting extra grain from the stores in Hostau. That surplus was nearly gone, and who could guarantee that the Americans would think it important to support the Spanish Riding School? This old institution might be seen as nothing more than a relic of a defeated order, as outdated as the Austro-Hungarian Empire itself.

As Podhajsky passed through the stables, greeting each of the horses by name and handing out lumps of sugar, he lingered at the stalls of Pluto and Africa. Pluto, the young stallion with so much potential, and Africa, with his unusually sensitive temperament. They were alive and they were healthy, but would they ever perform again? Would the world ever have an opportunity to see the brilliance that these two animals had to offer?

Outside the quiet stables, the Americans were rushing around in a fever pitch of preparations. Rumors were rife that even more important military dignitaries were going to arrive at the Arco Castle the following day. Later the same day, one of Podhajsky's riders came barreling up to him. "There is an American officer inquiring after you," the rider said, out of breath. "He wants to see you immediately. He saw you ride in the Olympics and he wants to meet you and see how you are doing!"

Podhajsky felt his heart leap just a little. Perhaps he would finally find a sympathetic ear for his cause?

Hurrying down to the stables, he found the American major who had asked for him by name, remembering his incredible ride at the Berlin Olympics. Just then, the same Brigadier General Collier who had brushed him off earlier arrived in the stables with the corps commander, General Walton Walker. The major immediately started to tell the generals that they were in the presence of an Olympic athlete— a celebrity in the equestrian world. Podhajsky observed them with cautious hope. So far, he and his men had tried to avoid attracting notice, lurking around the stables, unsure where they stood.

Walker and Collier listened attentively; then Walker spoke up with an idea. His boss was coming up for a look around the next day, and Walker thought he'd like to see Podhajsky's stallions. Everyone knew that George Patton had a strong interest in horses. Could Podhajsky possibly put on a show for the general? Tomorrow?

When Podhajsky heard the well-known name of General Patton, famed leader of the Third Army as well as a fellow former Olympian, he felt a brief moment of elation that was replaced swiftly by crushing doubt. Under normal circumstances, the riders prepared for their shows for months. The last days had been so tumultuous that the stallions had been forced to remain cooped up in their stalls. How could they possibly be ready for a show tomorrow? Still, Podhajsky knew that to protect the horses, he needed friends in high places. Without any further hesitation, he said yes to the general's suggestion.

Pleased with the outcome of their conversation, Podhajsky returned to the castle, where, just as he entered, he noticed that American soldiers were clearing out a large room to ready it for use as a mess hall.

Podhajsky's hair stood on end. Behind the furniture in the large room lurked his riders' hastily hidden Wehrmacht uniforms. If the Americans came upon the uniforms, they might take his riders for enemy soldiers and arrest them as POWs—then who would look after the horses? All would be lost. For a moment, he froze in a panic. What should he do?

Then he saw that his wife was already one step ahead of him. Verena had offered to help with the cleanup, and now, looking studiously calm, she walked out of the room with a laundry basket full of curtains and cushions balanced on her hip. With no more than a slight nod, she signaled to her husband that the cast-off uniforms were hidden in her basket.

That night, the first of the American occupation, Podhajsky barely slept. His bed was a child's cot that did not fit his long legs, but even worse, his mind was spinning with worries about the show that he had promised to put on.

Getting the attention of an American in the high command was his very best shot at securing help for the school, but how could he put together a worthy demonstration on such short notice? Whenever the white stallions performed, it always looked effortless, but that was their sleight of hand. Each performance was actually the culmination of the meticulous work of many highly specialized people, each one doing his job with the devotion of a monk.

The next morning, Podhajsky realized that General Walker was equally worried about the performance going off well. Having surveyed the stables, the courtyard, and the dismal condition of the riding hall with great dismay, he had engaged a veritable army of volunteers to help out. One group cleaned the courtyard and indoor riding hall; another cut up branches to hide the dilapidated walls of the hall's interior; a third helped to remove the saddles and riders' show uniforms from where Podhajsky had hidden them behind a hollowed-out wall.

Podhajsky knew that all of this was only window dressing. General Patton was coming to see the Lipizzaner perform, and for the horses and riders, this would be the command performance of their lives.

But how could they possibly be ready? They were missing a number of riders—the ones whom the army had pressed into military service. But even with the participation of those available, the show would demand so much of the horses. Like all highly trained athletes, the stallions could not be kept at peak training except during brief periods of time. But recently their life had been topsy-turvy and their training had been haphazard at best. The casual observer might not know the difference, but an experienced horseman could. And Patton would be watching the performance with the keen eye of an expert.

If Podhajsky had tried to contemplate everything that had happened to him in the last few weeks—his struggle for permission to leave Vienna, the terrifying flight with the horses on the trains, the long night finessing the local Nazis into not fighting back when the Americans arrived, the moment when he stepped out of the hated Wehrmacht uniform and shoved it behind the furniture, his intense relief that the war was finally over coupled with a knowledge that he and his horses were exiled from their home and might not ever be able to return—it would have completely overwhelmed his emotions. Instead, Podhajsky plunged into preparation for the show. He put Pluto and Africa through their paces, testing to see what each was willing to give. Pluto was flighty, as usual, but capable of brilliance, and Africa needed twice as much praise as the average horse, so hard did he try to please his master. Despite all the disruption and lack of proper training, Podhajsky found that his horses seemed to sense the urgency and responded by offering their best. He watched each of his riders and the horses in turn and was able to map out a program for the performance— one that took into consideration the small space, the reduced number of riders, and the degree of difficulty of the movements being asked of their mounts. He simply could not demand too much when the horses weren't ready.

It was a tremendous relief when Podhajsky learned that afternoon that Patton's visit had been delayed for a few days. Given a brief reprieve, Podhajsky and his riders sped into motion. They unpacked the loudspeakers used for piped-in music and, with the help of the soldiers, strung up electric lights that shone cheerfully inside the dreary riding hall. Podhajsky saw that General Walker was frequently at ringside, watching them train, and that he seemed to want to linger there. Evidently, the stallions had won their first fan.

Normally, the castle's large courtyard was packed with refugees hawking looted goods, but on the day Patton was set to arrive, it stood empty except for a single sentry posted at each entrance.

Finally, the military entourage arrived with a sweep of pomp and circumstance. First came the regimental colors of the 4th Armored Division and the XX Corps, flanked by military police. Directly behind the colors came Under Secretary of War Robert Patterson, with General Patton by his side. Patton strode in with the confident air of a conquering commander, raising his hand as he passed the row of riders

GENERAL PATTON, COLONEL PODHAJSKY, AND UNDER
SECRETARY OF WAR ROBERT PATTERSON TOUR
THE STABLES IN ST. MARTIN, AUSTRIA.

lined up to greet him. Then he and his coterie entered the riding hall and assumed their places on the raised dais that had been set up for them.

It was time for the performance to begin. Podhajsky gave his riders one final appraising glance. Each uniformed man sat astride a horse that he knew with an intimacy that rivaled any in the animal-human realm. Each rider had trained his stallion from the time he was a young horse. Each knew his mount's quirks and temperament, his strengths and weaknesses. Each pair communicated with a touch so deeply ingrained that it felt like intuition. These were love affairs, sure enough. These riders had devoted their entire lives to their horses and to the fine art of riding them. That was why they were here, still together. Now was their moment to prove what they were worth.

A million thoughts whirled through Podhajsky's mind. Not just: *Will they be good enough?* but also, deeper down: *Even if they're good enough, will anyone care?* Would these strangers, these foreigners, be able to fully recognize the animals' extraordinary gifts?

The art of classical riding was one of subtlety. While audiences were always impressed to see the leaps and jumps that were the airs above the ground, true horsemen knew that the real achievement of the Spanish Riding School was its exaltation of harmony, peace, and symmetry: the seemingly effortless display that, paradoxically, could be achieved only after years of training and selfless dedication on the part of horses and riders alike. Podhajsky put his faith in the fact that Patton was a horseman, but even more than that, he put his faith in his horses and in the spell they seemed to cast. Podhajsky thought of the final words of the doomed General Weingart: *The horses will work their magic with the Americans, just like they did with everyone else.*

Podhajsky had chosen Neapolitano Africa to lead the quadrille, the most important position on this most important of days.

The music started.

Gone were the ornate frescoes and crystal chandeliers of the Winter Riding Hall. Gone were the soaring ceilings with the huge paned windows several stories overhead, designed to direct the sunlight so there was never any glare. Gone was the portrait of Charles VI smiling over the unbroken tradition of excellence he had founded three centuries earlier.

Here, in the dressed-up dreariness of the small riding hall in St.

Martin, everything would be boiled down to its essence—riders and horses and the way they moved together.

General George Smith Patton sat on the viewing platform, watching this special performance that had been put together to entertain him. Patton and Patterson had flown up to St. Martin in a Piper Cub to visit the XX Corps. It was only upon arriving that they had learned of the presence of the white stallions and the Spanish Riding School. Patton would also learn that he and their Austrian director had something very important in common—Patton had competed in the modern pentathlon in the 1912 Olympic Games in Stockholm, and Podhajsky had competed in dressage in 1936. So much had changed for both of the men since then, but the love for horses had not diminished in either of them.

Two riders opened the show with a pas de deux, a choreographed pair performance. From his position near the gate through which the riders entered, Podhajsky could see that the sequence was proceeding flawlessly, but his gaze kept flitting back to General Patton in an effort to analyze his expression. The general appeared blasé, almost bored, as he watched. Podhajsky may not have known that this style of equestrianism was far removed from the kind of riding that Patton was used to. The American school favored the so-called forward method, where the horses moved in a more "natural" way, with head and neck extended. The training of the collected horse—which kept its hindquarters well beneath, its crest high, and the nose almost perpendicular to the ground, its gaits well controlled between the rider's hand, leg, and seat—was primarily a European art. For a foxhunter and polo player like George Patton, this style of riding was quite foreign. It was as if a rock-and-roll fan had been invited to listen to a string quartet. The general's expression was hard to read—it looked like he wasn't paying close attention. But soon enough, the pas de deux accelerated in complexity, and Podhajsky noticed that Patton and the other Americans leaned forward and started to focus.

Next was the quadrille, in which the horses performed in formation, as tightly choreographed as a drum corps. Surely this would make an impression. The precision and beauty of synchronization had long bewitched spectators. There is something simply mesmerizing about the precision of a marching band, a tableau of synchronized swimmers, a line of dancing Rockettes. Mounted on Africa, Podhajsky led off this display of ultimate horsemanship: eight horses and eight riders performing in absolute synchrony. General Patton sat up on the viewing stand, his face stern. Still, Podhajsky thought he detected an air of interest.

When the quadrille ended, Podhajsky patted Africa, rubbed his neck, and whispered a word in his ear. The horse had performed perfectly, even in these inelegant conditions.

While the horses were being prepared for the next segment, their saddles and cloths being exchanged by the efficient grooms, Verena came back to the staging area and whispered to her husband: She was sure that Patton and the others were enjoying the program. The general no longer looked bored—he was paying close attention, and the other spectators appeared enthralled.

If Patton and Podhajsky had known each other personally, the two Olympians most likely would have recognized in each other an intense and unbridled persistence. Just as Podhajsky knew how to put on an equestrian show, Patton himself was once in charge of the army's biggest equestrian spectacle—the Society Circus, held every year at Fort Meyer, Virginia. Patton's demonstration had showcased some of the army's most advanced trick riding—highly skilled acrobatics executed on horseback, such as Roman riding and monkey drills. Back in peacetime, presidents and ambassadors, senators and movie stars, had come out to watch this annual event. But all of that was long in the past for Patton, who had willingly turned away from his passion for horses to push the army through the technological advances that had helped the Allies win the war. Still, Patton, of all people, had an idea of how much work it took to put on a show such as this one.

As he watched the stallions circling the arena, he wasn't quite sure what to think. What surprised the general most was that the riders appeared to be healthy adult males—he wondered how these men had somehow escaped battle. As Podhajsky's spectacle unfolded in front of him, he was not completely won over.

To perform the finale, Podhajsky had again chosen Africa. He hoped that he had made the right decision: This was the first time his excitable stallion had ever performed alone. Silently, with just a light touch of the reins, the pressure of his legs, and his weight in the saddle, Podhajsky communicated with his stallion, his partner in crime, his companion: This was the most important moment of both of their lives.

The riding hall looked presentable, festooned with fresh-cut branches and thoroughly cleaned, and even the makeshift viewing stand looked ceremonial, with the brilliant ribbon-studded uniforms of the brass hats seated there. But nothing here was as grand as the hall in Vienna. The electric lights cast shadows; the music sounded muffled and tinny.

Still, as Podhajsky gave his beloved mount the signal to enter the ring, he knew that what made his horse magnificent was not the splendor of his surroundings but the deep beauty of his spirit. Most people in the audience would never know anything about these horses or the hardships they had suffered, but instinctively, they would understand that this performance was a manifestation of humanity's attraction to the most exalted principles: beauty and harmony, peace and mutual understanding. Each of these qualities seemed to have been lost in the struggle, chaos, and overwhelming sadness of the war. Podhajsky believed that these horses could help people, just for a moment, tap into the sublime. No matter that Africa had never performed alone, nor that these were unfamiliar surroundings. When a man communicates with a horse, he speaks the language of love, and in this manner, he speaks to all of humankind.

Podhajsky made a split-second decision to ride in the most advanced classical style. He crossed his reins into his left hand so that he controlled only the lower, or curb, rein. With the other hand, he held his whip straight up in an elegant flourish. Now he and his horse needed utter trust between them.

As soon as they'd entered the small hall, Podhajsky had dwelled in a circle of concentration that included only him and his horse. Always brilliant in his movements, Africa sparkled with animation today. The Americans on the sidelines were riveted and could not take their eyes off the pair. Podhajsky stole a glance at the general's face and saw that Patton was falling under the horse's spell. While they performed, time seemed suspended. Podhajsky and Africa passed seamlessly through intricate maneuvers—pirouettes, flying lead changes, lateral movements—not looking like man and beast, or master and servant, but appearing as one. Podhajsky realized that the enthusiasm of the assembled spectators was growing as each exercise that Africa performed was met with a staccato of applause. Podhajsky felt the harnessed power of the stallion beneath him; Africa somehow seemed to sense that he was dancing for his life.

Then the ride was over.

Podhajsky and Africa turned up the center line of the arena, directly toward Patton, who was seated in the middle of the viewing stand. First, they approached in the movement known as *passage*—a floating trot where the horse exaggerates the suspension of each stride. Then Podhajsky collected the stallion into a *piaffe*, an even more arduous movement, in which a horse lifts his feet and trots in place.

At last they came to a halt. Neapolitano Africa stopped completely square, his hooves lined up as if standing on an invisible line. Podhajsky doffed his bicorne hat and looked directly at General George Patton, who stood and returned a salute.

As Podhajsky later wrote in his memoir, "It was one of the most important moments in my life. In a little Austrian village in a decisive hour two men faced each other, both having fought for the Olympic crown for their countries. . . . Although they now met on such un-

PATTON SALUTES THE LIPIZZANER DURING A
PERFORMANCE IN ST. MARTIN, AUSTRIA.

PATTON SPEAKING TO PODHAJSKY AT THE CLOSE OF
THE PERFORMANCE IN ST. MARTIN, AUSTRIA.

equal terms, the one as a triumphant conqueror in a war waged with such bitterness, the other as a member of a defeated nation."

"Honorable Mr. Secretary and General," Podhajsky said in English. "I thank you for the honor you have done the Spanish Riding School. This ancient Austrian institution is now the oldest riding school in the world, and has managed to survive wars and revolutions throughout the centuries, and by good fortune, has lived also through the recent years of upheaval." None of those assembled knew just how true that was. Among the numerous heartbreaks of this terrible war, the innocent horses shot, abused, and killed would not rank among the worst atrocities—but somehow, the killing of innocent beasts, domesticated animals who existed only for man's beauty and pleasure, seemed to highlight the barbaric and depraved depths to which man had allowed himself to sink.

To give himself courage, Podhajsky tried to imagine that a remnant of the Olympic spirit of peace and cooperation hung over this moment while he looked at the general as vanquished to vanquisher.

"The great American nation," Podhajsky continued, "which has been singled out to save European culture from destruction, will certainly interest itself also in this ancient academy, which with its riders and horses presents, as it were, a piece of living baroque, so I'm sure I shall not plead in vain in asking you, General, for your special protection and help; for protection for the Spanish Riding School. . . ."

Patton at first seemed a bit surprised by Podhajsky's words. He paused and whispered something to the under secretary of war. Turning back to Podhajsky, he said, "I hereby place the Spanish Riding School under the official protection of the American army in order to restore it to a newly risen Austria."

At midnight on May 8, 1945, the Germans would officially surrender and the war in Europe would be over.

But for Podhajsky and Africa, the war ended the moment they strode together from the ring, having triumphed over their own fear and uncertainty, to step together into a new age.

THE CRAZIEST CARAVAN
IN THE WORLD

HOSTAU, CZECHOSLOVAKIA,

MAY 15, 1945

Two weeks after his moonlight ride on King Peter's horse, Captain
Tom Stewart looked around the stable courtyard in Hostau, Czechoslovakia, with wonder. Even in a world gone crazy with war, nowhere
on the planet had a scene unfolded that was quite like this one. Prince
Ammazov, leader of the Cossacks, was mounted on one of his Russian
Kabardins. He sported a tall *papakha* sheepskin hat and a long sheepskin
cape. His ten-year-old daughter, already an expert rider, was mounted
beside him on a sturdy Panje pony. The remainder of his Cossack
troop, all in traditional garb, circled around, keeping watch over the
horses. The German former staff of Hostau, now American POWs
wearing civilian clothing, stood by with checklists, calling out instructions. Ragged-looking grooms—former POWs who were now free
but had nowhere to go—held on to the lead ropes of their precious
charges. Battered American jeeps, armored cars, and tanks were parked
around the perimeters. Uniformed American GIs, most of whom had
little experience with horses, worked together to ready hundreds of
the world's most beautiful animals for departure. Some of the old cavalry hands had volunteered to go with the Cossacks as outriders, and
these soldiers were saddling up their chosen mounts. Hundreds of
prancing, dancing, snorting, whinnying horses looked around with
bright eyes, eager to set off, unaware how very much this journey

would change their lives. A herd of jeeps, armored cars, and a couple of tanks were ready to gallop alongside. Some of the trucks were loaded down with horse equipment—halters, bridles, and harnesses. Others were laden with people's household possessions. Everyone was leaving. Only Rudofsky, the former stud farm master, was planning to stay behind.

THE FIRST DAYS OF THE AMERICAN occupation had been harrowing for Rudofsky. Cut off from his family in nearby Bischofteinitz, he had anxiously awaited news of their fate. Not until after May 5, when the American 38th Infantry had taken the town, had he heard the frightening story about how young Ulli had hidden with his classmates inside the walls of the local castle as the American tanks approached. With the guns pointed straight at them, the boy's teacher had handed him a strip of white cloth and pushed him outside in front of the others,

COSSACKS.

whispering, "Americans don't shoot children." Fortunately, Ulli had survived the war unscathed, but Rudofsky was reluctant to abandon the boy, whose father was still missing—either dead or interned in a Russian prison camp. Besides, Rudofsky was convinced that with the Nazis defeated, Czechoslovakia had no more enemies, and its future looked bright. Prior to the war, Czechoslovakia had been a democracy, and Rudofsky believed it would become one again—a place with room for all.

Lessing tried to talk him out of staying. The two men carried on heated conversations out of earshot of the Americans.

"You are naive," Lessing said. "The Czech partisans are proxies of the Bolsheviks. They hate Germans—with good reason—and you are an ethnic German."

Rudofsky was adamant. He had done his duty to ensure the safety of the horses. He would not abandon his family. He would follow the horses only as far as the border.

"Why should I leave the country of my birth?" Rudofsky whispered to Lessing. "What have I to fear when I know I've never harmed a single Czech in my life? My family is here, my mother is too sick to travel, my brother's wife and children look to me for support . . ."

As the rest of the crew prepared for departure from Hostau, Rudofsky kept busy, carefully checking off each item of equipment on a detailed inventory, in particular making sure that every one of the purebreds was accompanied by an official copy of his pedigree. Rudofsky knew that for the horses to be valued properly, and eventually returned to their rightful owners if possible, their bloodlines would need to be clearly documented.

While Rudofsky checked over his lists, Quinlivan and Stewart watched nearby as American soldiers sorted the horses into groups that would travel together, gently coaxing the most pregnant mares and the spindly newborn foals to walk up improvised loading ramps. At last, perhaps the most unlikely caravan in history was ready to set off.

HANK REED HAD BEEN planning for this moment for days. In the best of circumstances, moving more than three hundred horses overland was complicated. To do so under the current conditions was like tackling a Chinese puzzle. Reed had plenty of experience with large-scale horse operations. In his Fort Riley days, a hundred-mile horseback trek was all in a day's work. But here, where everything was improvised and only a few of the soldiers knew anything about riding, the task would be infinitely harder to pull off. Moving so many horses without the proper equipment was fraught with danger. The jerry-rigged trucks might be hazardous. The stress of the journey might send the pregnant mares into labor. The horses might not cooperate. What was more, the crew assembled to move the horses was a motley assortment of people, many of whom had been sworn enemies just a few weeks earlier. To top it all off, Reed had agreed that for humanitarian reasons, families who wanted to hitch a ride with the caravan could come along, bringing their children and personal belongings.

Reed had given the job of fitting out the trucks to Fort Riley veteran Quin Quinlivan. Gifted with a sharp mind for technical tasks, the lieutenant jumped into the job with enthusiasm, devising ways to use the equipment they had to best accommodate the precious horses. He and his men built the ramps they needed for loading and improvised snow fences to raise the sides of the flatbeds. These makeshift trucks were hardly the padded train cars or specially fitted-out horse trailers normally used to transport valuable equines, but they were the best the men could do. Only the mares closest to foaling and the newborns too young to walk would ride in the trucks. The rest of the horses would be safer traveling on foot, herded in groups—cowboy-style—across the border.

The horses would have to caravan as far as Kötzting, a small town not far from the border where the Americans were holding and processing German prisoners of war. Reed had sent Kroll to secure stabling and pasture for the horses, and he had come back with a glum report. The local stables and cowsheds would be woefully inadequate for sensitive purebreds; the available pasture around Kötzting would support their three-hundred-odd horses for only a few weeks. Reed told Kroll that this would have to do. Eventually, though, they would need to find a more suitable long-term solution.

Reed knew that the technical difficulties of transporting the horses were outweighed by the delicate political situation. Since entering Czechoslovakia, Reed and the 2nd Cavalry had been dancing a tricky two-step with the Russians. After the capture of the stud farm at Hostau, the 42nd Squadron had moved farther into Czechoslovakia,

leaving only a skeleton crew to guard the horse farm, and established a headquarters in the town of Nepomuk. About twenty-five miles east of Hostau, Nepomuk was situated on the line agreed upon by the Russians and other Allies, beyond which the Americans would advance no farther. Patrols from the 42nd first made contact with Russian forces advancing west on the evening of May 8. That same night, Reed had a confrontation with a Russian general who claimed that his orders were to keep moving west into territory already held by American troops. Reed had stood up and, sternly shaking his finger, told the Russian in no uncertain terms that he should not advance because American guns were still loaded. In that instance, the Russian had agreed to detour around the American-held town.

The situation on the ground in western Czechoslovakia remained confusing and chaotic as the two giant armies, Russian and American, crowded up against each other, sharing space with terrified local citizens, floods of newly captured prisoners of war, and roadways filled with lines of weary refugee families fleeing west. Mob violence broke out, with instances of execution-style killings of suspected German collaborators. Even some elements of the American infantry had at one point threatened to start shelling the farm in Hostau. As Reed later recounted in sworn testimony, "They took a dim view of this island of mixed Americans and Germans." In this atmosphere, Reed knew that the horses needed to be moved quickly into American-held territory before the 2nd was ordered to pull back over the border. Once that happened, Reed would have no say about what became of the horses. A Czech representative had already visited the farm, seeming eager to make a claim that the horses belonged to the Czechoslovakian government—a claim that Rudofsky, the only man with knowledge of the horses located at Hostau before the war, roundly disputed. Reed knew that sorting out the provenance of these purebreds would call for diplomatic palaver between nations and would have to come later. The Americans could provide protection on the roadways leading out of Hostau, but the dangerous part would be to get the horses safely across a border manned by Czechoslovakian guards.

Reed knew that if he messed this up and the horses didn't make it back to Germany in one piece, he would go down in history as the most inept cavalryman ever let loose in Europe. He would not just disappoint General Patton, he would create a public relations night-

QUINLIVAN
WITH
WITEZ AT
HOSTAU.

mare. All of this lurked in the back of his mind as he oversaw the complicated preparations. But there was even more to what drove Reed to nail down every detail. He had carried his men all the way through the war and out the other side. Rescuing these horses was the last big job that he had been given—and he was determined to see it through.

WHEN ALL WAS READY, Tom Stewart climbed aboard the lead jeep alongside a major who carried the order of march. As leaders of the procession, they headed off first, followed closely by trucks transporting the precious mares and foals.

A thunder of hoofbeats filled the air as this improbable parade crowded Hostau's narrow main street. Placid white mares, frisky colts, bounding Arabians, and stocky Russian horses passed in front of the Church of St. James, heading out of town. From the truck beds, tiny foals struggling to balance on spindly legs peered with wonder through the slats of the vehicles' improvised sides.

Witez set off eagerly, eyes bright, tail aloft. On his back, one of the cavalry riders, a cowboy who hailed from Idaho, looked like he was having the time of his life. Few of the horses stabled at Hostau, horses used for breeding, were trained to be ridden under saddle, but Witez was one. The bay had been given the important job of riding herd on the young stallions, the group that would be most excitable. Quinlivan was mounted on Witez's stablemate, the gray Arabian Lotnik, and rode with the older stallions.

Reed and his men had planned out each stage of the ride and marshaled all of the manpower at their disposal. It was hard to believe that just two weeks earlier, Stewart and his men had fought their way into Hostau. Now, in addition to the men of the 2nd Cavalry, hundreds of American soldiers lined the streets to allow them to pass safely. At each intersection, American vehicles guarded the roads.

Yet the group had barely gotten started when trouble began to brew. Before they'd left the village limits, the young stallions got too close to the mares, and the handlers lost control. Quinlivan steadied Lotnik as he watched a couple of stallions break loose from the group and gallop away. The horses hightailed it across the fields, back in the direction of the stables. There was no time to send someone after them—every hand was needed in the caravan; they would have to retrieve them later.

Tom Stewart stayed up front in his jeep, sticking close to the trucks. The motorized vehicles could have made the trek in under a day, but they moved along slowly, keeping pace with the groups of horses traveling on foot. The road crossed flower-studded meadows, plunged them deep into forest and then back out along sunny trails. When night fell and it was too dark to keep riding, the groups slept in barns along the route as Lessing and Kroll circulated among the groups tending to the horses that needed attention. Many were footsore, unaccustomed to walking so far.

The second day was bright and clear. Rudolf Lessing, mounted on Indigo, rode toward the front of the first large herd. Before long, they could see a small burg in the distance, and Lessing's heart skipped a beat when he realized that soon they would cross the border between Czechoslovakia and Germany. They were headed toward the town of Furth im Wald, a medieval cluster of buildings along the Chamb River. An elegant arched bridge led over the river into the village. Once they crossed the bridge, they would be in Bavaria, now officially an American protectorate.

Above the town gate that led to Furth im Wald hung a shield with a gruesome medieval depiction of a white horse's severed head. According to local legend, a notorious bandit knight once tried to evade prison by mounting his white horse and charging toward the gate at a gallop. However, the alert gatekeeper dropped the gate's iron grating to stop him, decapitating the horse and thwarting the robber-knight's escape plot. Now men and white horses had to hope that the gate would not slam shut in front of them, as it had in the legend. The riders could see the spires of the town in the distance, but the caravan still faced the obstacle of crossing the horses over a border manned by Czechoslovakian guards.

As the first group of horses and riders approached the checkpoints, Lessing saw an armed Czech border control officer manning a large red-and-white-striped gate. As the caravan got closer, the border guards ordered the gate shut, then gathered in front of it, pointing their guns directly at the men and horses. Stewart's jeep and the horse-laden trucks were idling, and soon the first group of horses caught up and began prancing and pawing, not understanding why they couldn't move forward. Lessing, staring down at the guns as he reined in Indigo, quickly saw the danger. The second group of horses was not far behind; if the mares and stallions got too close, all hell would start, and some of them might bolt. Lessing grew increasingly nervous. He had heard many stories of unruly, scared horses being gunned down by frightened or trigger-happy soldiers. The Czech partisans manning the barricades were shouting that the horses could not go through. The Americans had no permission to remove horses or any other property from Czechoslovakian territory. Lessing knew that these were not Czech horses—all of them had been brought from other countries, and they were now under American control. But as a German prisoner of war, Lessing was afraid to say anything for fear of making matters worse.

A moment later, he saw the second group of horses appear in the distance. To his relief, he spotted Quinlivan and Lotnik trotting toward the group to join Stewart in asking the border guards what the holdup was. The men repeated the litany—the horses could not leave Czech territory. The Americans had no authority here. Quinlivan sized up the situation. He saw hot tempers, pointed guns, and snorting and pawing horses whose coiled energy was about to explode. Stewart nodded, and Quinlivan swiftly took the matter in hand. He radioed the tanks, which had just pulled up at the tail of the convoy, and told them to point their guns directly at the barricades.

"Open that gate, or I'll open it for you," Quinlivan said firmly. The guns and guards faced off. The only sound was the muffled clatter of horses' hooves. Then the surly border guard jerked his head and the barrier lifted.

Galloping and trotting, dancing and prancing, showing the gaits for which they were so rightly famed, the white horses streamed forward, the sunlight glinting across their backs, across the bridge, and over the border into the American protectorate in Germany.

Among the surging horses, Witez's burnished bay coat also stood out. Throughout the ride, he had been the perfect mentor. He seemed to be telling the frisky young stallions to settle down and get a move on, that this was serious business. Only after the last horse had passed the barriers did Quinlivan follow on Lotnik.

At the border, Hubert Rudofsky stood straight and tall in his unfamiliar civilian clothes, holding a clipboard. With a businesslike demeanor, he checked off the name of each horse, every one of which he knew by sight, as they passed. As the last of the purebreds passed through the gate, Rudofsky placed a crisp checkmark next to the name. With a heavy heart, he turned around and went home.

When he returned to Hostau, the long aisles of the whitewashed stables stood empty and hushed. Since the days of the Imperial Dragoons, these halls had rung with the sounds of a busy stable—the ring of hammer on anvil when the blacksmith labored, the hollow stamping of hooves on straw, the rattle of polished silver curb chains as horses shook their heads in high spirits, the gentle whinnies that echoed far and near as grooms approached with buckets full of oats. Now the air seemed drained of sound, leaving only a hollow emptiness.

At forty-eight years old, Rudofsky had nowhere to go but back to his mother's house in the neighboring town of Bischofteinitz. At least his nephew, Ulli, who had held the white flag as he surrendered to the American forces, would be eager to welcome him home.

ON THE AFTERNOON OF May 16, when Stewart, Quinlivan, and Lessing finally arrived in Kötzting, Germany, with more than three hundred exhausted, footsore purebreds, they could not have found a setting less hospitable for sensitive, pampered horses. The small town was bursting at the seams. The 111th Panzer Division, the same mighty tank division that the 2nd had fought during the battle of Lunéville, had surrendered en masse to the Americans on May 7. The 2nd Cavalry would have to process each and every soldier—give him a medical exam, fingerprint him, draw up his discharge papers, all under the seal of the 2nd Cavalry. Even processing five hundred men per day, the task would take over a month to complete. For now, the seventeen thousand German prisoners of war were encamped under guard in empty fields. Adding to the chaos was a flood of refugees—German speakers who had fled Bohemia and Silesia in advance of the Russians and now sought shelter anywhere they could find it. Even the citizens of the town were squeezed into cramped quarters, as every house billeted American soldiers. In the narrow, hilly lanes, shouting matches quickly escalated into street brawls, and petty thieves circulated, preying on the downtrodden and vulnerable.

Despite their fatigue from the journey, the horsemen had no time to rest. The barns, cowsheds, and pastures that Kroll had located for them were scattered around the nearby countryside. All of the horses had made the journey safely, but as Lessing, Quinlivan, and Stewart surveyed the poor conditions in Kötzting, they knew they still faced a mighty challenge—to keep the horses fed, watered, and safe from thieves would take the utmost vigilance from a force already spread thin with other demands.

Hank Reed was not on hand to witness their arrival; his headquarters remained in Czechoslovakia. He had taken over the castle belonging to Baron von Skoda, owner of the Skoda Works, one of Germany's biggest providers of arms and explosives during the war, making sure that this important facility did not fall into rogue hands during the time of turnover. Soon, the Americans would be retreating from Czechoslovakia, leaving the territory to the Russians. But in the meantime, Reed was required to keep boots on the ground and guns loaded until the Third Army—the 2nd Cavalry included—was ordered to retreat.

For Reed and his men, nothing could diminish what they had accomplished in rescuing these four-footed beauties. All of the horses were safe in American territory, not a single one hurt on the ride. Back in '42, when Reed had taken command of the 2nd Cavalry, it had seemed that the force's days of equestrian valor were behind them forever. But today, the regiment known by the code name Thoroughbred had earned a place among its honored mounted forebears.

THE LIPIZZANER FAREWELL

KÖTZTING, BAVARIA, GERMANY,
MAY 16–21, 1945

For the first time in his life, Alois Podhajsky was flying—aloft in General Collier's personal military airplane en route to 2nd Cavalry headquarters at the Skoda Castle, in Zinkowy, Czechoslovakia. The Austrian was on his way to meet the man who had saved his Lipizanner: Colonel Hank Reed. Podhajsky's mission was to inspect the horses that the 2nd Cavalry had just brought to Kötzting, and to pick out his mares and foals for transport back to Austria.

Podhajsky was understandably nervous. He had received the barest of information—only that the mares from Piber were believed to be among the horses recently captured by the 2nd Cavalry. Were they safe and healthy? Had any been lost? Podhajsky did not know. As he looked out the airplane window, an appealing panorama spread out below him; from such a distance, he could detect no traces of the war that had ravaged the Continent for six straight years. As the small plane approached its destination, Podhajsky could see the vast grounds of the castle of Baron von Skoda, surrounded by acres of ornamental gardens. The small plane circled over a meadow, then made a perfect landing on the castle's grounds.

Awaiting Podhajsky's arrival was an American major who escorted him into the opulent baroque building. They walked briskly through a maze of long hallways, past American sentries in olive drab stationed at the entrances to vast rooms hung with highly varnished oil paintings in gilded frames. The major led Podhajsky to a comfortable bedroom and invited the traveler to make himself at home. He informed the Austrian that the commander of the 2nd Cavalry, Colonel Reed, would join him for dinner. At six P.M., the major returned and escorted him to meet the colonel.

Podhajsky was introduced to a man with a warm smile and friendly manner who immediately set him at ease. Podhajsky was surprised and flattered that Reed had invited him to sit at the officers' table in the mess. During dinner, the two men discussed their favorite subject— horses. Reed told Podhajsky that he had recognized the Austrian's name. The head of the riding school at Fort Riley, Colonel Tuttle, a member of the 1936 Olympic team, had greatly admired Podhajsky's dressage performance in Berlin. Upon returning to Fort Riley, Tuttle had named one of the school's horses after the Austrian—they called him "Podhorski."

Reed then filled in the Austrian on what had transpired over the course of the last two weeks. He explained that the Americans had captured the stud farm intact, but that the farm lay in territory that now belonged to the Russians. Fearing that the Americans would soon pull back and the Russians would seize the horses or the Czechoslovakians would claim them as Czech property, Reed had made the difficult decision to move them overland to the village of Kötzting, in Germany. Fortunately, the horses had arrived safely, but conditions were dangerous—he wanted to return the Lipizzaner to Austria as soon as possible.

Podhajsky explained to Reed that there was just one hitch. Not all of the Lipizzaner in Hostau had come from Austria—some had been brought there from the stud farm in Lipica, Italy; others had come from the royal Lipizzaner stud of Yugoslavia; still more had been brought from other locations. Reed was alarmed to hear of this unexpected complication, having anticipated that all of the Lipizzaner would be returned to Vienna.

THE NEXT MORNING, REED and Podhajsky set out for Kötzting—a drive of about forty miles—in Reed's jeep, with O'Leary at the wheel. Their route took them southwest through the Czechoslovakian countryside. The spring day was breathtaking, with flowers studding the verdant meadows and a few high clouds hanging in a clear blue sky. As they drove, they passed buildings plastered with banners declaring, "We Greet the Red Army!" No similar signs welcomed the American forces.

Reed noticed the Austrian staring at the pro-Soviet banners. "The inhabitants of this country do not love us much and can hardly wait for us to leave," he said to Podhajsky. "Now you can see why I moved the horses to Bavaria as quickly as I could." Reed did not have to say more.

As they drove, Reed told Podhajsky that the arrangements for the horses in and around Kötzting were makeshift and temporary, and that there was not enough fodder to support the local population of horses, much less the new arrivals. Reed explained that the horses had been parceled out in twos and threes into pastures and cowsheds that were entirely unsuitable to such valuable bloodstock. His men reported that the horses had arrived safely, but he could not vouch for their condition since. So, as they approached, Podhajsky was nervous, fearing the worst.

When they arrived, they were greeted by Lessing, overworked and exhausted but eager to welcome his former colleague. Lessing and Podhajsky had met the previous year, when the Austrian visited Hostau to check on his mares. Their relationship had been cordial, as the two had discussed the horses' welfare over coffee in the veterinarian's home. Though Lessing still considered the Austrian his friend, he saw the scarlet armband that Podhajsky wore to signal loyalty to his country, and was surprised that Podhajsky refused to shake his hand or look him in the eye. Lessing was hurt by the treatment—they had shared a love of horses, and both had worn the Wehrmacht uniform. But their common past could no longer overcome the politics that had come between them: Lessing was a defeated German, Podhajsky was a liberated Austrian, and this fact made their personal circumstances entirely different. Lessing was an American POW, and the director of the Spanish Riding School was a free man.

As Reed, Lessing, and Podhajsky toured the stables, Podhajsky instantly recognized the mares from Piber, calling out to them by name. The white horses looked up and whinnied when they saw the familiar face. Podhajsky walked among them, easily picking out the ones branded with a P and a crown over it. There were 219 Austrian mares in all. Forty or so Lipizzaner that did not come from Austria had been brought to Hostau from Yugoslavia and Italy, and some had been foaled at Hostau, but Podhajsky pointed out that each horse's provenance could be readily determined by its brands. Hank Reed knew that courts and tribunals would decide where these horses should end up—for now, he just needed to get them out of Kötzting. He asked Podhajsky to take all of the purebred Lipizzaner to Austria for safekeeping until their proper final destination could be sorted out.

Podhajsky reflected on the situation in St. Martin. Already, he had trouble caring for his seventy stallions. Could he really agree to take so many more horses and be responsible for them? He hesitated only a minute before agreeing to find temporary homes for the Lipizzaner from Lipica and from the royal Yugoslavian stud farm. This would leave behind about fifteen Lipizzaner, those gathered from other places. The following day, Podhajsky returned to St. Martin in General Collier's airplane, determined to find enough stabling in and around St. Martin for all of the new horses. Reed had promised they would arrive within a week.

ON MAY 22, QUINLIVAN and Lessing prepared to load the Lipizzaner onto the trucks that would transport them from Kötzting to Podhajsky's home base at the Arco Castle, a distance of sixty miles. At Reed's behest, the Americans had assembled forty German trucks. Each would transport about fifteen of the 219 mares and foals being returned to Austria; the rest carried POWs to act as grooms, as well as food and supplies for the horses. German prisoners of war had been conscripted to drive the trucks and to serve as grooms for the journey. Members of the 2nd Cavalry accompanied the convoy in motorcars and jeeps.

Quinlivan and Lessing supervised the loading of the mares, making sure to steady them as they walked up the makeshift ramps. Some of the horses walked sedately, others took the ramp in a single bound, and still others seemed hesitant and needed to be coaxed. As soon as the last horse was loaded, the Americans gave the signal for the convoy to move off. What was left of the group of captured horses—including the Arabians from Janów Podlaski and the remaining Lipizzaner—would soon be taken by the 2nd to a captured German stud farm where Reed had found room for them. Witez had survived his long journey in remarkably good condition. He had shed his winter coat, and dapples spread across his haunches like faceted jewels. His mane was silken, his eyes bright, his spirited expression undampened. The stallion's fate remained in the hands of the 2nd Cavalry.

SINCE RETURNING FROM HIS visit with Reed, Podhajsky had spent the week desperately looking for stabling for the mares. On the night of May 22, he got a phone call from the XX Corps headquarters telling him that the mares were being delivered by truck to a nearby airfield—that very night. They would be there by ten P.M. Podhajsky forgot his fatigue and headed directly to the spot. The night was cold and clear and very dark; the floodlights that once lit the fields no longer functioned. The only illumination on that moonless night came from the thick blanket of stars that glittered in the sky. Podhajsky paced anxiously, suddenly brimming with energy. Ever since the Germans had taken the mares out of Austria, he had wondered if they would ever return. In only moments, the Lipizzaner mares would be reunited with their homeland.

SOON HE HEARD A low rumble, and the convoy of forty trucks began to roll onto the airfield, their headlight beams crisscrossing in the darkness. While waiting for the trucks to arrive, Podhajsky had prepared a ramp, set at a slant against a small rise; he had planned to ask the drivers to back their trucks up to the ramp, one by one, so the horses would not have to jump from the elevated flatbed of the truck all the way to the ground. But the field was dark, and the drivers couldn't see well enough to back up to Podhajsky's ramp. Instead, they all pulled up helter-skelter and turned off their ignition.

As soon as the drivers cut the engines, the horses got restless, kicking against the thin boards that enclosed them. Someone suggested waiting until dawn to unload, but Podhajsky could see that the mares were already getting panicky. They would have to improvise something and hope for the best. Unfortunately, the ramp that Lessing and Quinlivan had used to load the horses had been accidentally left behind in Kötzting, and Podhajsky's was unsuitable unless propped against the hillside. One of the trucks was equipped with a short ramp used for loading gasoline cans, but it was not long enough to reach all the way from the truck bed to the ground. Instead of leading the mares off the trucks, they would have to push them down to the end of the short ramp, where each horse would jump to the ground in the dark. Though the setup was far from perfect, it would have to do. Two trucks pulled around to illuminate the unloading area with their headlights. The mares, some calm, some impatient, skidded down the ramp one by one, jumping and sometimes stumbling as they came off the end. When one truck was unloaded, they moved the ramp to the next one.

Then one of the broodmares panicked and bolted ahead of her groom, jumping off the ramp with a terrible twist. She landed with a thump, and then, squealing and snorting, hopped forward on three legs. In the pale headlights, the men could see her fourth leg dangling at an awkward angle. Podhajsky's heart thudded heavily. He approached her quietly and coaxed the panicked mare to let him examine her. A quick check revealed the worst possible outcome. The mare, Trompetta, had fractured her cannon bone—a fatal injury. She had made it all the way back to Austrian soil, but she would never make it back to the barn. Podhajsky's serious mien revealed none of the grief that seized him. With his pistol and a steady hand, he took the mare out of her misery. That night marked the last shot fired in the Lipizzaner's war.

The rest of the mares were unloaded without mishap, and within a few hours, each was stabled in a fresh bed of straw in one of the barns that Podhajsky had managed to secure. It was near dawn when the POWs finally drove away and he was able to fall into his bed, exhausted.

The tumultuous arrival of the mares in the new Austria only served to highlight how difficult was the path that lay ahead of him. Yes, he had the horses, and yes, Reed and Patton had fulfilled their promises. But now more than three hundred mares and stallions were counting on him—a worn-out forty-seven-year-old citizen of a defeated nation—to keep them safe. The country of Austria would need to reinvent itself, and the Spanish Riding School, too, would need to find a new path to assure its future.

PART FOUR

Homecoming

For over a thousand years Roman conquerors returning from the wars enjoyed the honor of a triumph, a
tumultuous parade. In the procession came trumpeters
and musicians and strange animals from conquered
territories, together with carts laden with treasure and
captured armaments. . . . A slave stood behind the
conqueror holding a golden crown and whispering in
his ear a warning: that all glory is fleeting.

—FROM THE FILM *PATTON*

LIPIZZANER BEING LOADED INTO A
CRATE AT BREMERHAVEN DOCKS.

THE SUPER HORSES
ARE OURS

The war was over, but the scheming, conniving, and fighting over Germany's purebred horses had just begun. During the past six years, Hitler had systematically seized Europe's finest equine specimens. Pound for pound, these four-footed treasures were among the most valuable assets captured by the Americans, and perhaps no others commanded men's imaginations quite like these gallant and beautiful creatures.

By late May 1945, Germany was jammed with pedigreed horses. Some of these had been seized from occupied countries. Others were the tattered remnants of herds whose owners had fled west with them overland and been lucky enough to evade the Russians, survive the hardships of the trek, and make it across the German border. All of them required food and shelter.

The American army, exhausted after its long fight across Europe, now had the task of trying to reestablish a functioning government, ensure basic services for citizens, discharge German prisoners of war, and sort through a vast muddle of displaced people and property. Among all of these demands, sorting out the fate of the horses was a minor one, and yet, unlike works of art that could remain crated and stored until a resolution was found, these animals needed immediate care and attention.

In Kötzting, Reed had an urgent situation on his hands. The horses from Hostau would soon run out of feed. Even after 219 Lipizzaner had been returned to Podhajsky in Austria, more than a hundred rescued purebreds remained, with nowhere to go. Reed knew that these horses were Polish, Yugoslavian, and Russian in origin, but no one could explain precisely how they had ended up in Hostau; nor did anyone seem to have authority to negotiate a return to their rightful owners—if such owners could be found. Hoping to prevent the horses from being sold off, he tried to find uses for them, distributing those that were suitable for everyday riding to 2nd Cavalry officers. He sent five mounts to General Patton at Third Army headquarters, and still more than ninety horses remained, including the Arabians from Poland, Witez and Lotnik.

Eager to get them safely out of Kötzting, Reed sent the remaining horses to Mansbach, a captured German stud farm about two hundred miles to the northwest. There, Quinlivan, Lessing, and Kroll found well-appointed stables with roomy box stalls and green pastures. For the first time since leaving Hostau, the horses had safe, fenced pastures to graze in and room to stretch their legs. However, finding adequate food was a problem. As Lessing later explained, "We didn't even have enough oatmeal to feed our children, yet for the horses we demanded half a ton of oats." At least Witez and the other rescues were no longer in immediate danger, but Reed knew that if given the order, he would have to take his men off the task of looking after the horses, and if that happened, the horses would likely be sold to the highest bidder—even if that bid came from the slaughterhouse.

THE HORSES WERE SAFE for the time being. The next order of business was to determine whether their seizure had been lawful. On June 16 and 17, Reed, Stewart, and Hubert Rudofsky were called to Third Army headquarters to testify in front of the inspector general of the Third Army, Clarence C. Cook. Rudofsky's testimony proved powerful. He explained that when he returned to Czechoslovakia from Poland in 1944, not a single horse remained at Hostau from the bloodstock that had been there before the German arrival; some had been moved to other stud farms. Most of the young horses, he presumed, had been sent out as warhorses when they reached the age of four. Rudofsky swore under oath that the horses' pedigrees were accurate and that none of the horses belonged to Czechoslovakia. Reed and Stewart made the same assertion. Cook concluded that the horses' capture was lawful and that the purebreds could be claimed as spoils of war.

Now that the horses belonged to the U.S. Army, the question of what to do with them remained. For the overtaxed American army, every aspect of caring for them was difficult, from procuring scant grain to finding trustworthy workers to care for them. Fortunately, Reed, Patton, and the other experienced cavalry officers understood that something needed to be done for these horses—and fast. But the prospect of anything happening quickly enough to help seemed remote. Ever since the Louisiana Maneuvers back in 1941, the War Department had established a firm position that horses were not a high priority. With the intense demands on the ground in Germany, and the need to ship home combat veterans as quickly as possible, the plight of the horses seemed unlikely to garner much attention.

A stroke of good fortune occurred for the horses when, in early August 1945, Colonel Fred Hamilton was appointed chief of the army's Remount Service. Hamilton, a forty-nine-year-old Fort Riley veteran, was a passionate horse lover with a firm belief in continuing the army's role in breeding horses. He was about to be presented with a once-in-a-lifetime opportunity.

As soon as Hamilton took up his new position, he got word of the incredible cache of purebred horses in the hands of the American army. General Patton, who was on leave in the United States at the time, met with Hamilton, explaining that four major German military breeding farms, as well as the German Army cavalry school—where its top show horses were stabled—were in a state of near emergency. Millions of dollars' worth of irreplaceable bloodstock were at risk. With so many other pressing concerns, Patton's men were finding it difficult to be responsible for the horses' security. Most were not suitable for riding or recreational purposes—they were breeding horses, the foundation upon which an army would build up its military might. Not even the world's recent entry into the atomic age had changed these two soldiers' view that horses were valuable military assets. As Hamilton wrote in a later report, "It should be remembered that the horse still plays a vital part in the military establishment of these . . . countries. They are not in a position to become highly motorized or mechanized and will doubtless continue with many horses in their military establishment. Any return of horse-breeding stock, therefore, should be looked upon as contributing to the military potential of these . . . countries, as well as to the military potential of Russia." With the support of Patton and several "horse-minded senators," including Tom Stewart's father, Hamilton pressed to see the situation for himself and make a decision about what to do.

ON AUGUST 21, 1945, Colonel Hamilton received orders to report to Europe to inspect all horse facilities captured by the army in Germany. Hamilton's first stop was the stud farm at Mansbach. He was impressed by the magnificent Polish Arabians that Reed and his men had captured, but he was unsure where the horses belonged. He knew little of the tragic true story of the Arabians from Janów Padlowski. Had Hamilton had access to the full story, he would have realized that there were Polish citizens who cared greatly for these horses and were hoping to secure their return to their native land. But Hamilton knew only what he had learned from the horses' German captors—people who, it later became evident, were eager to cover up a good part of their role in Poland during the war. Added to this misinformation was the Americans' suspicions of Russia's intentions, and their belief that those claiming to act on behalf of Poland or Yugoslavia were actually puppets of the Bolsheviks hoping to seize the horses to build up Soviet military capacities.

By the end of his monthlong tour of Germany and Italy, Fred Hamilton had made a decision. He believed that the best of the horses should be shipped to America to be used in the army's remount program. In his official report, he wrote, "In my opinion, if the US does not acquire shipment of this breeding stock, in the near future it will be completely lost to the horse world. The Europeans are not in a position to maintain stock; [they] must sell some of it, and certain nations to the east are eager to acquire it by any means, legal or otherwise."

Even with Hamilton's strong recommendation, this would be no easy task. Cargo space in ships returning from Europe was at an absolute premium. The continent was teeming with soldiers eager to return home, and then there were massive amounts of American equipment that needed shipment as well. Could Hamilton possibly convince the powers that be in the War Department to commit manpower and space to *horses*?

In Mansbach, the summer of 1945 passed peacefully for the men and horses—Quinlivan and Lessing had developed a close friendship, riding together every day. In spite of the relative calm, providing adequate care for the refined horses was not easy. No one was more aware of the challenges than Rudolf Lessing. He not only looked after the horses under the care of the 2nd Cavalry; he also made rounds in the surrounding countryside, offering help wherever it was needed. Throughout the summer of 1945, Lessing toured the surrounding area in an enormous black BMW-21 convertible coupe with two carburetors and a red leather interior, seized from the Nazis and sold to him at a nominal fee as an essential worker. It was a great car but for one problem: It was a gas-guzzler, and Lessing was allotted only thirty liters of gas per week. Every Monday, he had to wait in line to tank up at the American depot. He was fortunate, since only a select few got this provision—doctors, veterinarians, and truckers who carried essential goods.

For the first two days after filling his tank, he circulated throughout the local farm country, looking after the animals of impoverished local farmers. People were so destitute that he took to keeping a milk pail in his car so he could ask to be paid in fresh milk if the farmer had no cash. By Wednesday, Lessing's tank of American gas would have run out, and he would need to buy gas on the black market from German truck drivers who transported the supplies that came in from America by ship—food, clothing, and chewing gum. The truck drivers drove into the woods, siphoned off gas from their large tanks, and sold it for cigarettes. This way, Lessing was able to keep on his rounds all week, which to him was vital, given the deplorable conditions for animals. People were scrounging to get by, never knowing in the morning where their dinner would come from, much less where to find food for their animals.

Often, Lessing was called out to help a draft horse get to its feet using a large sling; the gentle giants pulled coal wagons up and down large hills, and when they were not fed enough, they got tired and lay down from sheer exhaustion, and then they had trouble standing up. Rudolf would then get an urgent call asking him to come hoist a big horse back to its feet. Lessing dreamed of a future when people could once again ride horses for pleasure and sport, but every day presented so many challenges that it was hard to imagine when that time would come. For this reason, he supported passing control of the remaining horses permanently to the Americans. Witez, in his stable, seemed settled enough, but no decision had been made about his ultimate fate. After all of the efforts made to round them up, these horses would not survive the tumultuous postwar period unless a concrete plan was made for their benefit. It was becoming increasingly clear that if Hamilton couldn't find a way to ship the horses to the United States, the army could not be responsible for their care much longer.

Throughout the summer, a stream of visitors came to Mansbach. Liselotte, the stud farm assistant from Janów in Poland who had cried on the platform as Witez departed, was relieved to find the stallion alive and well. Even Gustav Rau, who had ridden out the war at a German remount depot in northern Germany, came to visit his former charges—as a civilian, he was free to continue with his life. His role during wartime in the stud farm administration of Poland would be largely swept under the rug. Sadly, in later years, as the Polish government was able to regroup and start to press a case for a return of the horses seized by the Germans, Gustav Rau would become the chief source of misinformation about them—preventing any hope that the seized Arabians from Hostau would ever be returned to their homeland.

As the summer of 1945 drew to a close, the 2nd Cavalry's role in caring for the horses was also coming to an end, as Reed passed responsibility for the horses to Colonel Hamilton. The end of the war had brought no lessening of Reed's responsibilities. Patton had put him in charge of the newly formed constabulary force patrolling the tense border region of Germany; one of Reed's first actions was to mount some of the MPs on horseback. He had plenty of work but more opportunity to relax than before, and his carriage, pulled by a pair of Lipizzaner coach horses, was a familiar sight around his new headquarters near Munich. After so many long, lonely months at war, his wife, Janice, had joined him in Germany. But the last few months had also seen a stream of deeply felt farewells: The men of the 2nd Cavalry had grown so close that some felt like members of his own family—none more so than the faithful young man who had saved his life three times, Jim O'Leary. On the day of O'Leary's departure, Hank wrote a letter to the young man's mother back in Chicago. In it, he said, "I have no sons. Had I one, I could wish nothing more but that he be a son as fine as yours."

On September 1, Tom Stewart's time for departure arrived. In May, Stewart had been awarded the Bronze Star for bravery, honoring his mission to Hostau. But he did not consider himself a hero. The memories of his comrades lost in the fields had affected him profoundly, deepening his natural reserve. Witez, with his velvety nose and proud expression, helped remind Stewart of the good he had accomplished. Almost two years after his departure from New York Harbor aboard the *Mauretania,* Tom Stewart was heading home at last, knowing he had done everything he could do on behalf of the horses.

After Stewart's departure, the only remaining member of the 2nd Cavalry still with the horses was Lieutenant Quinlivan. On September 19, 1945, he received top-secret orders from the War Department: He had been selected to join a special delegation headed by Colonel Fred Hamilton. The group—rounded out by another cavalry officer, a horse trainer from Paramus, New Jersey, and two veterinarians—now formed the crack team known as "the horse detectives." Their mission was to select the best of the best of the captured horses for shipment to America.

For the next three weeks, these horse experts toured the four captured German stud farms and examined the top-flight show horses belonging to the German Army equestrian team. At each stop, the team evaluated the horses' conformation, temperament, and performance, pored over pedigrees, and scrutinized often dubious bills of sale purporting to show German ownership of horses seized from other countries. Any horse whose private ownership or unlawful seizure could be determined was excluded from the Americans' acquisition. At each stop, the horse detectives needed to outwit Germans who, naturally, tried to hide their best stock. By the end of September, Hamilton and the horse detectives had selected 150 horses, including the Lipizzaner

سعادة الدنيا على ظهور الخيل

"OH LUCK OF THE WORLD ON BACK OF THE HORSES"

One Horsepicturebook

of

ARAB-LIPPIZAN-THOROUGHBRED HORSES

IN U.S. ARMY STUD FARM MANSBACH GERMANY

PRESENTED TO

Colonel

CHARLES H. REED

C.O. SECOND CAV. GROUP

by

DR. LESSING   DR. KROLL

PHOTOGRAPHS BY R. LESSMANN HANNOVER · SKETCHES BY BARONESS FALKENSTEIN

1945

REED RECEIVED AN ALBUM OF
PHOTOS OF THE RESCUED HORSES.

mare Madera, the refined gray Arabian Lotnik, and the 2nd Cavalry favorite, Witez. By his own account, Hamilton had strived to select horses neither for dollar value nor for pedigree but for qualities most suitable in the army's breeding program. Even so, among his selections were some of the world's most valuable racehorses, a choice that would engender no small measure of controversy. But, for the time being, Hamilton felt confident that he had picked the very best horses for the benefit of the horses, the army, and by extension, the American people.

KNOWING THAT THE HORSES were soon to be dispersed, Reed made a final visit to the stables at Mansbach. He was relieved to see how well cared for they were, and that they bore no traces of the harrowing last days of the war. Pleased with the Germans' loyalty and skilled work, Reed had invited Lessing and Kroll to join the horses on the trip to America, where the veterinarians would have a chance to start a new life. Kroll, who was single, readily agreed to the offer, but when Lessing learned that his family could not accompany him, as the berths on the ship were reserved for staff, he agonized for weeks over what to do. Reed assured him that he could establish himself in America and send for his family at a later date, but after much reflection, Lessing decided to stay with his family and let the Americans and his beloved horses leave without him.

In honor of his efforts, Hank Reed presented Lessing with a letter of commendation, praising him for his outstanding service. For Reed, Lessing and Kroll had prepared a leather-bound photo album full of pictures of the horses. A majestic photograph of the Lipizzaner stallion Neapolitano Slavonia graced the cover. Across the top, carefully inscribed in Arabic script and then translated into English, was printed a simple proverb: "Oh luck of the world on back of the horses." Hank Reed slowly turned the pages, looking through the photos of the foals, mares, riding horses, and stallions. One of the captions read, "The Lipizzaner galloping across the field at sunset, like something out of a fairytale . . ." Politics, prejudice, avarice, and intolerance had riven a brutal divide between the countries of these men; the grace of these horses had already started to knit them back together. The former enemies parted as friends.

DEPARTURE!

BREMERHAVEN, GERMANY,
OCTOBER 1, 1945

Out on the busy docks at Bremerhaven, among the battered ship containers, an improbable scene was unfolding. Sturdy white Lipizzaner, slender blue-blooded Thoroughbreds, high-crested Arabians, and a single Cossack horse circled nervously on the docks, tugging on the lead ropes held tightly by uniformed American soldiers, as each awaited its turn to be loaded into a slatted wooden crate just large enough to hold a single animal, then hoisted through the air to the deck of a ship. As the gears started grinding and the slatted wooden crate lifted off, each horse's hooves left the ground of a continent that had raised and proudly fostered his breed for centuries, but now no longer had a home for him.

The Liberty ship *Stephen F. Austin* would be carrying more than sixty men, some of whom had waited expressly for a chance to ride with the precious cargo of 151 of the world's most beautiful horses. Down in the hold, the crew had built individual box stalls for the stallions. The mares were placed in narrow standing stalls, and the foals were grouped in small pens. Like almost everything else in those postwar days, the setup had an improvised quality. As the horsemen settled the horses into their quarters, up on deck, the jubilant soldiers leaned against the ship's railings with grins on their faces. They had anticipated this day since the moment they'd set foot on this continent back in the summer of 1944. At long last, they were headed home.

A FEW DAYS EARLIER, the horses had boarded the trains that would carry them to the German port of Bremerhaven. From the 2nd Cavalry, only Quin Quinlivan would accompany the horses on their transatlantic crossing. Also shipping out with the purebreds was German veterinarian Wolfgang Kroll. Lessing wanted to travel with them to the docks to help oversee their departure. The three former enemies had slept on the hard floors of boxcars during the trek to Bremerhaven, heating up their C rations over Sterno burners in order to keep an eye on the horses. One of Arabian mares, Gospa, had foaled during the rail journey. The men had opened her boxcar in the morning to see a tiny Arabian peering out from her mother's side. Most wonderful of all was the telltale misshapen star on her forehead. This little filly would be Witez's first offspring to grow up in America.

WITEZ'S FOAL TROTS ALONGSIDE HIS MOTHER.

For Rudolf Lessing, watching the horses depart was bittersweet. He knew that when the ship and crew embarked, he would return home empty-handed. The mission he had started the previous April, when he had ridden across the border into Germany, had at last come to an end. From here on out, the fate of the horses rested with the American army. Lessing's love and constant care for these precious animals would reverberate down the line of equestrian aficionados on two continents for generations to come. In return, he asked for absolutely nothing. Lessing was going home to his wife and children, a home where he would again face a limited gas allotment and keep a milk pail in his car's backseat for payment in kind as he went about his dawn-to-dark routine of helping animals in need. When the last crate had left the dock, and the beloved horses that he would never see again had departed for distant shores, Rudolf Lessing turned around and went home.

MEN CLUSTERED ON DECK and the spirits were high as the *Stephen F. Austin* pulled out of the port of Bremerhaven on October 12, 1945. Sailing along the coast of Holland, they could see windmills in the distance, and the seas were calm. But the soldiers were edgy—these waters were laced with lethal undetonated mines. A Norwegian ship, passing near their route on the same day, had just had its rudder blown off. The silent but deadly gray waters slipped past their ship and its unique cargo. Each man breathed a sigh of relief when at last they sailed out of the dangerous corridor without mishap. Down below, Quinlivan made sure the horses were fed, watered, and not getting themselves into any trouble. In the best of circumstances, with ample exercise and fresh air, stallions can be a handful. Here in the hold of the ship, the horses would be cooped up for the entire crossing, which was expected to last about twelve days. Keeping them calm would be a big job. Crouched in the hold, Quinlivan spent hours looking after the tiny foal that had been born on the train. The veterinarians had been worried about her—she was frail, and her survival was uncertain. Still, the sun was shining, and all aboard were hoping for a peaceful trip. It was hard to believe, but in just a few days, these horses that Quinlivan had been watching over since the last days of the war would be safe in America.

BUT ABOUT FIVE DAYS into the journey, as they entered the Bay of Biscay, the seas got heavier, and the ship started to roll. The Liberty ship

THE HORSE DETECTIVES ON THE DECK OF THE
STEPHEN F. AUSTIN EN ROUTE TO AMERICA, OCTOBER 1945.

was constructed to carry ten thousand tons of cargo—the 151 horses stabled belowdecks took up the allotted cargo space but were not nearly heavy enough (horses weigh about 900 to 1,200 pounds each) to provide good ballast. The ship started to buck and toss. As Quinlivan described it, "The old ship would nose down so far the screws would come clear out of the water and the whole ship would vibrate." Some of the men started to get seasick. Those less prone to it, among them Quinlivan, picked up the slack.

At first, the horses seemed better off than the men in the rough seas. The four-legged animals could balance even when the men were hardly able to stand. Quinlivan and the team hovered around the horses, making sure they were okay. But as the storm increased in violence, even the horses began to lose their equilibrium. Belowdecks, it felt like a roller coaster. One moment, the ship would plunge downward, forcing the horses to brace themselves. When the ship hit the bottom of each swell, it smacked so hard that the planks underneath them shook. A moment later, the same cycle started again. Staggering from horse to horse, the men stroked their sweaty coats and whispered words of reassurance. The animals reared against their restraints, throwing up their heads and yanking on their cross ties. Separated by narrow planks that were lower than their heads, the horses saw their stablemates' distress, which fed their own as the ship tossed them from side to side in their small enclosures. Only Witez, as balanced as a cat, shifted but never seemed to panic. When Quinlivan approached him, he blew a puff of warm breath across the soldier's cheek, as if to say, "Don't worry about me."

The weather grew worse; winds whipped across the decks at seventy-five miles an hour, and the ship was making no headway. At the helm, the captain's compass wasn't working; he struggled to navigate using backup equipment. Hoping to find the shortest route to the other side, he decided to head the ship directly into the storm. But as soon as he did, the vessel started pitching dangerously from side to side. Taking a breather from the horses up on deck, Quinlivan was shocked by the storm's intensity. The ship, too light to hold its course in heavy seas, was knocked on its beam ends, listing sharply with each churning wave. As the ship rolled into a wave's trough, Quinlivan could see the next one towering sixty feet above his head. A moment later, the next wave would grab the ship, propelling it up until he saw the churning ocean an equal depth below. Barely able to stand, Quinlivan staggered back to the hold to see how the horses were faring.

In the cargo hold, the lights had blown out and it was pitch-dark. Quinlivan could hear the bone-chilling sounds of stallions screaming, hooves clanging against metal and boards, and mares whinnying. Each time the ship rolled, the horses were flung back and forth against the wooden planks that separated them. When a particularly giant wave sent the ship almost horizontal, the planks separating the horses finally splintered, and they were thrown out into the hold.

Quinlivan bolted into action to save the horses. With just the light of a single lantern, he climbed into the midst of the fray; the rest of the men followed close behind him.

In the small pool of light afforded by the lantern, they shuddered at what they saw. The force of the storm had knocked the horses clear of their enclosures and piled the priceless stallions in a heap. They were fighting and kicking one another in a flashing tangle of bared teeth, sharp hooves, and flaring nostrils with flashes of white coats lighting up and then disappearing in the dark. The mares were thrown from their enclosures as well, and timbers crashed down on top of them, injuring several. The terrified horses were just as dangerous to the men as the bullets they had so recently escaped.

Still, Quinlivan's men thought nothing of their own safety. Pushing away any thought of fear, they moved into the tangle, trying frantically to separate the animals before they killed one another. All of the miles traversed, all of the danger faced, all of the lives risked and even lost to save these horses—all of it was on the verge of being wasted.

Quinlivan set about looking for Gospa's foal, fearing the worst— just a few days old, the tiny foal could easily be killed by the flailing hooves of a furious stallion. Miraculously, she was unscathed: Gospa had managed to stand guard, shielding her precious charge with her body. Next, Quinlivan made his way to Witez. Even in the chaos, the stallion seemed to understand that panicking would only make matters worse. Quinlivan stroked the horse's nose for a moment, whispering a quiet word of thanks. Witez, the chieftain, had been bred to maintain his composure in the fury of battle—and here on the *Stephen F. Austin,* he had won his warrior's stripes.

By the time the men got the horses separated, many of the animals were bloody and covered in cuts. They trembled, nostrils trumpeting, eyes white-edged. The captain had managed to turn course, steering them around the storm; the ship had ceased its violent pitch and roll. The exhausted horsemen had no time to rest. The veterinarians squatted on the straw floor, improvised sterile fields laid out in front of them, and sutured up the horses' wounds with steady hands while men held flashlights to illuminate the work.

Finally, after hours of constant attention, the animals were sewn up and bandaged and the jerry-rigged stalls rebuilt. The horses were spent, and the men were so exhausted that they could hardly stand. But all of them were going to survive.

The seas slowly calmed, and finally, after the past few days' fury, Quinlivan had a few moments to spend up on deck. The ocean had turned to a tranquil turquoise filigreed with seaweed; off in the distance, Quinlivan spotted porpoises cavorting. But he knew that the calm seas did not spell the end of their troubles. The captain's detour around the storm had thrown them off course. The crossing, which was originally supposed to take ten to twelve days, had been extended to over two weeks. Safely on the other side of the tempest, the horsemen faced a different sort of emergency—their stores of hay and grain were running dangerously low. Horse feed was so scarce in Germany that they had been allotted the bare minimum needed for the journey.

Trying to make their fodder last as long as possible, the horsemen made the risky decision to bulk out the remaining feed with bedding straw. The sensitive animals, already debilitated by the rough passage, did not respond well. One horse after another got sick, their guts twisting with painful colic—a dangerous intestinal condition that often proves fatal to horses. Again, the men were huddled belowdecks, this time watching the frantic horses kicking at their distended bellies. Horses are unable to vomit, so Quinlivan soothed horses writhing in pain as a veterinarian threaded a hose through the nostril of each sick animal, attempting to pump its stomach. One by one, the horses started to recover. Two days before reaching port, they ran out of feed. If the trip had lasted any longer, some of the horses might not have survived.

On October 28, 1945, the *Stephen F. Austin* and its exhausted cargo of men and beasts pulled up to the dock in Newport News, Virginia. Sixteen days on the high seas, through a battering storm, with inadequate feed, had left the horses looking weary and battle-worn—their cuts and nicks not yet healed, their coats dull, and their bodies thin— but they had made it.

The first to board the ship was Colonel Fred Hamilton, chief of the Army Remount Service. Back stateside, he had been preparing for the horses' arrival, and he was eager for a report. "How many were lost?" he asked.

"None," Quinlivan reported proudly. "In fact, we gained one." One of the mares had foaled two days out from Newport News, her foal joining Gospa's as the tiniest additions to the group. Quin had left Bremerhaven with 151 stallions, mares, and foals, and arrived in Virginia with 152.

28.

THE RIDERLESS HORSE

The gloomy news spread like wildfire. On December 9, 1945, General George S. Patton had been seriously injured in a car accident in the Rhineland. Like everyone in Europe and America, Hank Reed was shocked to hear the news. At first nobody could quite believe that the seemingly invincible warrior had suffered such a fate, and for the first few days, the newspapers continued to report that Patton was improving. But at his bedside in a military hospital in Heidelberg, the reality was quite different. He had suffered a fractured spine and was paralyzed from the neck down. When his doctor came to talk to him, Patton, the consummate cavalryman, had only one question: "Will I ever ride again?"

AT THE TIME OF PATTON'S ACCIDENT, six months had passed since the raid on Hostau; in a surprising twist of fate, the rescued horses were safely settled in Hank Reed's native Virginia while he remained in Germany to set up a constabulary force. But Colonel Reed's involvement with horses had continued as he developed a mounted brigade to patrol the rugged border region that stretched between Germany and Czechoslovakia—the same area that Stewart and Lessing first crossed on horseback. Reed's project demonstrated that horses had a continuing utility in the army, even if in a limited way. Patton, in his role as military governor of Bavaria, had supported Reed's decision.

———

DURING THE SIX MONTHS prior to Patton's accident, emotions had been running high on a subject that mattered deeply to both Patton and Reed—the horse's role in the postwar army. With only a few exceptions, no American horses had been used in combat during the hostilities. Nevertheless, the role of the horse in the army—the riding school at Fort Riley, the prestige of the equestrian events, and the ceremonial mounted color guards—were so central to the force's history that many could not imagine the army without them.

Patton had been drawn into the debate. In July, Colonel Thomas J. Johnson, head of the American Remount Association, had written to Patton, requesting his help with the "present, thoughtless discrimination in the Army against horses and mules." Johnson told Patton, "Your opinions on this subject will have more effect than those of anyone living." Patton wrote to his friend General Jacob Devers, head of Army Ground Forces in Washington, pleading with him to retain a role for horses. Patton reminded Devers of the outstanding records of polo players in combat and said, "Otherwise, we will have nobody in the next war who knows anything about an animal." The outstanding combat performance of horse-trained cavalry officers like Hank Reed appeared to prove Patton's point; but outside the ranks of the former horse cavalry, no one seemed to be listening.

More than any other individual, Patton had been instrumental in drumming up support for the captured horses that had safely landed in America, but he did not live long enough to see what became of them. Thirteen days after his automobile accident, on December 21, 1945, George Patton died at age sixty of a pulmonary embolism. According to the wishes he had expressed to his wife, Beatrice, he was to be buried alongside his men at the Third Army Cemetery in Luxembourg.

Hank Reed had a final service to perform in Patton's honor. On December 22, he received orders to report to Luxembourg. Like Patton, Reed had been stationed at Fort Myer, adjacent to Arlington National Cemetery, for several years before the war and thus had been trained in the somber protocol for an army funeral. It was his duty to organize the color guard and the horses at what would be one of the most watched military funerals in history.

―――

THE DAY OF PATTON'S funeral was dark, with a cold, steady drizzle falling on the mourners, some black-clad, others in full dress uniform. Reed had attended to every single detail, carefully preparing the black horse that would follow the casket through the streets of Luxembourg City. One of the lessons drilled into the funeral delegations at Fort Myer was that to properly honor the fallen, the tiniest details mattered. Reed and his men did not sleep all night as they went over the parade routes, briefed leaders, and instructed the drivers for the procession that would wind through the streets of a city liberated by the Americans a year earlier.

Heads of state and high-ranking military officers followed as the flag-draped coffin passed through the cobblestone streets of the somber, wintry city on the back of a half-track. The route was lined with mourners, while reporters from all over the world jostled for position. Patton's widow, Bea, clad in a thick black fur coat and cloche, followed the coffin in the first car. The cortège, wending slowly through the narrow streets of Luxembourg city from the train station to the Hamm

PATTON'S FUNERAL PROCESSION,
LUXEMBOURG CITY, DECEMBER 1945.

cemetery, swelled with the trappings of the powerful military force that Patton had led: Massive armored cars and powerful tanks rolled along in formation, showcasing the technological might of the United States Army. The band played "The General's March" at the tempo of a dirge; as the coffin passed, mourners doffed hats to the great leader.

Following the half-track bearing Patton's coffin came the caparisoned horse, a tradition that dated back to the rites for fallen warriors during the time of Genghis Khan. The black horse wore Patton's saddle, draped with black crepe. In the stirrups, the general's high boots were placed, their toes facing backward. In all the solemn fanfare, it was the quiet dignity of the riderless horse that symbolized this tragic loss: a symbol that all present could intuitively understand, no matter what their native language.

The victorious general was laid to rest alongside his men, and with his death, it seemed that the end of an era had come. The man who had, during the 1912 Olympics, run, swum, fenced, shot at a target, and jumped a horse to demonstrate his fitness as a soldier, had departed a world that had changed almost beyond recognition during his lifetime. It was a world that the consummate horse lover Patton had helped to create—a world in which wars were fought with the tanks and motorized vehicles so mightily on display. In this world, the parading black horse so carefully appointed for the ceremony had become a relic of the past. Hank Reed and the men of the cavalry had lost a friend, a leader, and the army's most passionate defender of horses.

THE VICTORY PARADE

FRONT ROYAL, VIRGINIA,

APRIL 7, 1946

A soft sunshine beamed down on the kelly-green pastures surrounding the Aleshire Army Remount Depot in Front Royal, Virginia. Under mild blue skies, slicked-up servicemen soothed high-strung horses. Tweedy-looking horse experts and women in bright spring dresses chattered in excited tones while they perused the exotic names and pedigrees of the horses that would be put on display today, April 7, 1946. The parade of captured horses was turning out to be one of the most talked-about equine spectacles in recent memory. During the war, most major horse events had been curtailed—racehorses were kept off trains to make room for the troops, and the big horse shows had been canceled because so many young men were in uniform. But today the war was over, the Allies had won, and the equestrian world was abuzz with the news that Uncle Sam had not just removed the Nazi scourge but also made off with a king's ransom of horses.

His face shaded by a broad-brimmed campaign hat, Captain Quinlivan passed quietly among his four-footed friends, whispering soothing words. The horses responded with soft whinnies and friendly nudges, pleased to see a familiar face among the throngs of strangers flooding the grounds of the Aleshire depot. Quinlivan smoothed manes and fiddled with halters, determined that "his" charges would put their best foot forward on this important day. For months since their arrival, the European imports had been sheltered from view—a mini–Manhattan Project of secrecy right in the very heart of America's horse country. All that time, rumor, speculation, and interest had been brewing, and today the public would see these spectacular purebreds for the first time. The event had drawn a large crowd of interested spectators, as well as a gaggle of journalists from the local and national press corps.

In the year following the end of the war, stories about captured horses continued to seize headlines. A few months before Patton's death, a photograph of the general riding Favory Africa, a Lipizzaner stallion intended as a gift for Japanese emperor Hirohito, had circulated widely in the press. Meanwhile, in Tokyo, a young GI had actually discovered Hirohito's personal mount, a white Arabian, hidden away in a stable. The soldier had been granted permission to ship the captured stallion back to California, where they now made regular appearances at horse shows and rodeos.

But the horses brought over from Europe were no circus horses, and the army had been determined to keep the clamoring crowds away until they were ready to be seen. Colonel Voorhees, the commanding officer of the Remount Depot, had kept all of the European horses cloistered inside the grounds. "While we were trying to pull them into shape," he said, "only a few outsiders were allowed to see them. Horsemen all over the country were screaming to be allowed in, but it would have been like running rubberneck busses through a hospital ward."

The horses' arrival had not been free from controversy. Drew Pearson, muckraking columnist for *The Washington Post,* had issued a public scolding, implying that the animals had taken berths from soldiers awaiting their chance to ship home. Some argued that the German horses' blood might taint that of the American-breds—an argument that held traces of the old eugenicist theories that had driven Rau's breeding enterprise. At the same time, members of the American Jockey Club were fighting over whether to allow the German horses into the American Thoroughbred registry. Colonel Fred Hamilton, who had painstakingly cleared the horses and checked their pedigrees before taking them from Germany, then flown home to be the first to greet them in America, was frustrated. If the horses could not be registered, their value to the American horse-racing industry, which allowed only Thoroughbreds with registered bloodlines to compete, would be ruined. The Americans had gained control of these horses by defeating Nazi Germany; now, ironically, Nazi-style arguments related to the purity of their blood were being marshaled against them.

All of this bickering had gone on in the press; no one in America outside a select group of cavalrymen had actually laid eyes on these much-talked-about horses. The animals were bound to make a stunning impression. Lotnik's pearlescent coat gleamed. Witez, the chieftain, shone bright as flame. Quinlivan was as well groomed as his four-footed companions, looking spruce in his cavalry uniform, his eyes lit up with a twinkle of pride. Of the entire group from the 2nd Cavalry, Quinlivan was the only one who would be an eyewitness to this important day—their introduction to the American public. Having long since fallen in love with his charges, Quinlivan would share them with the world at long last.

At two P.M., in the large outdoor arena of the Front Royal complex, it was time for the parade to begin. Clustered at ringside, people jostled while eagerly flipping through their programs. A hush fell over the crowd as cavalrymen began to lead the horses, one by one, across the viewing area. As the slender, light-footed Thoroughbreds came prancing by, avid racehorse breeders swapped notes about their European racing records. Everyone present agreed that the one they were calling "Hitler's Horse," Nordlicht, a past winner of the German Derby, was Hamilton's most valuable import in monetary terms. The last horse to be led out was Witez. From the large irregular white star that set off his big dark eyes to the white feet up to his fetlocks, from the kingly way that he held his head aloft to the power of his perfectly formed hindquarters, the stallion made an indelible impression. The assembled horsemen nodded and murmured in appreciation as Quinlivan noted their response to his favorite with satisfaction. Even among an extraordinary collection of horseflesh, this genuine descendant of a pureblooded desert-bred Arabian was a one-of-a-kind beauty.

The final event of the parade of horses was a driving display: Four Lipizzaner mares, fully decked out in their brass-studded imperial harnesses, circled the arena pulling an imperial coach. As they trotted around the large enclosure with their natural high-stepping stride, the brass fittings of their harnesses glinted in the mild spring sunshine. Most of the people in the stands were completely unfamiliar with the Lipizzaner breed. Alongside the lanky Thoroughbreds, the white horses looked stocky and compact, their Roman noses, a sign of their elegant breeding, unappealing to American taste. Nor did the audience know anything of the intricate dressage moves and impressive "airs above the ground" leaps that had made these horses so famous in Europe. A cavalry lieutenant drove the four-in-hand with panache, and the audience was impressed at the novel sight—but even so, the Lipizzaner were unable to seize the spectators' interest like the more familiar Thoroughbreds.

When the parade was over, reporters and photographers from *Life, Reader's Digest,* and *Collier's* snapped photographs and asked questions about the horses' trip to America. One soldier who had traveled aboard the *Stephen F. Austin* quipped, "Noah was lucky. He had only one stallion. We had seventy." Madera, the princess of Piber, with her foal by her side, pricked up her ears as a reporter from *Stars & Stripes* snapped her picture; the magazine would run her photograph alongside the story of her journey to America, with the caption: "America's Sweetheart Horse."

Certainly, there would have been eager prospective buyers for many of the rescued horses among the well-heeled crowd assembled to see them on parade, but these refugees were not for sale. They remained the property of the United States Army. In April 1946, Colonel Hamilton's Remount Service was still operating five major horse-breeding operations in addition to the one in Front Royal. Now Hamilton's plan was to disperse the horses among the different depots. Only the Thoroughbreds would remain at Front Royal. Quinlivan had been reassigned to Fort Robinson, Nebraska. Witez was being shipped to Pomona, California. After spending almost a year together, the friends had their marching orders: They were going separate ways. On his last day at Front Royal, Quinlivan lingered an extra moment with the chieftain to say goodbye. Witez's exquisitely tapered ears flicked back and forth, and Quinlivan could hear the deep, throaty whinny of the Polish-bred Arabian following him as he turned around and moved on to his next assignment.

FINDING A HOME

Alois Podhajsky stood in the center of an empty riding hall in Wels, Austria, scanning its once familiar contours. Deep parallel lines bracketed his slim lips; bags pillowed under his eyes. Around him whispered ghostly echoes of creaking leather, cadenced hoofbeats, and the commanding voices of exacting riding masters. It was here, at this dragoon barracks, that Podhajsky had started his career as a cavalry soldier. Now weathered but still possessed of an Olympian's athletic form, Podhajsky was among the lucky ones: He had survived. Older, less hopeful, but no less determined, he looked resignedly at the changes the war had wrought on this familiar place.

The once well-appointed edifice had been stripped almost bare—windows, doors, light fittings, and electric circuits were gone, sold off on the black market. The building had only recently been vacated after serving as a shelter for war refugees. What remained was in a sorry state, but Podhajsky, having grown accustomed to improvisation, believed that this dilapidated former barracks might be the best place for the stallions' new permanent home.

A year had passed since Podhajsky and his stallions had fled the elegant Spanish Riding School. For now, a return to Vienna remained impossible. Peace had brought stability to Austria, but the country remained under Allied occupation, divided into sectors controlled by the United States, Great Britain, France, and the Soviet Union. Vienna was likewise divided, although its center was designated as a shared international zone. Thanks to Patton's decree in 1945, the Lipizzaner and the Spanish Riding School had been granted American protection, their safety and ongoing support assured as long as they remained within the American zone. And so the centrally located Imperial Stables stood empty. The Winter Riding Hall was being used to store props from the National Opera House. Podhajsky's dream of returning the horses to their rightful place in Vienna had not dimmed, but for the meantime, he requested permission to relocate them to Wels. Here, with adequate stabling and a large riding hall, he hoped that they could gradually reestablish a state of normalcy and routine.

By April 1946, the move was complete, stallions and mares settled in their new quarters, the school cleaned up and repainted. For the first time since leaving Vienna with the horses, Podhajsky could free his mind from questions of daily survival. As he put the stallions and riders back on a training footing, he found comfort in the familiarity of their daily program. He still had no money, no support, and no real long-term plan. Though this outcome was not what he had expected when he fled Vienna under a hail of bombs, Podhajsky knew the prewar world was gone, and with it the infrastructure that had supported the school. He needed to invent a new future for the horses.

HALFWAY ACROSS THE GLOBE, in Pomona, California, Witez cantered along a hillside trail, kicking up small puffs of dust with each stride. His coat shone with a coppery fire; his black tail floated behind him like plumes of blowing smoke. On his back, his groom and rider, Joe Benes, was riding western-style, holding the braided leather reins in one hand; a Stetson shaded his eyes from the bright West Coast sunshine. Citrus groves and ornamental rose gardens spread out below them. Behind them soared the snowcapped San Gabriel Mountains. After traveling halfway across the globe, the Arabian stallion appeared to have landed in paradise.

The Pomona Remount Depot, where Witez now lived, was the jewel in the army's crown. A million-dollar property (in 1940s dollars), it was the former home of W. K. Kellogg, one of the world's foremost breeders of purebred Arabian horses.

Kellogg's romance with the Arabian had begun during his hardscrabble boyhood in Michigan. His family owned an old nag named Spot; he and his brothers and sisters used to pull themselves up on Spot's tail and stand on his back, sometimes two or three at a time. One day, a neighbor scolded young Kellogg about bothering Spot, telling the boy that the horse was part Arabian, "the most regal breed of horses the world has ever known."

This simple interaction led to a lifelong fascination for Kellogg. In 1925, he spent $250,000 on 377 acres in Pomona to establish an Arabian breeding farm. The Kellogg Ranch soon became a popular Southern California attraction, winning legions of fans who learned to appreciate the refined desert breed. Every Sunday, the ranch sponsored Arabian shows for the general public, featuring parades and trick riding. Hand-tinted postcards and samples of Kellogg's cornflakes were handed out to the visitors. Dignitaries, from royalty to celebrities like Gary Cooper, Mary Pickford, and Olivia de Havilland, visited the ranch. In 1927, Charles Lindbergh did a flyover in the *Spirit of St. Louis*. Ronald Reagan posed for publicity photos there. The most famous of the Kellogg Arabians was a white stallion named Jadaan, who appeared with Rudolph Valentino in six movies, starred in the Rose Parade, and had his own plush box stall adjacent to one of Hollywood's ornate movie palaces. He was even taken to Santa Anita to be photographed with the statue of California's other most famous horse—Seabiscuit. In 1932, with great fanfare, Kellogg donated the ranch property, six hundred thousand dollars, and eighty-eight purebred Arabians to the University of California for the founding of an institute of animal husbandry. Will Rogers emceed the dedication ceremony, which was attended by twenty-two thousand people. Kellogg had only one precondition: that the Sunday Arabian shows must be continued.

In 1942, Kellogg was deeply moved when an Arabian breeder in England sent him letters describing how her horses were endangered during the Battle of Britain. Inspired to make a contribution to the war effort, Kellogg strongly encouraged the university to donate the ranch and all of its horses to the United States Army. Kellogg believed that his brave and intelligent Arabians would be useful to the military, but the Quartermaster Corps took possession of the ranch just as the army began dismounting its troops in earnest.

In 1946, when Witez arrived in Pomona, he was stabled in one of the finest Arabian horse-breeding establishments in the world. Even among these celebrity Arabians, the Polish chieftain immediately attracted attention. The Remount Service offered him at stud; Witez quickly proved his strength as a sire. By 1947, out of a crop of thirty-two foals, eight were the offspring of Witez. One local rancher, who had bred two of his mares to Witez and owned two of the stallion's foals, wanted desperately to buy him. But the horses belonged to the Quartermaster Corps and were not for sale.

Despite his success as a remount stallion, Witez's future remained in question; the army's commitment to horse breeding was wavering. With the passing of Patton in 1945, the horse had lost its most powerful ally. No young, ambitious person in the army wanted to be known for his fervor for horses. Most of the old "hit the leather and ride" folk had retired and moved into civilian life. In Washington, Colonel Fred Hamilton continued to plead on behalf of the Remount Service. But privately, Hamilton was feeling hopeless. He had managed to convince the War Department to cede precious America-bound cargo space to the horses by arguing that they were more valuable by the cubic foot than any other possible cargo. But that value had yet to be proved. As if the tempest at sea on the *Stephen F. Austin* were a harbinger of things to come, the horses had faced nothing but problems since their arrival.

The head of the Army Remount Depot in Pomona, Colonel F. W. Koester, had been a persistent advocate for the Arabians during his tenure. In 1946 and 1947, Koester fought for the animals' pedigrees to be authenticated so the horses could be registered. If they were not, they would be classed as grade horses and lose all of their value for breeding. But American breeding organizations continued to voice skepticism about authenticating the bloodlines of horses seized in wartime. As the one soldier who had been with the horses at each step of their transfer from Hostau to Bremerhaven to the United States, Quinlivan gave a sworn affidavit as to the horses' identities and the manner of their capture, and to the trustworthiness of the Germans—Lessing and Rudofsky—who had vouched for the authenticity of their pedigrees. Through the efforts of Colonel Koester, both Witez and Lotnik were eventually registered with the Arabian Horse Registry of America, assuring their continuing value as sires. Throughout 1947, the Pomona Remount Depot thrived, as crowds of four to five thousand people attended the Sunday Arabian shows and delegations from China, India, and Saudi Arabia came to tour the state-of-the-art ranch and to admire

Witez and the rest of the world-famous Kellogg Arabians. But Colonel Koester was set to retire at the end of 1947, leaving no one to advocate for the horses.

To make matters worse, several European countries—Hungary, Poland, and Yugoslavia—had filed suits claiming that their horses had been seized unlawfully. Hoping to avoid ruffling diplomatic feathers, the State Department recommended that the horses be returned to their countries of origin. In response, the Senate Armed Services Committee began to hold hearings in 1947. A delegation (including Tom Stewart's father, Senator Tom Stewart of Tennessee) went to the Aleshire Remount Depot in Virginia to inspect the "war booty" horses (mostly Thoroughbreds) remaining there. Some of the horses of Hungarian origin, including the famous Thoroughbred Taj Akbar, were sent to the port of New Orleans to be boarded on a cargo ship for Europe, but in a sudden reversal, the Senate Armed Services Committee blocked the decision and ruled that the horses were legitimate spoils of war. The wrangling over the rescued horses' fate kept them in the news, but the underlying problem had no clear solution. Two years after the end of a horseless war, no one had been able to marshal a convincing argument that the army should continue to breed them.

As bureaucrats in Washington, D.C., debated the horses' future, newspapers fed public interest. In 1947, a reporter from *The Christian Science Monitor* visited the Pomona Remount Depot. Of Witez and Lotnik, he wrote, "They like to be looked at. They back up a little so you can appraise more carefully their classic beauty, and then come close so you can pat them and perhaps donate a lump of sugar. War captives yes, but world citizens to any lover of fine horses." In his photograph, Witez, the "famous Arabian stallion," stood on a loose lead with his ears pricked forward, looking out toward the mountains in the distance. Above his picture ran the bold headline: "Fine European Horses Captured by Army Pose Problems."

31.

THE WAR ORPHANS

As 1948 drew to a close, three years had passed since the war had been won at the cost of more than four hundred thousand American lives. The troops were home and the veterans, like the characters in the popular 1947 movie *The Best Years of Our Lives,* had bottled up their stories and gotten on with their business. The men of the 2nd Cavalry had scattered across America, picking up the pieces of the lives they had left behind during the war years. Some, like Captain Quinlivan, were still in the army; others, like Tom Stewart, had been discharged and were trying to find their footing in the civilian world. Many of them had cut out newspaper and magazine articles about the horses' triumphant arrival in Newport News, but as the years passed, the men lost track of the horses, and the memory of the wartime rescue was tucked away with the rest of their war souvenirs.

By this time, the 231 horses imported to America by Fred Hamilton and the horse detectives, in two separate shipments in 1945 and 1946, had met a variety of fates. Although none of the transported horses had been intended for sale, support for the Remount Service quickly began to dwindle, and by late 1946, Hamilton had been required to auction off most of the Thoroughbreds at Front Royal. His promise of the Thoroughbreds' great value was not borne out. The refusal of the American Jockey Club to register the Thoroughbreds had greatly diminished their worth. Of the sixty-four imported by Hamilton, only four—among them Nordlicht—would be registered. A syndicate headed by Christopher Chenery (of the family who would later own Secretariat) bought the famed German Thoroughbred for $20,300, a relatively high price tag for a stallion at the time. But without registration papers, the majority of these horses' descendants could not be raced, significantly limiting their value. As a result, most of the horses that had been captured to such great fanfare just a few years before had mostly gone on to ordinary lives in private hands.

The army cavalry had a last hurrah when it cobbled together an equestrian team to ride in the 1948 Olympics in London. In November of that year, the Army Equestrian Team made their final public appearance at the National Horse Show in Madison Square Garden. When members of the Dutch team spotted a couple of their own horses in the American stables, the army handed them back to their rightful owners. Meanwhile, cavalry veterans were offered a chance to purchase army horses at a discount. Quite a few took advantage of the offer to buy strings of horses and establish riding academies. The future of equestrian sports from here on in would be civilian. Still, a few of the horses from Hostau, including Witez and Lotnik, remained with the Remount Service, their destiny uncertain, their plight unknown to most of the men involved in their rescue.

On July 1, 1948, the Defense Department, under the order of President Truman, formally transferred its remaining Remount Depots with all of their livestock and equipment to the Department of Agriculture. Army horsemen hoped the transfer of the Pomona Remount Depot would preserve its unique Arabian breeding program. But with lightning speed, the horse lovers' hopes were dashed. The Agriculture Department declared that its budget would not support any horse-breeding operations. They planned to sell off all remaining animals immediately. The number of horses in the army had already dropped precipitously, from the more than 200,000 horses in 1941 to just 327 in 1949. At Fort Riley, the soldiers lovingly cared for some of the distinguished beloved retired horses from the army's competitive equestrian days. At the Pomona Remount Depot, only Kellogg's prized Arabians, the imports from Janów Podlaski, and nine Lipizzaner remained.

Witez had lived through the bombings of wartime, but now, in his formerly peaceful home, a new sort of battle ensued. The former Kellogg Ranch had turned into the center of a storm of controversy, pitting horse lovers and animal rights activists against bean counters in Washington. As soon as the Department of Agriculture assumed control of the Pomona Remount Depot, their staff began a ruthless process of selection, culling the Arabian herd. Many of the able-bodied animals were sold off. Older mares and stallions, in good health but past their prime for breeding, were targeted for euthanization. Only the cream of the crop remained.

Arabian lovers, horrified by this callous treatment, started rescue operations, determined to save as many of the beautiful animals as possible. Sometimes they succeeded. When Raseyn, a twenty-two-year-old stallion and well-loved veteran of the Sunday shows, was discovered to be sterile, he was slated to be destroyed. A local humane horse advocate spirited him off the grounds (even the official history of the ranch declared that no one knew how she had pulled it off) and gave him a new home. In a letter to W. K. Kellogg, she wrote, "Your darling Raseyn is happy here, I'm sure. Once in a while, he puts his head against me as much to tell me that he loves me. The feeling is mutual. I have been feeding him small pans of chopped carrots, ground hay, ground grain, and added vitamins every three hours, and now he puts up his head and speaks whenever I get near his corral."

Other aged horses were not so lucky. Jadaan, Valentino's horse, was euthanized, his skeleton donated to the school of veterinary medicine at the University of California, Davis, his hide promised (but never delivered) to the Cody Museum in Wyoming. Kellogg, by then eighty-eight years old and blind, was reported to be heartbroken by this turn of events. He had donated the ranch "with no strings attached," believing the horse-breeding operations would continue in perpetuity. With each passing day, the horse group shrank—some sold, others put down, and some lucky ones given refuge by kindhearted fans. As long as the Kellogg Ranch remained in the army's hands, there had been great reluctance to sell off the rescued horses—a public relations disaster for the army as well as a sentimental one—but with the changing of the guard, the bureaucrats in the Agriculture Department had no such scruples. Lotnik, once the pearl of Hostau, was sold to a local horseman to be used as a pleasure horse.

By the fall of 1948, only the most valuable horses in the Kellogg stables remained. Among these was Witez. In October 1948, even these horses—the most valuable of all—were to be sold off in a closed-bid auction, until this announcement faced a prompt and noisy backlash. Horse organizations and interested individuals sent off a flurry of telegrams to President Truman, a slew of critical articles appeared in Southland papers, delegations of powerful horse advocates met with California governor Earl Warren, and an ambitious young congressman named Richard Nixon made a personal plea to the Department of Agriculture. Petitioners believed that the ranch and its herd should be kept together and another organization should take over—one committed to continuing its mission. Hoping to tamp down the controversy, the Department of Agriculture changed tack. Rather than auction the remaining animals, they decided to move them to Fort Reno, Oklahoma, where the horse-breeding operations had not yet been fully curtailed. Many assumed that the horses would be quietly sold away from the prying eyes of the Southern California press, though this had not been publicly stated. One thing was clear: The War Assets Administration had designated the horses as surplus government property. The United States government was not in the horse business any longer, and these animals, products of the most refined pedigrees in the world, were about as valuable to them as a bunch of cast-off tires from an old-model jeep.

ON DECEMBER 1, 1948, the Pomona ranch appeared serene, its palm trees silhouetted against the gray San Gabriel Mountains, as uniformed officers watched a line of horses parading toward a waiting railcar. The gathered horse handlers were clearly downcast, reluctant to see their stunning charges loaded for departure. The Arabians stepped lightly across the dusty train yard, seeming too regal for these ordinary surroundings. The mild California sunshine shone upon their fine coats, bringing out the copper, silver, and gold. A gaggle of reporters and press photographers had gathered to witness the dispersal.

Four mares with foals at their sides loaded first, then four yearling stallions, one six-year-old, one ten-year old, and a pure white Lipizzaner coach horse. As each horse was safely stowed into the specially made box stalls in the train cars, the handlers who were staying behind exited the train with somber expressions and empty hands.

At the very back of the line, last to load, stood Witez. With his large dark eyes, he paused, looking at the assembled crowd like a monarch surveying his subjects. Joe Benes let the lead rope loose so that Witez could show his well-shaped head and sculpted muzzle to best advantage. As cameras flashed, the stallion flicked his curved ears forward, their delicate tips pointing inward. Benes waited until the photographers had finished, then clucked softly. The chieftain followed him into the shadowy boxcar without looking back.

After Witez was settled in the train, Benes offered him a sugar lump, then planted a kiss on the animal's soft muzzle, lingering an extra moment at his side. But the train's engine was revving, and Benes, who had been caring for this stallion and riding him daily since his arrival from Front Royal in 1946, had no choice but to unclasp the lead rope, coil it over the hook next to Witez's improvised stall, and walk away.

Had anyone noticed, as he boarded the train, the brand just behind the stallion's left shoulder? Witez still wore the mark of his birthplace in Poland: a royal crown. But that had not protected this knight, this chieftain, this warrior. This train to nowhere rattled east all the same.

The next day, the papers ran the headline "Kellogg Herd Slashed Again." At the end of 1947, Colonel Fred Hamilton, who had worked so hard to bring the captured horses to the United States, had retired from the army on disability at the age of fifty-one. Publicly, he remained an outspoken advocate for horses. Privately, he had taken to calling these last remaining horses "the war orphans."

THE AUCTION

In the spring of 1949, Witez was in his prime, glowing with health and vitality. But the eleven-year-old Polish chieftain, the stolen treasure of the Third Reich, star of the Kellogg Arabians, was a precious jewel in a tarnished setting—especially today, May 25, when he stood in a dusty corral with the number 131 pasted on his hip.

Just a few short months after Witez arrived in Fort Reno, Oklahoma, away from the inquisitive eyes of the California press, the Department of Agriculture made a decision to close down the last vestiges of the army's remount program and sell off the remaining horses.

The auction of exotic Arabians and Lipizzaner had attracted a motley assortment of prospective buyers. A movie company, a circus, and a variety of local ranchers had gathered to cast bids on these formerly priceless horses; news of the sale was not widely publicized, so those most aware of the horses' true value had not heard of the impending sale.

Witez couldn't have looked more out of place. Of all the destinations on his long journey, this one, ending on the dusty plains of Fort Reno, was the most desolate. Witez had arrived without a single familiar face to greet him. No one knew this glorious stallion's extraordinary story.

However, it turned out that one of the veterans of the 2nd Cavalry was in Fort Reno on the day of this terminal sale. Shortly before the auction started, a slight dark-haired man moved quietly past the corrals where the horses were lined up, ready to enter the showground. The man's step was soft but purposeful. He was looking for an old friend, a companion he once loved and watched over.

Each horse lined up here was sleek and refined—and each had a number stuck to his hip. The dark-haired man passed them by almost without looking; there was only one he wanted to see.

And only one horse grew still at the sound of the approaching footsteps, then flicked a single tapered ear forward. Yes, maybe, no? The single ear flicked back again, then a fine-boned head turned, deep brown eyes lighting up in recognition.

The veteran first heard the deep, full-throated whinny and then saw the face—the dark eyes set off by an irregular white star, the curved ears that seemed almost to touch when he pricked them forward. The man leaned up against the wooden fence, and the stallion approached. The Arabian extended his nose. His nostrils fluted, showing delicate pink inside. With a shiver of recognition and joy, Captain Tom Stewart put out his hand.

Stewart, the man whose midnight ride had set the stage for the rescue of the horses from Hostau, had not seen any of them since September 1945. He had been honored for his bravery in the raid, yet after a few months at home in Bethesda, like many veterans, he had found the transition to civilian life difficult. Still haunted by the friends he had lost and the brutality he had witnessed, he had trouble fitting into the social whirl afforded a senator's son. A few months after returning home, he confided in his sister, Betty Ann, that he needed to get away for a while—he needed time to think. The serious young man set off on a cross-country sojourn, hitchhiking across the American West, stopping to work as a day laborer pumping gas or washing cars when he needed to earn some money. As if guided by a divine hand, his journey had brought him here to Fort Reno to see his old friend Witez for the last time. Stewart was in no position to buy him—standing there at the dusty ringside, he could only hope that this horse, for whom much had been sacrificed, would find a loving home.

A few minutes before ten A.M., the prospective buyers moved away from the pens where they had been inspecting the horseflesh and clustered around the railing of a large sandy arena, their eyes shaded by broad-brimmed hats, their feet shod in scuffed western boots. People murmured and flipped through the program as they waited for the horses to be led out.

An auctioneer called out in drawn-out syllables, "One-thirteee-one." Witez raised his head, his forelock rakishly sweeping across the white star on his forehead. He pranced forward, holding his black tail proudly aloft. Prospective buyers studied the program, a typescript pamphlet of a few pages with a cover that read: *Agriculture Remount Service. Catalogue of Horses to be sold at Public Auction. 10:00 am. Wednesday, May 25th, 1949, Fort Reno, Oklahoma (4 miles West of El Reno on hwy. 66).* Inside was just the barest information: *Hip # 131, a bay stallion, foaled in 1938, 15 hands, son of Ofir and Federajca. Certified by the Arabian Horse Club No. 3933.* That was it.

Nowhere in the brochure did it tell of a frightened young groom daubing mud on the colt's sides, hoping to escape notice from the advancing Russians. Nowhere did it mention boarding a train to Czechoslovakia while a tearful young woman named Liselotte waved goodbye, or parading in the rain on a muddy field in front of a group of Nazi grandees, his lead rope held by a black-clad POW. Nor did it mention a gentle-handed veterinarian, Rudolf Lessing, who risked his life to try to save him. No mention was made of Tom Stewart, the soft-voiced captain who had accompanied Lessing under cover of darkness to secure his surrender. Nowhere was written the name of Quin Quinlivan, who had crouched in a dark ship's hold, trying to keep the stallion safe during a rough transatlantic journey. Fred Hamilton's name did not appear; nor did that of the late George Smith Patton; perhaps most surprising of all, no mention was made of the respected 2nd Cavalry colonel Hank Reed, the right man in the right place at the right time to save this horse's life. A chain of loving hands had passed the horse along virtually since his birth, trying to keep him safe from the danger that surrounded him. But none of those people had been able to hold on to him. The people who knew him, who cared for him, had never been allowed to own him. Since the moment of his birth, Witez had belonged to faceless bureaucracies: the government of Poland, the Third Reich, the United States Army, and now the Department of Agriculture.

The ranchers scanned the horse from forelock to fetlock, appraising his graceful swanlike neck and delicate-featured face, so unlike that of the compact muscular American Quarter Horse that was the popular breed in these parts. They squinted and chewed on bits of straw; it was hard for Stewart to tell what any of them was thinking.

As Witez circled the ring, high up in the bleachers, a man in a white cowboy hat clutched a sweaty hand around his rolled-up program as his heart beat faster. Back at his barn in Calabasas, California, he had two young colts that would grow up to be just like their sire. This was Earle Hurlbutt, who had been pestering for permission to purchase Witez but was never given the chance—until now. Ever since the stallion had left Pomona back in November, Hurlbutt had kept his ear to the ground, hoping to get some news of him. It was only by coincidence that he ended up hearing that the last lot of twenty-odd Arabians sent from the Kellogg Ranch would be auctioned off in Oklahoma. Without giving it a second thought, Hurlbutt hopped in his car and drove east, hoping to get there on time.

For a moment, the horse held everyone in a spellbound hush. Tom Stewart watched with his heart in his throat. He knew nothing of the man in the white hat, but he did know that the 2nd Cavalry's beloved mascot needed to go to a good home. Although he had no money in his pocket, Tom Stewart was rich in faith, and up in the grandstands, he said a silent prayer.

The auctioneer's high-pitched twang took off at a fast gallop as he opened the bidding. Hurlbutt soon noticed that he was not the only bidder; as the price went up in five-hundred-dollar increments, a few of the others dropped out, and soon Hurlbutt was bidding against a single other man. Hurlbutt had a weather-beaten face with kind blue eyes, the craggy landscape of a rancher who has spent his entire life in the wind and sun. As he increased the dollar amount with a raise of his index finger, his face showed no emotion, but inside, he was a nervous wreck. Very soon, he would reach his top bid, and the other rancher had given no sign of slowing up.

Witez had never been sold before, and it was hard to imagine putting a dollar price on his worth. But Earle Hurlbutt knew that he had reached his limit. He made his final bid—eight thousand one hundred dollars—adjusted the brim of his hat, and then, reluctant to face the disappointment of being outbid, climbed down off the wooden bleachers and walked away.

A man ran up and tapped him on the shoulder, asking where he was going. "You bought yourself a horse," he said.

That May day in 1949 was when Witez finally got his discharge papers and joined civilian life. The bloody shoulder on his mother had marked the stallion as a warrior, and for eleven years, as his life was buffeted by armies and war, it had seemed more of a curse than a blessing. That spring day in Oklahoma, the curse was broken at last. For the first time in his life, Witez would have a home of his own.

When Tom Stewart realized that the war orphan had found a loving owner, his heart flooded with relief. Here was tangible evidence that his wartime efforts had come to something good. From that day forward, Stewart's heart lightened; the horse he had worked so hard to save had helped to set him free.

THE WIDOW'S ROSE

On October 3, 1950, eight men wearing brown double-breasted jackets, buckskin riding breeches, and bicorne hats gathered at a New York pier as the *American Importer* docked. Standing a bit apart from the other riders, his lined face lit up with anticipation, was fifty-two-year-old Alois Podhajsky, who had arrived in the city a few days earlier on his first transatlantic flight. The weather was mild and the sky was bright blue. A few scattered clouds floated high above the New York skyline, which glittered at their backs. Behind the waiting riders, a throng of reporters and photographers clustered to photograph this moment: The famed white Lipizzaner stallions had come to America.

Soon the first stallion appeared on the gangplank, the polished brass of his leather halter jingling as his hooves thumped on the ramp. He raised his head, flicked his ears, and trumpeted his pink-and-black-speckled nostrils, taking in the clanging hubbub of the pier: belching steamships, noisy tugboats, and shouting dockworkers. Picking a familiar face out of the crowd, he lowered his head and let out a warm whinny. At the sight of his beloved Africa, Alois Podhajsky hurried to the horse's side, whispering a word of greeting, then passing him a sugar lump and kissing him on the nose. Soon all fourteen of the stallions stood in a line, their coats gleaming in the bright afternoon sunshine. Around them, flashbulbs popped and reporters called out

questions, but Podhajsky paid them little mind until he had finished his series of greetings. The friendly and intelligent stallions were pricking up their ears and looking around, seeming to mug for the cameras, while the uniformed riders, posing with the horses, tried to maintain dignified demeanors as the gaggle of the cameramen yelled out, "Smile!"

Dressed in a dark business suit and a gray fedora, the president of the American Horse Show Association, Brigadier General Alfred G. "Tubby" Tuckerman, was there to greet the visitors. He stopped to pose for a photograph with Africa, grasping the halter as Podhajsky offered the horse a carrot. Africa's expression looked as if he were so amused by the whole scene that Podhajsky couldn't help but break into a rare smile. Soon, the horses were loaded into vans and transported to the Kenilworth Riding School in nearby Rye, a suburb in Westchester County, to stretch their legs and warm up for their big American debut.

The next morning, more than fifty photographers showed up to watch the first schooling session. Riders put their horses through their paces while members of the press swarmed around, snapping pictures from all angles and calling out questions. By the end of the week, photos and rapturous articles had appeared across the nation, describing the dancing white stallions; a newsreel of the Lipizzaner demonstrating the airs above the ground sped around the world, the narration translated into twenty-eight different languages.

Since moving the horses to Wels in 1946, Podhajsky had painstakingly worked to gain fans for them, taking them to perform exhibitions in Switzerland and Ireland, even giving a demonstration ride in Wembley Stadium during the London Summer Olympics in 1948. Podhajsky had learned that the graceful magic woven by the white horses could win friends and influence faster than any human could ever hope to. Let them *piaffe, passage,* and pirouette. Let them *courbette* and *capriole;* the horses' eloquent silent language turned out to be universal. This was Podhajsky's strategy to keep the school alive.

FOUR WEEKS AFTER ARRIVING in New York, on November 6, 1950, Alois Podhajsky stood in a receiving line in the sweeping Grand Ballroom at the Waldorf Astoria Hotel, one of the city's most elegant establishments, as the guest of honor at the National Horse Show Ball. The ornate hall bubbled with a brilliant collection of military officers, international riders, and members of New York society who crowded the wide expanse of polished floor and the two levels of balustrades. Women bedecked in couture evening dresses and men sporting scarlet riding jackets with hunt club pins on their lapels lined up to express their best wishes to Colonel Podhajsky.

The colonel, solemn and courtly, gave no hint that his mind was elsewhere: in the basement stables of Madison Square Garden, where the white stallions were being readied for tonight's dress rehearsal. Podhajsky had been instructed to include all of the airs above the ground in rapid succession, followed by the school quadrille, in the truncated space of twenty-five minutes; he worried about the technical difficulty of achieving this in an unfamiliar arena under the flash of spotlights. He longed to be with the horses right now, walking among them, attuning himself to their humors, instead of making chitchat with this seemingly endless line of guests. The scheduling inside Madison Square Garden was so tight that they had to wait until after the ice had melted from a figure-skating performance before the arena was ready for dress rehearsal. Determined to give his stallions a chance to become acquainted with the arena, he was going to bow out of dinner and make a mad dash across town to hurriedly mount up.

The next night, thirteen stallions assembled in the cramped schooling area in the basement of Madison Square Garden, their white coats glowing in the close, dusty air. One stallion, Africa, was missing from the lineup. Podhajsky's favorite had contracted a fever. He would recover, but tonight he needed to rest. Instead, Podhajsky's second mount, Pluto, would have to do double duty, taking on all of Africa's roles as well as his own. Podhajsky flitted nervously among the horses, giving the grooms instructions for minor adjustments, offering a reminder or two to the riders and a reassuring whisper to each horse.

Seated in the arena above them, a crowd of more than twenty thousand people had gathered to watch the show. In the reserved boxes at ringside, men and women in evening dress chatted softly in expectation of the white stallions' entrance, while up in the cheaper seats, crowds of spectators waited, completely unaware of what kind of show the Spanish Riding School of Vienna would perform. The disorganized sounds of the ringside string orchestra warming up added to the hubbub. During the previous night's rehearsal, Verena Podhajsky had sat with the string orchestra, explaining to the musicians exactly how to time the music to the horses' movements. In the center of the vast arena, jeeps circled hurriedly, deftly removing the fences used for the jumping classes, then running a harrow to smooth out the sandy surface. Finally, the ring crew set out tubs of flowers to mark a square for the stallions' performance.

Podhajsky could feel Pluto's coiled nervous energy as he prepared to enter the large unfamiliar space, made spookier (for horses) by the uneven lighting that striped the ground with shadows. Podhajsky stroked the stallion on the neck to soothe him, tightened his fingers on the reins, and closed his lower legs around the horse's barrel. This stallion had cowered under a hail of bombs in Vienna under siege; he had accepted reduced rations when food was scarce; he had put up with rattling across war-torn Austria in an unadorned boxcar and stood without panicking during the horror of an unsheltered air raid outside a train station. Through all of that, one man had stayed with him. One man had been there to reassure him, to watch over him, to ride him, and to communicate with him in his own silent language.

As the pair entered the enormous arena, the bright lights made the horse's white coat glow as if lit from within. The babble of twenty thousand people was swiftly replaced by an expectant silence. Pluto tensed; he flicked a single ear back, intent upon his rider. From the orchestra at ringside came the familiar strains of a Viennese waltz, and the pair broke into a canter. Despite the strange surroundings, the unfamiliar sounds and sights and smells that greeted them at every turn, Pluto and Podhajsky listened only to each other. The pair seemed to float upon the air. At last, they halted in the dead center of the arena, and as the strains of music ended, a collective spellbound hush replaced it—until at last the quiet was broken by a thunderclap of applause. The rest of the program passed in a carefully choreographed blur as stallions and riders perfectly executed their complicated routines. The crowd watched in awe while the choreographed white stallions flew into the air or posed as still as porcelain statues.

At the end of the program, the announcer came on with a special piece of news. An honored guest had come to watch the horses perform.

Podhajsky and Pluto rode at the head of a single column of horses and riders, with each white stallion an even ten paces behind. When they reached the center of the arena, they pulled abreast and halted. The ring crew rolled a red carpet out onto the tanbark, then General Tuckerman emerged from the sidelines, escorting a small elderly woman whose graying hair was swept up in an elegant coif. She walked slowly toward the center of the arena, her hand resting on the general's arm.

Podhajsky and Pluto rode toward her. Halfway across the arena, the colonel halted and dismounted, leaving Pluto unattended as he approached the honored guest on foot. Pluto followed his master for a few paces, stopped, and looked back at the horses, as if to say, "What am I supposed to do?" With twenty thousand pairs of eyes trained upon him, Pluto stood perfectly still, his reins looping loose, and waited. Suddenly, the horse all but disappeared. The entire arena was plunged into darkness as a single spotlight encircled the two people standing in the arena: Colonel Podhajsky and Bea Patton, the general's widow.

In the dark, the crowd was utterly still.

"I am very happy to be able to show you the horses that General Patton, a great American soldier, saved for Austria," Podhajsky said.

"I would give anything if only my husband could be standing here instead of me, for he loved the Lipizzaner so much," Mrs. Patton replied.

As an explosion of photographers' flashbulbs lit up around them, Mrs. Patton handed Podhajsky a single red rose.

BEA PATTON PRESENTS A SINGLE ROSE TO
ALOIS PODHAJSKY AT THE NATIONAL HORSE SHOW
AT MADISON SQUARE GARDEN, 1950.

THE BIRTHDAY PARTY

A radiant blue sky spread over the Calarabia Ranch, and the gates to the well-kept spread were flung wide open. Above Witez's stable, a flag flew, denoting that the prince was at home. The beloved King of the Ranch was having a birthday party. The party featured a carrot cake and a host of fans from near and far who had come to pay their respects to California's most famous purebred Arabian. The Hurlbutts were calling the party "This Is Your Life: Witez," after the TV show of that name in which people were fêted by gathering old friends and acquaintances. They had collected comments about Witez from many of his past acquaintances in both Europe and America.

Witez was twenty-seven years old, but his shiny coat, playful manner, and bright eyes were testaments to his excellent health. When Witez arrived in America in 1945, most people had never heard of the Arabian horse. Since then, the breed had gained many fans and was now revered among children for its role in the best-selling *Black Stallion* series and the award-winning book *King of the Wind*. All over America, when horse-loving girls closed their eyes and imagined an Arabian stallion, they were probably picturing Witez. His illustrated likeness was featured in the books *Album of Horses* by Marguerite Henry and *All About Horses* by Margaret Cabell Self, two of America's best-loved equestrian writers. Famed illustrator Wesley Dennis painted a well-known portrait of Witez's lost mother, Federajca, with the foal Witez resting at her side in the straw at Janów in Poland. Breyer released a horse statuette modeled on Witez. The Hurlbutts lovingly tended to his fan clubs, answering letters from children and corresponding with people in Europe who remembered him and were happy to know that he had found a peaceful home. Perhaps the most heartfelt reunion took place when Liselotte traveled all the way from Germany to see him. Back in the dark days of the war, it would have been impossible to imagine that this reunion could ever happen.

Witez never returned to his birthplace, and this was the cause for much sadness among the Polish people. Their country was one of the hardest hit by the war: It was the location of the most infamous Nazi extermination camps—Auschwitz, Sobibor, Treblinka, and more; it was invaded by both Russia and Germany; and Hitler's murderous intent had been to enslave or murder almost all of its people. Over fifteen percent of Poland's population died during the war. Animals fared little better. Its Arabian horse stock—once a point of pride for the country—was decimated, approximately eighty percent of the horses lost. After the war ended, its Soviet "liberators" started a second brutal period of totalitarian occupation, which lasted for another forty years.

In spite of these difficulties, Janów Podlaski rebounded once again. During the 1980s, when Poland was gradually withdrawing from the Russian stranglehold and the Solidarity movement was growing in strength, the annual Arabian sale at Janów Podlaski was one of the few bright spots in the Polish economy. And the people of Poland did not forget Witez. His image graced a postage stamp, and many argued that he never should have been sent to America in the first place. There were those who begged for his return—but in the Cold War era, that demand was impossible to meet.

In the end, Witez was like so many others who seemed to have been born in the wrong place at the wrong time. He was a prince with a royal brand on his shoulder, but he was also a refugee. Perhaps that was why he became so beloved. Witez had been hurled into a maelstrom for which he bore no responsibility and over which he had no power. Like so many others at that terrible time, he ended up having to start from scratch in a new place, and like so many others, he was lucky to have found kindness and a new home among strangers. Perhaps, like his human counterparts, Witez never forgot his hunger for home, but he thrived in his adopted country.

WITEZ IS IN FINE FORM AT CALARABIA RANCH
IN CALIFORNIA.

ON HIS TWENTY-SEVENTH BIRTHDAY, as he dined on carrot cake and accepted the love and praise from the gathered well-wishers, Witez still had the regal good looks that had brought him so much fame. His dappled coat shone and his tail floated on the soft California breeze. As he cavorted for his fans in the pastures of Calarabia, the chieftain had never looked more content.

35.

A MIGHTY GOOD AMERICAN

On April 7, 1980, thirty-four years to the day after the European horses paraded at Front Royal, Virginia, a message radiated across long-distance phone lines from coast to coast as old army buddies called one another, their voices shaking with the sad news. Hank Reed had been their leader, their mentor, and their father figure. None of the survivors could really believe that he was gone.

Colonel Reed left his regiment on August 12, 1947, to report for duty with Army Ground Forces (later the Army Field Forces) in Fort Monroe, Virginia. In 1948, he was nominated for promotion to brigadier general but chose to retire and take over his family's textile business following his father's death. Hank Reed's right hand, injured in the battle of Lunéville, never did quite recover. There was "something a little funny about it," although he wouldn't tell you why unless you asked. Like most men of his generation, Hank Reed did not like to talk about the war. But in his library, along with his books and souvenirs from his days in Germany, a single item rested in the place of honor: his army helmet, nicked and battered in a silent testimony to its owner's wartime journey across a bleeding continent.

When he returned home from service overseas, Reed found his two beloved polo ponies, Tea Kettle and Skin Quarter, healthy and well tended in the pastures of the family farm at Stanford Hill. He and his

COLONEL
CHARLES
HANCOCK
REED.

wife, Janice, built a house in the countryside near Richmond, where they had room for horses. His two polo ponies stayed with him for life and peacefully passed away of old age in the late 1950s. In addition, Reed had adopted an Arabian mare, Hedschra, and shipped her back from Germany. Reed's hand may not have been what it used to be, but he rode his horse every single day.

By the early 1960s, the white stallions whose bloodlines Reed had helped to save had become world-famous, their every move followed by adoring fans and the press. They had starred in a Walt Disney movie called *Miracle of the White Stallions,* in which Robert Taylor played Alois Podhajsky. If you watch closely, you might see a scene flash by in which an unpolished American fellow is eating a bowl of oatmeal while getting a report about the horses: That unsung hero is Hank Reed. The Disney version of the story makes it look like General Patton was solely responsible for the rescue of the horses, but the men of the 2nd Cavalry knew better.

Around the time the movie came out in 1963, Ferdinand Sperl hosted a 2nd Cavalry reunion at the Pere Marquette Hotel in Peoria, Illinois, where he was the general manager. When the men asked Reed, who had been an adviser on the movie, why he hadn't corrected the record to explain that he was responsible for saving the horses at Hostau, he shrugged and, with the typical modesty of a good soldier, just said, "Let it be."

While Reed had returned to a quiet private life, Alois Podhajsky was somewhat of a celebrity, regularly entertaining dignitaries and heads of state. Both Queen Elizabeth II and Jackie Kennedy had visited the stables in Vienna and watched the horses perform. In 1963, in conjunction with the Disney movie's release, the stallions flew to the United States in resplendent comfort on a transatlantic airline for a whirlwind tour of major American cities. Podhajsky had grown accustomed to long lines of people clamoring to get his autograph. Now, in addition to the horses nibbling up his sugar treats, he seemed to have the whole world eating from his palm.

During this trip to America, there was an unfinished piece of business for Podhajsky to attend to. On the first night of the horses' grand tour, in Philadelphia, a delegation of officers involved in the horses' rescue walked into the ring, dressed in civilian suits. Hank Reed, his face lit by a spotlight, stepped out from the group and strode into the center of the arena. His hair was mostly silver, but nobody could mistake the hint of American swagger or his mile-wide smile.

ALOIS PODHAJSKY PERFORMS FOR
FIRST LADY JACQUELINE KENNEDY IN 1961.

After nineteen years, Colonel Reed and Alois Podhajsky stood face-to-face in the spotlight. Forgetting all protocol, the two men, overcome with emotion, threw their arms around each other, and thunderous applause rose to the rooftops as the two former soldiers, who had once worn the uniforms of opposing nations, shared a heart-felt embrace.

IN 1972, TWENTY-SEVEN YEARS after the war had ended, Reed and a group of veterans from the 2nd traveled to the American Military Cemetery in Luxembourg. It was Reed's first visit since that long-ago day of Patton's funeral procession. The cemetery's brilliant green swards held the graves of 5,070 fallen soldiers. Reed and the other members of the 2nd Cavalry had gone on with their lives in the years since the war, but each had left a piece of himself on that field of white crosses and Stars of David. The faces of the fallen—the young husband Jim Pitman, the teenager Raymond Manz—were alive in the memories of the men who had served alongside them.

Reed laid a wreath on Patton's grave, then silently stepped away from the other men. One of the veterans followed, worried that Reed was ill.

"Is something wrong?" he asked gently.

Reed shook his head. "I knew the general for so long and so well. It's hard to believe that he is truly gone."

Respectfully, the men drew away from their commander, leaving him space to reflect. Apart from the group of veterans, Hank moved from headstone to headstone, laying a single red carnation on the grave of each member of the 2nd Cavalry who was buried there.

THE SKIES OVER THE Hollywood Cemetery in Richmond, Virginia, were a brilliant blue the day Hank Reed was buried. Twenty men from his regiment had come from all over the country to pay their final re-spects. The lead pallbearer was Jim O'Leary, his faithful driver; over the years, the two had stayed in touch. After the ceremony, Reed's widow told O'Leary that there was something her late husband wanted him to keep. To the sergeant from Chicago who steered with his arms akimbo, who first met Hank Reed in South Carolina in the spring of

1942, Mrs. Reed presented Reed's West Point class ring, worn thin from almost fifty years of use.

Standing around the flag-draped casket as it was lowered into the ground, silver heads bowed and eyes flooded with tears, these veterans gave final salutes. From the moment these men had first seen Hank Reed as he jumped up on the stand in Fort Jackson, South Carolina, promising that they would add battle streamers to their regimental flag, he had seemed to them immortal. The man being laid to rest had trained them to be soldiers and then led them into battle, never abandoning them, pressing on through tragedy and heartbreak, and eventually leading them to victory. The lives of all the men gathered there were inextricably intertwined with, and all of their lives connected to, their proudest accomplishment: the rescue of the horses. Even those unable to travel to the cemetery that day—Tom Stewart and Quin Quinlivan—seemed to be standing among these good men who gathered one last time.

At the graveside, one of the men was heard to mutter, "A mighty good American was buried today."

They remembered Hank Reed as they had first known him: forty-two years old, with his Sam Browne belt, the crossed cavalry swords pinned on both lapels; his hair parted down the middle and carefully slicked back, his smiling eyes and uncreased face reflecting a life that had been largely devoid of hardship. In those days, Hank Reed had two good hands, the right one callused from swinging a polo mallet. He had the loose walk and the big-hearted gaze of a horse-loving cavalryman.

One of his men described him as an "astute, hard-bitten, regular Army Colonel: pragmatic, sensible, focused on getting the job done." But once upon a time, back in April 1945, he had been an idealist, a dreamer, a believer in far-fetched possibilities. He had listened to the pleas of men who should have been his enemies, and decided to act. Because of that single moment when he set aside doubt, the horses had been saved.

World War II is still the most destructive event ever to have occurred in human history, with estimates of the total death toll as high as sixty million, or 2.5 percent of the world's total population. The irreparable loss to civilization that resulted from people being slaughtered and entire cultures being obliterated is impossible to measure.

DURING A LIPIZZANER TOUR OF AMERICA IN 1964,
REED VISITS WITH AN OLD FRIEND.

Against the backdrop of all this wreckage, the saving of the horses was a small thing; and yet as Hank Reed's men instinctively knew, it was only through individual acts of compassion that the world was able to climb out of the trough it had dug for itself and attempt to find its way into a more peaceful future.

Later, when people asked why he had decided to save the horses, Colonel Reed's answer was simple: "We were so tired of death and destruction. We wanted to do something beautiful."

THE VETERANS

A thousand lights illuminated the sand arena as the crowd sat in hushed expectation. In just a few moments, everyone in the audience would have an opportunity to see a timeless, graceful spectacle. From a darkened gap behind long velvet curtains, twelve prancing horses emerged. The riders wore brown jackets with six rows of brass buttons; each horse's coat gleamed pure white. As the steeds entered with military precision, their brass-plated bridles glittered under the spotlights. Viennese waltzes were piped over the loudspeakers and the horses seemed to dance in rhythm to the music.

As always, the sight of the stallions entering the arena caused the gathered spectators to catch their breath. But tonight was special, because in the front row sat three honored guests: two Germans, Hubert Rudofsky and Rudolf Lessing, and American Lou Holz, a representative of the 2nd Cavalry Association. Of the thousands gathered in the auditorium tonight, only these three truly understood that in the darkest hour of the twentieth century, the princely horses and their centuries-old tradition had come close to obliteration. If only those in the audience could see the world through the eyes of these three octogenarians, then the performance, already brilliant, would seem almost magical.

After the performance, the three men walked into the center of the arena. Sixty years after the men had exchanged their uniforms for civilian clothes, their aged frames still reflected the upright posture of their military pasts; their faces were solemn and dignified, and each one had a sheen of tears on his wrinkled cheeks.

A uniformed rider presented each man with a plaque and a porcelain statuette, then stepped away so that all twelve riders could doff their hats in salute.

"Tonight," said the announcer, "the horses dance for you."

THE SPANISH RIDING SCHOOL TODAY

There is a timeless quality to the Spanish Riding School in Vienna. Nowadays, the school resides at the heart of a bustling modern city that still boasts Old World charm. Tourists flock to see the horses perform: The formal performances sell out months in advance, and tickets to watch the morning rehearsals are sometimes standing room only. Sunlight softly filters through the high palladium windows, and the crystal chandeliers, once dismantled piece by piece and hidden away by Alois Podhajsky, hang again in resplendence from the frescoed ceilings. As the horses practice their timeless movements, the riders continue to share their technique the same way they always have, through word of mouth handed down in an unbroken chain that goes back hundreds of years. That chain of wisdom, based on partnership, love, and kindness, has lasted much longer than any of the successive governments that have controlled this institution.

Go to visit the horses in their stables, and for a moment, you might think you're back in the Habsburg Empire. You might expect to see Alois Podhajsky coming around the corner, calling out to each of his beloved stallions by name. Perhaps you will think for just a moment that you have seen Neapolitano Africa or Pluto Theodorosta, looking over their stall doors with lively eyes, ready to whinny a friendly greeting to their friend and master. But no.

Podhajsky, Africa, and Pluto are gone. But their memory lives on. Every time a rider mounts a Lipizzaner, he reflects some of the wisdom that Alois Podhajsky passed along, wisdom that he acquired in more than six decades of working with horses; and each stallion retains some of the genetic makeup passed down through the lines of the original six stallions. Each horse is still named according to his bloodline and wears a brand that denotes his lineage, as has been the custom for hundreds of years. The Spanish Riding School shows a reverence for tradition but has also repeatedly proved that it is able to reinvent itself. One of the biggest changes since Podhajsky's day is that some of the riders are women.

In the end, it is not only the horses' DNA that determines their ability to perform the brilliant quadrilles and statuesque poses. It is not the gender or race of the riders, nor any precise quality of the bloodstock alone, that allows such extraordinary achievement. In 1945, in a time of war, it was a love of horses that enabled men to rise above their differences and find a way to cooperate. And so it is at the Spanish Riding School today. The discipline embodied in the long, quiet, dignified partnership between man and beast is a feat of deep cooperation and silent harmony; it is the antithesis of the Nazi philosophy that once threatened to destroy this beautiful legacy.

FEMALE RIDERS AT THE SPANISH RIDING SCHOOL.

EPILOGUE

WHAT BECAME OF THEM?

COLONEL FRED L. HAMILTON

Fred Hamilton deeply regretted that the demise of the army's remount program occurred during his tenure as head of the Army Remount Service. He was heartbroken that the horses he had brought from Europe, which he had dreamed would have a lasting effect on American horse breeding, mostly failed to live up to their promise in their adopted country. His disappointment is reflected in his labeling of the rescued horses sold off by the Department of Agriculture as "the war orphans." Witez's storybook ending in America was a bright spot in this otherwise mostly unsuccessful attempt to elevate American horse breeding by importing captured European horses.

WOLFGANG KROLL

Wolfgang Kroll was known for his tall tales, so the truth of his exploits before and after the war may never be fully known. After traveling with the horses to America, Kroll returned to Germany, where he got a job working with Lipizzaner horses in the circus. Having managed to secure a letter of recommendation from George Patton himself, he eventually returned to America, where he ended up working at the San Diego Zoo. He then left California and moved to Chicago, where he worked for the Department of Agriculture as an inspector in a meatpacking plant. Along the way, he told people stories about his involvement with the Camel Corps, his days fighting alongside the partisans in Yugoslavia, the hours he spent playing cards with General Patton, and his involvement with the rescue of the Lipizzaner. As incredible as those stories may have seemed, the part about helping to rescue the Lipizzaner was absolutely true.

RUDOLF LESSING

The large farm where Rudolf Lessing grew up was situated east of the partition between East and West Germany. After the war, his parents' lands were confiscated and collectivized. His once affluent family lost everything. Lessing remained with his wife and children in West Germany, continuing to work as a veterinarian. Throughout the rest of his life, he donated his time and knowledge to help rebuild the German horse industry, which had been largely destroyed during the hostilities. After the best of the captured horses were shipped to America, Lessing worked to find homes for the ones from Hostau that had been left behind, in particular the rough-and-ready Russian Kabardins and Panje ponies that the Americans were not interested in importing. Lessing remained friends with the men of the 2nd Cavalry Association, especially Quin Quinlivan, even traveling to America to attend one of their reunions. In 1986, he was recognized at a special performance of the Spanish Riding School and given a medal of honor by the Austrian government.

WILLIAM DONALD "QUIN" QUINLIVAN

Quin Quinlivan, who ran off at the age of seventeen from his home in East Dubuque, Illinois, to join the cavalry, was one of the army's last mounted soldiers. After bidding goodbye to his friend Witez at Front Royal in 1946, he was assigned to the Quartermaster Corps at Fort Robinson, Nebraska, then transferred back to Germany in 1947. On the Europe-bound ship, he met his future wife, Rita McDonald. They were married in Augsburg, Germany, in 1947. In 1949, when Witez was sold at auction, Quinlivan was in Germany, serving as a member of one of the army's last mounted units, fondly known as the Bowlegged Brigade. After he was discharged in 1949, Quinlivan and his wife settled in Los Angeles. He followed the stories about Witez and was delighted by the stallion's growing fame.

Quinlivan never gave up his love for animals. Throughout his life, he adopted unwanted animals—dogs, a bird, even a Shetland pony. Quinlivan saw the Lipizzaner perform once: In 1964, along with Hank Reed, he was part of the 2nd Cavalry delegation invited to Philadelphia to see Podhajsky and the Spanish Riding School. At Quin's funeral in 1985, an Austrian military attaché hand-delivered a floral wreath to honor his contribution to the Lipizzaner and the Spanish Riding School. The Quinlivan family paid more than their fair share to the defense of their nation. Quin's older brother was killed in 1940; his younger brother perished in Korea. Undeterred by their history of sacrifice, Quin's pride in his time in the army no doubt inspired his children, three of whom followed his footsteps into military service. In 1991, his daughter Maureen Nolen, a nurse and army major, was honored during a performance of the Lipizzaner stallions in Nevada. The ornamental swords that were surrendered to Quin that long-ago day in Hostau are still in the family.

GUSTAV RAU

After the war was over, Gustav Rau became one of the most influential horsemen in Germany. He was the first postwar head of the German Olympic Equestrian Committee, and he was revered for discovering the great German horse Halla, the only show jumper ever to win three Olympic gold medals (1956 individual and team, 1960 team). Given credit for rebuilding the German horse industry twice—once after World War I and once after World War II—he was honored repeatedly for his contributions to equestrianism in Germany until his death in 1954. The highest equestrian honor in Germany is called the Rau Medal, and in Munich, there is a street named after him, Gustav Rau Strasse, near the Riem Thoroughbred racecourse. But as recent scholarship has uncovered more about Rau's role in the stud farm administration during the Third Reich, his legacy has become more controversial. Some defend him for his part in safeguarding horses during the war, and it is true that the horses within Rau's dominion in general fared better than those in the pathway of Russian troops. More recently, as German scholars have documented his wartime activities, some have demanded that the street and the prize be renamed due to his activities during the National Socialist period.

HUBERT RUDOFSKY

The last time Hubert Rudofsky ever performed with the Lipizzaner was on Hitler's birthday, in April 1945, in a grand arena festooned with brilliant scarlet Nazi banners that were wilting in the rain. By the end of the summer of 1945, the American GIs billeted in Bohemia had left, and with them, any semblance of order for the Rudofsky family. The Germans were the hated oppressors during the war. Now the postwar Czech government made the decision to expel all ethnic German citizens, even those, like the Rudofskys, whose families had lived in Bohemia for centuries. All citizens of Bischofteinitz were ordered to leave behind all of their possessions except one suitcase and were herded into a "resettlement camp" in the Czech town of Domazlice. Conditions in the camp were difficult, and Rudofsky's mother died there; her family blamed her death on medical neglect. Rudofsky avoided the harsh treatment reserved for suspected Nazi collaborators due to his standing in the community and his official paperwork showing that he had co-operated with the Americans. All of Lessing's predictions had come true. Six months after the horses galloped across the border into Bavaria, everyone involved in the rescue was a free man except Rudofsky.

The stables at Hostau remained silent, eerie, and empty. The coaches, the white horses, the busy riders and grooms, all were like a half-remembered dream that had slipped away. The rooftops of the stables caved in, and nettles grew up around the buildings. Nobody remembered that this was a place where horses once danced. The church in Bischofteinitz where Rudofsky turned heads as he strode down the center aisle in his cavalry uniform had fallen into decrepitude—many of its treasures had been looted, most of its windows were broken. But one delicate stained-glass window improbably survived: Its leaded inscription read, "In the war year 1916, the Rudofsky family offers this window in the hopes that their son will return safely from the war."

After enduring eighteen months in a resettlement camp, Rudofsky was released without being charged with any crime. By that time, his sister had left for America, taking his nephew and niece with her. He relocated to Germany, but never regained his former status in the horse world. Four years after the war's end, Rudofsky and Lessing ran into each other at an equestrian event. Rudofsky confided to his friend that his life's greatest regret was that he had declined Reed's offer to stay with the Americans. Still, he managed to build a new life for himself, eventually securing employment at the Donnauworth stud farm in Bavaria and loaning his expertise to Arabian horse breeders all over the world. He also amassed an impressive collection of paintings of Arabian horses, most of which are now housed in the German Museum of the Horse in Verden, Saxony. For a long time, Rudofsky's role in the Lipizzaner rescue was largely unknown. The Germans' role in securing the horses' rescue was swept under the rug, and the Spanish Riding School distanced itself from its wartime association with the German military. Finally, those wartime animosities started to lessen. In 1986, Rudofsky and Rudolf Lessing were honored at one of the Spanish Riding School's performances. Six months later, that performance aired on Austrian TV. That night, perhaps content that his sacrifice had finally been recognized, Hubert Rudofsky died in his sleep.

ULRICH (ULLI) RUDOFSKY

The world that Ulrich Rudofsky had grown up in was all but obliterated by the war. His father, a physician serving on the Eastern Front, spent close to three years as a prisoner of war. He was released but not long after committed suicide, leaving Ulrich's mother alone to manage two young children. After the Americans left Czechoslovakia and her brother-in-law Hubert was imprisoned, Ulli's mother had no choice but to take her two children and flee their home with only a few possessions. She managed to bribe a driver to carry them across the border to Germany. At the border, a Czech border guard tried to stop their departure, but an American military policeman intervened and they were allowed to cross, thus escaping internment in the crowded resettlement camp. But the local Germans did not welcome the refugee mother and children back into Germany proper. They had their papers ripped up by a city official, and the boy and his family spent a terrifying month, March 1946, hiding in a stinking cow stable near Schönsee, Germany.

Ulli and his mother and sister eventually emigrated to the United States. After graduating from college, Ulli served in the American army in Germany, patrolling the border but unable to cross the Iron Curtain to the east to see the home he had been forced to leave behind as a ten-year-old. Now a retired pathologist and miniature-shipbuilding enthusiast, he lives near Albany, New York.

FERDINAND SPERL

Swiss-American Ferdinand Sperl, a naturalized citizen of the United States, never lost his enthusiasm for the adopted country he had bravely served. After the war was over, he moved to Peoria, Illinois, where he returned to his first profession of hotelkeeper, taking over as managing director of the Pere Marquette Hotel. Sperl retained his fame in the small town of Kötzting in Germany, where he was remembered for having provided rescued Lipizzaner horses for a traditional local festival just after the German surrender. He returned to Kötzting for the fiftieth anniversary of that celebration, and while there, he was stunned to find that two women in the hotel's restaurant remembered him; when they were schoolgirls, Sperl had come across them as they were fleeing Czechoslovakia on foot with their teachers in April 1945, and he had saved their lives. After this chance meeting, Sperl and the two women remained friends for the rest of his life.

TOM STEWART

Captain Tom Stewart returned to private life after the war. He met his beloved wife, Anne, and together they raised three children. Always humble, he never demanded credit for his daring midnight ride on King Peter's horse in the company of Rudolf Lessing. Throughout the following years, he demurred whenever he was asked to stand in the limelight, especially when it came to his role in rescuing the horses. Finally, in 1996, the modest veteran allowed the Spanish Riding School to honor him for his contributions to preserving the Lipizzaner. During an American tour, he was invited to one of their performances, and in the stables, he was able to visit the descendants of the beautiful animals he had saved. In 2001, he was awarded a National Gold Award by Austria for his wartime role in rescuing the Lipizzaner. One of the longest-lived of the main players in the horse rescue, he passed away in 2006 at the age of ninety-six, more than sixty years after he made that fateful moonlit ride. "The little minister" taught Sunday school at his local church throughout his life.

THE HORSES

LOTNIK

Lotnik was auctioned off by the Department of Agriculture in 1948 and purchased by a man who intended to use him as a pleasure horse. When the buyer got divorced, Lotnik was abandoned, eventually housed in squalid conditions in an ill-kept stable. Fortunately, several years later, the retired former head of the Pomona Remount Depot stumbled across the stallion and recognized him as the pearl of Hostau. Purchased by Bob Aste of the Scottsdale Arabian ranch in 1963, Lotnik lived out the rest of his life on Aste's farm and was a successful sire.

WITEZ

The chieftain never left his final home at Calarabia except for a brief stay at the ranch of Arabian horse breeder Burr Betts in Colorado from 1960 to 1964. He lived a few months past his twenty-seventh-birthday bash before he died peacefully while sleeping in his pasture. The sign from his days at the Mansbach Stud Farm that reads "Witez, Field Headquarters" hangs in the International Museum of the Horse in Lexington, Kentucky.

THE PLACES

FORT RILEY, KANSAS

Once the preeminent horse cavalry locale in America and one of the best in the world, Fort Riley, Kansas, is now home to the 1st Infantry Division, known as "the Big Red One." Horses remained at Fort Riley until 1950, when the last few were led off the base and given refuge for life at the personal ranch of Colonel John Wofford, a member of the 1932 Olympic equestrian team. As these last horses left the hallowed stables at Fort Riley, grown men in uniform, most of them hard-bitten veterans of World War II, lined the streets with tears in their eyes to bid these last chargers, the tail end of a centuries-old tradition, a final farewell. But the spirit of horses remains at Fort Riley. As a fitting tribute to the contribution of horses to the American military, the U.S. Cavalry Memorial Foundation offers individuals the opportunity to memorialize their favorite equine companion with a plaque bearing its name mounted and displayed at the U.S. Cavalry Memorial Research Library located in Fort Riley.

JANÓW PODLASKI

The green-roofed stables of Janów Podlaski are peaceful now, still home to some of the finest Arabians in the world. The town fills up every year for the sale of purebred Arabians that draws horse lovers from around the world. Eighty percent of Poland's Arabians perished between 1938 and 1945, but the stallions Stained Glass and Grand Slam, after fleeing Rau's stud farm in 1944, passed through Dresden during the bombing and were saved by two brave Poles. At the end of the war, the stallions were returned to Poland, forming the nucleus from which the country rebuilt its Arabian breeding program. The stables of Janów Podlaski reopened in the autumn of 1950. Old-timers may still say how much they mourn the loss of their favorite son, Witez, but they probably also know that the stallion was an ambassador for the Polish Arabian and helped increase the breed's renown all over the world.

HOSTAU/HOSTOUŇ

The stud farm at Hostau (now called Hostouň in the Czech language) has been divided up and no longer serves as a horse farm. The mansion where Rudofsky made his home is now a school for delinquent juveniles, and the once elegant horse stables have fallen into disrepair. Shortly after the war, all ethnic Germans in Czechoslovakia either fled or were forcibly evicted from their homes, leaving behind the majority of their possessions, which were seized by the Czech government and redistributed to its citizens. The ethnic Germans, for complicated reasons that had much to do with history that predated the war, had shown enthusiastic support when Hitler invaded Czechoslovakia in 1938, annexing the Sudetenland as the first step in his brutal war of expansion. The local Czech and Jewish populations suffered greatly under Nazi rule. Because the Germans fought a war of aggression, little sympathy was reserved for their hardship in the aftermath. The loss of the Bohemian Germans' homeland, where their families had lived for centuries, was painful. For many years, due to the closed border between Czechoslovakia and Germany, families who had fled were unable to return to their childhood homes. But with the loosening of restraints after the end of the Soviet era, there has been renewed interest on both sides, Czech and German, in exploring their shared history. There has been increasing interest in the story of the magical Lipizzaner who once lived there, and just a few years ago, a bronze memorial plaque was installed that tells that story in three languages: Czech, German, and English. Citizens in Hostouň dream of restoring the horse farm to its original grandeur and attracting tourists to visit this place where, in the middle of a terrible war, a few men reached past their natural enmity, their different-colored uniforms, and their warring countries to try to do something that was simply good.

ACKNOWLEDGMENTS

To tell a story spanning two continents and more than eight decades is a giant undertaking, and I could not possibly have done it without the help of many people. My greatest debt, without any doubt, is to the families of the veterans who so generously shared their photo albums, old letters, scrapbooks, and personal memories: Reed Johnson; Maureen Quinlivan Nolen; Margaret, Dennis, and Kathleen Quinlivan; Fran Sperl Cannon; Helen Stewart Raleigh; Martha and Virginia Ratliffe; Anne Stewart; Sandi Slisher Konicki; James Hudson Pitman Kelsey; Rick Rudofsky; Kathy O'Leary; and Betty Ann Dunn.

Special thanks to the trustees of the National Sporting Library & Museum in Middleburg, Virginia, who supported me with a John H. Daniels Fellowship in 2010. It was during that time that I first stumbled across a pamphlet describing a parade of Lipizzaner horses in Virginia, which piqued my interest in this fascinating story. Thank you to Bill Cooke, director of the International Museum of the Horse in Lexington, Kentucky, for access to the unparalleled collection of materials about Witez II, and for his great graciousness in helping me with my research. Thanks also to E. Lee Shepard and Jamison Davis at the Virginia Historical Society for their able assistance with the Charles Hancock Reed papers, and to librarians Katherine Staab and Caryn Romo at the W. K. Kellogg Arabian Horse Library in Pomona, California, for their assistance in locating valuable resources. Thank you to Herwig Radnetter, Karin Nakhai, and the staff of the Spanish Riding School in Vienna for answering so many questions, and for my fascinating visit to the school. Thank you to both Suzanne Christoff at the United States Military Academy Library and Ryan Meyer at the Reed Museum in Vilseck, Germany, for help with historical documents and photographs. Thank you to Esther Buonanno of Tempel Farms for answering questions about the American Lipizzaner and to John H. Daniels Fellow Earl Parker, who graciously shared his research with me. I'm especially indebted to the cheerful and indefatigable Ann Trevor, who sleuthed out a wealth of archival resources for me.

A very special note of gratitude is due to Rick Rudofsky and to Joseph, Isolde, and Reinhold Gruber, who gave me the once-in-a-lifetime experience of touring Germany and the Czech Republic with them as they shared their memories of and reflections on what it was like to live through the events of 1945. Thank you to Balcar Balthazar for sharing Czech perspectives, and to Susi Rudofsky for her vivid recollections of visiting the Lipizzaner horses as a child.

Thank you to Pam Gleason for her expertise about polo and to Robert J. Chambers for his knowledge of carriage driving. Thank you to Victoria Carson for her insights into horse welfare and suggestions for sources. A very special word of thanks to Olympian Jim Wofford, who shared his special insights into the men who served in the twentieth-century cavalry and his memories of Fort Riley.

For help with research, thanks to Nora Alalou for her map-drawing expertise, to Hannah Alalou for assistance with photo research, and to Kimmi Pham and Emily Letts for helping to compile the bibliography. Thank you to Hans Shoeber, Ely Grinwald, Alexandra Lang, Jonathan Larson, and Irene Flotzinger for expert assistance with German-language translation and to Basia Musik Moltchanov for assistance with Polish pronunciation and translation. Thank you to Iris Busch and her father, Josef Reinhold, for assistance in locating sources from Germany. Many thanks to Daniela Rapp, for her ready (and speedy) assistance with German pronunciation.

It takes many people to make a book, and I'm grateful to the outstanding team at Ballantine for all of their work. I am deeply indebted to my brilliant editor, Susanna Porter, whose patience, meticulousness, and gift for narrative structure helped me chisel out this story from the giant rock of information. A special note of thanks goes to Priyanka Krishnan, whose insightful reading of the first draft helped so much to hone the structure of the story. Thanks to Kim Hovey, Steve Messina, Rachel Kind, Robbin Schiff, and Cheryl Kelly, who have gone above and beyond for me so many times.

Great thanks as well to my agent, Jeff Kleinman of Folio Literary Management, whose enthusiasm, kindness, and quick mind make my writing life and my stories better in so many ways.

Much love to my writer buddies who make it all bearable: Lauren Baratz-Logsted, Jon Clinch, Renee Rosen, Danielle Younge-Ullman, Jessica Keener, Karen Dionne, Melanie Benjamin, and Darcie Chan; to Andrew Grant for his special insight into wartime animal stories; and to the brilliant Tasha Alexander, who will read a draft at any time of day or night and always says the right thing.

Love and gratitude to my mother, Virginia Letts, who listened as I read each draft out loud, and whose comments, while sparing, were always insightful. And as always to my patient and wonderful family, Ali, Joseph, Nora, Hannah, and Willis, who rarely complain about burnt dinners, and never suggest that I get a real job.

A special word of appreciation to Marguerite Henry, whose book *White Stallions of Lipizza* inspired my lifelong fascination with the Spanish Riding School. And most of all a heartfelt thank-you to all of the wonderful men, women, and children who love horses and have written me letters, called me, invited me to speak or visit book clubs, and engaged in wonderful conversations on social media. Above all, it was your passion for great equestrian stories that encouraged me to tackle the story of the white stallions.

A NOTE ABOUT SOURCES AND PLACE-NAMES

In order to retell this story, I relied on first-person accounts, published books and monographs, and archival material in both English and German. Many of the participants wrote their own unpublished first-person accounts of what transpired during the mission. The broad outline of each account is the same, but in some particulars the accounts differed. Where there are discrepancies, I've tried to acknowledge them in the endnotes. All material within quotation marks is either a direct quotation or derived from a conversation that was reported later by one of the participants. In cases where the dialogue is a paraphrase, I've tried to include the exact words in the notes.

A few books that gave me a deeper understanding of the time and place include *The End* by Ian Kershaw, which helped me understand the conditions in Germany as the war was ending; *Orderly and Humane* by R. M. Douglas, for background on the German Bohemians; and *Two Lives in Uncertain Times* by Wilma and Georg Iggers, for prewar life in Bohemia. For life in the twentieth-century cavalry and the army's move from mounted to mechanized warfare, I relied upon *The Twilight of the U.S. Cavalry* by Lucian K. Truscott Jr., and *Through Mobility We Conquer* by George Hofmann. For background on Witez's life, I drew upon *The Romance of the Kellogg Ranch* by Mary Jane Parkinson, and *And Miles to Go* by Linell Smith, as well as the film *Path to Glory* from Horsefly Films. For detailed information about the Spanish Riding School and the Lipizzaner horses, I drew upon *The Lipizzan Horse* by Georg Kugler and Paula Boomsliter. And for the life of Alois Pod-hajsky, I drew upon his own writings, in particular, his memoir *My Dancing White Horses*. For further reading on the interplay between beliefs about genetic inheritance and Lipizzaner horses, I would recommend *Brother Mendel's Perfect Horse* by Frank Westerman, and for a full picture of the relationship between horse sports and National Socialism in Germany, *". . . Reitet für Deutschland": Pferdesport und Politik im Nationalsozialismus* by Nele Maya Fahnenbruck.

For place-names, I've chosen to use the German names used during the time that the story takes place. Many of these have changed, as these towns are now located in the Czech Republic and have Czech names.

In the course of writing this book, I had many touching conversations with the descendants of these World War II soldiers, but the words that I believe marked me the most were those of the son of James Harold Pitman, who was only a baby when his father was killed in the war. He said, "I hope you can bring him alive again." I have tried.

NOTES

PROLOGUE: BOMBARDMENT

xvii **On the grounds of the Hofburg:** Podhajsky, Alois. *My Dancing White Horses* (New York: Holt, Rinehart and Winston, 1965), pp. 95–96.

PART ONE: THE EUROPEANS

CHAPTER 1: AN UNLIKELY OLYMPIAN

3   **Equestrian art:** *The Complete Training of Horse and Rider in the Principles of Classical Horsemanship* (Garden City, NY: Doubleday, 1967), loc. 220.

3   **On June 12, 1936:** *Die Reitkunst der Welt an den olympischen Spielen 1936. L'Art équestre du monde . . . International Equitation, Etc.* (Nachdruck der Ausgabe Berlin 1938) (Hildesheim, Germany: Olmse, 1978), pp. 70–148.

3   **Nero, a gangly brown Thoroughbred:** Podhajsky, *My Dancing White Horses,* p. 30.

4   **"You're finished":** Ibid., p. 29.

4   **Today, they entered the arena:** Ibid., p. 35.

4   **He resembled a boy:** Ibid., p. 32.

6   **The crowd assembled to watch:** *The XIth Olympic Games, Berlin, 1936: Official Report* (Berlin: Wilhelm Limpert, 1937), p. 880.

7   **"Excited applause":** Podhajsky, *My Dancing White Horses,* p. 34.

7   **The Nazis, in a clever propaganda move:** "The Nazi Olympics, Berlin," United States Holocaust Memorial Museum. United States Holocaust Memorial Council, www.ushmm.org.

8   **To mark this importance:** *The XIth Olympic Games,* p. 880.

8   **Clad in a dark suit:** *Die Reitkunst der Welt an den olympischen Spielen 1936,* p. 375.

8   **This fifty-six-year-old:** Fahnenbruck, Maya. *". . . Reitet für Deutschland": Pferdesport und Politik im Nationalsozialismus* (Göttingen, Germany: Die Werkstatt, 2013), pp. 231–32.

9   **The press had called:** Podhajsky, *My Dancing White Horses,* p. 41.

9 **Nero once was flighty:** Podhajsky, Alois, *My Horses, My Teachers* (North Pomfret, VT: Trafalgar Square), 1997, p. 85.

9 **"Don't be nervous":** Ibid., p. 77.

9 **When the ringmaster gave the signal:** *The XIth Olympic Games,* p. 888.

9 **For more than a year:** Podhajsky, *My Dancing White Horses,* pp. 21–22.

10 **He extracted a sugar lump:** Ibid., p. 41.

10 **When the German judge realized:** Ibid.

10 **Later, when Gustav Rau:** *Die Reitkunst der Welt an den olympischen Spielen 1936,* pp. 1–4.

10 **the 1936 results have remained:** DiMarco, Louis, "The Army Equestrian Olympic Team," www.louisdimarco.com/armyeques.doc.

10 **"His appearance had attracted notice":** *Die Reitkunst der Welt an den olympischen Spielen 1936,* p. 105.

CHAPTER 2: THE MASTER OF ALL HORSES

12 **On May 8, 1938:** "Reich Equestrians Arrive for Shows. German Party to Visit Sport's Centers. Group Attends Races at Belmont," *The New York Times,* May 10, 1938.

12 **Despite his generally jovial air:** Brandts, Ehrenfreid. *Pferde zwischen den Fronten: Polnische Staatsgestüte und das Schicksal des Hengstgestüts Drogomysl/Draschendorf unter deutscher Besatzung 1939–1945* (Muich: Zugvogel Verlag Wenzel, 2007), p. 11.

12 **Accompanying Rau:** "Reich Equestrians Arrive for Shows."

12 **ready to commence an itinerary:** Ibid.

13 **Rau had begun developing:** Fahnenbruck, ". . . Reitet für Deutschland," p. 111.

13 **After World War I:** Ibid., p. 118.

13 **Hitler's National Socialists:** Ibid., p. 232.

14 **On the cover of its April 3, 1933, issue:** Westerman, Frank. *Brother Mendel's Perfect Horse: Man and Beast in an Age of Human Warfare* (London: Vintage Digital, 2012), p. 105.

14 **That same season:** "Hitler Watches Germans Win Equestrian Event," *The New York Times,* February 10, 1934.

14 **On May 24, 1933:** JM correspondence.

15 **"a whole race":** Fahnenbruck, ". . . Reitet für Deutschland," p. 169.

15 **As minister of food and agriculture:** Ibid. Rau stepped down after only one year; his decision was rumored to be due to his refusal to cooperate with the National Socialists.

15 **Reaching beyond its title:** Fahnenbruck, ". . . Reitet für Deutschland," p. 167.

16 **Rau's dream was that the German nation:** Ibid., p. 112.

16 **The first event:** "Reich Equestrians Arrive for Shows."

16 **"From concept to completion":** Moran, Paul, "Destination Immortality: At Belmont Park Nothing Matters but the Horse and the Test at Hand," www.belmontstakes.com/history.

16 **In truth, Belmont's Jockey Club:** *The Right Blood: America's Aristocrats in Thoroughbred Racing* (New Brunswick, NJ: Rutgers University Press, 2001), pp. 25–48.

17 **At Belmont Park, the races were run:** "Destination Immortality."

17 **Belmont Park was not the only place:** Kevles, Daniel, *In the Name of Eugenics: Genetics and the Uses of Human Heredity* (New York: Knopf, 1985), loc. 1259–1301.

18 **In 1930, Alfred Frank Tredgold:** "They Say," *The New York Times,* October 26, 1930.

19 **Sysonby's scientific contribution:** "Sysonby's Body Exhumed, Museum of Natural History Takes on Great Horse's Skeleton," *The New York Times,* July 12, 1906.

19 **From 1908 to 1933:** Kevles, *In the Name of Eugenics,* loc. 1756.

21 **In 1921, to great fanfare:** "Dawn Man Appears as Our First Ancestor," *The New York Times,* January 9, 1927.

21 **In August 1932:** "Eugenics Conference Opens Here Today," *The New York Times,* August 13, 1932.

21 **After a day of sightseeing in Manhattan:** "Reich Equestrians Arrive for Shows."

22 **Standardbred racing, perhaps not surprisingly:** *Journal of the History of Biology* 35 (2002), pp. 43–78.

22 **From Goshen, Rau's group:** "Reich Equestrians Arrive for Shows."

22 **Off Reisterstown Road:** Krista, "Sagamore Farms: New and Improved," *Baltimore Fishbowl,* May 17, 2013.

23 **In his notes on the 1936:** *The XIth Olympic Games,* p. 881.

23 **The Americans had started their program:** Livingston, Phil, and Ed Roberts. *War Horse: Mounting the Cavalry with America's Finest Horses* (Albany, TX: Bright Sky Press, 2003), pp. 15–55.

23 **At Rau's Olympics:** DiMarco, "The Army Equestrian Olympic Team."

24 **In 1938, the peacetime German Army:** Fahnenbruck, ". . . Reitet für Deutschland,"* p. 287.

24 **In the blueprint forged:** Brandts, *Pferde zwischen den Fronten,* p. 10.

CHAPTER 3: THE POLISH PRINCE

25 **Inside one of the stud:** Smith, Linell, *And Miles to Go: The Biography of a Great Arabian Horse, Witez II* (Boston: Little, Brown, 1967), p. 9.

25 **It was an old Polish word:** Ibid., p. 23.

26 **The first mentions of Arabian horses:** Schiele, Erika, *The Arabian Horse in Europe: History and Present Breeding of the Pure Arab* (London: Harrap, 1970), pp. 139–76.

26 **Bolshevik marauders:** Luft, Monika, "The Lots of Arabian Horses in Poland, Part 1: The World War I and the Bolshevik Invasion." *Arabians Horse Mag.* www.polskiearaby.com, March 21, 2011.

26 **The stud farm's assistant director:** Pawelec-Zawadzka, Izabella. "Andrzej Krzysztalowicz." *Magazyn z M do M,* January 1998.

27 **The dam, a gray mare:** Smith, *And Miles to Go,* p. 10.

27 **After days of wavering:** Luft, Monika, "The Lots of Arabian Horses in Poland, Part 2—World War II." *Arabians Horse Mag.* www.polskiearaby.com, April 6, 2011.

28 **The long line of 250:** Pawelec-Zawadzka, "Andrzej Krzysztalowicz." See also *Path to Glory: The Rise and Rise of the Arabian Horse.* Directed by Jen Miller and Sophie Pegrum. Horsefly Films, 2011.

29 **Devastated, Stanislaw Pohoski:** Luft, "The Lots of Arabian Horses in Poland, Part 1."

29 **Silently, Kristalovich pulled out his pistol:** Pawelec-Zawadzka, "Andrzej Krzysztalowicz."

30 **After three exhausting days of trekking:** Ibid.

30 **With renewed hope:** Ibid.

30   **Orange flames stood out:** Ibid.

30   **Not seeing any alternative:** Luft, "The Lots of Arabian Horses in Poland, Part 2."

30   **unable to find an intact bridge:** Pawelec-Zawadzka, "Andrzej Krzyształowicz."

30   **On September 25:** Luft, "The Lots of Arabian Horses in Poland, Part 2."

30   **On the morning of October 5:** Ibid.

31   **Kristalovich watched in horror:** Luft, "The Lots of Arabian Horses in Poland, Part 2." See also *Path to Glory.*

31   **The troops torched the stables:** Luft, "The Lots of Arabian Horses in Poland, Part 2."

31   **Only after the war:** Ibid.

31   **Gustav Rau, dressed in his Sumatra greatcoat:** Ibid.

32   **In the words of Hans Fellgiebel:** Brandts, *Pferde zwischen den Fronten,* p. 119.

32   **With the organizational skills:** Luft, "The Lots of Arabian Horses in Poland, Part 2."

32   **Even so, eighty percent:** Ibid.

33   **But Kristalovich's passion:** Pawelec-Zawadzka, "Andrzej Krzyształowicz."

33   **The Arabians seized at Janów:** Luft, "The Lots of Arabian Horses in Poland, Part 2."

33   **His sumptuous lodgings:** Westerman, *Brother Mendel's Perfect Horse,* loc. 1936.

33   **He bragged:** Ibid., loc. 1918.

33   **The high-handed chief:** Ibid., loc. 1914.

34   **Those who knew Rau:** Brandts, *Pferde zwischen den Fronten,* p. 10.

CHAPTER 4: RAU'S DOMINION

36   **Out the window:** Arnold, Dietbart. *Gespräche mit einem Pferdemann* (Bremen: Pferdesport-Verlag Rold Ehlers, 1995), p. 64.

36   **"They're gassing the Jews":** Ibid.

36   **If the Germans win this war:** Ibid.

37   **Karl Koch, the camp commander:** Fahnenbruck, *". . . Reitet für Deutschland,"* p. 306.

37   **The most notorious was on the grounds:** Westerman, *Brother Mendel's Perfect Horse,* loc. 2009.

37   **The Germans were churning:** Fahnenbruck, *". . . Reitet für Deutschland,"* p. 287.

37   **Together with Lessing:** Brandts, *Pferde zwischen den Fronten,* pp. 10–15.

37   **Rau's acquisitiveness focused:** Fahnenbruck, *". . . Reitet für Deutschland,"* pp. 286–87.

37   **He sent one of his adjutants:** "Goodbye to Landstallmeister Ekkehard Freilinghaus," DVM, *NASS News: The Official Newsletter of the North American Shagya-Arabian Society,* Summer/Fall 2008.

37   **Rau sent some:** Rudofsky, Hubert, "The Fate of the Lipizzaner During the War Years, 1941–1945," UR papers.

37   **Others were fanned out:** JM, correspondence with author.

38   **At first, Rau traveled:** Brandts, *Pferde zwischen den Fronten,* p. 10.

38   **Only twenty-six, Lessing:** Arnold, *Gespräche mit einem Pferdemann,* p. 6.

38   **Lessing hailed from Mecklenburg:** Ibid.

38   **As a young man:** Ibid., p. 63.

38   **At eighteen, he decided:** Ibid.

38 **His father advised him:** Ibid.

38 **Later, he would characterize:** Ibid. "We young people at that time followed this mass delusion."

38 **After graduating from the veterinary:** Ibid., pp. 40–44.

38 **The experience had marked Lessing deeply:** Ibid.

38 **While most people tend to associate:** Fahnenbruck, ". . . *Reitet für Deutschland,*" p. 287.

39 **In spite of his father's:** Arnold, *Gespräche mit einem Pferdemann,* p. 63. "When I was eighteen, my father voluntarily became a Nazi, even though my father warned me. My father was not a Nazi. He said, right then, in 1934, the Nazis are going to war. He was right. He had foreseen it. I only realized this in 1943 when I was in Poland."

39 **But as he later described:** Ibid.

39 **The social and sporting realm:** Fahnenbruck, ". . . *Reitet für Deutschland,*" pp. 288–91.

39 **In 1940, the Polish occupation police:** Ibid., p. 289.

39 **The *Black Corps:*** Ibid., p. 291.

39 **Gustav Rau had come:** Ibid., pp. 288–91.

40 **One day in 1942:** Arnold, *Gespräche mit einem Pferdemann,* pp. 63–64.

40 **Speaking about Auschwitz:** Ibid., pp. 64.

41 **One day, Hermann Fegelein:** Ibid.

41 **Despite the mayhem that rocked Poland:** UR interview. Lessing visited Poland after the war in his capacity as a horse expert. He reported that in the stud farm's visitor log from the war years, only the SS officers' names were crossed out.

42 **Lessing realized that Rau:** Arnold, *Gespräche mit einem Pferdemann,* p. 53.

CHAPTER 5: THE SPANISH RIDING SCHOOL OF VIENNA

43 **Africa was high-strung:** Podhajsky, *My Horses, My Teachers,* p. 137.

43 **This was the first horse:** Podhajsky, *My Dancing White Horses,* p. 67.

43 **According to the school's ancient traditions:** HR interview.

44 **They had been lavished:** Podhajsky, *My Dancing White Horses,* p. 58.

44 **The beauty and order apparent:** Ibid., pp. 51–60.

44 **Realizing that he could not:** Ibid., p. 63.

45 **He was painfully aware:** Ibid., p. 86.

45 **But Germany's takeover of Austria:** Ibid., p. 87.

45 **But Podhajsky was hearing:** Ibid., pp. 87–88. In his memoirs, Podhajsky says that none of his school stallions were taken out of Austria, but in fact, two school stallions were located in Hostau for breeding purposes (see Rudofsky, "The Fate of the Lipizzaner During World War II").

45 **The Winter Riding Hall was:** Isenbart, Hans-Heinrich, Emil M. Bührer, and Kurt Albrecht, *The Imperial Horse: The Saga of the Lipizzaners* (New York: Knopf, 1986), pp. 99–103. A brochure for the Spanish Riding School, dated 1942, pictures the Winter Riding Hall with Nazi swastika flags affixed to the central pillars.

46 **When the riding hall was:** Ibid.

46 **The purebred Lipizzaner:** Ibid.

47 **These snow-white horses:** Ibid.

47 **For the achievement:** Morgan, M. H., *The Art of Horsemanship by Xenophon* (London, 1894), p. 64.

48 **At the Spanish Riding School:** Isenbart et al., *The Imperial Horse*, pp. 184–98; and HR interview.

48 **At the Spanish Riding School:** Sternthal, Barbara, *The Lipizzans and the Spanish Riding School Myth and Truth* (Vienna: Brandstätter, 2010), p. 68.

49 **For centuries, these beautiful creatures:** Ibid., pp. 37–42.

49 **The cataclysmic Great War:** Ibid., pp. 43–44.

50 **In 1938, when Austria:** Podhajsky, *My Dancing White Horses*, pp. 51–53.

50 **In 1934, there were 176,034 Jews:** "Vienna," United States Holocaust Memorial Museum, United States Holocaust Memorial Council, August 18, 2015.

50 **In July 1942, Podhajsky set off:** Podhajsky, *My Dancing White Horses*, p. 86.

51 **Broodmares and young foals:** See *Legendary White Stallions*, DVD, for an excellent overview of the life of young Lipizzaner in Piber. See also Sternthal, *The Lipizzans and the Spanish Riding School*, pp. 51–55.

51 **Conveniently, this allied him:** ". . . *Reitet für Deutschland*," pp. 168–70.

52 **Podhajsky was left feeling:** Podhajsky, *My Dancing White Horses*, p. 87.

52 **After returning to Vienna:** Ibid., p. 88.

52 **He was unaware that Rau:** Westerman, *Brother Mendel's Perfect Horse*, loc. 2240.

53 **In early October, unbeknownst to Podhajsky:** Podhajsky, *My Dancing White Horses*, p. 88.

53 **The long-range plan:** Isenbart et al., *The Imperial Horse*, p. 38.

53 **In a panic, he immediately petitioned:** Podhajsky, *My Dancing White Horses*, pp. 89.

53 **Arriving on the grounds of Hostau:** Ibid., p. 89.

54 **In Podhajsky's words:** Ibid.

54 **While he was not in fact a doctor:** JM correspondence with the author.

54 **As Podhajsky had discovered:** Podhajsky, *My Dancing White Horses*, p. 88.

54 **Shortly after his return to Vienna:** Ibid., pp. 88–89.

55 **Also sixty-one, General Schulze:** Jarymowycz, Roman, *Cavalry from Hoof to Track* (Westwood, CT: Greenwood, 2008), p. 185.

55 **Schulze, who had a peaceable:** Podhajsky, *My Dancing White Horses*, p. 88–90.

55 **Aware of his deficiencies as an orator:** Ibid.

55 **"Your ideas are antiquated":** Ibid., p. 90. "He pronounced my ideas old-fashioned."

56 **Podhajsky accused Rau:** Ibid.

56 **Back at Hostau:** Ibid., p. 91.

56 **In just a few weeks:** Ibid., p. 69.

56 **On this night, Podhajsky:** Ibid., p. 70.

57 **As Podhajsky would later learn:** Fahnenbruck, ". . . *Reitet für Deutschland*," p. 306.

CHAPTER 6: THE HIDDEN STUD FARM

60 **The stud farm at Hostau:** Peter, Brigitte, "Hostau 1945: Die Rettung der Lipizzaner—Wagnis oder Wunder? Die Rettung der weissen Pferde am Ende des II. Weltkrieges." *Zyklus* 2–4 (1982).

60 **In addition to the main complex of stables:** Ibid.

61 **Throughout 1942, he:** Rudofsky, Hubert, "The Fate of the Lipizzaner Horses," unpublished manuscript, UR papers.

61 **Austrian-born Hitler's goal:** Adolf Hitler, *Mein Kampf* (Boston: Houghton Mifflin, 1943).

61 **Gustav Rau believed that these intelligent:** Westerman, *Brother Mendel's Perfect Horse,* loc. 2340.

61 **As a young man:** Ibid., loc. 1954.

61 **Despite evidence of mounting technological:** Fahnenbruck, ". . . *Reitet für Deutschland,*" pp. 112–17. See also Westerman, *Brother Mendel's Perfect Horse,* loc. 1944–1972.

62 **As head of the Polish stud farm:** Brandts, *Pferde zwischen den Fronten,* p. 11.

62 **As the war continued to escalate:** Ibid.

62 **He had predicted:** Peter, "Hostau 1945."

62 **Without access to a modern understanding of genetics:** Westerman, *Brother Mendel's Perfect Horse,* loc. 2243–2244.

63 **Rau wrote, "We have to promote . . .":** Fahnenbruck, ". . . *Reitet für Deutschland,*" p. 169.

64 **As a civilian, Rudofsky:** UR, interview.

64 **Now a colonel:** Ibid.

64 **He owed his love:** "The man originating from the Sudetenland found a new home in Boxberg. Horse-breeding became a vocation for stablemaster Hubert Rudofsky. His service as a stud director is known here and around the world." Undated clipping, UR papers.

64 **At the war's end:** Ibid.

64 **In peacetime, Rudofsky was a civil servant:** Ibid.

64 **When the Germans occupied:** Hubert Rudofsky, UR papers.

65 **Soon after, Rudofsky:** Ibid.

65 **Rudofsky acquitted himself:** "The man originating from the Sudetenland."

65 **The ability to drive a four-in-hand:** RJC, interview.

66 **One turn-of-the-century enthusiast's:** *Outing,* May 1897, p. 107.

66 **On the day of the parade:** "H. Rudofsky Album," UR papers.

66 **Lining up along the railings:** Arnold, *Gespräche mit einem Pferdemann,* p. 63.

66 **The parade began:** "H. Rudofsky Photo Album," UR papers.

67 **As they circled:** Ibid.

67 **A few people pulled out:** Ibid.

67 **The grounds of the stud farm:** Arnold, *Gespräche mit einem Pferdemann,* p. 63.

67 **The SS officer:** Ibid.

67 **"You have no authority . . .":** Ibid. "Rau went to them and said, 'If you do this then you will regret it. I will make a huge spectacle.' . . . Rau had an advantage that he could say that the stud farms were all under the power of the Wehrmacht and this event was a Wehrmacht event under his command."

67 **When the time came:** H. Rudofsky photo album.

68 **The doctors were unable to find:** Rudofsky medical reports, UR papers.

68 **Within Rudofsky's own family:** UR interview.

68 **His father's first cousin:** Iggers, Wilma and Georg, *Two Lives in Uncertain Times: Facing the Challenges of the 20th Century as Scholars and Citizens* (New York: Berghahn Books, 2006), p. 7.

69 **His younger brother:** UR interview.

69 **His younger sister:** Ibid.

69 **Privately, Rudofsky disdained:** Ibid.

69 **Being closer to home:** Ibid.

69 **The devout Rudofsky:** Ibid.

69 **When he stopped:** Ibid.

70   **The stables full of white horses:** UR interview; and SR correspondence with author.

70   **When they arrived at Hostau:** Ibid.

70   **This carriage master:** UR interview.

71   **The day-to-day routine:** Isenbart et al., *The Imperial Horse*, p. 52.

72   **Rudofsky was a consummate:** Podhajsky, *My Dancing White Horses*, pp. 88–89.

72   **During 1944, Alois Podhajsky:** Peter, "Hostau 1945."

72   **Verena Podhajsky:** Ibid.

72   **But Podhajsky's relationship with Colonel Rudofsky:** UR interview.

72   **Rau's program at Hostau:** Westerman, *Brother Mendel's Perfect Horse*, loc. 2445.

72   **At special "birth clinics":** *Daily Mail* (London), January 9, 2009.

CHAPTER 7: PODHAJSKY'S CHOICE

74   **In this peaceful setting:** Podhajsky, *My Dancing White Horses*, p. 94.

75   **One view was that the school:** Ibid.

75   **After wrestling with the dilemma:** Ibid.

75   **Alois Podhajsky stood:** Ibid.

76   **Noticing that each of the stallion's performances:** Ibid., p. 95.

76   **On May 24, 1944:** Ibid.

77   **No one, neither man nor beast:** Ibid.

77   **After several years of being well treated:** Ibid.

77   **By the summer of 1944:** Ibid., pp. 95–96.

78   **To Podhajsky, it seemed:** Ibid., p. 96.

78   **Secretly, throughout that fall:** Ibid., pp. 94–106.

79   **He had fulfilled his obligation:** Ibid.

80   **Podhajsky was reluctant:** Ibid.

80   **"Is the situation with the Lipizzaner under control?":** Ibid., p. 101.

80   **"Due to the danger to the horses":** Ibid. The conversation between von Schirach and Podhajsky is related on pp. 101–2.

82   **Unfortunately, the twenty-two Hungarian Lipizzaner:** JM correspondence with author.

CHAPTER 8: HORSES IN PERIL

83   **In early May, they received orders:** Smith, *And Miles to Go*, p. 155.

84   **As the train lurched:** Ibid.

85   **Already the newly established:** Brandts, *Pferde zwischen den Fronten*, p. 117.

85   **At the stallion depot in Drogomyśl:** Brandts, quoted in Westerman, *Brother Mendel's Perfect Horse,* loc. 61.

85   **In May 1944:** Brandts, *Pferde zwischen den Fronten*, p. 119.

85   **In late June, Rau:** Ibid.

85   **Rau persuaded a retired cavalry officer:** Ibid.

86   **Late at night, in the quiet of his home:** Pawelec-Zawadzka, "Andrzej Krzyszstałowicz."

86   **Hans Fellgiebel, the farm's German director:** Ludwig, Dieter. "Inge Theodorescu—eine große Pferdefrau lebt nicht mehr," ludwigs-pferdewelten. de, April 12, 2010. See also Brandts, *Pferde zwischen den Fronten*, p. 121.

86   **In the end, Kristalovich:** Pawelec-Zawadzka, "Andrjez Krzyształowicz."

86   **On July 1, ninety-six:** Brandts, *Pferde zwischen den Fronten*, p. 119.

86 **Trucks loaded with sandbags:** Ibid.
86 **Nineteen days later:** Ibid.
87 **A few days later, Hans:** Ludwig, "Inge Theodorescu." See also Brandts, *Pferde zwischen den Fronten*, p. 121.
87 **The horses he had shipped to Sohland:** Brandts, *Pferde zwischen den Fronten*, pp. 119–20.
87 **As a motley assortment of local farmers:** Ibid., p. 119.
88 **six months after fleeing Janów:** Ibid.
88 **In spite of the lack of sufficient staff:** Luft, "The Lots of Arabian Horses in Poland, Part 1," p. 56.
89 **Defying their own exhaustion:** Ibid.
89 **As they approached the city:** Toland, John, "Death Descends on Dresden," *The Last 100 Days* (New York: Bantam), ww2warstories.tripod.com. See also "Eyewitness Götz Bergander Recalls the Bombing of Dresden," German History in Documents and Images, Nazi Germany (1933–1945), germanhistorydocs.ghi -dc.org/section.cfm?section_id=13.
89 **Green tracers:** Toland, "Death Descends."
89 **In the words of an eyewitness:** "Eyewitness Götz Bergander."
90 **Jan Ziniewicz, strong and wiry:** Luft, "The Lots of Arabian Horses in Poland, Part 2," p. 58.
90 **Kristalovich, traveling with the mares and foals:** Pawelec-Zawadzka, "Andrjez Krzyształowicz."
90 **The group congregated in Weisser Hirsch:** Brandts, *Pferden zwischen den Fronten*, pp. 119–20.
91 **Just as he prepared to leave:** Ibid.
91 **There were fewer than fifty:** Luft, "The Lots of Arabian Horses in Poland, Part 2."

CHAPTER 9: THE ESCAPE

92 **The scene down at the Franz Joseph:** See Podhajsky, *My Dancing White Horses*, pp. 103–6, for Podhajsky's description of his flight from Vienna with the stallions.
93 **Podhajsky hurried through the covered walkway:** Ibid., p. 103.
95 **People crowded around:** Ibid., p. 105.
96 **He had fallen in love:** Podhajsky, *My Horses, My Teachers*, p. 24.
97 **For two straight hours:** Podhajsky, *My Dancing White Horses*, p. 105.
97 **The stationmaster ran out and shouted:** Ibid.
97 **Podhajsky felt the boxcars roll:** Ibid., p. 106.
97 **By nightfall, they had escaped:** Ibid.

PART TWO: THE AMERICANS

CHAPTER 10: MACHINE VERSUS HORSE

103 **Under the wide blue Kansas skies:** CH Reed papers, VMA.
103 **Just three years ago:** "Reich Equestrians Arrive for Shows."
103 **At that time, the young officer:** CH Reed papers, VHA.
103 **On February 9, during a radio speech:** "Give Us the Tools," Radio Broadcast, February 9, 1941, www.winstonchurchill.org.

104   **The U.S. Army Remount Service:** Waller, Anna L., "Horses and Mules in the National Defense," 1958.

104   **A group of Americans:** "Arabians Are Given to War Department," *The New York Times,* October 19, 1941.

104   **A short while later:** "Kellogg Arabian Horse Farm Turned Over to Army," *Los Angeles Times,* November 2, 1943.

104   **The Kellogg ranch:** "W. K. Kellogg Arabian Horse Ranch," *Los Angeles Times,* January 2, 1931.

104   **On August 10, 1941, the men of the 10th:** "Crack 10th Cavalry Marks 75th Anniversary at Riley," *Baltimore Afro-American,* August 10, 1941.

105   **Here, where a sign near the officers' quarters:** Truscott, Lucian K., Jr., *The Twilight of the U.S. Cavalry: Life in the Old Army, 1917–1942* (Lawrence: University Press of Kansas, 1989), p. 76.

105   **Major Hank Reed:** CH Reed Papers, VHA.

105   **Hank was born on a gentleman's farm:** RJ, interview.

106   **The real action was happening out at Fort Knox:** Hofmann, George, *Through Mobility We Conquer: The Mechanization of U.S. Cavalry* (Lexington: University Press of Kentucky, 2006), pp. 209–38.

106   **In the 1920s, it sent a young cavalry officer:** JW interview.

106   **At West Point, his fellow cadets:** Yearbook page, CH Reed Papers, VHA.

106   **As a student, he was average:** "Commissions Given 122 at West Point," *The New York Times,* June 14, 1922.

106   **The West Point superintendent:** Ibid.

107   **He and the other young graduates:** Ibid.

107   **Reed would be heading:** CH Reed Papers, VMA.

107   **In 1930 and 1931, he showed off:** CH Reed Papers, VMA. In sworn testimony given on June 17, 1945, Reed said, "I was a member of the Olympic Equestrian team but I wasn't good enough to be allowed to compete."

107   **That year, he was also selected:** CH Reed papers, VHA.

107   **At the beginning of the year:** Truscott, *Twilight of the Cavalry,* pp. 80–83.

108   **Lessons on fording rivers on horseback:** *A Cavalry Team Crossing an Unfordable Stream,* Training Film #14, War Department, 1933.

108   **The cavalry training manual also described:** The Cavalry School of Fort Riley, Kansas, Horsemanship and Horsemastership, cited in Ottevaere, James, *American Military Horsemanship: The Military Riding Seat of the United States Cavalry, 1792 Through 1944* (Bloomington, IN: AuthorHouse, 2005), p. 263.

108   **A young African-American recruit:** "Transcript of Interview with Dr. Elvin Davidson on April 4, 2000, at the University of Tennessee in Knoxville, TN, with Kurt Piehler," Veterans History Project, American Folklife Center, Library of Congress.

108   **Equitation, defined by the army:** Ottevaere, *American Military Horsemanship,* p. 103.

108   **Training included instruction:** Ibid., p. 122.

108   **As described by a journalist:** "Now Men on Horseback Team Up with Machines," *Life,* April 1941, p. 86.

109   **Hank walked and talked and moved:** JW interview for insights into the mindset of career cavalrymen.

109   **Throughout the 1920s and '30s, the army cavalry:** Hofmann, *Through Mobility We Conquer,* pp. 201–57, for a detailed discussion of the debate over mounted versus mechanized cavalry.

110 **In 1939, a new chief of cavalry:** "Arms Before Men," *Time,* August 22, 1938.
111 **"cushion pushers":** "Now Men on Horseback Team Up with Machines."
111 **On April 21, 1941, a handsome cavalry soldier:** Ibid., pp. 88–89.
111 **The article opened:** Ibid., p. 88.
112 **"That is the reason I've been pouring":** "Crack 10th Cavalry."
112 **"When we fight an enemy . . .":** Ibid.
112 **Speaking later about the 10th:** Davison, Michael S., "The Negro as Fighting Man," *The Crisis: A Record of the Darker Races,* published under supervision of NAACP Public Relations, February 1969.
112 **On Monday, September 15, 1941:** "Big Maneuvers Test US Army," *Life,* October 6, 1941, pp. 33–43.
112 **Congress had handed over:** Gabel, Christopher R., "The US Army GHQ Maneuvers of 1941," Center of Military History, United States Army, 1992, p. 51.
113 **Louisiana was not only the proving ground:** Hofmann, *Through Mobility We Conquer,* pp. 277–79.
113 **Especially since 1931, their status:** "Tenth Cavalry Act as Flunkeys for White Polo Players," *Baltimore Afro-American,* June 22, 1940. See also "Buffalo Soldiers on the Eve of War, at Fort Leavenworth in the Early 1930s and 40s." Interviews conducted by George E. Knapp, Combat Studies Institute, U.S. Army Command and General Staff College, Fort Leavenworth, Kansas, April 1991.
113 **The unabated rain:** Hofmann, *Through Mobility We Conquer,* pp. 277–79.
114 **While the press focused their cameras:** Rickey Robertson, "The Last Cavalry Horse," www.sfasu.edu.
114 **They also noticed:** Ibid.
114 **For a while, it seemed as if the horse:** Ibid.
114 **Among the horse cavalry:** Hofmann, *Through Mobility We Conquer,* pp. 277–79.
115 **"He lost it all":** Ibid., p. 287.
115 **On February 21, 1942, Colonel Davison:** CH Reed, letter from Colonel Davison, from the personal collection of Reed Johnson.
115 **Reed was no Luddite:** RJ interview.

CHAPTER 11: A HORSELESS COMMANDER

116 **Reed had brought his two polo ponies:** RJ interview.
118 **Just eight days later:** "Second Cavalry Reactivated at Fort Jackson Ceremonies," *The State,* January 12, 1943, in Lambert, A. L., and G. B. Layton, *The Ghosts of Patton's Third Army: A History of the Second U.S. Cavalry.* Compiled, edited, and published by Historical Section, 2nd Cavalry Association, 1946.
118 **The mounted 2nd had been deactivated:** Boese, Sam, "A WW2 Remembrance of an Old 2nd US Cav Trooper, 1941–1945, a Personal Account," history .dragoons.org.
118 **Reed evoked the 2nd's:** "Second Cavalry Reactivated."
119 **They would look to the lieutenant colonel:** "Second Cavalry Association Newsletter, Thoroughbred #59" (Summer 1980), CH Reed Papers, VHA.
119 **By January 22, the new recruits:** Lambert and Layton, *The Ghosts of Patton's Third Army,* p. 33.
119 **Soon, they were arriving twenty-four hours a day:** Ibid.
121 **Some of the recruits were so young:** KO interview.
121 **Everyone in the 2nd Cavalry:** Ibid.
121 **Among this mass of soldiers:** EAD interview.

122   **Tom had taken a shine to one:** Ibid.

122   **Tom cloaked himself:** Ibid.

122   **His nickname was "the little minister":** Ibid.

122   **One day, Tom came home from school:** Ibid.

122   **On May 25, 1943, it was humid:** Lambert and Layton, *The Ghosts of Patton's Third Army,* p. 37.

123   **When the men finally reached:** Ibid.

123   **For a while, it had seemed:** Ibid., p. 51.

123   **On March 20, 1944, a small group:** Ibid., p. 52.

123   **A high-speed liner, the ship did not travel:** Ibid., p. 53.

123   **On April 30, the ship arrived:** Ibid.

123   **At an anonymous rural station:** Ibid.

CHAPTER 12: AMERICA'S FIGHTIN'EST GENERAL

125   **On May 31, 1944, a restless crowd:** Lambert and Layton, *The Ghosts of Patton's Third Army.* My description of Patton's speech to the XII Corps is drawn from "A General Talks to His Army" (expunged; as reported by Sgt. Griffin), pp. 55–59.

126   **Then a captain:** Ibid., p. 55.

126   **Pundits joked:** pbs.org/thewar/detail_5217.htm, retrieved 1/12/15.

126   **An estimated five million tons:** "D-Day, June 6th, 1944," www.national ww2museum.org/learn/education/for-students/ww2-history/d-day-june-6 -1944.html, retrieved 1/16/15.

126   **The buildup had started:** Ibid.

126   **The door to the black car:** Lambert and Layton, *The Ghosts of Patton's Third Army,* p. 55.

127   **"We are here," he said:** Ibid., p. 56.

127   **Though Patton was eighteen years:** "Army Team Fete Visiting Polo Players: Participants Are Guests at Dinner in Army-Navy Club," *The Washington Post,* 1936.

127   **Once, while playing:** D'Este, Carlo, *Patton: A Genius for War* (New York: HarperCollins, 1995), p. 313.

127   **Another time, he fell so hard:** Totten, Ruth Ellen Patton, and James Totten, eds., *The Button Box: A Daughter's Loving Memoir* (Columbia: University of Missouri Press, 2005), p. 258.

127   **Patton, like many others in the army:** D'Este, *Patton: A Genius for War,* p. 313.

128   **"Men, this stuff we hear":** Province, Charles M., "The Famous Patton Speech, Part II, the Speech," www.pattonhq.com.

128   **Major Pitman hadn't seen his wife:** JHPK interview.

129   **He remembered the moment:** Ibid.

129   **Since the days of his boyhood:** Ibid.

129   **"You are not going to die":** Lambert and Layton, *The Ghosts of Patton's Third Army,* p. 56.

129   **Patton continued with his speech:** Province, Charles M., "The Famous Patton Speech, Part I, the Background," www.pattonhq.com.

130   **"We are advancing constantly":** Ibid.

130   **"Remember this," he said:** Ibid.

130   **"No, sir, you can look him straight":** Ibid.

131   **The next six weeks were a frenzy:** Lambert and Layton, *The Ghosts of Patton's Third Army,* pp. 59–65.

131 **On the morning of July 16, Jim Pitman:** Ibid.
131 **The convoy's thirty-one ships:** Lambert and Layton, *The Ghosts of Patton's Third Army*, pp. 69–70.
132 **But Pitman was summoned:** Ibid., p. 69.
132 **By eight P.M., the convoy had sailed:** Ibid.
132 **The doctor diagnosed:** Ibid.
132 **But at eleven P.M., red flares shot up:** Ibid.
132 **With few options available:** Ibid.
132 **When they landed, Pitman's first:** Ibid.

CHAPTER 13: TWO HANDS AND A PURPLE HEART

134 **Today, he was en route:** Lambert and Layton, *The Ghosts of Patton's Third Army*, pp. III–12.
135 **The mission of the 2nd Cavalry:** Herron, Francis, "The Ghosts of Patton's Third Army," *Warweek,* November 11, 1944.
135 **Today, as Reed surveyed the valley:** Lambert and Layton, *The Ghosts of Patton's Third Army*, p. III.
135 **"Sir, the commanding general of the Twelfth Corps":** Ibid.
135 **Without missing a beat:** Ibid.
136 **In November 1944, Francis Herron:** Herron, "The Ghosts of Patton's Third Army."
136 **An officer from the 2nd:** Ibid.
136 **In the words of one captain:** Lambert and Layton, *The Ghosts of Patton's Third Army*, p. 80.
137 **One such incident occurred:** Ibid., p. 119.
137 **In the words of cavalry historian:** Hofmann, *Through Mobility We Conquer,* p. 330.
137 **Between August and September:** Burkhard, Marianne, "Ferdinand Sperl, 1918–2006: The International Life of a Swiss Hotelkeeper" *SAHS Review* 45 (February 2009), pp. 18–19.
137 **Between camps, Reed led his command:** Ibid.
137 **Always in danger of a surprise:** Ibid.
138 **In the chill early morning of September 18, 1944:** Lambert and Layton, *The Ghosts of Patton's Third Army*, pp. 145–61.
138 **Just two weeks earlier, Pitman:** Ibid., pp. 106–7.
139 **Colonel Reed was telling:** "James H. Pitman 1940 Cullum Number 2006, September 18, 1944. Died in Lunéville, France," www.westpoint.edu.
139 **Trained to perform under duress:** JHPK interview.
139 **He radioed the coordinates of a meeting place:** Ibid.
139 **Just as Pitman stepped:** Ibid.
139 **At that same instant:** Ibid.
139 **Jim O'Leary picked his way:** KO interview.
139 **But as they gathered around Reed:** "Thoroughbred #59."
140 **As the daylight waned on September 18:** Dickerson, Bryan J., "The Battles of Luneville: September 1944," *Military History Online,* www.militaryhistoryonline.com/wwii/articles/luneville.aspx.
140 **So many of their vehicles:** Lambert and Layton, *The Ghosts of Patton's Third Army*, pp. 154–55.
140 **Each time a shell hit:** Ibid., p. 155.

140 **Reed was sent to Paris for surgery:** "Thoroughbred #59."
140 **But when visitors came:** Ibid.
140 **By December 1944, he was back:** Ibid.
140 **To each officer and soldier:** FS papers.
140 **Out of the blue, a single piece:** Lambert and Layton, *The Ghosts of Patton's Third Army*, p. 212.
141 **Though James:** Dickerson, "The Battles of Luneville."

PART THREE: THE MISSION

CHAPTER 14: ARMIES CLOSING IN

145 **Along a country lane:** Podhajsky, *My Dancing White Horses*, p. 109.
146 **They were not its only inhabitants:** Ibid.
146 **The village was full to the bursting point:** Ibid., pp. 108–9.
147 **As Podhajsky described:** Ibid., p. 109.
147 **It was General Erich Weingart:** Ibid., p. 112.
147 **But the general reassured him:** Ibid., p. 111.
147 **General Weingart continued:** Ibid.
147 **Only later would he learn:** Ibid., p. 112.
148 **Trying not to draw attention to himself:** Ibid., pp. 110–11.
148 **As their tense vigil continued:** Ibid., p. 110.
149 **But late at night, as Lessing:** Arnold, *Gespräche mit einem Pferdemann*.
149 **The veterinarian lent a hand:** Peter, "Hostau 1945."
149 **In mid-March 1945:** Ibid.
149 **They had fled:** Brandts, *Pferde zwischen den Fronten*, p. 117.
150 **Every detail of the stud farm director's:** UR interview.
150 **Next to Rudofsky:** Peter, "Hostau 1945" refers to the mysterious visitor by the name "Walter H"; however, it was most likely that Rudofsky was aware of the colonel's real name, Luftwaffe Oberstleutnant Walter Hölters, director of a group of interrogators of captured Russian pilots known as "Auswertestelle Ost" or "Duty Station East." For a description of Hölters, see Dolibois, John S., *Pattern of Circles*, pp. 72–73. Also JD correspondence with the author.
151 **A tasseled gold-threaded Arabian headdress:** Peter, "Hostau 1945."
152 **"Vienna has already fallen":** Ibid.
152 **"I've spent time on the Eastern Front":** Ibid. See also Reese, Mary Ellen, *General Gehlen and the CIA Connection* (Fairfax, VA: George Mason University Press, 1990), p. 45. Hölters despised the Russians because his daughter was raped by a Russian and later committed suicide.
152 **Trakhenen, Germany's famed "city of horses":** "The History of the Trakhener Horse," trakehners-international.com/history/index.html.
152 **Germany's greatest Thoroughbred:** "The Story of Alchimist," www.horsyme.com/Alchimist.html.
152 **Just a week previously, he had:** Peter, "Hostau 1945."
152 **"You must make contact":** Ibid.
153 **Rudofsky had sensed:** JD correspondence with the author.
153 **After instructing Rudofsky:** Peter, "Hostau 1945."
153 **His loyalties lay close to home:** UR interview.
154 **The safest thing for the horses:** Sperl, "IPW Team 10," p. 3.

CHAPTER 15: THE PHOTOGRAPHS

156   **A German Luftwaffe intelligence group:** Sperl, "IPW Team 10," p. 2.

156   **When they ran out of gas:** Ibid.

156   **They were calling:** Ibid.

156   **Reed's commander at XII Corps:** Ibid.

156   **Reed summoned Captain Ferdinand Sperl:** Ibid. Sperl was a naturalized Swiss-American, but his grandparents came from Bohemia, and he had visited the area as a child.

157   **Sperl was known as a wit:** Burkhard, "Ferdinand Sperl, 1918–2006," p. 21.

157   **Among them, the six men:** Ibid., p. 20.

157   **When they set up camp:** Ibid.

157   **He showed Sperl a location:** Ibid., p. 2.

157   **"There are about twenty men hiding up there":** "A small Luftwaffe Intelligence Group had been evacuated from Berlin, about twenty officers and men, and was now installed in a Hunting Lodge just across the border in Bohemia, called Dianahof."

158   **Because these were high-value captures:** Burkhard, "Ferdinand Sperl, 1918–2006," p. 2. (Sperl said they would be taken to London, but in fact the men were transported to Revin, France: JD correspondence.)

158   **Sperl named the mission:** Ibid., p. 1.

158   **The next day, April 26, around noon:** Ibid., p. 2.

158   **He looked to be about fifty:** Dolibois, *Pattern of Circles,* loc. 1569.

158   **He particularly noted:** Ibid.

158   **A hotelier by trade:** Burkhard, "Ferdinand Sperl, 1918–2006."

158   **His "field office" was a lot more humble:** Ibid., p. 20.

158   **"What brings you here?":** "I.P.W. Intelligence Team 10," pp. 2–3.

158   **"I come here on urgent business":** Ibid., p. 3. "He had come under a White Flag as a parliamentarian with 'Urgent Information.'"

158   **"Oberst Walter H.":** On p. 2, Sperl refers to him as Colonel Walter O. X. (no last name). Hölters's signature is visible on a note reproduced in Peter, "Hostau 1945."

159   **But the wallet was not entirely empty:** Ibid., p 3.

159   **Instead of family members:** Ibid.

159   **"I took these photographs":** Ibid.

159   **"Did you come here from Hostau?":** Ibid.

159   **"I'm a lover of horses":** Ibid.

160   **"I'm a meteorologist"** Ibid.

160   **This Colonel H.:** Ibid.

160   **"These are no ordinary horses":** Ibid.

160   **Hank Reed had arrived:** Dyer, George, *XII Corps, Spearhead of Patton's Third Army,* XII Corps History Association, 1947.

161   **He scrutinized a photo:** Peter, "Hostau 1945," photo of Rudofsky with Colonel Hölters and Lotnik.

161   **With Sperl acting as interpreter:** Ibid., p. 3.

161   **If they met Reed's demands:** Ibid.

161   **There, they would not be treated:** Ibid.

161   **If the plan went off as promised:** Ibid.

161   **He would bring Sperl to Dianahof:** Ibid.

161   **There were only a few checkpoints:** Ibid.

162 **He did not know if:** Ibid.

162 **The German colonel explained:** Ibid.

162 **Reed and Sperl exchanged:** Ibid.

162 **Waiting until dusk:** Ibid., p. 4.

162 **The forest was spooky:** Ibid.

162 **When they arrived:** Photo in author's personal collection.

163 **Saying that he wanted to speak:** "IPW Team 10: Account of His Negotiations at Dianahof," p. 4.

163 **Between the work of preparing the convoy:** Ibid., pp. 4–5.

164 **The German colonel was nattily attired:** Dolibois, *Pattern of Circles,* loc. 1558.

164 **As soon as Sperl rounded a bend:** Ibid.

164 **He radioed ahead:** "IPW Team 10," p. 5.

164 **Back at headquarters, Reed invited Hölters:** Charles Hancock Reed, "The Rescue of the Lipizzaner Horses: A Personal Account." Virginia Historical Society, 1970.

165 **First, on two sheets of lined paper:** "IPW Team 10," p. 5. See also Peter, "Hostau 1945" for an image of this letter.

165 **Hölters sent his personal valet off:** "IPW Team 10."

CHAPTER 16: THE PLAN

166 **Lessing listened thoughtfully:** Peter, "Hostau 1945." See also Arnold, *Gespräche mit einem Pferdemann,* p. 9.

167 **Lessing was to ride horseback:** Peter, "Hostau 1945."

167 **Lessing should take along a groom:** Ibid.

167 **In the close quarters:** Arnold, *Gespräche mit einem Pferdemann,* p. 63.

168 **As they got closer to the edge of the forest:** Ibid., p. 10.

168 **Lessing inquired:** Peter, "Hostau 1945."

168 **The forester offered the use:** Ibid.

168 **Lessing decided:** Ibid.

169 **"Hands up!":** Arnold, *Gespräche mit einem Pferdemann,* p. 10.

169 **He wasn't sure what it might mean for him:** Peter, "Hostau 1945."

169 **Even though he had not been expecting:** Ibid. In Peters, Lessing is quoted as saying that he decided "to use the hour in the American station to find out as much as he could and to explain the situation openly."

170 **"The horses are in danger":** Sperl, p. 5, reports that Lessing explained, "Many of the horses might be killed in such an undertaking."

170 **"Regardless of what you decide":** Arnold, *Gespräche mit einem Pferdemann,* p. 9.

170 **Reed gave no sign:** "IPW Team 10," p. 3.

170 **American troops were forbidden from advancing:** Dyer, George, "XII Corps, Spearhead of Patton's Third Army, 14 March–9 May, 1945," p. 103.

170 **The continuing cold, the muddy roads:** Ibid.

171 **"You must be: a horse master":** Patton, George, "The Cavalryman." The Patton Society Research Library.

CHAPTER 17: DRESSED UP AS A PLENIPOTENTIARY

172 **The veterinarian said:** Stewart, Thomas, "An Account of the 2nd Cavalry Taking the Remount Depot in Hostau, Czechoslovakia, and the Return of a Breeding Band Held There to Austria," unpublished manuscript, 1990, AS papers.

173   **Tom Stewart had been planning:** EAD interview.
174   **One harrowing day, while the 2nd:** Ibid.
174   **Instead, he was ordered:** Ibid.
174   **"Colonel Reed wants to borrow":** Stewart, "An Account of the 2nd Cavalry."
174   **Stewart arrived just in time:** Ibid.
174   **Stewart didn't know at the time:** Ibid.
174   **When Stewart arrived:** Ibid.
175   **Far from being flattered:** Ibid.
175   **Before Stewart had much chance:** Ibid.
175   **At the same time, he set Sperl:** Ibid.
175   **"Be careful," Reed cautioned:** Ibid.
175   **"The note says 'emissary' ":** Ibid.
176   **In addition to the three pass notes:** Ibid.
176   **"Captain Stewart must be returned":** Peter, "Hostau 1945."
176   **"If he fails to return by the deadline":** Ibid.
176   **The moment the preparations were completed:** Ibid.
177   **By the time Stewart and Lessing arrived:** Stewart, "An Account of the 2nd Cavalry."
177   **His buddies pitched in:** Ibid.
177   **"You don't have to go":** Ibid.
177   **"Don't worry, that's one of ours":** Ibid.
178   **But once Stewart put his weight in the stirrup:** Ibid.
178   **A ribbon of moonlight snaking:** Ibid.
178   **Before they had gone far, Stewart's horse:** Peter, "Hostau 1945." (Stewart's personal account omits any mention of a fall.)
179   **Eventually, they reached a barricade of brush:** Ibid.
179   **"That horse doesn't jump," Lessing called out:** Ibid.
179   **Lessing took Stewart straight:** Ibid.
179   **The general had told Reed:** Ibid.

CHAPTER 18: CHANGE OF HEART

181   *No Americans!:* Stewart, "An Account of the 2nd Cavalry."
181   **Colonel Rudofsky had been in favor:** Peter, "Hostau 1945."
181   **His fellow veterinarian:** Brandts, *Pferde zwischen den Fronten*, p. 117.
182   **"My hands are tied," Rudofsky said:** Peter, "Hostau 1945." See also "IPW Team 10," p. 5.
182   **"Our misfortune has made us mature":** "Our Hitler. Goebbel's 1945 Speech on Hitler's 56th Birthday. German Propaganda Archive," research.calvin.edu.
183   **"How is it that you are negotiating with":** Peter, "Hostau 1945."
184   **According to historian Ian Kershaw:** Kershaw, Ian, *The End: The Defiance and Destruction of Hitler's Germany* (New York: Penguin), 2012, p. 310.
184   **"Sir, discipline, obedience":** Peter, "Hostau 1945."
185   **"I will not let the American leave again":** Arnold, *Gespräche mit einem Pferdemann.*

CHAPTER 19: LESSING TAKES CHARGE

186   **Soon, they arrived at a company command:** Stewart, "An Account of the 2nd Cavalry."
187   **"like the cat had gotten into the cream":** Ibid.

187   **He told Lessing that:** Arnold, *Gespräche mit einem Pferdemann*, p. 13.
187   **They had no chance:** "IPW Team 10," p. 6.
187   **To solve this problem:** Peter, "Hostau 1945."
187   **Stewart, hastily disguised:** Ibid.
187   **Seated at a bare table:** Ibid.
188   **"The Americans wish to assist you":** Stewart, "An Account of the 2nd Cavalry."
188   **After his perusal was completed:** Ibid.
188   **"The Americans' goal is to safeguard":** Ibid.
188   **"You never should have acted independently":** Peter, "Hostau 1945."
189   **"Oh, really?":** Ibid.
189   **"I fell for beautiful phrases":** Ibid.
189   **"Okay, fine. Do whatever you want":** Ibid.
189   *Herr General Schulze:* Peter, "Hostau 1945."
190   **Once at Hostau, Lessing:** Ibid. Weisenberger called ahead to let Schulze know that he had given his approval. Arriving in Hostau, General Schulze provided a pass note that Lessing and Stewart were able to use to cross the border.
190   **At first, the house appeared deserted:** Ibid.
190   **When he arrived, he found:** Stewart, "An Account of the 2nd Cavalry."
190   **When Stewart had not appeared:** "IPW Team 10," p. 6.
190   **When Kroll arrived:** Ibid.
190   **He had received Patton's terse reply:** Reed, "The Rescue of the Lipizzaner Horses."
190   **On April 28:** Blumenson, Martin, *The Patton Papers* (Boston: Houghton Mifflin, 1972), p. 694.
191   **Lessing waited for Kroll for several hours:** Peter, "Hostau 1945."
191   **As the trail he was riding along:** Ibid.
191   **The baron quickly relayed the news:** Ibid.

CHAPTER 20: THE TANKS ARE COMING

193   **Reed had divided the task force into three parts:** Reed, "The Rescue of the Lipizzaner Horses."
193   **Stewart had a funny feeling:** Stewart, "An Account of the 2nd Cavalry," p. 8.
194   **General Schulze, whose arrival:** Peter, "Hostau 1945."
194   **It was then that Rudofsky saw General Schulze:** Ibid.
194   **In the past few days, the Hitler Youth:** UR interview.
194   **Just last week, Rudofsky had:** Ibid.
195   **Hastily, Rudofsky:** Peter, "Hostau 1945."
195   **Grasping another white sheet:** Ibid.
195   **In command of one platoon:** MNQ, DQ, MQ interviews.
195   **Quinlivan had a soft core:** Ibid.
195   **He had grown up in a devout Catholic family:** Ibid.
196   **Forced to double back:** Reed, "The Rescue of the Lipizzaner Horses."
197   **Between them, they held:** "Quinlivan Account," p. 3.
197   **A moment later, the Americans drove through:** Ibid.

CHAPTER 21: THE FALLEN

198   **He headed out in his jeep:** Arnold, *Gespräche mit einem Pferdemann*, p. 13.
199   **Now the pair from Hostau confronted:** Ibid.

199 **"Give back the watches":** Ibid.

200 **Along the narrow thoroughfare:** Reed, "The Rescue of the Lipizzaner Horses."

200 **Reed could not help but notice:** Stewart, "An Account of the 2nd Cavalry," p. 10.

200 **Reed offered Rudofsky a seat in his jeep:** Peter, "Hostau 1945."

201 **One young private, as he stood gazing:** "Vito's Story: Letter from Sergeant Vito Spadafino, Troop A, 42nd Squadron, 2nd Cavalry Regiment," history .dragoons.org.

202 **An early-morning American patrol:** "Charles Reed, Sworn Testimony, June 17, 1945," NARA RG 165, Entry 418, Box 921.

202 **Meanwhile, out in the field near Rosendorf:** "Raymond Manz, Tribute," Army: Together We Served, army.togetherweserved.com, accessed October 6, 2015.

202 **Raymond Manz was still a few days:** Ibid.

203 **Around the same time:** Stewart, "An Account of the 2nd Cavalry," p. 9. See also "Charles H. Reed Sworn Testimony."

203 **Colonel Reed and three other officers of the XII Corps:** "XII Corps, Spearhead," p. 107.

203 **The day before, General Patton:** Ibid., p. 109.

204 **Reed stood at attention, eyes forward:** Ibid., p. 107.

CHAPTER 22: THE AMERICANS

205 **Shortly after Podhajsky had received:** Podhajsky, *My Dancing White Horses*, p. 112. My description of the American occupation of St. Martin is drawn from pp. 107–26.

206 **Thinking quickly, he devised a scheme:** Ibid., p. 113.

206 **Podhajsky was startled that the men:** Ibid.

207 **"But I have orders to close them":** Ibid.

207 **Podhajsky unbuttoned his German uniform jacket:** Ibid.

207 **Half an hour later, Podhajsky's phone rang:** Ibid.

207 **When Podhajsky entered their office:** Ibid.

208 **Podhajsky felt the cool stock of his pistol:** Ibid.

208 **In the calmest voice he could summon:** Ibid., p. 114.

208 **But the *Kreisleiter*:** Ibid.

209 **At Podhajsky's signal, his riders:** Ibid., p. 115.

210 **Knowing that he needed the Americans' protection:** Ibid., p. 116.

CHAPTER 23: THE GENERALS

212 **For months before the evacuation:** Podhajsky, *My Dancing White Horses*, p. 110.

212 **Later the same day:** Ibid., p. 116.

212 **Just then, the same Brigadier General Collier:** Ibid.

214 **The next morning, Podhajsky realized:** Ibid., p. 117.

215 **It was a tremendous relief:** Ibid., p. 118.

215 **Podhajsky saw that General Walker:** Ibid.

215 **First came the regimental colors:** Ibid.

217 **It was only upon arriving:** Blumenson, *The Patton Papers.*, p. 696.

217   **From his position near the gate:** Podhajsky, *My Dancing White Horses*, p. 119.
217   **The general's expression was hard to read:** Ibid.
218   **While the horses were being prepared:** Ibid.
218   **Patton himself was once in charge:** Totten and Totten, *The Button Box*, pp. 133–34.
218   **What surprised the general most:** Blumenson, *The Patton Papers*, p. 697.
219   **Podhajsky made a split-second decision:** Podhajsky, *My Dancing White Horses*, p. 119.
220   **As Podhajsky later wrote:** Ibid.
221   **"Honorable Mr. Secretary and General":** Ibid. See also Blumenson, *The Patton Papers*, p. 697.
221   **"The great American nation":** Podhajsky, *My Dancing White Horses*, p. 119.
222   **Turning back to Podhajsky, he said:** Ibid., p 120.

CHAPTER 24: THE CRAZIEST CARAVAN IN THE WORLD

224   **Not until after May 5:** UR interview.
224   **With the guns pointed straight:** Ibid.
225   **"You are naive," Lessing said:** "Recording of conversation between W. D. Quinlivan and Rudolf Lessing during Second Cavalry Association Reunion, 1995," QF papers.
225   **As the rest of the crew prepared:** "Sworn Testimony of Hubert Rudofsky, June 17th, 1945," NARA RG 165, Entry 418, Box 921.
226   **To top it all off, Reed had agreed:** Peter, "Hostau 1945."
226   **Gifted with a sharp mind for technical tasks:** MQN interview.
226   **He and his men built the ramps:** "Quinlivan Account."
226   **The rest of the horses would be safer:** Peter, "Hostau 1945."
226   **The local stables and cowsheds:** "Charles H. Reed, Sworn Testimony."
227   **That same night:** "IPW Team 10," p. 9.
227   **As Reed later recounted:** "Charles H. Reed, Sworn Testimony."
227   **A Czech representative:** "Sworn Testimony of Jindrich Basta," NARA RG 165, Entry 418, Box 921.
227   **a claim that Rudofsky:** "Sworn Testimony of Hubert Rudofsky," NARA RG 165, Entry 418, Box 921. In his 1970 account of the rescue, Reed describes Basta's visit as "stealthy," and "apparently to connive with Czech born Lt Colonel who was second in command when we arrived," seeming to refer to Rudofsky; however, Rudofsky was first in command at Hostau, and in his sworn testimony, he clearly stated that none of the horses were Czech property. The Czech interest in the stud farm was natural, and because Czechoslovakia was treated as an ally, the Americans did not have the right to remove Czech property from Germany; however, the stud farm at Hostau had been seized by the Germans, and all of the horses on the farm had been brought there from other countries.
228   **When all was ready:** Stewart, "An Account of the 2nd Cavalry," p. 11.
228   **On his back, one of the cavalry:** Ibid.
228   **Quinlivan was mounted:** Ibid.
229   **Yet the group had barely gotten started:** Arnold, *Gespräche mit einem Pferdemann*, p. 16.
229   **Tom Stewart stayed up front in his jeep:** Stewart, "An Account of the 2nd Cavalry." Per Tom Stewart's account, he rode King Peter's Lipizzaner some, but made most of the trip riding in a jeep.

230 **As the first group of horses and riders**: Peter, "Hostau 1945." See also Arnold, *Gespräche mit einem Pferdemann*, pp. 16–17.

230 **"Open that gate, or I'll open it for you"**: Arnold, *Gespräche mit einem Pferdemann*, p. 17.

231 **At the border, Hubert Rudofsky stood**: Stewart, "An Account of the 2nd Cavalry," p. 11. Some sources state that upon returning to the stud farm at Hostau, Rudofsky was immediately arrested; however, Rudofsky was left in charge of the horses, and the Americans returned to the farm to bring out additional horses on May 17. After the American departure, the farm was commanded by Czech national Jindrich Basta. Rudofsky continued his duties until June 1, 1945.

231 **The IIIth Panzer Division**: "IPW Team 10," pp. 22–24.

232 **He had taken over the castle**: Ibid., pp. 8–9. See also "Letter," CH Reed Collection, VHA.

CHAPTER 25: THE LIPIZZANER FAREWELL

233 **For the first time in his life**: Podhajsky, *My Dancing White Horses*, p. 127.

233 **The Austrian was on his way**: Reed, "The Rescue of the Lipizzaner Horses."

233 **As he looked out the airplane window**: Podhajsky, *My Dancing White Horses*, pp. 127–28.

233 **Awaiting Podhajsky's arrival was an American major**: Ibid., p. 128.

234 **Podhajsky was surprised and flattered**: Ibid.

234 **Upon returning to Fort Riley**: "Cole Heads Army Riders. Team in Training at Fort Riley for Three Horse Shows," *The New York Times*, September 25, 1938. In his memoirs, Podhajsky states that the horse named Podhorski was ridden by Reed's brother, but Reed did not have a brother. Reed himself may well have had an opportunity to ride the horse named Podhorski.

234 **Fearing that the Americans**: "Charles H. Reed, Sworn Testimony."

234 **Not all of the Lipizzaner in Hostau**: "Quinlivan Account." Podhajsky did not want any Yugoslavian Lipizzaner.

234 **The next morning, Reed and Podhajsky**: Reed, "The Rescue of the Lipizzaner Horses," p. 4.

235 **"The inhabitants of this country"**: Podhajsky, *My Dancing White Horses*, p. 129.

235 **Their relationship had been cordial**: Arnold, *Gespräche mit einem Pferdemann*, p. 17.

236 **Podhajsky reflected on the situation**: "Quinlivan Account."

237 **On the night of May 22**: Podhajsky, *My Dancing White Horses*, pp. 131–32. See also Arnold, *Gespräche mit einem Pferdemann*, for Lessing's account.

237 **The only illumination**: Podhajsky, *My Dancing White Horses*, p. 131.

237 **While waiting for the trucks**: Ibid.

238 **Then one of the broodmares**: Ibid. See also Arnold, *Gespräche mit einem Pferdemann*, p. 17, for Lessing's account.

PART FOUR: HOMECOMING

CHAPTER 26: THE SUPER HORSES ARE OURS

242 **In Kötzting, Reed had an urgent situation on his hands:** Stewart, "An Account of the 2nd Cavalry," p. 11. See also Reed, "The Rescue of the Lipizzaner Horses," and Arnold, *Gespräche mit einem Pferdemann,* p. 11.

242 **Eager to get them safely:** Stewart, "An Account of the 2nd Cavalry," p. 11. Stewart was flown ahead to inspect the facility.

242 **As Lessing later explained:** Arnold, *Gespräche mit einem Pferdemann,* p. 17.

242 **On June 16 and 17:** "Rudofsky, Stewart, Reed, Sworn Testimony."

242 **He explained that when he returned:** "Rudofsky, Sworn Testimony."

243 **Cook concluded that the horses' capture was lawful:** NARA.

243 **As soon as Hamilton took up his new position:** Waller, "Horses and Mules."

243 **As Hamilton wrote in a later report:** "Request for Information re Horses Taken from Germany, 27 Feb 1947," NARA NND 785095.

244 **With the support of Patton:** Waller, "Horses and Mules."

244 **Hamilton's first stop:** "Request for Information."

244 **He was impressed by the magnificent:** Ibid. Hamilton specified that at the time of his first visit, the horses were actually in the hands of the troops, and that the situation was confusing, as the Allied Reparations Commission had not yet been established.

244 **But Hamilton knew only:** Ibid. Hamilton's chief informant for the status of the Polish horses, including Witez and Lotnik, was Gustav Rau; Hamilton referred to him as a "world-famous horse expert" whom he "had not reason to doubt." Rau claimed that the Arabians from Janów had been purchased legally by Germany after being looted by Polish farmers during the Russian invasion of Janów.

244 **Added to this misinformation:** Ibid. Hamilton also stated that he never spoke to Count Stefan Adam Zamoyski, a member of Poland's government in exile who had been appointed to handle Poland's affairs in horse breeding. Hamilton stated that the count's intentions were viewed with suspicion and that he was denied entry into the American zone. Zemoyski is credited with saving the lives of Witez's half brothers, Wielki Szlam (Grand Slam) and Witrzaj (Stained Glass), and helping to repatriate them to Poland.

244 **In his official report, he wrote:** "Report of Official Travel, 16 May, 1946," NARA NND 785095.

244 **Cargo space in ships returning from Europe:** "The Super Horses Are Ours," Mannix, Daniel P., *Collier's,* August 17, 1946.

245 **Quinlivan and Lessing had developed a close friendship:** "Quinlivan and Lessing, Conversation" (audio recording), QF papers.

245 **Throughout the summer of 1945:** Arnold, *Gespräche mit einem Pferdemann,* p. 27.

246 **For this reason, he supported passing control:** Ibid., p 17. See also Podhajsky, *My Dancing White Horses,* p. 130. Podhajsky reported that Lessing wanted all of the Lipizzaner to go to America, as he felt they had a better chance of survival there.

246 **Even Gustav Rau:** Arnold, *Gespräche mit einem Pferdemann,* photograph of Rau in Mansbach, with horses.

246 **Sadly, in later years, as the Polish government:** "Request for Information."

246 **The end of the war:** "Reed Service Record," CHR Collection, VMA.

247 **Hank wrote a letter to the young man's mother:** "Letter from CHR," KO papers.

247 **But he did not consider himself:** EAD interview.

247 **On September 19, 1945, he received top-secret:** "Special Orders, #187," Quinlivan family papers.

247 **The group—rounded out by another cavalry:** Mannix, "The Super Horses." After Stewart's departure, the command of the Mansbach Stud Farm was under Major Weldon Slishar.

247 **For the next three weeks, these horse experts:** "Request for Information."

247 **At each stop, the team evaluated the horses' conformation:** Mannix, "The Super Horses Are Ours."

247 **Any horse whose private ownership or unlawful seizure:** "Request for Information."

247 **At each stop, the horse detectives:** Mannix, "The Super Horses Are Ours."

248 **By his own account, Hamilton:** Ibid. See also Waller, "Horses and Mules."

249 **Pleased with the Germans' loyalty:** Peter, "Hostau 1945."

249 **In honor of his efforts, Hank Reed:** Ibid.

249 **For Reed, Lessing and Kroll had prepared:** "One Horsepicturebook of Arab-Lipizzan-Thoroughbred horses, presented to Colonel Charles Reed, CO Second Cavalry Group," RJ papers.

249 **A majestic photograph:** Ibid. Neapolitano Slavonia was one of two Lipizzaner stallions transferred to Mansbach. He died of a heart attack shortly after his transfer.

249 **Across the top:** Ibid.

CHAPTER 27: DEPARTURE!

250 **The Liberty ship *Stephen F. Austin*:** Mannix, "The Super Horses Are Ours."

251 **A few days earlier, the horses had boarded:** Ibid.

251 **The men had opened her boxcar:** Ibid.

252 **Sailing along the coast of Holland:** "Quinlivan Shipboard Diary," QF papers.

252 **The veterinarians had been worried:** Mannix, "The Super Horses Are Ours."

253 **As Quinlivan described it:** "Quinlivan Account," p. 6.

253 **One moment, the ship would plunge downward:** Mannix, "The Super Horses Are Ours."

254 **Only Witez, as balanced as a cat:** "Quinlivan Account," p. 7, states, "the Arabians were the best behaved."

254 **The weather grew worse:** Ibid., p. 6.

254 **the captain's compass wasn't working:** Ibid., p. 7.

254 **As the ship rolled into a wave's trough:** Ibid., p. 6.

254 **In the cargo hold, the lights:** Mannix, "The Super Horses Are Ours." First into the hold after the horses piled up was the commanding officer, Major Weldon Slisher.

254 **The force of the storm had knocked the horses clear:** "Quinlivan Account," p. 7.

255 **Quinlivan set about looking for Gospa's foal:** "Quinlivan Shipboard Diary." Quinlivan reports, "little foal is doing better."

255 **By the time the men got the horses separated:** Mannix, "The Super Horses Are Ours." See also "Quinlivan Account," p. 7.

255   **The ocean had turned to a tranquil:** "Quinlivan Shipboard Diary."
256   **Safely on the other side of the tempest:** "Quinlivan Account," p. 7.
256   **Trying to make their fodder last:** Ibid.
256   **Horses are unable to vomit:** Smith, *And Miles to Go,* p. 190.
256   **"How many were lost?" he asked:** "Quinlivan Account," p. 7.
256   **"None," Quin reported proudly:** Ibid.

CHAPTER 28: THE RIDERLESS HORSE

257   **At first nobody could quite believe:** See, for example, "Patton Continues to Gain." *The New York Times,* December 19, 1945.
257   **But at his bedside in a military hospital:** For an account of Patton's injury and death, see Blumenson, *The Patton Papers,* pp. 817–35.
258   **With only a few exceptions:** Waller, "Horses and Mules."
258   **In July, Colonel Thomas J. Johnson:** Blumenson, *The Patton Papers,* p. 728.
258   **"Otherwise, we will have nobody":** Ibid.
258   **Thirteen days after his automobile accident:** Ibid., p. 832.
258   **On December 22, he received orders:** Lambert and Layton, *The Ghosts of Patton's Third Army,* pp. 327–29.
258   **Reed had been stationed:** RJ interview.
259   **The day of Patton's funeral was dark:** Blumenson, *The Patton Papers,* p. 835.
259   **Reed and his men did not sleep all night:** Lambert and Layton, *The Ghosts of Patton's Third Army.*

CHAPTER 29: THE VICTORY PARADE

261   **Tweedy-looking horse experts:** Mannix, "The Super Horses Are Ours."
261   **For months since their arrival:** Ibid.
262   **Meanwhile, in Tokyo:** "American Gets 'Emperor's Horse'" *The New York Times,* December 13, 1945.
262   **"While we were trying":** Mannix, "The Super Horses Are Ours."
262   **Drew Pearson, muckraking columnist:** "Drew Pearson on the Washington Merry-Go-Round," *The Washington Post,* November 2, 1945.
262   **Some argued that the German horses' blood:** "The Thoroughbreds from Germany. Not a Shadow of a Doubt," *The Blood Horse,* November 9, 1946, clipping from the collection of the International Museum of the Horse.
262   **Colonel Fred Hamilton, who had painstakingly:** "Response to a Request for Further Information."
263   **in the large outdoor arena:** "A Parade of Horses," clipping from a collection of documents related to the cavalry, National Sporting Museum, Middleburg, VA.
263   **The final event of the parade:** Mannix, "The Super Horses Are Ours."
264   **One soldier who had traveled:** Ibid., quoting Major Weldon Slisher.

CHAPTER 30: FINDING A HOME

265   **It was here:** Podhajsky, *My Dancing White Horses,* p. 151.
265   **The once well-appointed edifice:** Ibid.
266   **By April 1946, the move was complete:** Ibid.
266   **The Pomona Remount Depot:** Parkinson, Mary Jane, *The Romance of the Kellogg Ranch: A Celebration of the Kellogg/Cal Poly Pomona Arabian Horses, 1925–2000*

(Pomona: W. K. Kellogg Arabian Horse Center, California State Polytechnic University, 2001). The most complete source for the history of the Kellogg Ranch.

267 **One day, a neighbor scolded:** *The Original Has This Signature: W. K. Kellogg* (Battle Creek, MI: W. K. Kellogg Foundation, 1989), p. 21.

267 **In 1925, he spent:** *Inland Valley Daily Bulletin,* September 25, 2004.

267 **In 1927, Charles Lindbergh:** Parkinson, *The Romance of the Kellogg Ranch;* Chavez, Stephanie, "Horse Lovers Head for the Shrine," *Los Angeles Times,* July 13, 2001.

267 **In 1932, with great fanfare:** "State May Get Kellogg Ranch," *Los Angeles Times,* March 31, 1932. See also Parkinson, *The Romance of the Kellogg Ranch,* pp. 200–207.

267 **In 1942, Kellogg was deeply moved:** Parkinson, *The Romance of the Kellogg Ranch,* pp. 280–83.

268 **By 1947, out of a crop of thirty-two foals:** Ibid., p. 349.

268 **One local rancher:** Ryan, Dixie, "Witez II and Earle," *Horse Magazine* (Summer 1977).

268 **He had managed to convince:** Mannix, "The Super Horses Are Ours."

268 **In 1946 and 1947, Koester fought:** Parkinson, *The Romance of the Kellogg Ranch,* pp. 336–37.

268 **As the one soldier:** Ibid.

268 **Throughout 1947, the Pomona Remount Depot:** Ibid., pp. 344–47.

269 **To make matters worse:** NARA RG 260 USACA, Box 102.

269 **In response, the Senate Armed Services Committee:** Ibid. See also Hevenor, Phillip. "Senators Hold Hearings on Ownership of Blooded Horses Taken in Europe," *The Washington Post,* November 30, 1947.

269 **A delegation (including Tom Stewart's):** "War Booty Horses Viewed by Eight Officials," *The Washington Post,* December 7, 1947.

269 **In 1947, a reporter:** "Fine European Horses Captured by Army Pose Problems," *The Christian Science Monitor,* December 7, 1947.

269 **Of Witez and Lotnik, he wrote:** Ibid.

269 **Above his picture ran the bold headline:** Ibid.

CHAPTER 31: THE WAR ORPHANS

270 **Although none of the transported horses:** "Request for Information."

271 **A syndicate headed by:** "How Did a German Derby Winner End up in Louisiana?" Bloodstock in the Bluegrass, fmitchell07.wordpress.com, March 10, 2010.

271 **On July 1, 1948, the Defense Department:** Parkinson, *The Romance of the Kellogg Ranch,* p. 349.

271 **The number of horses:** " 'Ghostly' Stables Show Army's Shift," *The New York Times,* November 4, 1949.

272 **As soon as the Department of Agriculture assumed control:** Parkinson, *The Romance of the Kellogg Ranch,* pp. 356–65.

272 **In a letter to W. K. Kellogg:** Ibid., p. 362.

272 **Other aged horses were not so lucky:** "Jadaan, the Sheik, and the Cereal Baron," Cal Poly Pomona Special Collections, cpp.edu/~library/special collections/history/jadaan.html.

272 **Kellogg, by then:** Parkinson, *The Romance of the Kellogg Ranch,* p. 356.

272 **Lotnik, once the pearl of Hostau:** Kowalcyzk, *Tennessee's Arabian Racing Horse Heritage* (Mt. Pleasant, SC: Arcadia, 2007), p. 54.

272 **By the fall of 1948, only the most valuable:** Parkinson, *The Romance of the Kellogg Ranch,* pp. 356–64.

273 **On December 1, 1948, the Pomona ranch:** "New Removals Slash Kellogg Herd. Nineteen Horses and Colts Depart by Rail. President May Be Urged to Check Exodus,"*Los Angeles Times,* December 1, 1948.

274 **The next day, the papers ran:** Ibid.

274 **Privately, he had taken to:** "This Is Your Life: Witez," undated unpublished manuscript, Arabian Horse Collection, International Museum of the Horse. See also "Even Atom Age Can't Displace Old War Horse. Animals Are Still Needed, Retired Officer Warns," *Chicago Daily Tribune,* February 23, 1948.

CHAPTER 32: THE AUCTION

275 **In the spring of 1949, Witez:** "Agriculture Remount Service: Catalogue of Horses to Be Sold at Public Auction," Pamphlet, National Sporting Library Collection.

275 **A movie company, a circus:** "Royal Horses Will Be Sold," *The Washington Post,* November 20, 1947.

275 **However, it turned out that one of the veterans:** "Quinlivan Account."

276 **the deep, full-throated whinny:** Ibid.

276 **Still haunted by the friends:** Ibid.

276 **A few months after returning home:** Ibid.

278 **As Witez circled the ring:** "Witez II and Earle."

278 **"You bought yourself a horse":** *Calarabia: The Story of the Hurlbutts and Witez II,* video, Arabian Horse Trust, 1989.

CHAPTER 33: THE WIDOW'S ROSE

280 **On October 3, 1950, eight men:** "Horses Arriving from Europe for the Garden Show," *The New York Times,* October 10, 1950.

281 **The friendly and intelligent stallions:** Podhajsky, *My Dancing White Horses,* p. 210.

281 **Dressed in a dark business suit:** "Horses Arriving from Europe."

281 **Soon, the horses were loaded into vans:** Podhajsky, *My Dancing White Horses,* p. 210.

281 **By the end of the week:** Ibid., p. 211.

281 **Since moving the horses to Wels:** Ibid., pp. 170–205.

281 **Four weeks after arriving:** "Horse Show Ball Has Gala Throng," *The New York Times,* November 6, 1950. See also Podhajsky, *My Dancing White Horses,* p. 217.

282 **The colonel, solemn and courtly:** Ibid., pp. 217–18.

282 **One stallion, Africa, was missing:** Ibid., p. 214.

283 **During the previous night's rehearsal:** Ibid., p. 217.

283 **At the end of the program:** Ibid., p. 221.

284 **The ring crew rolled:** Ibid.

284 **"I am very happy":** Ibid.

284 **"I would give anything":** Ibid.

CHAPTER 34: THE BIRTHDAY PARTY

286 **The Hurlbutts were calling the party "This Is Your Life: Witez":** "This Is Your Life: Witez," unpublished manuscript.

287 **In spite of these difficulties:** Trimborn, Harry, "Polish Breeders of Prize Arabians Fear National Turmoil," *Los Angeles Times,* June 18, 1982.

288 **On his twenty-seventh birthday:** "This Is Your Life: Witez," IMH.

CHAPTER 35: A MIGHTY GOOD AMERICAN

289 **On April 7, 1980, thirty-four years:** "Second Cavalry Association Newsletter, Thoroughbred #59, Summer, 1980," RJ papers.

289 **There was "something a little funny":** RJ interview.

289 **But in his library:** "untitled photo album," RJ papers.

289 **When he returned home from service:** Ibid.

290 **In addition, Reed had adopted:** "Fred Hamilton, Description of Horses Shipped from Europe, 1945," "Memorandum for Major Geldart, May 1947," NARA NND 785095 RG 92, Entry 1890.

290 **Reed's hand may not have been:** RJ interview.

290 **Around the time the movie came out:** Klein, Jerry, "Second Cavalry Reunion," CH Reed Collection, VMA.

291 **While Reed had returned:** Podhajsky, *My Dancing White Horses,* pp. 229–55.

291 **On the first night of the horses' grand tour:** RJ interview.

292 **In 1972, twenty-seven years after:** "Thoroughbred #59."

292 **"Is something wrong?":** Ibid.

292 **Twenty men from his regiment:** Ibid.

292 **To the sergeant from Chicago:** Ibid.

293 **At the graveside, one of the men:** Ibid.

293 **One of his men described him:** Ibid.

294 **"We were so tired of death and destruction":** Foster, Renita F., "Saving the Lipizzaner: American Cowboys Ride to the Rescue." *Armor,* May–June 1998, p. 22.

CHAPTER 36: THE VETERANS

296 **"Tonight, the horses dance for you":** Performance of the SRS, Vienna, 1986, video, UR papers.

BIBLIOGRAPHY

INTERVIEWS AND PERSONAL CORRESPONDENCE WITH AUTHOR

Robert J. Chambers (RJC)
Fran Sperl Cooper (FS)
Bryan Dickerson (BD)
John S. Dolibois (JD)
Elizabeth Ann Dunn (EAD)
Pam Gleason (PG)
Reed Johnson (RJ)
Sandra Slisher Kanicki (SSK)
James Hudson Pitman Kelsey (JK)
Jan Maiberg (JM)
Maureen Quinlivan Nolen (MQN)
Kathy O'Leary (KO)
Dennis Quinlivan (DQ)
Margaret Quinlivan (MQ)
Herwig Radnetter (HR)
Ulrich Rudofsky (UR)
Anne Stewart (AS)
James Wofford III (JW)

FAMILY PAPERS

Fran Sperl Cooper (FS papers)
Reed Johnson (RJ papers)
Sandra Slisher Kanicki (SSK papers)
James Hudson Pitman Kelsey (JHPK papers)
Kathy O'Leary (KO papers)
Quinlivan Family (QF papers)

Ulrich Rudofsky (UR papers)
Stewart Family (SF papers)

ARCHIVAL COLLECTIONS

The International Museum of the Horse, Arabian Horse Collection (IMH)
Kellogg Arabian Library (KAL)
National Archives and Research Administration (NARA)
National Sporting Library (NAS)
Reed Museum
United States Military Academy
Virginia Historical Association (VMA)

WORKS CONSULTED

"255,700 Men in U.S. Army; Only 2954 Are Colored." *Baltimore Afro-American*, December 15, 1934.
"2d Cavalry Regiment." *The Dragoon* I (July/August 2012).
"8-Year-Old German Stallion Brings Top Price at Auction." Undated clipping (IHA).
Agriculture Remount Service Catalogue of Horses to Be Sold at Public Auction. Fort Reno, Oklahoma, 1949 (NAS).
Allen, David. "Pomona's K Is for a Man Who Was Truly Grrreat!"*Inland Valley Daily Bulletin*, September 25, 2004.
Allen, Robert S. "Patton Visioned as Unit of Cavalry." *The Salt Lake Tribune*, 1946, 4.
"American Gets 'Emperor's Horse.'" *The New York Times*, December 13, 1945.
"Arabian Horse Breeding Farm to Change Hands." *Los Angeles Times*, 1947.
"Arabian Horse Display Draws Many Tourists." *The Washington Post*, 1942.
"Arabian Horses Given to War Department Club Act to Help Defense and Preserve the Strain." *New York Times*, October 19, 1941.
"Arabian Horses Given to War Department." *The New York Times*, 1941.
"Arco-Valley Held as Foe of Hitler." *The New York Times*, 1933.
"Arms Before Men." *Time*, August 22, 1938.
"Army and Rambler Polo Fours Victors." *The New York Times*, 1922.
"Army Team Fete Visiting Polo Players: Participants Are Guests at Dinner in Army-Navy Club." *The Washington Post*, June 11, 1936.
"Army to Get Lipizzaner Stallion." *The New York Times*, 1964.
"Army to Increase Its Horse Cavalry." *The New York Times*, 1940.
"Army to Use Arabian Stud Farm." *The New York Times*, 1943.
Arnold, Dietbert. *Gespräche mit einem Pferdemann* (Bremen: Pferdesport-Verlag Ehlers, Gmbh, 1995).
"Athletes Spurred by Reich Officials." *The New York Times*, 1935.
"Austria." United States Holocaust Memorial Museum, www.ushmm.org.
"Average American No Adonis to Science." *The New York Times*, August 22, 1932.
Bartlett, Arthur. "The War Horse Comes Back: Military Experts Said the Cavalry Was Dead." *The Sun*, 1941.
"The Battles of Lunéville: September 1944." *Military History Online*, www.military historyonline.com.
"Drew Pearson on the Washington Merry-Go-Round." News Release, Bell Syndicate, November/December 1945.
Betts, Burr. "★Witez II." *The Arabian Horse Journal*, July 1977.

"Big Maneuvers Test US Army." *Life,* October 6, 1941.

Black, Edwin. *War Against the Weak: Eugenics and America's Campaign to Create a Master Race* (New York: Four Walls Eight Windows, 2003).

Blumenson, Martin. *The Patton Papers* (Boston: Houghton Mifflin, 1972).

Boker, John R., Jr. "Report of Initial Contacts with General Gehlen's Organization." *Forging an Intelligence Partnership: CIA and the Origins of the BND, 1945–1949* (CIA History Staff, Center for the Study of Intelligence, European Divison, 1999).

Brandts, Ehrenfried. *Pferde zwischen den Fronten: Polnische Staatsgestüte und das Schicksal des Hengstgestüts Drogomysl/Draschendorf unter deutscher Besatzung 1939–1945* (Munich: Zugvogel Verlag Wenzel, 2007).

"Brilliant Setting for Society Circus." *The Washington Post,* 1922.

Brown, Gordon. "Meet Vast, Army Wonder Horse Which Can Gallop Backward." *The Washington Post,* 1940.

Case, Carole. *The Right Blood: America's Aristocrats in Thoroughbred Racing* (New Brunswick, NJ: Rutgers University Press, 2001).

Catalogue of Thoroughbreds, Property of the U.S. Remount Service to Be Sold by Public Auction at Aleshire Quarter Master Depot (Remount), Front Royal, Virginia. Pamphlet, 1946 (NSP).

Chavez, Stephanie. "Horse Lovers Head for the Shrine." *Los Angeles Times,* 2001.

Clark, Alfred E. "Charles H. Reed, 79, the Colonel Who Rescued Lipizanner Horses." *The New York Times,* 1980.

Clay, Steven E. "US Army Order of Battle 1919–1941." *Combat Studies Institute Press* II (2010).

"Clinical History of Crime." *The New York Times,* 1925.

"Cole Heads Army Riders." *The New York Times,* 1938.

Cole, Hugh M. *European, Mediterranean, Middle East Theaters of Operations* (Washington, D.C.: United States Army Center of Military History, 2002).

"Commissions Given 132 at West Point." *The New York Times,* 1922.

Corrigan, Joseph E. "They Say." *The New York Times,* 1930.

Cullum, George W. *Biographical Register of the Officers and Graduates of the U.S. Military Academy,* Vol. VII (Chicago: R. R. Donnelley & Sons Company, 1931).

Daley, Arthur J. "Largest U.S. Team in History, 395, Will Compete in Olympic Games." *The New York Times,* 1936.

Daniell, Raymond. "Pity for Germans Grows in U.S. Ranks." *The New York Times,* 1945.

Daume, Anja. *Galoppieren gegen den Wind: Gestütsgeschichte Mansbach: Vision & Wirklichkeit* (Norderstedt, Germany: Books on Demand, 2009).

Davis, Susan. "Operation Cowboy." *Sports Illustrated,* October 16, 1995.

De Amicis, Albert. *General George S. Patton, Jr., and the U.S. 2nd Cavalry (Patton's Ghosts of the Third Army),* University of Pittsburgh's Graduate School of Public and International Affairs, July 17, 2008.

D'Este, Carlo. *Patton: A Genius for War* (New York: HarperCollins, 1995).

"Die Lipizzaner und der Kötztinger Pfingstritt 1945," *601 Jahre Kötztinger Pfingstritt.* Author's personal collection.

DiMarco, Louis A. "The Army Equestrian Olympic Team." Louis DiMarco home page, www.louisdimarco.com.

———. *War Horse: A History of the Military Horse and Rider* (Yardley, UK: Westholme Publishing, 2008).

Dolibois, John. *Pattern of Circles: An Ambassador's Story* (Kent, OH: Kent State University Press, 1989).

————. Interview with John Dolibois, May 11, 2000, RG-50.030*0408, United States Holocaust Memorial Museum, collections.ushmm.org.

Douglas, R. M. *Orderly and Humane: The Expulsion of the Germans After the Second World War* (New Haven, CT: Yale University Press, 2012).

"Dressage Experts." *The New Yorker,* November 5, 1950.

Dyer, George. *XII Corps Spearhead of Patton's Third Army.* Report, 1945.

"Eugenics Conference Opens Here Today." *The New York Times,* August 13, 1932.

"Europe Is Offering an Extensive List of Fall Attractions." *The Christian Science Monitor,* 1938.

"European Horses Captured by Army Pose Problem." *The Christian Science Monitor,* December 3, 1947.

Evans, Richard J. *The Third Reich at War* (New York: Penguin Press, 2009).

"Even Atom Age Can't Displace War Horse. Animals Still Needed, Retired Officer Says."*Chicago Daily Tribune,* February 23,1948.

"Eyewitness Gotz Bergander Recalls the Bombing of Dresden." *German History in Documents and Images,* Nazi Germany 1933–1945, ghi-dc.org.

Fahnenbruck, Nele Maya. *". . . Reitet für Deutschland": Pferdesport und Politik im Nationalsozialismus* (Göttingen, Germany: Die Werkstatt, 2013).

Foster, Renita. "American Cowboys Ride to the Rescue." *Armor,* 1998, 22–23.

Frederic, Sondern. "The Wonderful White Stallions of Vienna." *Reader's Digest,* April 1963.

Freilinghaus, Eckkehard. "Hubert Rudofsky ein Grandseigneur der Welt des Pferdes." *Trankhener Hefte,* undated, from Rudofsky family papers.

————. "Hubert Rudofsky." *Arabische Pferde,* 151.

"Ft. Myer Society Circus Is Success; Two Shows Today." *The Washington Post,* 1933.

"Gen. Patton Helped Save Famed White Stallions." *The Washington Post,* 1966.

"German Army Jumpers Win the Lion's Share of Horse Show Honors." *Brooklyn Daily Eagle,* December 13, 1930.

"German Horse Wins at Garden." *The Washington Post,* 1946.

"German Visitors Learn Their ABCs of Trotting at Goshen." *Middletown Times Herald,* 1938.

Godfrey, A. H. "Driving Four-in-Hand." *Outing,* May 1897, 107–12.

Golden, Chris, ed. "History, Customs and Traditions of the 'Second Dragons,' the Oldest Continuously Serving Mounted Regiment in the United States Army." In *2d Cavalry Association* (Newton, MA: 2d Cavalry Association, 2011), 1–56.

"Gustav Rau Led Olympic Riding Team." *The New York Times,* December 6, 1954.

Hanlin, J. J. "The General and the Horses." *The American Legion Magazine,* 1963, 22–43.

The Heimatbrief: A Newsletter Magazine of the German Bohemian Heritage Society 17 (March 2007) and 19 (September 2008).

"Here for the National Horse Show." *The New York Times,* October 3, 1950.

Herr, John K. *The Story of the U.S. Cavalry 1776–1942* (Boston: Little, Brown, 1956).

Higgins, Alice. "From the Near East to the Far West." *Sports Illustrated,* March 11, 1963.

Hitler, Adolf, trans. Ralph Manheim. *Mein Kampf* (Boston: Houghton Mifflin, 1943).

"Hitler Watches Equestrians Win Show." *The New York Times,* February 10, 1934.

Hofmann, George F. *Through Mobility We Conquer: The Mechanization of U.S. Cavalry* (Lexington: University Press of Kentucky, 2006).

Holt, Carlyle. "America Builds an Army. Cavalry Horse Just Like His Rider Gets 13 Weeks of Basic Training." *The Boston Daily Globe,* January 9, 1943.

Holz, Louis T., ed. "Thoroughbred: Second Cavalry Association." *Newsletter #59,* Summer 1980.

"Horse Show Ball Is Set for Nov. 3." *The New York Times,* 1950.

"Horses Arriving from Europe for the Garden Show." *The New York Times,* October 1, 1950.

"Horses Held Booty." *Chicago Daily Tribune,* January 14, 1948.

Hughes, Allen. "Lipizzaner at the Garden." *The New York Times,* 1964.

Iggers, Wilma, and Georg Iggers. *Two Lives in Uncertain Times: Facing the Challenges of the 20th Century as Scholars and Citizens* (New York: Berghahn Books, 2006).

"Imported Horses Attract Throng at Front Royal." *The Washington Post,* 1946.

Isenbart, Hans-Heinrich, Emil M. Bührer, and Kurt Albrecht. *The Imperial Horse: The Saga of the Lipizzaners* (New York: Knopf, 1986).

"James H. Pitman 1940 Cullum Number 2006, September 18, 1944. Died in Lunéville, France." www.westpoint.edu.

Keane, Michael. *Patton: Blood, Guts, and Prayer* (New York: Regnery, 2012).

"Kellogg Arabian Horse Farm Turned Over to Army." *Los Angeles Times,* November 2, 1943.

"Kellogg Farm Fate in Brannan Hands." *Los Angeles Times,* December 2, 1948.

Kershaw, Ian. *The End: The Defiance and Destruction of Hitler's Germany, 1944–1945* (New York: Penguin Press, 2011).

Kevles, Daniel J. *In the Name of Eugenics: Genetics and the Uses of Human Heredity* (New York: Knopf, 1985).

Keyser, Tom. "Aging GI Reflects on WWII Rescue of Lipizzaner Stallions." *Laredo Morning Times,* 2005.

"King of the Wing Review." *The New York Times,* November 14, 1948.

Knapp, George. "Buffalo Soldiers at Fort Leavenworth in the 1930s and Early 1940s: Interviews Conducted by George Knapp." Combat Studies Institute, U.S. Army Command and General Staff College, April 1991.

Kochanski, Halik. *The Eagle Unbowed* (New York: Penguin, 2013).

Kowalczyk, Andra. *Tennessee's Arabian Horse Racing Heritage* (Charleston, SC: Arcadia, 2007).

Kugler, Georg, and Paula Boomsliter. *The Lipizzan Horse: A Guide to Vienna's Spanish Riding School and Lipizzaner Museum* (Florence, Italy: Bonechi, 2002).

Lambert, A. L., and G. B. Layton. *The Ghosts of Patton's Third Army: A History of the Second U.S. Cavalry.* Compiled, edited, and published by Historical Section, 2nd Cavalry Association, 1946.

Leerhsen, Charles. *Crazy Good: The True Story of Dan Patch, the Most Famous Horse in America* (New York: Simon & Schuster, 2008).

Legendary White Stallions, DVD. Directed by Michael Schlamberger. PBS, 2013.

"Letter." Charles Hancock Reed to Mrs. O'Leary, September 29, 1945 (KO papers).

Livingston, Phil, and Ed Roberts. *War Horse: Mounting the Cavalry with America's Finest Horses* (Albany, TX: Bright Sky Press, 2003).

Loch, Sylvia. *The Royal Horse of Europe: The Story of the Andalusian and Lusitano* (London: J. A. Allen, 1986).

"Los Angeles Briefs." *Los Angeles Times,* May 5, 1946.

"The W. K. Kellogg Arabian Horse Ranch." *Los Angeles Times,* January 2, 1931.

Ludwig, Dieter. "Inge Theodorescu—eine große Pferdefrau lebt nicht mehr," ludwigspferdewelten.de, April 12, 2010.

Luft, Monika. "The Lots of Arabian Horses in Poland, Part 1: The World War I and the Bolshevik Invasion." *Arabians Horse Mag.* www.polskiearaby.com, March 21, 2011.

———. "The Lots of Arabian Horses in Poland, Part 2—World War II." *Arabians Horse Mag.* www.polskiearaby.com, April 6, 2011.

MacCormac, John. "Austria Will Send Famed Horse Unit." *The New York Times*, 1950.

MacDonogh, Giles. *After the Reich: The Brutal History of the Allied Occupation* (New York: Basic Books, 2007).

Malone, Michael. "Stolen by the Nazis: The Tragic Tale of 12,000 Blue-Eyed Blond Children Taken by the SS to Create an Aryan Super Race." *Daily Mail* (London), January 9, 2009.

"The Man Originating from the Sudentenland Found a New Home in Boxberg." Undated clipping (UR papers).

Martin, Frank Wayne, and Nancy Martin. *Patton's Lucky Scout: The Adventures of a Forward Observer for General Patton and the Third Army in Europe* (Milwaukee: Crickhollow Books, 2009).

McGuire, Phillip. *Taps for a Jim Crow Army: Letters from Black Soldiers in World War II* (Santa Barbara, CA: ABC-Clio, 1983).

McLaughlin, Kathleen. "Patton Gives Up Army to Truscott." *The New York Times*, 1945.

Michael, John. *Fort Myer* (Charleston, SC: Arcadia, 2011).

Morgan, M. H. *The Art of Horsemanship by Xenophon* (London, 1894).

"Mrs. Patton's Fall Is Fatal." *The Sun*, October 1, 1953.

"Name Adolf Held Banned for German Police Horses." *The New York Times*, 1943.

NASS News: The Official Newsletter of the North American Shagya-Arabian Society, September 2008, 1–14.

"National Defense: Horses on Wheels." *Time*, August 19, 1940.

"The Nazi Olympics Berlin 1936." United States Holocaust Memorial Museum, August 18, 2015.

"New Problem for Senate: 234 Horses." *The Washington Post*, December 2, 1947.

"New Removals Slash Kellogg Ranch Herd." *Los Angeles Times*, 1948.

"Now Men on Horseback Team Up with Machines." *Life*, April 21, 1941, 86–93.

"Ocean Travelers." *The New York Times*, 1938.

"Official Denies Horses Booty." *The Washington Post*, December 12, 1947.

"Operation Cowboy: The Saving [*sic*] the Lipizzaner Horses by Troop A, 42nd Squadron Mecz 2nd Cavalry Group (The Ghosts of Patton's Third Army)," www.gjt.cz.

O'Shaughnessy, Edward J., Jr. *The Evolution of the Armored Force, 1920–1940* (United States Army War College, 1993).

"Our Hitler (1945)." German Propaganda Archive,www.calvin.edu.

Parker, Earl, Ph.D. "The Remount Service and Its Stallions: Rescue of the WWII Hostau POWs and of the Lipizzans, Part I." *Haute École* 20, no. 4 (Summer 2012).

Path to Glory: The Rise and Rise of the Polish Arabian Horse. Directed by Jen Miller and Sophie Pegrum. Horsefly Films, 2011.

"Patterson Arabians." *Arabian Horse World*, June 1977.

Pawelec-Zawadska, Izabella, "Andrzej Krzyształowicz," *Magazyn z M do M*, January 1998.

Peter, Brigitte. "Hostau 1945: Die Rettung der Lipizzaner—Wagnis oder Wunder? Die Rettung der weissen Pferde am Ende des II. Weltkrieges." *Zyklus* 2–4 (1982).

Piekałkiewicz, Janusz. *The Cavalry of World War II* (New York: Stein and Day, 1980).

Podhajsky, Alois. *The Complete Training of Horse and Rider in the Principles of Classical Horsemanship* (Garden City, NY: Doubleday, 1967).

———. *My Dancing White Horses* (New York: Holt, Rinehart and Winston, 1965).

———. *My Horses, My Teachers* (North Pomfret, VT: Trafalgar Square Publishing, 1997).

Powell, Horace B. *The Original Has This Signature: W. K. Kellogg* (Battle Creek, MI: W. K. Kellogg Foundation, 1989).

"Question of Ownership of Captured Horses: Hearings Before a Subcommittee of the United States Senate. Eightieth Congress. First Session. December 3–23, 1947." United States Government Printing Office, 1947.

"Prize Horses Seized in Hungary to Be Sold." *The Washington Post,* November 21, 1947.

Ragan, Jean. "A Horse and His Friend." *The Denver Post,* April 30, 1961.

Rau, Gustav. *Die Reitkunst der Welt an den olympischen Spielen 1936. L'Art équestre du monde . . . International Equitation, Etc.* (Hildesheim, Germany: Olms Presse, 1978).

"Reich Equestrians Arrive for Shows. German Party to Visit Sport's Centers. Group Attends Races at Belmont." *The New York Times,* May 10, 1938.

Rendel, John. "10,000 See Horse Show Opening; Mexican Girl Wins Feature Jump." *The New York Times,* 1950.

Robinson, Ruth. "Lipizzaner Stallions, Due May 19, Attract Big Benefit Parties." *The New York Times,* 1964.

Robson, Seth. "Czech Republic Pays Tribute to WWII Heroes. Memorial to Honor Soldiers Who Saved Lipizzaners, POWs." *Stars and Stripes,* April 9, 2006.

"Rommel's Arabian Horse in Windsor Castle Stable." *The New York Times,* 1946.

Rosmus, Anna. *Czech Incursions: Foreign Horses Going Home* (Anna Elisabeth Rosmus, 2014).

"Royal Horses Will Be Sold." *The Washington Post,* November 20, 1947.

Schoomaker, Eric B., and Russell J. Czerw. *The United States Army Medical Department Journal,* 2009.

"Scientists Display Heredity Control." *The New York Times,* 1929.

Shirer, William L. *The Rise and Fall of the Third Reich: A History of Nazi Germany* (New York: Simon & Schuster, 1960).

Smith, Krista. "Historic Sagamore Farm: New and Improved." *Baltimore Fishbowl,* May 17, 2013.

Smith, Linell Nash. *And Miles to Go: The Biography of a Great Arabian Horse, Witez II* (Boston: Little, Brown, 1967).

"Society Circus at Fort Myer Begins Friday." *The Washington Post,* 1932.

"Stallion Brings $20,300; Young Pawley Gets German-Bred Nordlicht at Auction." Undated clipping (IMA).

Steen, Andrew K. "W. R. Brown's Maynesboro Stud." *Modern Arabian Horse,* September 12, 2012, 44–51.

Sternthal, Barbara. *The Lipizzans and the Spanish Riding School Myth and Truth* (Vienna: Brandstätter, 2010).

"Sysonby's Body Exhumed." *The New York Times,* 1906.

Tavel, Emilie. "Hungary Asks U.S. to Return Thoroughbred Horses." *The Christian Science Monitor,* December 4, 1947.

Tedesco, Vincent J., III. "'Greasy Automations' and 'The Horsey Set': The U.S. Cavalry and Mechanization, 1928–1940." Master's thesis, Pennsylvania State University, 1995.

"The Thoroughbreds from Germany. Not a Shadow of a Doubt." *The Blood-Horse,* November 9, 1946.

Thurtle, Phillip. "Harnessing Heredity in Gilded Age America: Middle Class Mores and Industrial Breeding in a Cultural Context." *Journal of the History of Biology,* 2002, 43–78.

Totten, Ruth Ellen Patton, and James Patton Totten. *The Button Box: A Daughter's Loving Memoir of Mrs. George S. Patton* (Columbia: University of Missouri Press, 2005).

Trimborn, Harry. "Polish Breeders of Prize Arabian Horses Fear National Turmoil's Impact." *Los Angeles Times,* 1982.

Truscott, Lucian K., Jr. *The Twilight of the U.S. Cavalry: Life in the Old Army, 1917–1942* (Lawrence: University Press of Kansas, 1989).

"Um die 50. Lipizzaner sollen dabei gewesen sein." *601 Jahre Kötztinger Pfingstritt.* Author's personal collection.

Waller, Anna, *Horses and Mules in the National Defense* (Washington, D.C.: U.S. Army Quartermaster Corps, 1958).

"Use Army Horses in Polo." *The New York Times,* 1922.

" 'War Booty' Horses Viewed by 8 Officials." *The Washington Post,* December 7, 1947.

Westerman, Frank. *Brother Mendel's Perfect Horse: Man and Beast in an Age of Human Warfare* (London: Vintage Digital, 2012).

Wiener, Tom. *Forever a Soldier: Unforgettable Stories of Wartime Service* (Washington, D.C.: National Geographic Society, 2005).

Wilson, Paul. *Himmler's Cavalry: The Equestrian SS, 1930–1945* (Atglen, PA: Schiffer, 2000).

"The W. K. Kellogg Arabian Horse Ranch." *Los Angeles Times,* January 2, 1931.

The XIth Olympic Games, Berlin, 1936: Official Report (Berlin: Wilhelm Limpert, 1937).

Zaloga, Steve, and Tony Bryan. *Lorraine 1944: Patton vs. Manteuffel* (Oxford, UK: Osprey Military, 2000).

IMAGE CREDITS

Page xv: courtesy of Ulrich Rudofsky
Page 1: ullstein bild
Page 5: author's collection
Page 14: Foto Deutsches Pferdemuseum e.V.
Page 20: Library of Congress
Page 34: courtesy of the International Museum of the Horse,
    Lexington, Kentucky
Page 46: ullstein bild
Page 49: Associated Press
Page 52: courtesy of Reed Johnson
Page 60: courtesy of the Reed Museum, Rose Barracks,
    Vilseck, Germany
Page 65: courtesy of Ulrich Rudofsky
Page 68: courtesy of Ulrich Rudofsky
Page 71: courtesy of Ulrich Rudofsky
Page 77: Mondadori Portfolio
Page 101: courtesy of the Virginia Historical Society
Page 110: courtesy of the Virginia Historical Society
Page 118: courtesy of the Virginia Historical Society
Page 120: courtesy of the South Caroliniana Library,
    University of South Carolina, Columbia
Page 130: courtesy of Jim Hudson Pitman Kelsey
Page 143: courtesy of Ulrich Rudofsky
Page 150: courtesy of Ulrich Rudofsky
Page 151: courtesy of Ulrich Rudofsky
Page 157: courtesy of Fran Sperl Cooper
Page 167: courtesy of Ulrich Rudofsky
Page 173: courtesy of the Stewart family
Page 201: courtesy of the Reed Museum, Rose Barracks,
    Vilseck, Germany
Page 215: courtesy of the General George Patton Museum and
    Center of Leadership, Fort Knox, Kentucky
Page 220: courtesy of the General George Patton Museum and
    Center of Leadership, Fort Knox, Kentucky

INDEX

Page numbers in *italics* refer to illustrations.

PHOTO: © TED CATANZARO

ELIZABETH LETTS is the *New York Times* bestselling author of *The Eighty-Dollar Champion;* two novels, *Quality of Care* and *Family Planning;* and one children's book, *The Butter Man.* An equestrian from childhood, Letts represented California in the North American Junior Championships as a teen. She currently lives in Southern California.

elizabethletts.com

Facebook.com/eightydollarchampion

Twitter: @Elizabeth Letts

ABOUT THE TYPE

This book was set in Bembo, a typeface based on an old-style Roman face that was used for Cardinal Pietro Bembo's tract *De Aetna* in 1495. Bembo was cut by Francesco Griffo (1450–1518) in the early sixteenth century for Italian Renaissance printer and publisher Aldus Manutius (1449–1515). The Lanston Monotype Company of Philadelphia brought the well-proportioned letterforms of Bembo to the United States in the 1930s.